James Madison
Rules America

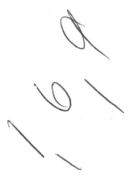

James Madison Rules America

The Constitutional Origins of Congressional Partisanship

William F. Connelly, Jr.

ROWMAN & LITTLEFIELD PUBLISHERS, INC.
Lanham • Boulder • New York • Toronto • Plymouth, UK

Published by Rowman & Littlefield Publishers, Inc.
A wholly owned subsidiary of The Rowman & Littlefield Publishing Group, Inc.
4501 Forbes Boulevard, Suite 200, Lanham, Maryland 20706
http://www.rowmanlittlefield.com

Estover Road, Plymouth PL6 7PY, United Kingdom

British Library Cataloguing in Publication Information Available

Library of Congress Cataloging-in-Publication Data

The hardback edition of this book was previously cataloged by the Library of Congress as follows:

Connelly, William F., 1951–
  James Madison rules America : the constitutional origins of congressional partisanship / William F. Connelly, Jr.
    p. cm.
  Includes bibliographical references and index.
  1. Constitutional law—United States. 2. United States. Congress—History. 3. United States. Congress—Decision making. 4. Political culture—United States—History. 5. Politics, Practical—United States—History. 6. Separation of powers—United States—History. 7. United States—Politics and government. I. Title.
  KF4930.C66 2010
  328.73'0769—dc22

                                                              2010002988

ISBN 978-0-7425-9965-9 (cloth : alk. paper)
ISBN 978-0-7425-9966-6 (pbk. : alk. paper)
ISBN 978-0-7425-9967-3 (electronic)

∞™ The paper used in this publication meets the minimum requirements of American National Standard for Information Sciences—Permanence of Paper for Printed Library Materials, ANSI/NISO Z39.48-1992.

Printed in the United States of America

Dedicated with love and admiration
to Benjamin and Caroline,
who understand that liberty
and self-government
begin with governing oneself.

Contents

Acknowledgments

This book would not have been possible without a great deal of assistance. I appreciate Washington and Lee University's institutional support, including and especially the encouragement of two of the finest academic administrators with whom a faculty member could possibly work, Dean Larry Peppers and Associate Provost Bob Strong. John and Marilyn Boardman have also been notably generous in their support of my work over the years. I am grateful for the support and inspiration of the Center for the Constitution at James Madison's Montpelier as well.

Jon Sisk, Darcy Evans, Melissa Wilks, and Julia Loy at Rowman and Littlefield have been quite helpful, as have the anonymous reviewers they recruited. The administrative assistance and patience of Lynda Bassett De Maria and Jennifer Ashworth at Washington and Lee University is appreciated, as is the assistance of many students over the years including Sam Langholz, Jason Robinson, Ingrid Schroeder, Danielle Simonetta Maurer, Lauren Willson Lawson, Ruth Hill Yielding, Greg Papeika, Caitlin Mullen, Harrison Gates, Richard Cleary, Alexandra Utsey, Chris Martin, and Greg Franke. I am grateful, too, for the many Washington and Lee students in my courses over the years, who patiently listened and responded thoughtfully as I explored many of the ideas in this book.

I am especially grateful to my graduate-school teachers and colleagues. James W. Ceaser will no doubt recognize in these pages his enormous influence on my understanding of American politics, as well as any limitations in my ability to appreciate his insight. Ceaser has been a true mentor and friend. Charles O. Jones, Henry J. Abraham, Michael J. Malbin, Randy Strahan, Dan Palazzolo, and Don Wolfensberger have contributed to my understanding of American politics each in his own way. David K. Nichols was an ideal fellow graduate-school student and later colleague. David's voracious appetite for learning and ceaseless willingness to question every argument I ever made taught me as much as anyone in graduate school. Last but not least, I cannot thank enough my coauthor on many other projects, Jack Pitney, who has been a friend, mentor, and my best editor. I continue to learn from Jack over two decades after we first met on the fourth floor of the Longworth House Office Building where we served at different times as American Political Science Association (APSA) Congressional Fellows.

My thanks also to Irving Louis Horowitz and Transaction Press, who in 2002 originally published chapter 4 in modified form as the introduction to a new edition of Woodrow Wilson's *Congressional Government*. *Southeastern Political Review* and Blackwell Publishing originally published chapter 3 in modified form as "Newt Gingrich—Professor and Politician: The Anti-Federalist Roots of Newt Gingrich's Thought," *Southeastern Political Review* 27, no. 1 (March 1999): 103–27.

Finally, I have two principal and enduring debts to acknowledge: one to my parents, whose love and support have been unfailing; and the other to my wife, Rebecca, and our two children, Benjamin and Caroline, for their love, understanding, and patience as I worked on this project.

As authors commonly do, I accept full responsibility for the limitations of this study.

Introduction

There is no right answer to that question.

—Dick Cheney

$\mathbf{A}$s a young Congress scholar, I did not readily understand then-congressman Dick Cheney's answer to my question, "Should the minority party in the House adopt a strategy of compromise or confrontation in seeking to advance their agenda and ambition?"

No right answer? How was that possible given that members of Congress, and perhaps especially "permanent minority" House Republicans in the 1980s and early 1990s, spent so much time arguing about precisely this question? "Old guard" House GOP leaders such as Bob Michel urged accommodation and compromise with majority Democrats. Yet backbench "young turks" like Newt Gingrich sought to rouse House Republicans to revolution using confrontational tactics.

WHO WAS RIGHT? MICHEL OR GINGRICH?

As chairman of the House Republican Policy Committee at the time, and later conference chair and Whip, Cheney stood somewhere between Michel and Gingrich—or at least that was the common perception. In fact, Cheney personified the challenge facing congressional party leaders, especially those in the House minority: compromise or confrontation? Bipartisanship or partisanship? Seek common ground with the other party or stand on principle? Be part of the *government* or part of the *opposition*?

The young Dick Cheney worked as White House chief of staff under moderate Republican president Gerald Ford. When divisive Vice President Spiro Agnew had to resign, congressional leaders urged Watergate-tainted President Richard Nixon to replace him with the more conciliatory Ford. After Nixon's departure, Ford believed his own presidency was "a time to heal," as he titled his autobiography. Cheney's reputation as a moderate followed from his tenure under Ford. Later when Cheney was elected to the House from Wyoming, congressional journalists and scholars perceived him as a House "institutionalist," who placed the interest of the House above personal ambition and partisanship.[1] Yet later in his career, while he was serving as George W. Bush's vice president, critics saw Cheney as a polarizing figure inclined to stoke partisan fires. Bipartisan compromise or partisan confrontation? No right answer?

Gerald Ford, Cheney's mentor, once observed, "The job of the minority is to become the majority." But how? By adopting a strategy of compromise or confrontation? Bipartisanship or partisanship? By being part of the government or part of the opposition?[2]

THE ARGUMENT

The argument of this book is that the Constitution governs contemporary congressional party politics. Evidence to this effect can be found in the fact that congressional party leaders constantly face a constitutional conundrum, a strategic dilemma defined, at least in part, by the Constitution: compromise or confrontation, bipartisanship or partisanship, pursue policy or play politics, advance the party's agenda or the party's ambition, be part of the government or part of the opposition? This conundrum has its roots in the Constitution; therefore, to understand contemporary congressional party politics, especially the strategic dilemma facing legislative party leaders, we must understand the constitutional playing field. We must begin with the Constitution.

An understanding of the constitutional rules of the game influences both our theory and practice of contemporary congressional party politics. Political scientists and political journalists must appreciate the constitutional context of legislative party politics in order to fully grasp majority- and minority-party machinations. Similarly, congressional party leaders must understand the institutional playing field and constitutional rules of the game if they hope to succeed in advancing their party's ambition and agenda. How effectively we comprehend the constitutional playing field influences how effectively we understand and practice contemporary congressional party politics.

Specifically, we must understand the constitutional separation of powers as more than merely the checks and balances as is often presumed.

Just as the Constitution humbles and empowers presidents and Congress, depending often on the time and circumstances, so, too, does the separation of powers humble and empower majority and minority parties in Congress. A case in point is the above-cited "government or opposition" constitutional constant. This conundrum constantly confronts the majority and minority parties in Congress with both challenges and opportunities as they decide whether to be part of the government or part of the opposition, whether to play the politics of compromise or confrontation, bipartisanship or partisanship. This dilemma may be especially acute in the House.

Congressional partisanship—and the way partisanship plays out in congressional politics—is rooted in the Constitution. In our separation-of-powers system, neither party is ever simply the government or the opposition, unlike the British parliamentary system, where each party knows where it stands. This quandary persists for congressional parties whether under conditions of so-called unified or divided government. The quandary is obvious under divided government. For example, House majority leader Tom Foley (D-WA) observed during the second Reagan administration, "There are two minorities in the House—the Democratic minority vis-à-vis the administration and the Republican minority vis-à-vis the House."[3]

Yet even under so-called united party government, the majority party may occasionally break with a president of their own party, as House Democrats did with Clinton on the North American Free Trade Agreement (NAFTA) in 1993, and as House Democrats found themselves tempted to do with President Obama's Afghan war strategy in 2009.[4] In the latter case, a *Washington Post* headline said it all: "Obama vs. Own Party on Troop Increase."[5] In both instances, minority Republicans worked more cooperatively with the Democratic president than did his own majority party. Sometimes the minority party must accept governing responsibility; sometimes the majority party must resort to playing opposition. Arguably, the Constitution invites compromise and confrontation from both parties at all times. *not just minority*

The complex constitutional "government or opposition" conundrum splits both parties into internal party factions continuously disagreeing over the appropriate legislative strategy. These intraparty disagreements often inform and define party leadership fights within both parties, for example, in the transition from Michel to Gingrich or Gephardt to Pelosi. Since there may not be a simply right answer to this strategic dilemma, party leaders must struggle endlessly to manage factionalism within their own ranks, just as James Madison intended. The challenge Speaker Pelosi faces today, Speaker Gingrich confronted in the 1990s. Before either party can hope to govern the country and Congress, they must first govern themselves. Madison has made this task difficult—not to say impossible.

Both parties must constantly be part of the government and part of the opposition, must campaign *and* govern, must advance their ambition in order to advance their agenda, while advancing their agenda in order to advance their ambition. Madison may deserve the blame or credit for the "permanent campaign" in American politics.

The Constitution confronts congressional party leaders with a daunting electoral and legislative predicament.

CHALLENGING THE CONVENTIONAL WISDOM

Contrary to the conventional wisdom among many political scientists, the Constitution counts. Institutions matter. Constitutional institutions affect behavior. The argument that the Constitution governs political behavior runs contrary to the opinion of Woodrow Wilson, perhaps James Madison's most worthy opponent across two centuries. Wilson and Progressive scholar Herbert Croly were part of the behavioral revolution within political science. In *Progressive Democracy*, Croly sought to "liberate democracy from the bondage of law."[6] Wilson thought the Constitution was essentially irrelevant to congressional behavior: "Institutions are the creatures of opinion."[7] Wilson also sought to demonize disagreement.

Today are we all Wilsonian in our understanding—or misunderstanding—of American politics? This is critical since how we understand politics influences how we practice politics. Arguably, today we may do congressional party politics better than we understand congressional party politics. For this reason, we must return to the Constitution. To understand contemporary congressional party politics, we must take the Founders seriously. We must examine the arguments of both the Federalists and the Anti-Federalists, along with Alexis de Tocqueville's synthesis of the two. We must take seriously the arguments of both Madison and Wilson.

In doing so, we will come to appreciate how institutional and constitutional structures practically and concretely affect legislative behavior by establishing the political playing field. Our parties are creatures of our constitutional system. Evidence supporting this insight can be found in the unending intraparty debates over the strategic dilemma identified above and in party leadership fights premised on this "compromise or confrontation" conundrum. The Constitution, specifically the separation of powers, presents congressional party leaders with a seemingly impossible task.

Contrary to the conventional wisdom, however, the separation of powers is not merely reducible to the checks and balances. Today's presumption that the separation of powers *is* the checks and balances has its roots in Progressive theory, especially that of Woodrow Wilson. Wilson's Whig-like view of the separation of powers as merely the checks and balances assumes the constitutional system contains a bias against change contributing to gridlock and precluding progress. There is an element of truth to this Progressive assumption, but it may be only half the truth. The separation of powers humbles both political branches and both political parties, but the same separation of powers also empowers both branches and both the majority and minority parties. The Founders sought to create limited, but effective, government. The Federalists were not content with the ineffective government of the Articles of Confederation. In its place, they designed the constitutional separation of powers to promote stability *and* energy—to impede change *and* advance innovation.

An example might be seen in how the 1997 budget accord followed upon the 1995–1996 budget showdown/shutdown. Gridlock gave way to governing. The former may have been the predicate for the latter.

As applied to congressional party politics, the assumption that the separation of powers is little more than the checks and balances may support the conclusion that majority parties lose their majorities rather than minority parties winning their majorities. There is probably a large element of truth to this opinion. In our constitutional system, the minority party in the Senate clearly has leverage, but so, too, may the minority party in the House. While the minority party in the House often may need the majority party to provide the opening, majority parties frequently do provide just such an opening because governing is hard. Congressional Democrats' 2009 struggle over health-care reform provides a case in point. One year after the GOP was presumed dead following their 2008 election setbacks, Republicans once again were resurgent. Minority parties are not powerless in our separation-of-powers system; they need not just wait until the majority party fails. Arguably, then, a minority party needs to offer creative alternative policy proposals even if there is initially little hope they will pass. Yet given the constitutional conundrum facing the minority in the House, they frequently debate among themselves whether they need to provide such alternatives. In fall 2009, minority House Republicans felt compelled to offer alternatives to Democrats' health-care reform legislation. Both the majority and minority parties must constantly engage in a balancing act between compromise and confrontation, bipartisanship and partisanship.

Contrary to the conventional wisdom today, partisanship is potentially constructive and constitutionally permissible; it is a normal, natural, and necessary part of our political system. If it is "evil," as some insist, it is a necessary evil. Politics—including partisan politics—is how we do policy; campaigning and governing go hand in hand. Politics is rarely far removed from policymaking; campaigning is inextricably part of governing. Congress, for example, must at all times be responsive and responsible.

Partisanship and bipartisanship are two halves of a whole, two sides of the same coin. We can never fully sort out the blame for partisanship, or for the use of confrontational tactics, or for the irresponsible playing of politics. Woodrow Wilson was right in noting that the separation of powers precludes strict accountability. Thus, the blame game is endless and often is itself a form of partisanship. Speakers Gingrich and Pelosi have both promoted confrontation and compromise as they saw fit, including in their majority-winning efforts to become Speaker.

Partisanship and bipartisanship are not simply in the eye of the beholder. There is probably always an element of truth to the charge that a party is being partisan since parties are partisan—or partial—by their very nature. Indeed, politics is partisan.

Some say the Founders were anti-party. Yet James Madison concluded that "parties seem to have a permanent foundation in the variance of political opinions in free states." Indeed, Madison observed, "The Constitution itself . . . must be an unfailing source of party distinction."[9] It is tempting to concur with Madison and conclude that congressional partisanship to this day is rooted in the Constitution.

Some say the Founders did not expect political parties to form, that parties formed much later in American history. Yet in a 1792 essay titled "A Candid State of Parties," Madison outlines the state of parties at the time in three periods: during the Revolutionary War, during debate over ratification of the Constitution, and following the establishment of the federal government under the new Constitution. Madison concludes this "third division" is "natural to most political societies" and likely will endure.[10] Perhaps even to this day? Of course, "A Candid State of Parties" is arguably a partisan tract, just as was *The Federalist*. Madison, as "the Founder," was a statesman, a politician, a serious political theorist, and a partisan.

Certainly, the Founders' practice of their principles in the first decade of the new republic suggests that they were hardly anti-party. Their ardent partisanship during the 1790s, discussed in chapter 7, provides evidence that partisanship is a normal, natural, and inevitable part of our politics.

Today many lament the "permanent campaign" along with polarizing partisanship, yet both are constitutionally permissible—and may be normal. Partisanship may be greater today than during the relatively quiescent 1950s, the baseline often used to measure heightened partisanship today. In the 1950s, however, political scientists were lamenting the excessively local, parochial, and pluralistic character of our politics. Our parties were said to be "Tweedledee and Tweedledum." The discipline of political science famously called for a more disciplined and responsible two-party system with parties providing a choice not an echo. Perhaps we should be careful what we wish for?

The pluralism of the 1950s and the partisanship of today may both be normal and permissible as argued in chapter 9. Indeed, the potential for pluralism and "conditional party government" may be contained in our constitutional order. Perhaps American politics oscillates between an all-politics-is-local pluralism and an all-politics-is-national approximation of party government. Perhaps our politics oscillates across the decades, as witness the disaggregation of the 1950s and the polarization of today. Or perhaps our politics oscillates within presidential terms. For example, the bipartisanship of George W. Bush's first term—who can forget Teddy Kennedy and President Bush smiling broadly at one another over passage of the No Child Left Behind Act?—contrasts with the partisanship during his second term. Perhaps American politics alternates within congressional terms, with the first year of a new Congress producing more policy, while the second year gives way to politics as the next election approaches. Finally, perhaps American politics fluctuates depending on the issues. For example, partisan warfare in the 2008 election year gave way repeatedly to bipartisan cooperation on Capitol Hill to deal with the looming economic and financial crises. The media made much of partisan conflict in 2008, yet little noted bipartisan cooperation when it occurred.

Both pluralism and party government are, of course, paradigms or perspectives within political science. Each captures part of the complexity of our constitutional system debatably, and thus neither is ever the dominant paradigm in political science. There may be a reason rooted in the Constitution for the oscillating of our politics and for these competing perspectives within political science.

In Federalist No. 10 Madison notes that the "principal task of modern legislation" is the regulation of "various and interfering interests," which "involves the spirit of party and faction in the necessary and ordinary operations of government."[11] Madison's Constitution incorporates both the "mischiefs of faction" and the "spirit of party." American politics encompasses both intense minorities and aspiring majorities, both minority factions (interest groups) and majority sentiment—often given voice by majoritarian parties. The Constitution checks and balances special interests and political parties. The Constitution, however, also embraces and empowers interest groups and political parties.

Arguably, the struggle among contending interest groups both constitutes and corrupts our politics. Similarly, partisan confrontation between political parties both constitutes and corrupts politics. Congressional politics may be a pendulum swing between "pluralism" and "party government," encompassing compromise and confrontation, bipartisanship and partisanship. The ebb and flow of partisanship is a natural part of our constitutional system that in and of itself provides evidence of the dynamic, rather than static, character of the separation of powers.

THE 2008, 2009, AND 2010 ELECTIONS

Were it not for Republicans, Democrats would never win an election; were it not for Democrats, Republicans would never win an election. Is this true?

Following Barack Obama's 2008 election victory coupled with significant gains by congressional Democrats building on their hard-earned 2006 majorities, prognosticators seemed ready to declare the GOP all but dead. Of course, just four years earlier in the aftermath of George W. Bush's 2004 reelection victory, including GOP retention of their congressional majorities, the chattering class had then raised doubts about Democrats' vital signs. President Bush's White House political guru, Karl Rove, declared 2004 to be the advent of a Republican realignment. Two years later, Democrats won majorities in the House and Senate. Rumors of the demise of either party are often premature.

In the 2009 off-year election, the purportedly moribund Republican Party found new life in the tea-leaf readings of gubernatorial elections in Virginia and New Jersey. Ten months into Barack Obama's reign, some were ready to declare the king is dead. Republicans were eagerly anticipating the 2010 midterm elections since the outlook seemed increasingly promising. Minnesota governor and Republican presidential hopeful Tim Pawlenty credited President Obama with providing the GOP an opening, insisting Democrats had misinterpreted the 2008 election results as a mandate: "When one party has total power, they are prone to overplay their hand," he noted. "They did it in a real hurry, and they did it with boldness and a great deal of lack of wisdom and restraint. They've delivered us a new opportunity more rapidly than even the more optimistic amongst us expected."[12]

Republican political consultant Mike Murphy declared "the Obama honeymoon is officially over," and he advised congressional Democrats to begin thinking about a "bipartisan approach" and "compromise."[13] President Obama, Murphy argued, ran as a "post-partisan politician," but Democrats "got a little drunk on power and they've governed as a one-party liberal party. It's been more of the Democratic dogma, particularly in the House under Pelosi," especially with their "one-party health care plan." Murphy insisted, "[I]f the Democrats try to do this alone and ideologically, it's going to be very painful for them politically."[14] This GOP strategist urged congressional Republicans to adopt a centrist, bipartisan approach on health care in order to win the independent voters Democrats had alienated. Murphy cited House GOP Whip Eric Cantor as espousing bipartisanship. Meanwhile, nonpartisan election analyst Rhodes Cook began comparing the 2010 midterm election to 1994 when House Democrats lost their forty-year "permanent majority."[15]

The phoenix-like revival of supposedly down-for-the-count political parties raises questions about congressional party electoral and legislative strategy. The health-care reform fight in the 111th Congress provides a good example of the strategic conundrum facing congressional party leaders.

The decision by Democrats to advance comprehensive, nonincremental health-care reform may by its very nature be partisan especially when it involves fundamental questions about the proper role of government. Not surprisingly, Republicans recommended against comprehensive reform: "Let's don't try to change the whole system at once," counseled moderate senator Lamar Alexander.[16] Conservative columnist Michael Gerson declared, "If the president—opposed by a majority of Americans, with almost no support from the other party—imposes an ideologically divisive health reform, it will smack of radicalism, reinforce polarization and may cede the ideological center to Republicans for years to come."[17] *Washington Post* columnist David Broder, a proponent of bipartisan politics, cited political scientist William Schambra, who maintained that Democrats' "highly rational, comprehensive approach" to health-care reform "fits uncomfortably with the Constitution."[18] Earlier comprehensive progressive reform efforts by Jimmy Carter on energy and Bill Clinton on health-care resulted in failure.

During the House floor debate, Democrats, according to the *Washington Post*, "cast the vote as a long-overdue opportunity to provide affordable health coverage to tens of millions of people and as the final pillar of economic security, alongside Social Security and Medicare. Republicans cast it as the ultimate government overreach, an assault on American liberty that would drive the nation deeper into debt."[19] Again, comprehensive reform augmenting the role of government inevitably promotes polarizing partisanship between the two parties. It also may exacerbate factional tensions within the majority party. Flash points in the debate over Democrats' House and Senate health-care reform bills—the public option, abortion, taxes, Medicare cuts, increased deficits—presented Democratic congressional party leaders with problems within their own party as well as between the two parties.[20]

The fight within the two parties—for example, between Blue Dogs and Progressive Caucus House Democrats—may often be as critical as the fight between the two parties. Party leaders sometimes wonder, with friends like these, who needs enemies? Managing factionalism is a challenge for congressional party leaders who frequently have their hands full with internal party divisions.

DEMOCRATS' DILEMMA

As the majority party in the 111th Congress, Democrats found attempting to govern tough; in advancing health-care reform, they were especially "mired in division."[21] Their earlier success in recruiting moderates to run in 2006 and 2008 in order to build their majority ironically compounded their strategic dilemma.[22] Still, Speaker Pelosi displayed skill and tenacity in managing intraparty factionalism over health-care reform on issues ranging from the public option to abortion during fall 2009.[23] As a member of the liberal wing of her caucus, she found herself frequently saying "no" to her liberal friends.[24] She did so, according to *National Journal*'s Richard E. Cohen, because Pelosi believed "failure is not an option" for Democrats on health-care reform.[25]

This mantra became an article of faith among congressional Democrats. The lesson of the defeat of "Clinton Care" prior to the 1994 election, according to many Democrats, was that failure would only prove they were not ready to govern, thereby alienating their base and resulting in electoral disaster. Congressional Democrats were so convinced by this interpretation of history that they were willing to pass health-care reform in the Senate using budget reconciliation at the risk of seriously exacerbating already-high partisan tensions.[26] Michael Barone articulated the dilemma facing Democrats: "There is a prevailing assumption around town that failure to pass major health care legislation would be political death. But passing a law that produces a horrible mess could be even more electorally deadly."[27] Once again, the majority party may face a damned-if-you-do, damned-if-you-don't strategic dilemma.

RESURGENT REPUBLICANS?

While Democrats were caught between a rock and a hard place in trying to govern, Republicans were learning that it is easier, albeit only marginally so, to be united in opposition. At the opening of the 111th Congress, Republicans were busy calibrating their role as the opposition, striving to find the "right blend of cooperation and defiance."[28] House Republican leader John Boehner insisted, publicly at least, that Republicans could not simply be the "Party of No," and "must offer solutions to voters' problems." He vowed to find "common ground" with Democrats. His Senate counterpart, Mitch McConnell, pledged to be "a respectful, loyal opposition."[29]

Yet "internal divisions" within the Grand Old Party raised doubts about bipartisanship. Some in the conservative wing of the party perceived the "instinct" to "compromise" as collaboration or worse—capitulation. Party leaders were caught between principle and pragmatism. The *Wall Street Journal*'s Naftali Bendavid said Republicans faced "a central challenge: re-energizing party loyalists while beginning to win back the centrists who had just rejected them so decisively" in the 2008 election.[30] Not surprisingly, Republicans concluded they should "adopt different strategies for different bills." According to the *Washington Post*'s Dan Balz, in seeking a "path to revival," Republicans also had to maneuver between "the conservative grass-roots" and "swing voters," between "populist conservative forces" and "party regulars," between "conservative insurgents" and the "party establishment."[31] They needed to work on recruitment and message; they needed candidates and new ideas—but which candidates and which ideas?

As the minority party in Congress, Republicans suffered the fate of the party out of the White House in our separation-of-powers system: they were unable to speak with one voice. Consequently, Republicans often found themselves defined in the media as much by tea party protestors and angry August town-hall meetings as by their elected leaders in Congress. House GOP Whip Eric Cantor sought the high ground of principles and ideas by founding, along with Jeb Bush and others, the awkwardly titled National Council for a New America. Election analyst Charlie Cook quickly rained on that parade, suggesting new ideas did not matter for the out party: "They're going to succeed in the short term by throwing rocks and by attacking."[32]

The GOP soon became identified as the "Party of No" on health-care reform, the Democrats' key legislative initiative. They provided an almost perfectly unified phalanx in opposition during floor consideration in November 2009.[33]

In doing so, Republicans were perhaps taking their cue from Nancy Pelosi, who successfully brought Democrats out of twelve years in the minority in 2006. Pelosi did so, arguably, by borrowing in turn from Newt Gingrich's playbook leading up to the 1994 House Republican "revolution." Apparently the "Party of No" knows something about winning majorities?

In the 109th Congress leading up to the 2006 election, Pelosi-led Democrats said "no" to President George W. Bush's efforts at Social Security reform, tax reform, and immigration reform:

> Whatever the merits of Bush's plans for Social Security reform, tax reform, or immigration reform, one fact stood out: the Republicans had nothing positive to present to the country. Unified control of government had not allowed Republicans to achieve their aims, but it would allow Democrats to hold Republicans to blame.[34]

The parallels between Democrats' opposition on Social Security reform in the 109th Congress and Republicans' opposition to health-care reform in the 111th Congress are striking. In thwarting Social Security reform, were Democrats being partisan for the sake of partisanship—seeking to advance their ambition or their agenda? Were they acting out of partisanship or principled motives? Probably both. Similarly, on health-care reform in the 111th Congress, were Republicans being merely partisan or were they standing on principle? Again, probably both.

In both cases, the polarizing partisanship was all the more acute because the reforms raised fundamental questions about the role of government. Bush was said to be "privatizing" Social Security and rolling back the signature achievement of New Deal Democrats. Bush's efforts were in line with Ronald Reagan's efforts to limit the growth of government with his tax and spending policies, and in line with Newt Gingrich's "devolution revolution," including Welfare Reform in 1996. Obama's health-care reform effort expanding the role of government was billed as completing the project begun by Progressives, and in line with FDR's Social Security initiative and LBJ's Medicare reform. Clearly principle is at stake on both sides, but so, too, is ambition.

As *Politico*'s Jim VandeHei and Mike Allen outlined:

> The health care debate has brought all of this into stark relief. One thing Republicans and Democrats agree on is this: The best way for the GOP to win back the House is to do to health care what Democrats did to Social Security and other issues to win control in 2006: Energize the party by creating a unified front in opposition to the White House.
>
> "They're just trying to run the same playbook," said a Democratic Hill aide. "The way we took down Social Security, they're trying to do the same thing with health care. You take down the idea first, and then you go after the president. We went after Social Security privatization first, scaring seniors. That injured the president, and we came back."[35]

With health-care reform, Democrats may have been presenting congressional Republicans with the opening they need in 2010 when only a year earlier pundits declared the GOP comatose. The Gallup Poll's fall 2009 generic ballot found Republicans in a better position than prior to the 1994 election. Perhaps because Democrats had broken President Obama's post-partisan promise, the *Washington Post*'s "wrong track" poll numbers were similar to those prior to the 1994 and 2006 elections.[36] Election analyst Rhodes Cook was already asking, "The GOP: Poised for Another Quick Comeback?"[37] Cook compared the 2008 election with Democratic victories in 1964, 1976, and 1992. In all three instances, the Republican Party rebounded quickly, perhaps most notably in 1994. But Cook also raised the prospect of 2008 looking more like 1932 and the beginning of FDR's New Deal Democratic realignment. Republicans could not take anything for granted. Cook concluded, "At this point, it looks like the GOP's future could go either way."

So Republicans rolled the dice, called for a redo on health-care reform and urged a more incremental approach. Even Newt Gingrich was back with a plan he dubbed "A Growth Vision for Health Reform."[38]

Clearly, midterm elections are one way Madison empowers minority parties in Congress. The 1994 and 2006 elections provide clear examples, but so, too, may the 2010 election. Midterms often enable the out party to pick up seats, but the looming electoral pressure on the majority party can also provide the minority with leverage in the legislative process. Again, the Constitution governs contemporary congressional party politics. James Madison rules America: just ask Newt and Nancy.

ROADMAP

In what follows, chapter 1 refines the focus of the book, further defining the strategic conundrum confronting congressional party leaders particularly in the House. Chapter 1 places the argument of the book in the context of the contemporary practice of congressional party politics. In recent decades, two House leaders, Newt Gingrich and Nancy Pelosi, dealt effectively with the strategic dilemma confronting them, successfully leading their party from a minority to a majority. Chapter 1 also grounds the book in the literature on congressional party polarization. Chapter 2 focuses on the rise of Nancy Pelosi. Chapter 3 focuses on Newt Gingrich and his echoes of Anti-Federalist thought. Chapters 4, 5, and 6 respectively examine the ideas of Wilson, Tocqueville, and Madison. In many ways, Tocqueville provides a bridge between Federalists and Anti-Federalists, between Madison and Wilson. Chapter 7 considers the Founders' practice of their principles in order to bring a necessary historical and constitutional perspective to the topic. Similarly, chapter 8 explores more recent case studies of legislative party strategy. Finally, chapter 9 draws conclusions about the intimate connection between constitutional theory and contemporary political practice.

1

~

Congressional Party Strategy

Aﬆter the 2000 presidential elections, Democrats turned on themselves. During election postmortems even Democratic standard bearers Al Gore and Joe Lieberman, along with former president Bill Clinton, famously engaged in finger pointing, often blaming one another for advancing a failed campaign strategy.[1] In the aftermath of the 2002 midterm elections, dispirited Democrats again engaged in yet another round of the blame game, complete with scapegoating, infighting, and recriminations directed at their party leaders.

Following the 2002 congressional elections, of course, Democrats could not blame the "top of the ticket" since there was no top of the ticket. Naturally, they turned their fire on the next available target, congressional party leaders. Many blamed Senate Democratic leader Tom Daschle and House Democratic leader Dick Gephardt for their purported failure to compete effectively during the previous legislative session with Republican president George W. Bush on two central issues: tax cuts and war with Iraq. Daschle survived the criticism. Gephardt did not.

Subsequent to the midterm elections, Dick Gephardt stepped down as House Democratic leader having failed to lead his party out of the minority in four straight elections. During election postmortems, many argued that Democrats lost House and Senate seats in the midterm election because congressional Democrats failed to offer a clear alternative to President Bush on taxes and Iraq prior to the election. Democrats debated whether to be part of the "government" or part of the "opposition." They debated whether they should have stood on principle and confronted President Bush on tax cuts and war as their liberal wing wished, or

15

whether they should have adopted a more accommodating centrism in order to blunt GOP issues and appeal to swing voters.

The ensuing House Democratic leadership fight between Nancy Pelosi and Martin Frost highlighted their different approaches to legislative party strategy. Congresswoman Pelosi won in large part because a majority of Democrats wanted a bold new direction; they perceived her as best able to offer voters a choice rather than an echo of the Republicans. "We must draw clear distinctions between our vision of the future and the extreme policies put forth by the Republicans," Pelosi argued.[2] Frost responded, "The battleground seats in this country are in swing, marginal, moderate and conservative areas. If we want to write off all those seats, if we want to say 'We want to be to the left, and we want to be pure,' we will be a permanent minority party."[3]

A permanent minority? Clearly, House Democrats did not want to echo the House GOP by becoming the "permanent minority" Republicans were for forty years prior to their Newt Gingrich–inspired 1994 "revolution." Yet by 2004, House Democrats had served a full decade as the minority party in the House. The last time Democrats remained mired so long in the House minority was from 1919 to 1931 prior to FDR's New Deal Democratic realignment. At the opening of the 108th Congress some were beginning to worry that they might remain mired in the minority for the foreseeable future. Representative Jim Cooper (D-TN) noted House Democrats were getting accustomed to losing: "I go to too many meetings in Washington where the attitude among Democrats is how to lose gracefully. Too many Democrats never have served in the majority."[4] Almost preternaturally, House Democrats began mimicking the old "permanent minority" House GOP behavior in important ways.

During their forty years in the "permanent minority" wilderness, House Republicans seemed to develop a special fondness for circular firing squads; their favorite tactic at times seemed to be shooting themselves in the foot in order to bleed all over the Democrats.[5] House Republicans spent much time, energy, and angst following disappointing elections fighting among themselves and castigating each other over legislative party strategy. In their long tenure as a "permanent minority," Republicans had repeated opportunities to fight over leadership strategy. Such fights typically entailed challenges to House Republican leaders or blaming GOP presidents. Newt Gingrich's early 1990s challenge to Republican Leader Bob Michel is one such instance of the former.[6] House GOP insurgents' 1992 "win the House by losing the White House" strategy is an example of the latter.[7]

The 1994 House Republican "revolution" brought the GOP out of the "permanent minority" wilderness. The 2006 election did the same for House Democrats after twelve years in the minority. Newt Gingrich and

Nancy Pelosi were widely credited with executing successful—and quite similar—legislative strategies in leading their congressional parties into the majority.[8] How did these two recent House leaders successfully lead their parties from a minority to a majority? Each addressed effectively the strategic dilemma confronting congressional party leaders.

GOVERNMENT OR OPPOSITION?

In January 2003, Democrats found themselves on the horns of a dilemma, namely, whether to be part of the "government" or part of the "opposition." Any party wishing to gain or retain a majority must address this central strategic dilemma of congressional party politics. In the British parliamentary system, the majority party is the government and the minority party is the loyal opposition. Our separation of powers muddles this partisan calculus especially under conditions of divided government. Yet even when one party controls both the White House and Congress, the other party still confronts a complex conundrum.

At the opening of the 108th Congress, for example, Democrats faced a series of daunting questions. Should they play the "opposition" confronting, and perhaps obstructing, the GOP's efforts at playing "government"? Should they return to their liberal ideological base offering voters a clear alternative perspective, while mostly obstructing Bush initiatives? Should they follow the moderate Democratic Leadership Council's lead, adopting an accommodating centrism, working with Republicans, and appealing to moderate voters in swing districts? Or should they adopt a "third way" as Congressman Harold Ford suggested during his brief challenge to Pelosi for the minority leadership post?

In such a circumstance, minority party members may be damned if they do and damned if they don't. The first approach risks the irrelevance of Hooverism. Worse still, obstructionism may look like the politics of "no," giving voters little affirmative reason to embrace a merely confrontational party. Yet an accommodating centrism may cause a party to lose its principles *and* its base. The 108th Congress Democrats, for example, could ill afford to risk a mimicking me-too-ism offering Bush-lite, while playing the pale moon reflecting the dominant Republican sun. Either approach conceivably might risk relegating them to "permanent minority" status. Yet defining an appropriate third way may be easier said than done.

And what about the majority party? Following the 2002 midterm elections, the good news for the GOP was that they had won. The bad news, of course, was also that they had won. Under conditions of united Republican government following a clearly nationalized election, they arguably were the responsible governing party. Democratic National Committee chair Terry McAuliffe made precisely this point in speaking about President Bush who had actively campaigned for—and who was widely credited with promoting—united Republican government:

> The burden of leadership rests squarely on his shoulders. The president got what he asked for, and now he'll have to produce. . . . No more blame game. No more nonsense about a dysfunctional Senate. This is his sputtering economy; he must take responsibility for it. . . . The Bush era of responsibility starts today.[9]

Following the 2002 midterm elections, Republicans seemingly had the opportunity and the challenge of offering an attractive, coherent governing philosophy in hopes of augmenting their narrow majorities in the House and Senate in the next election. Presumably—and as we shall see, this presumption is presumptuous—congressional Republicans also wanted to help Republican president George W. Bush get reelected in 2004. Part of the challenge for the GOP was the need to coordinate Republicans in the White House, Senate, and House of Representatives: no mean feat given our separation-of-powers system.[10]

At the risk of getting ahead of the story discussed in chapter 2, it is worth noting that following the 2004 election, George W. Bush was still president, while congressional Democrats lost seats in both the House and the Senate. Of even greater symbolic significance, perhaps, Tom Daschle and Martin Frost both lost their reelection bids. Democrats on the Hill and in the hinterlands reportedly suffered from a new psychological malady, P.E.S.T. (postelection stress trauma). Did Hill Democrats adopt the right legislative party strategy following the 2002 election? Did they help or hurt themselves in the 2004 election with the tack they took following the 2002 election? Finally, does Nancy Pelosi, like Newt Gingrich before her, deserve credit for leading House Democrats to victory with a successful legislative party strategy in 2006?

LEGISLATIVE PARTY STRATEGY

Government or opposition? Compromise or confrontation? Is there a right answer to this question? As we shall see below, politicians spend a lot of time debating the question of legislative party strategy, and political journalists spill a lot of ink outlining and highlighting these interparty squabbles and intraparty debates. But does the question of legislative party strategy really matter?

Much of the political-science literature on congressional party leadership seems to question whether leaders matter, thus by implication calling into question whether leadership strategy, in particular legislative party-strategy, matters.[11] Did it matter that House Republicans sidelined Bob Michel and the "old guard," thereby making room for "young turks" like Newt Gingrich, in the late 1980s? Did it matter that House Democrats at the opening of the 108th Congress retired Dick Gephardt and elected Nancy Pelosi, presumably in hopes she would adopt a more principled, partisan, and confrontational stance toward President Bush and the GOP majority?

To answer these questions, we might begin by carefully defining the legislative party strategy question in concrete, practical terms. Specifically, we can sharpen and define the question by borrowing politicians' own words and by relying on their understandings of the strategic dilemma facing legislative party leaders. We can try to understand the question as they understand the question. We can take seriously what politicians, and their closest observers, political journalists, take seriously. Maybe party politicians and political journalists know what they are doing. If, as some political scientists seem to believe, leadership does not matter, then leadership fights do not matter. Neither therefore, does the "government or opposition" or the "compromise or confrontation" question matter. Why then do politicians and political journalists waste so much time, energy and ink debating it?

As political scientists we cannot assume we understand politicians better than they understand themselves. Politicians act as if party-leadership fights matter. They act as if such leadership contests turn on questions of legislative party strategy, earnestly debating the same. Can this strategic dilemma be of little consequence given how seriously politicians take it? Political scientists must take seriously what politicians take seriously. Empirical evidence that the legislative strategy question matters abounds in the actions, opinions, and words of politicians and their closest observers.

If legislative leaders like Newt Gingrich or Nancy Pelosi take seriously the question of legislative party strategy, then political scientists must also. If serious and long-time Congress watchers like the *Washington Post*'s David Broder, or *National Journal*'s Richard E. Cohen, or the *L.A. Times*'s Janet Hook take seriously the "government or opposition" or the "compromise or confrontation" question, then so, too, should political science. Taking seriously and trying to parse the strategic dilemma facing legislative party leaders is the purpose of this study. In endeavoring to pass legislation or in seeking to gain or retain a legislative party majority, how should congressional party leaders play politics and pursue policy? Should they adopt a posture of compromising bipartisanship or confrontational partisanship? Should they be part of the "government" or part of the "opposition"? Meeting this challenge and answering this question correctly requires an adequate understanding of the institutional and constitutional context and circumstances. Understanding the institutional context is critical, and such an understanding begins with the recognition that the constitutional separation of powers defines that institutional context. Party leaders, political journalists, and political scientists misunderstand constitutional context at their peril. For example, contemporary commentary on congressional party politics seems premised on the presumption that partisanship, especially when engineered by Republicans, is constitutionally suspect. Is it?

 The specific aim of this study is to examine how institutional context defined by the constitutional separation of powers affects the strategic calculus party leaders face.

For both parties, of course, the real challenge remains translating the strategic "government or opposition" question into concrete, practical legislative tactics on particular pieces of legislation. Often much is lost "twixt cup and lip," or in this case, between strategic vision and tactical floor battles.[12] Just as critical, the role of legislative party strategy must, of course, be understood in the context of other factors strongly influencing congressional elections, especially candidate quality. Such factors include retirement, recruitment, reapportionment, redistricting, fund-raising, get out the vote (GOTV) efforts and the long-term building of farm teams in state legislatures.[13] All these and more influence legislative party success in attaining majority status, but the purpose of this study is to focus intently on the influence of the constitutional separation of powers on party leaders' legislative strategic calculus. How does the institutional and constitutional playing field affect the calculus of party leaders? Does it make compromise or confrontation, bipartisanship or partisanship more appropriate?

The actions, opinions, and words of politicians may help political scientists better understand the true nature of the separation of powers. We can learn about separation of powers *theory* from the *practical* experience and *practical* insights of politicians. What is the connection between theory and practice, between institutions and behavior? Do institutions affect behavior? Does political theory, defined as differing perspectives on the separation of powers, matter? Do political-science paradigms, including the "party government" and "pluralist" perspectives on the separation of powers, matter? Do such ideas have consequences?

Asking politicians provides a good starting point for answering the above questions. Even though politicians, like all human beings, sometimes say one thing and do another, they act as if leadership fights matter. In the process, they earnestly debate legislative party strategy. Interview evidence suggests that competing ideas about legislative strategy do matter to politicians. Can the strategic dilemma really be of little consequence given how seriously politicians take it? We can begin to address the questions above by parsing the strategic challenge confronting legislative parties.

THE STRATEGIC DILEMMA

In the most general sense, the strategic dilemma confronting legislative party leaders takes the form of the choice between "government or opposition," "compromise or confrontation," or ("pursuing policy or playing politics." In popular parlance, it often takes the form of debates about bipartisanship and partisanship. To sort out this question further, it helps to think of legislative politics as *individuals* working in the context of political *institutions* to manage and mediate competing *interests* and *ideas*.[14] Congressional party leaders, operating within our separation-of-powers system, strive to balance competing interests, including factions, and competing ideas, including party principles, within and between the parties. To understand the strategic dilemma, therefore, we need to look at institutions, individuals, interests and ideas.

Institutions

Compromise and conflict exist broadly in all human affairs. The "government or opposition" calculus exists in both the British parliamentary system and Congress. The different constitutional forms of government, however, cast this legislative calculus in dramatically different terms. While in the British system one party is the "government," and the other is the "opposition," American parties do not have the luxury of such clear-cut roles.[15] Indeed, American parties in our separation-of-powers system find themselves hoisted on the horns of a more complex "government or opposition" dilemma. Are they inevitably both at all times? Further complicating the calculus is the necessary connection in the U.S. Constitution between the separation of powers, bicameralism, and federalism.[16]

Bicameralism first. A legislative branch consisting of coequal chambers, like the House and the Senate, naturally complicates the partisan calculus beyond the separation of powers between the president and Congress. House and Senate Democrats, and House and Senate Republicans, do not always see eye-to-eye with their copartisans in the "other body." As an American Political Science Association Congressional Fellow, I was privileged to sit in on joint Republican leadership staff meetings. The lack of cooperation, and lack of mutual understanding, was at times surprising. Similarly, my interviews of House and Senate Republican Policy Committee staffers in the 1980s revealed a remarkable chasm between copartisans in the two chambers.

The federal character of our constitutional system further complicates intraparty relations by reinforcing the separation of powers. Different electoral bases for presidents, senators, and House members tend to augment divisions and tensions between the branches and the chambers. Presidents naturally tend to adopt a more national perspective, contrary to the more parochial perspective members of Congress tend to adopt. Serious institutional analysis must ask whether the constitutional separation of powers concretely and practically affects leaders' decision calculus.

Individuals

Individual-level analysis can ask, does free agency exist and do leaders matter?[17] Does leadership strategy matter? Do leaders' understandings of legislative strategy and the separation of powers matter? For party leaders, are there practical consequences for understanding or misunderstanding the separation of powers and how it defines legislative strategy? The answer to all three questions is yes. Certainly during the Pelosi/Frost contest following the 2002 midterm election, leadership strategy seemed to matter to these two leaders and to rank-and-file members. Similarly, House Republicans fought tooth and nail during the 1980s over the proper legislative strategy for escaping their seeming "permanent minority" status. Central to Newt Gingrich's challenge to Bob Michel's leadership were questions of legislative strategy. These debates over legislative party strategy are inevitably premised on implicit or explicit understandings of the fundamental nature of the American political system and, in particular, the constitutional context defined by the separation of powers.

Some credit the 1994 electoral success of Newt Gingrich and the House GOP to his strategy of confronting Democratic president Bill Clinton and congressional Democrats during the 103rd Congress. Others suggest that Gingrich's later failure in the 1995–1996 budget showdown and government shutdowns was due to his unwillingness to compromise, his failure to make the transition from "campaigning" to "governing," and ultimately to his misjudging the fundamental nature of our political system.[18] The Gingrich example also raises questions about the personality and temperament of legislative leaders. Is there a connection between personality, style, and a leader's approach to legislative strategy? More so than Bob Michel, Newt Gingrich refused to accept the "go along to get along" approach to legislative politics. As an insurgent "backbench bomb thrower," Gingrich seemed more comfortable storming the majority House Democrats' Bastille than making the legislative trains run on time as Speaker. This wartime *consigliere* eventually had trouble managing the peace. Finally, congressional party-leadership *style* increasingly seems to require both an inside and an outside strategy; in the information age, "going public" may be a necessary strategy for legislative leaders as well as presidents.[19]

Ideas

Ideas include a party's principles, priorities, policies, and platform, or in general their understanding of the *ends* or purposes of government. The ideological leanings of our two broad-based, coalitional parties tend to range from moderate centrism to the more ardent approach of the liberal or conservative wings of the Democratic and Republican parties; though it is worth noting that today the ideological divide in the House between liberal Democrats and conservative Republicans is essentially complete. A yawning "empty center" or chasm exists between the two parties in the House.[20] Ideas might also entail competing opinions about the best *means* to advancing party principles whether by winning floor fights or by winning more seats in Congress.

Interestingly enough, there often seems to be a correlation between ideology and a willingness to adopt a stance of confrontation or accommodation toward the opposing party. The party extremes seem more inclined to opt for a legislative strategy of partisan confrontation, while moderates of both parties are often more willing to embrace bipartisan compromise.[21] Perhaps this is because moderates do not have far to reach across the aisle, though again, today there are seemingly fewer moderates in either party. On the other hand, tactical differences between ideological factions within each party at times seem tantamount to fundamentally different understandings of the nature of Congress and, therefore, of the nature of our constitutional separation of powers. Fights over legislative party tactics often seem premised on competing strategic visions that, in turn, are founded on differing understandings of the constitutional context of Congress. Liberal Democrats and conservative Republicans may be more inclined toward viewing Congress in terms of what political scientists call "party government," while centrists may be more amenable to working within the confines of the pluralism of "committee government." The former invites partisanship and confrontation, the latter approach tends to promote bipartisanship and accommodation. Do members' and leaders' different implicit understandings of the fundamental nature of congressional politics and the separation of powers matter? Are centrists in both parties correct in assessing the need for greater bipartisan compromise to advance their agendas and their ambitions, or are the more ideologically strident in both parties right in recognizing the need for partisanship as a constitutionally permissible and even necessary legislative strategy? Are pragmatic centrists or more ardent ideological partisans more accurate in their understanding of constitutional context and the proper approach to legislative party strategy?

Interests

Factions within legislative parties often differ on questions of legislative party strategy; for example, factional divisions were evident in the Pelosi/Frost and Gingrich/Michel leadership fights. Such factional divisions, however, are not limited to ideology; they can include generational and geographic divisions as well.

The generational divide often translates into a tactical division between the "old guard" and "young turks," between the "establishment" and the "revolutionaries." The late, long-time House Republican Barber B. Conable, Jr., observed,

> When new members come into a complicated institution like the House, they are likely to experience a high degree of frustration. Fresh from the People, highly motivated, anxious to get on with the business of saving the world, they find the key to legislative spots foreclosed by the elderly Establishment types. . . . Old as I am, I recall being a "young turk" at one point and participating noisily in a successful effort to change House rules which the Establishment found adequate. I learned a lot about the institution from the effort, vented my frustrations, and gradually became part of the Establishment myself. Youth presses age, provides a good deal of the dynamic and the dialogue, and eventually ages. Partisans may not like the tranquility of my view of these recent histories, but I find reassurance in the cycle of renewal.[22]

The "cycle of renewal," Conable implies, educates members to the natural tendency of members to adapt to a more incremental, less confrontational approach to legislating over time.

Another factional division within congressional parties involves region or geography, especially political geography. Members from heavily "blue" or heavily "red" states or districts may be more inclined to foment partisan divisions than members from marginal or swing seats. Whether a member hails from a safe or competitive district may influence just how partisan and confrontational they are willing to be.

Interests, Ideas, Institutions, and Individuals

Congressional party leaders must balance competing interests and ideas because legislative politics is about both interests and ideas. Congress is both a bargaining and a deliberative institution.[23] The legislative process includes bargaining and trade-offs among competing interests as well as principled deliberation and debate over grand principles. Members of Congress represent both local, parochial interests and national party principles. Congress is simultaneously pluralist and majoritarian—hence both slow incrementalism and partisan "revolution" characterize the legislative process, though perhaps at different times and on different issues. Congress embodies both "friction" and "fission."[24]

Congress can accommodate, albeit at different times, the all-politics-is-local "pluralism" of Tip O'Neill and the national "party government" strategy of Newt Gingrich's "revolution." Indeed, neither the "pluralist" nor the "party government" perspective alone fully captures the essence of the legislative process.[25] We see this "dual nature" of Congress in the competing committee and party-leadership structures.[26] Congress contains the potential for both "committee government" and "party government." Stated in terms of contemporary political-science paradigms, Congress exemplifies both pluralism and party government. Understanding the role of interests and ideas in Congress necessitates examining the importance of institutions and individuals as well.

As an institution Congress is constantly steeped in both politics and policy. As individuals, members are constantly engaged in both campaigning and governing. Indeed, politics and policy as well as campaigning and governing cannot be readily distinguished in principle or practice in American politics. For example, given the nature of our separation-of-powers system with its frequent and regular elections, Congress and its members seem to be on constant campaign footing.

At the same time, Congress and its members have a permanent responsibility for governing, a responsibility they share, of course, with the executive. The same cannot simply be said for the contemporary British Parliament. Once the majority party in the House of Commons "forms a government," Parliament essentially turns over its authority for governing to the executive, specifically the prime minister and his or her cabinet. It may not be too much of an exaggeration to say that once the prime minister and cabinet get the blessing of the queen to "form a government," Parliament all but extinguishes its own authority short of the next election or a potential future vote of no confidence in the "government."

Congress, on the other hand, never extinguishes its own authority, nor does the Constitution allow it to do so.[27] Congress may frequently look to the president for leadership or take cues from the executive, but Congress always remains part of the "government" and always retains responsibility for governing. Indeed, congressional parties and members, especially those with a president of their own party in the White House, are frequently torn between loyalty to the White House and loyalty to their congressional party leadership. Both parties, when confronted with a president of their own party in the White House, must constantly cope with a factional tension between presidential loyalists and congressional party loyalists.[28]

In short, Congress as an institution requires members and congressional parties to constantly govern and constantly campaign, to constantly pursue policy and constantly play politics. The complexity of this strategic dilemma confronting legislative parties is at the heart of many important books about American politics. We can sharpen our understanding of the strategic dilemma still further by examining the arguments in *Learning to Govern* by Richard F. Fenno, *Politics by Other Means* by Benjamin Ginsberg and Martin Shefter, and *The Permanent Campaign and Its Future* edited by Norman Ornstein and Thomas Mann, all written during the 1990s. Subsequently, the current decade has spawned a raft of studies on partisan polarization, including Ron Brownstein's *The Second Civil War*, Mann and Ornstein's *The Broken Branch*, and the Annenberg Democracy Project book titled *A Republic Divided*. All six of these books, on balance, seem to argue for a politics of bipartisan compromise over partisan confrontation. Implicitly, and in some cases explicitly, they conclude that our constitutional system requires above all an accommodating politics of bipartisan compromise. Are they right?

To hone our understanding of legislative strategy and the constitutional context legislative parties confront, we can begin productively by examining all six of the above books. Fenno first.

LEARNING TO GOVERN

In 1997, Richard Fenno concluded that "forty consecutive years as the minority party in the House left the Republicans, as of November 1994, totally without first-hand political experience of two essential sorts: experience in *interpreting* electoral victory and experience in *governing* the country."[29] Fenno argued that House Republicans overinterpreted their 1994 victory as a mandate for the Contract with America, and more importantly, they failed to learn to govern. Only through experience as the majority party—something House Republicans lacked in 1994—could Republicans gain the necessary "governing expertise." Such "expertise" about "the business of legislating"

> involves a practical grasp of lawmaking as a lengthy, incremental, multi-level, coalition-building process. And it involves a seasoned strategic sense in matters such as establishing priorities, negotiating outcomes across the separated institutions of government, and calculating feasibilities, trade-offs, and timing at every decision-making juncture.[30]

In *Learning to Govern*, Fenno defines governing as the careful, incremental, coalition-building of a pluralist system. Governing entails bargaining and trade-offs; governing means compromise and accommodation. While Fenno is at least partially right—indeed, probably in large part right—his definition of governing seems incomplete. Is that all there is to governing?

Does "learning to govern" mean merely learning to compromise—or does successful governing also sometimes entail partisan confrontation? Fenno criticizes Gingrich for his failure to compromise.

As a "permanent minority," House Republicans and their leader, Newt Gingrich, displayed plenty of talent in the politics of partisan confrontation. Some credit Gingrich's 1994 electoral success to his nationalizing the election through the politics of confrontation, including House Republicans' effort to defeat Hillary Clinton's health-care initiative, and their discipline in making House Democrats walk the plank on the vote to pass President Clinton's budget in the 103rd Congress. The House GOP's Contract with America was an explicit effort to nationalize the election by sharpening differences between the parties.

Was Gingrich's 1994 electoral success using a strategy of partisan confrontation premised on an accurate understanding of the institutional and constitutional playing field? As part of the minority, under conditions of united Democratic government, Gingrich apparently could play the politics of a full-throated partisanship—and win. However, Gingrich's later failings as leader of the new majority House GOP, Fenno implies, were premised on a failure to understand the need for a governing majority to compromise, and more generally a failure to understand how our separation-of-powers system works.

Fenno argues Newt Gingrich failed to "learn to govern" because he misjudged the nature of our political system including "the separated institutions of government."[31] Note that for Fenno, "learning to govern" includes understanding the fundamental nature of our constitutional system as defined by the separation of powers. Note also that in defining governing as, in large part, compromise and accommodation, Fenno argues, in effect, that the strategic-dilemma question at the heart of this study matters. Newt Gingrich's failure to understand the "compromise or confrontation" conundrum facing legislative leaders had, according to Fenno, concrete, practical legislative and electoral consequences. If individual leadership skills are not important, as some political scientists conclude, then why does Fenno's "learning to govern" matter?[32] Fenno's criticism of Speaker Gingrich suggests leadership matters, and leadership understanding of the separation of powers matters. To be successful, congressional party leaders need to understand the constitutional context within which they operate. So, too, do political scientists and journalists.

POLITICS BY OTHER MEANS

In their three editions of the popular book *Politics by Other Means*, Benjamin Ginsberg and Martin Shefter lament the fact that American elections seem to settle nothing, hence partisans continue sniping at one another between elections. Safely ensconced in their institutional redoubts, especially under conditions of divided government, the two parties continue playing "politics" rather than soberly pursuing "policy." Ginsberg and Shefter dislike the confrontational tactics of ceaseless "institutional combat," and they disdain the personal attack politics of what they term "revelation, investigation and prosecution" or "RIP."[33] Clearly, Ginsberg and Shefter are onto something. Many Americans today bemoan the bitter partisan politics of "red and blue" America along with the tawdry politics of personal destruction seemingly so commonplace in recent years. Yet one cannot help but wonder if the authors are judging American politics as wanting by contrasting our practice with an idealized vision of what politics ought to be borrowed from the "party government" viewpoint, a perspective articulated, for example, by Woodrow Wilson in *Congressional Government*.

Echoing historian Daniel Boorstin, Ginsberg and Shefter cite the "genius of American politics" as the "virtue" of "compromise," rather than the vice of "conflict."[34] Unfortunately, according to the authors, in the United States today "electoral success often fails to confer the capacity to govern," especially under conditions of divided government.[35] Inevitably, institutional combat ensues and individual politicians too often resort to the politics of personal attack against partisan foes. This raises a question: Is "politics by other means" inevitably part of the separation of powers since our constitutional separation of powers, unlike the British parliamentary system, surely bears considerable responsibility for elections failing to settle partisan conflict? Arguably both parties, even under conditions of united party government, still retain some responsibility for governing. Given the regularity and frequency of American elections, it is perhaps not altogether surprising that both parties remain on a permanent "war" footing, constantly "campaigning" and playing politics rather than earnestly pursuing policy.

At the same time, Ginsberg and Shefter make an important distinction between "institutional combat" and "RIP" tactics. Institutional combat may be perpetual in our separation-of-powers system since both major parties are constantly confronted with the "government or opposition" strategic dilemma. But must institutional combatants necessarily resort to "RIP" tactics and the politics of personal destruction? During an early 1990s interview, Congressman Vin Weber, a Gingrich comrade-in-arms, made an important distinction between the politics of principled partisan confrontation and the politics of personal destruction.[36] Weber wholeheartedly embraced Gingrich's confrontational politics, yet he criticized the manner in which Gingrich personalized political differences. Weber, for example, was reluctant to follow Gingrich's lead in attacking Speaker Jim Wright.

If "politics by other means" means *confrontational* tactics, then it may be a by-product of our separation-of-powers system. But if "politics by other means" means the "politics of personal destruction" or the criminalization of political differences, then it may not inevitably flow from our constitutional system. Rather, "revelation, investigation and prosecution" tactics may follow from other features of our politics, including the increasing role of the electronic media with its natural structural tendency to personalize politics.[37] Still, our constitutional separation of powers may bear some responsibility for the politics of personal destruction because our campaigns, given the nature of both congressional and presidential elections, tend toward personal candidacies rather than ideological party combat. After all, many have noted that personal attack politics is not altogether new.[38] One can cite the incendiary rhetoric leveled at Jefferson and Lincoln as prominent historical examples.

THE PERMANENT CAMPAIGN

In their edited volume, *The Permanent Campaign and Its Future*, Norman Ornstein and Thomas Mann seem to share in common with Ginsberg and Shefter a concern that politics never ends in America and that politics never fully gives way to governing. Our elections never seem to allow one party to "form a government," in Lloyd Cutler's phrase, nor do our elections ever simply seem to relegate the other party to the role of "loyal opposition."[39] Yet it may be fair to ask, is the "permanent campaign" a *permanent* feature of our separation-of-powers system? Since neither party is ever wholly the "government" or the "opposition," perhaps the constitutional separation of powers promotes the "permanent campaign" phenomenon. Even when one party controls the White House, Senate, and House, the minority party on the Hill, especially in the Senate with its tendency to empower all members, is never simply the "opposition." Our separation-of-powers system typically fails to distinguish neatly one party as the "government" and the other party as the "opposition." Consequently, "politics" remains perpetual, pervasive, and permanent.

In sum, the concerns Fenno, Ginsberg and Shefter, and Mann and Ornstein highlight are serious and significant; each perspective clearly includes a large element of truth. Nevertheless, a more comprehensive understanding of the separation of powers—one taken from *The Federalist*—can place all three arguments in perspective. One object of this book is to articulate a more complete understanding of the separation of powers. To anticipate, our separation of powers cannot be reduced to the checks and balances. The constitutional separation of powers limits the abuse of power while also providing for the effective use of power by creating three separate, independent, and powerful branches, each best designed to exercise its peculiar function: legislative, executive, and judicial.

The separation of powers thereby encompasses both friction and fission, both the "pluralist" bargaining, accommodation, and compromise of competing interests and the sharp, polarizing confrontation of party principles found in "party government." While our separation of powers may not provide for pluralism or party government in any pure sense; our constitutional system, with its built-in flexibility, can accommodate an approximation of the pluralist and party government paradigms. Our constitutional separation of powers provides for *neither and both* pluralism and party government. Consequently, both bipartisanship and partisanship—including sharpened partisanship—may be normal and appropriate in American politics.

The three books highlighted above, all published in the 1990s, provide a prelude to the explosion in recent years of new books and articles by political scientists and political journalists examining—and in most instances denouncing—partisan polarization and the "permanent campaign" in American politics. This veritable growth industry in the politics literature over the last few years has given birth to new terms of art, including party wars, second Civil War, off-center politics, fight-club politics, freak-show politics, contentious Senate, and broken branch.

Some of these new books, such as Barbara Sinclair's *Party Wars*, Nicol Rae and Colton Campbell's *Contentious Senate*, and Nelson Polsby's *How Congress Evolves* are rigorously objective political science.[40] Others seem to echo the partisan predilections of their authors as they, somewhat ironically, denounce partisanship.[41] For our purposes here in highlighting the seemingly growing perception that our politics suffers from bitter partisan polarization, we can focus on three recent studies in particular: Ron Brownstein's *The Second Civil War*, Thomas Mann and Norman Ornstein's *Broken Branch*, and the splendidly concise and precise summary review essay by Paul Quirk in *A Republic Divided* titled "The Legislative Branch: Assessing the Partisan Congress." First, however, in order to place the discussion of these three recent studies in context, we begin with political scientist Nicol Rae's comprehensive *Annual Review of Political Science* essay surveying the political parties literature over the past half century.

BE CAREFUL WHAT YOU WISH FOR

In his 2007 essay titled "Be Careful What You Wish For: The Rise of Responsible Parties in American National Politics," Nicol Rae provides a careful and thorough review of the literature and history of political parties since the early 1950s.[42] Beginning at least with the landmark American Political Science Association (APSA) study *Toward a More Responsible Two-Party Sys-*

tem penned by responsible-party—or party government—theorists including E. E. Schattschneider, political scientists lamented the lack of disciplined, British-style political parties in America. Ironically, Rae notes, the 1950s APSA report, with its call to arms in support of strong parties, was followed by decades of party decline, to the point where political scientists and journalists were declaring and lamenting, "The party's over," by the 1970s.[43]

Disalignment, disaggregation, decomposition, and demobilization were, according to Rae, the watchwords of the day for political scientists discussing political parties in the 1970s. Three decades later, the watchwords of the day for political scientists seem to be partisanship, polarization, "permanent campaign," and "politics by other means." As noted above, we are, according to some political scientists and journalists, in the midst of a second Civil War, characterized by off-center, freak-show, fight-club politics, complete with Congress as a broken branch.

ARE WE REALLY?

The 1980s and 1990s saw the rise of strong party leadership in Congress. By 2002 political scientist Barbara Sinclair could fairly raise the question "The Dream Fulfilled?" referencing the original 1950s APSA report with its responsible, disciplined British-style party government aspiration. How did we get here, especially given the decades-long decline of parties and the "formidable obstacles" to responsible parties built into our constitutional structure and individualistic culture? According to Rae, those obstacles include the separation of powers, federalism, bicameralism, the Electoral College, and our cultural predilection for limited government.[44] So how did we overcome these impediments to strong parties? Put differently, what are the causes of party polarization?

Rae cites the causes of heightened partisanship as including (1) primary-dominated nominating processes, especially in congressional elections; (2) gerrymandered redistricting, especially enhanced by computer modeling; (3) campaign-finance reform; (4) close elections, partisan parity, and narrow margins in Congress; (5) the culture wars, especially the religious divide in America; (6) the civil-rights revolution contributing to a southern realignment and the end of the solid South; (7) the growth of government and the concomitant increased stakes in our politics; (8) the growth in the role and number of interest groups and interest-group elites; and (9) the decentralization and fragmentation of the new media as the hegemony of the old media establishment eroded.[45]

Other commentators echo and supplement Rae's listing of causes. Barbara Sinclair cites (10) the decline in voter turnout augmenting the role of activists and pure partisans; along with (11) demographic shifts enabling some citizens to cocoon in exurbia.[46] Mann and Ornstein add

(12) the democratization and decentralization of Congress due to institutional reforms; (13) the fragmentation and increasing hyperpluralism of the media and interest-group systems, including the think-tank universe; and (14) the coarsening of our culture accompanying a generational shift in members of Congress.[47] In addition, Ron Brownstein mentions (15) the Internet and bloggers; and (16) the rise of political consultants as hired guns.[48] Finally, some commentators blame Republicans, especially Newt Gingrich, George W. Bush, and Karl Rove, for partisan polarization today.[49] For example, Mark Halperin and John F. Harris in *The Way to Win* identify "Bush Politics" as base-oriented, confrontational, partisanship politics, while associating "Clinton Politics" with the purportedly accommodationist centrism of the 1990s. They conclude their book with the seemingly nostalgic hope that "someday, an enlightened public will punish the politics of cynicism and destruction and reward the politics of creativity and civil dialogue. That truly will be the way to win."[50]

Since the 1970s, observes Nicol Rae, partisan polarization in the electorate has increased to the point that partisanship in the 2004 election proved to be the most intense in recent history. "In summary," he concludes,

> American national parties appear very healthy in all respects compared to their condition 30 years ago. They are more ideologically coherent, maintain viable and significant national organizations, are much stronger in Congress, and enjoy a stronger and more committed mass base of support. It would appear that the parties have gone at least some way toward the model envisaged by the authors of the 1950 report.[51]

Indeed, he argues, "party unity and the power of the party leadership in Congress is at its highest levels since the Gilded Age" preceding the Progressive Era.[52] Rae, along with other political scientists such as Barbara Sinclair, qualifies this observation by acknowledging the ongoing and as yet inconclusive debate between Morris Fiorina and his critics over whether partisan polarization and the "culture war" are elite or popular phenomena.[53] Rae seems to agree with Fiorina, however, in noting "the potentially unhealthy side effects—partisan rancor, political polarization, policy stasis" that accompany greater partisanship today.[54] Amplified partisanship may have provided voters with a choice not an echo, Rae notes, but it also has raised the level of bitterness and invective, exacerbating conflict and undermining compromise according to many commentators.

For political scientists, there are two distinct, yet related questions, one empirical and the other normative. There exists clear evidence of partisan polarization, especially in Congress, yet it is more difficult for political science to evaluate the virtues and defects of greater partisanship. One way to address this question is by means of a longitudinal comparison of congressional partisanship across decades.

Are the party wars, freak show, fight club, and broken branch in fact new in American politics? Partisan polarization may not be new—in fact it may be the historical norm—according to Hahrie Han and David Brady in a *British Journal of Political Science* study titled "A Delayed Return to Historical Norms: Congressional Party Polarization after the Second World War."[55] The authors conclude, "The recent period of polarization mirrors patterns of polarization that have prevailed throughout most of congressional history. In fact, the truly unusual historical period is the bipartisan era immediately following the Second World War."[56] The reemergence of partisanship in the last few decades, they argue in their carefully documented study, is a return to the historical norm. The 1950s baseline so popular with critics of partisan polarization today may give us a distorted sense of what is normal in American politics. Harkening back to the Ozzie and Harriet days of quiescent politics born in part from Democratic supermajorities in Congress may not be the proper measure by which to judge our politics today. Might partisan confrontation and bipartisan compromise *both* be as American as Mom and apple pie?

THE SECOND CIVIL WAR?

Journalist Ron Brownstein's indictment of confrontational partisan politics in *The Second Civil War* provides a good case-in-point illustration of how commentators today protest partisan polarization. Even the title of the book makes the point, though at the risk of exaggerating or exacerbating precisely the problem the author identifies.

Brownstein begins by blaming the parties. While he is somewhat bipartisan in his criticism, he levels the lion's share of the blame at Republicans. Hyperpartisanship has, he tells us,

> some of its roots in the strategies liberals pursued in the first decades after World War II to promote more disciplined and ideologically unified parties. But over roughly the past fifteen years, the Republican Party has contributed more than the Democrats to the rising cycle of polarization in American politics.[57]

Newt Gingrich and George W. Bush come in for special approbation. Yet Brownstein recognizes that it takes two to tango in party politics, including when he explains the rise of "backbench bomb-thrower" Newt Gingrich:

> In the House, a more militant and unified Republican Party was the inevitable, if often unanticipated, consequence of a more unified Democratic Party. In that sense, Gingrich was [congressional party reformer] Richard Bolling's bastard son. . . . The cycle of action and reaction, like a gang war, spiraled toward ever higher levels of conflict.[58]

Former Democratic Speaker Jim Wright's efforts at creating Democratic "party government" in the House inspired House Republicans to shift from the politics of compromise to the politics of confrontation: "Wright's provocations drove more House Republicans away from Michel's congenial approach and toward Gingrich."[59]

Although there were clearly larger forces at work. The strategic calculus of party leaders must be understood in the larger context of the evolving political system.[60]

To Brownstein's credit, he does not simply blame our political parties for confrontational polarization; rather, he acknowledges the role of other key mediating institutions, in particular, interest groups and the media.

The explosion in the formation of new interest groups in the 1960s and 1970s "institutionalized conflict" and "guaranteed collisions," he argues; "the dominant ethos of the new groups was to resist compromise."[61] "After the interest-group upheaval that began in the 1960s, Washington was much more open, fluid and accessible. But it was also much more polarized."[62] As others have argued, "establishment" politics gave way to "movement" politics, and "hyperpluralism" contributed to "demosclerosis," or the hardening of political arteries.[63] In Brownstein's terms, the "age of bargaining" among elites, like the age of chivalry, faded away only to be replaced by the "age of hyperpartisanship."[64] Gridlock ensued.

Similarly the media, both old and new, according to journalist Brownstein, are part of the problem, not part of the solution. The new partisan media—for example, Rush Limbaugh and the Daily Kos—"fuels the flames of hyperpartisanship."[65] They are, he says, "both a product and a cause of today's polarized political culture."[66] The new partisan media "disparage compromise and applaud confrontation" while the "traditional mainstream media . . . often discourage compromise between the parties. Conflict invariably draws more attention from the traditional press than consensus."[67] One wonders if this does not also hold true for journalistic books like *The Second Civil War* or journalists John Harwood and Gerald Seib's recent volume *Pennsylvania Avenue: Profiles in Backroom Power.*

Brownstein sees the problem of our conflict-ridden, contentious politics as systemic and serious; interest groups, media, and parties all contribute to the polarization and together constitute a new American political system a long time in the making.[68] We are, he insists, at a "dangerous impasse."[69] It is worth quoting at length the following passage from Brownstein's book because it simultaneously outlines his argument and its limits:

> The central obstacle to more effective action against our most pressing problems is an unrelenting polarization of American politics that has divided Washington and the country into hostile, even irreconcilable camps. Compe-

tition and even contention between rival parties has been part of American political life since its founding. That partisan rivalry most often has been a source of energy, innovation and inspiration. But today the parties are losing the capacity to recognize their shared interest in placing boundaries on their competition—and in transcending it when the national interest demands. On some occasions—notably efforts to balance the federal budget and reform the welfare system under Bill Clinton, and an initiative to rethink federal education policy in George W. Bush's first year—they have collaborated on reasonable compromises. But for most of the past two decades the two sides have collided with such persistent and unwavering disagreement on everything from taxes to Social Security to social and foreign policy that it sometimes seems they are organizing not only against each other, but against the idea of compromise itself.[70]

The contentious polarization over the past two decades is dangerous because it impedes needed change in the national interest even though the political system has produced significant policy change: reforming welfare in 1996, balancing the budget in 1997, and reforming education in 2001. Competition and contention have produced "energy, innovation and inspiration" in the past, but today we are gridlocked and unable to serve the national interest.[71] Most significantly perhaps, Brownstein acknowledges that confrontational politics has been with us since the Founders. Might the Founders have built into our constitutional system both the capacity to impede change *and* advance innovation? Apparently we have experienced both stasis and energy over the past twenty years, though Brownstein and others seem not to be satisfied with the pace of change:

> Our politics today encourages confrontation over compromise. The political system now rewards ideology over pragmatism. It is designed to sharpen disagreements rather than construct consensus. It is built on exposing and inflaming the differences that separate Americans rather than the shared priorities and values that unite them. It produces too much animosity and too few solutions.[72]

Brownstein prefers compromise over confrontation, and he abhors gridlock. Hyperpartisanship has "inflamed our differences and impeded progress," causing "immobilization" and "stalemate."[73] Such polarization coupled with gridlock is "a recipe for alienation in large parts of the public."[74] We have "virtually lost the capacity to formulate the principled compromises indispensable for progress," consequently "the costs of hyperpartisanship vastly exceed the benefits."[75] Where Brownstein sees polarization and paralysis, Seib and Harwood see division and gridlock.[76]

Where have we heard this before? Not only has the problem been with us since the Founding, as Brownstein notes, but so, too, has the criticism he articulates. Neo-Progressives like Lloyd Cutler and James MacGregor Burns, and Progressives like Herbert Croly and Woodrow Wilson have leveled many of these charges for over a century. But they were not the first. Even before ratification of the Constitution, Anti-Federalist critics had similar complaints. The persistence of this line of criticism for over two centuries suggests that it may contain an element of truth, perhaps even a large element of truth. Still, we may want to ask, How have we managed to muddle through the past two centuries, perhaps especially the last two decades given the purported dangers of partisan polarization and paralysis?

Like fellow journalists Halperin and Harris in *The Way to Win,* Brownstein sees the transformation of our political system today as new and dangerous. We might fairly ask, is it really new and is it truly pathological? Or is it instead the return to a new normalcy? Without question the stakes in our politics are high, but is the sky really falling? Or is this the rough and tumble of a democratic people campaigning and governing as usual? In *Democracy in America* Alexis de Tocqueville makes it abundantly clear that politics in America is not always pretty.[77] What was true in the 1830s may remain true today.

Brownstein naturally turns to discuss cures for what he thinks ails us. He lists several ways to reform the political process including open congressional primaries, nonpartisan redistricting, campaign-finance reform, replacing the Electoral College with a direct national popular vote, changes in voter-registration laws, proportional representation in place of single-member congressional districts in the House, procedural changes to open the rules in the House and Senate, as well as others. One wonders, however, if further Progressive reforms are the answer, if in fact partisanship was in part the unintended consequence of earlier Progressive reforms.[78] Brownstein also raises the seemingly conservative idea of returning contentious social and cultural issues to the states by means of a reinvigorated federalism.[79] Although he suggests that institutional or procedural reforms alone are not enough.

Ultimately, we need "unifying leadership" willing to "take a leap of faith that a constituency for reasonable compromise still exists in America."[80] Perhaps Barack Obama's "post-partisan" presidency can provide the needed presidential leadership to rise above politics and overcome our confrontational partisanship. Although it is worth remembering that Bill Clinton and George W. Bush both promised to be uniters not dividers—and we still had the supposedly dangerous impasse of the past two decades. Still, Brownstein holds out the hope that a new president may be able to create consensus around a new political center.[81] Similarly, Harwood and Seib explicitly cite the potential 2008 promise of the "post-partisan" Obama.[82] Nevertheless, the first year of the Obama presidency witnessed plenty of partisan wrangling. At the same time, in 2009, President Obama seemed to appreciate just how powerful Congress is in our separation-of-powers system; it takes two institutions to legislate.

THE BROKEN BRANCH?

In their 2006 book *The Broken Branch* Thomas Mann and Norman Ornstein agree in large part with Brownstein, though they focus more directly on Congress. Congressional politics, they argue, is characterized by (1) corrosive partisanship, (2) the "permanent campaign," (3) confrontation rather than compromise, (4) a decline in deliberation, (5) gridlock more than legislative productivity, (6) dominance by the president, and (7) a lack of adequate legislative oversight. Partisan polarization and invective drown out serious and thoughtful deliberation. Campaigning trumps governing. The executive eclipses the legislature, hence Congress is no longer the "First Branch," as they insist the Founders intended, because it has ceded too much authority to the executive. Meanwhile, the Senate has become more like the House. In sum, the "broken branch" is broken in many ways:

> In recent years a number of factors—the two parties at parity and ideologically polarized, a populist attack on Congress that has weakened its institutional self-defenses, a more partisan press and interest group alignment, and an electoral environment making legislative activity subordinate to the interests of the permanent campaign—have conspired to encourage a decline in congressional deliberation and a *de facto* delegation of authority and influence to the president.[83]

Mann and Ornstein lament the "demise of regular order" including the "decline of committees" and the "decline of deliberation." The essence of Congress, they insist, is compromise.[84] They seem to long for the good old days of committee government in the 1950s when bipartisan compromise was the hallmark of Congress; rather than the partisan confrontation today.[85] They quote their 1992 *Renewing Congress* report: "'Compromise' and 'accommodation' are not dirty words but the very essence of 'getting things done' in a representative democracy."[86] Certainly compromise is not a dirty word, but is confrontation? In many ways, Mann and Ornstein echo Richard Fenno in *Learning to Govern*. The essence of Congress is compromise not confrontation, bipartisanship not partisanship, committee government not party government, governing not campaigning. But what if Congress is both?

If committees are the essence of Congress, why does the "dual Congress," as Davidson and Oleszek call it, have a parallel party structure? Mann and Ornstein may be in danger of identifying party government, or the congressional approximation thereof, as illegitimate. Why exactly is bipartisanship good and partisanship bad? Principled partisan competition can provide voters a choice and not an echo. Nor is partisanship necessarily antithetical to deliberation; it can, for example, sharpen choices for politicians and voters alike, thus contributing to public deliberation.

Mann and Ornstein's analysis in *The Broken Branch* raises other questions as well. Is it necessarily the case that moderation and centrism are always right? Are the best public-policy solutions invariably found in the middle of the road? Is Congress truly gridlocked and unproductive? David Mayhew's analysis in *Divided Government* raises doubts about this perennial charge leveled against Congress. While legislative productivity may not suffice when measured by the Progressive desire for activist government and change, sometimes not to act is to act.[87] At various times, both parties valiantly fight on principle to prevent passage of sweeping reforms with which they disagree.

politics good

Mann and Ornstein may be in danger of arguing that politics is the problem, when, as Larry Sabato likes to argue, "politics is a good thing."[88] Like Progressive reformers, do Mann and Ornstein want to take the politics out of politics? The term "broken branch" did not originate with them. The high priest of Neo-Progressive reform, Ralph Nader, may have first used the term in the early 1970s. In 1972 Congress scholar Richard Fenno wrote an essay titled "If as Ralph Nader Says, Congress Is 'The Broken Branch,' How Come We Love Our Congressmen So Much?"[89] In this study Fenno counsels journalists not to take Nader's lead and "to forego 'broken branch' type generalizations about Congress."[90]

The 1950s—when Republicans were the pale moon reflecting the dominant Democratic sun—may not be the ideal baseline for congressional behavior; such comparisons risk underestimating the value of party competition. As Han and Brady note above, the 1950s may not be the proper baseline for normal congressional behavior. And, as Brownstein notes, can't-we-all-get-along civility can be a way of avoiding as well as solving problems; the 1950s "consensus" on ignoring civil rights, for example, was a defect, not a virtue. Sometimes one needs to break the china in order to bring about needed change, whether that entails growing or shrinking the role of government.

Other questions arise while reading *The Broken Branch*. "The Constitution is most certainly not a charter for legislative supremacy," Mann and Ornstein note, and yet they insist that Congress as the "First Branch" is meant to be "first among equals."[91] The president is "not an equal" and is meant to be "subordinate" to Congress.[92] Yet their own thumbnail history of relations between the branches, including precedents set by early presidents, certainly does not seem to support the idea that the president is meant to be subordinate to Congress.[93]

Mann and Ornstein constructively cite Nelson Polsby's observation that Congress is meant to be a "transformative legislature," independent and powerful. The executive and judiciary, however, are also meant to be independent and powerful in our separation-of-powers system. The three branches cannot check and balance one another if each is not independent and powerful within its own sphere. Finally, in discussing "what is to be done" to mend the broken branch, the authors, like Brownstein, and Seib and Harwood, argue that presidential leadership "far more than any other kind, has the potential to alter the dynamic of institutional behavior."[94] If Congress is the "First Branch" why does it need the president to cure what ails it?

Similarly, why if Congress is the "First Branch" do Mann and Ornstein lament Newt Gingrich's experiment in congressional government?[95] Under Speaker Gingrich we briefly witnessed the most powerful Congress since czars Reed and Cannon—along with record popularity for the perennially least popular branch. Why not celebrate Gingrich's success? Perhaps it is because Gingrich's legislative overreach ultimately undercut his own presumption that Congress is the "First Branch." Congress as the Article One branch needs the presidency and vice versa. The Madisonian separation of powers includes three independent and powerful branches that, as we shall see, ironically need each other. No branch by itself is the government.

As with others before them, Mann and Ornstein compare Newt Gingrich to the Anti-Federalist critics of the Federalist Constitution, and the comparison is apt.[96] Speaker Gingrich, like the Anti-Federalists and the Woodrow Wilson of *Congressional Government*, was a legislative supremacist. The Federalist Constitution, of course, provides for nothing of the kind. The Articles of Confederation instituted legislative supremacy— and was found wanting by the Founders. The Federalist Constitution explicitly set about correcting this defect in the first American political system by creating a strong and independent executive and a strong and independent judiciary.[97]

During the ratification debate, the Anti-Federalists criticized the Federalist Constitution for subordinating the legislative to the executive and judicial branches. The Anti-Federalists certainly did not see the Federalists as legislative supremacists, even though they also failed to appreciate that the Federalist Convention created *three* powerful and independent branches. If neither the Federalists nor their Anti-Federalist critics understood the Constitution to promote legislative supremacy, why has the tendency to see Congress as the "First Branch" persisted throughout our history from the Whigs to Woodrow Wilson to Newt Gingrich to Mann and Ornstein? This persistent misunderstanding may arise from a failure to appreciate fully the fact that the Federalists created simultaneously limited, yet effective government. This central irony of the separation of powers admittedly is difficult to comprehend.[98] Woodrow Wilson, one of our most brilliant political scientists, saw in the Constitution—at different times in *Congressional Government* and *Constitutional Government*—the potential for a strong legislature and a strong executive. Yet he seemed to ignore the possibility that the Constitution provides simultaneously for both a strong Congress and a strong presidency.

When it comes to fixing the broken branch, Mann and Ornstein share something else in common with earlier critics of our constitutional system, including the Anti-Federalists and Woodrow Wilson; they turn to extra-constitutional solutions to resolve real or perceived defects in the existing order. Examples include their proposed independent Office of Public Integrity—an institution that arguably would exist outside our separation-of-powers system to police congressional behavior—and their Continuity of Congress proposal requiring a constitutional amendment.[99] No doubt Mann and Ornstein identify serious problems, but is it truly the case that the Constitution and the politics it engenders are inadequate to the challenges of today? A common lament of Progressive reformers, at least since Woodrow Wilson, has been that our constitutional system is incapable of responding to the exigency of modern times. Is it really? In particular, is our constitutional system seriously endangered by today's contentious and confrontational partisanship? Are we failing to govern ourselves as a nation?

One thing that clearly has changed since the Founding, of course, is the growth of government. As Mann and Ornstein note, today "Congress is much larger, more potent, and part of a federal government with remarkable scope and sweep."[100] The growth of the national government has been, at least since Woodrow Wilson, a key Progressive premise in calling for reform including constitutional reform. Such reforms have, in turn, provided the premise for further growth in government.

Perhaps the "permanent campaign" is due in part to the growth and permanence of governing. Given the growth of government and the greater stakes in our politics, perhaps it is not surprising that partisan rhetoric has becomes sharper. Indeed, over the past few decades, Republicans' shrill partisanship has been in part a response to this very growth of government. The confrontational politics of Ronald Reagan, Newt Gingrich and George W. Bush are, in part, an effort to curb or even roll back the growth of the federal government.[101] Is this why Republicans, more so than Democrats, sometimes appear to be on the offensive—and sometimes seem to adopt more offensive tactics?

Ultimately Mann and Ornstein acknowledge that the "contentious, partisan, name-calling Congress is nothing new in American politics"; they add that "some historians might argue that it is the norm."[102] If so, is it really illegitimate for Newt and Nancy to sharpen partisanship? A legislative strategy of confrontation worked for House Republicans in 1994 and House Democrats in 2006. Their practice calls into question the contention that partisan confrontation is out of bounds. So, too, as we shall see in chapter 7, does the practice of the Founders during the early years of the American republic.

Like Brownstein in *The Second Civil War*, Mann and Ornstein conclude that contemporary Congress is not living up to the expectations of the Founders. It is, of course, altogether fitting and proper that we judge our contemporary theory and practice by the light of the theory and practice of the Founders. Alexis de Tocqueville, for example, appropriately noted that Americans love to debate the Constitution and its origins. We should examine carefully the Founders' expectations for Congress. In fact, one central purpose of this book is to revisit the Founding; chapters 3 and 6 examine Anti-Federalist and Federalist thought respectively, while chapter 7 examines the political practice of the Founders during the first decade of the American republic.

Mann and Ornstein, like the Anti-Federalists and Woodrow Wilson before them, identify defects in our constitutional system. James Madison acknowledged many of the defects identified by his Anti-Federalist critics, and yet he went on to defend the Constitution's capacity to promote free and effective government. We may still have the same choice today: Federalist or Anti-Federalist, Madison or Wilson?

A REPUBLIC DIVIDED?

Paul Quirk's analysis in his 2007 literature-review essay "The Legislative Branch: Assessing the Partisan Congress" in many ways distills and sharpens the perspective of Mann and Ornstein. Congress is "mired in partisan warfare" and suffers from "sharp ideological conflict" and "ideological polarization."[103] In Congress, there has been a complete collapse of the center. The House, in particular, suffers from an empty center, with, as Sarah Binder notes, "virtually no ideological common ground" between the two parties.[104] In their voting behavior, there is daylight between the most conservative Democrat and the most liberal Republican in the House; consequently, Quirk concludes, the parties have lost the capacity to cooperate.

Such partisan conflict undermines important legislative principles such as deliberation, efficiency, and procedural fairness, Quirk argues.[105] Congress needs orderly procedures, careful, deliberate consideration of policy, and a fair chance for the minority party.[106] Congress needs regular order, not "procedural opportunism" by the majority party, as well as bipartisan cooperation and a return to the "tradition" of consensus-seeking "historically associated with American politics," according to Quirk.[107] The broken branch is broken because it suffers from conflict not consensus and because an overweening executive eclipses the legislative branch.[108] For Quirk, as for Mann and Ornstein, bipartisan compromise and cooperation are good, and partisan confrontation is bad.[109] Like Brownstein, and Mann and Ornstein, Quirk cites the theory and practice of the Founders in making his case against partisanship.[110]

Quirk, Brownstein, and Mann and Ornstein also prefer "conventional" committee-based deliberation rather than deliberation that takes place within political parties, as occurred for example when Republicans supplemented or supplanted standing committee deliberations with GOP task forces.[111] In *Congressional Government* Woodrow Wilson urges the majority party to form single-party legislative committees, in part to promote party responsibility. Arguably, deliberation can and does occur within party councils as well as within bipartisan standing committees.[112] Quirk acknowledges, too, that parliamentary party government worldwide "does not rely upon the capabilities that have been compromised in the contemporary Congress."[113] Parliamentary systems function effectively without bipartisan committees, a practice Woodrow Wilson thought worth emulating.

Deliberation can also take place between the parties on the floor, perhaps even during the course of high-decibel declamations across the center aisle. Why then is committee-based deliberation preferable? Is centrist bargaining and accommodation really the ideal? *PBS NewsHour* commentator David Brooks recently observed,

> When you go to a conservative dinner in Washington, there are academics, there are think-tankers, there are activists. When you go to a liberal dinner, there are academics, think-tankers, and activists. When you go to a middle dinner, a centrist dinner, there are a bunch of lobbyists.[114]

Regardless of whether Brooks is simply accurate in this observation, the point is telling. The politics of compromise and bargaining suffers from the defect of its virtue, just as responsible party government does. The ideal of pluralist accommodation may entail a special interest–dominated politics complete with lobbyists wining, dining, and—supposedly—bribing members of Congress. Yet Quirk is critical not only of the partisanship in Congress but also of the purported special-interest domination of legislative politics. Apparently, according to Quirk, Congress suffers from the excesses of both pluralism and party government. Quirk acknowledges, however, that the political-science literature does not support the public's "wildly exaggerated" image of Congress as dominated by special-interest lobbyists and politician action committees (PACs).[115] Might not the hoary tales of partisan excess also suffer from exaggeration at times? Are we really facing a "second Civil War"?

Like Brownstein, and Mann and Ornstein, Quirk cites various causes for the maladies afflicting the legislative branch including gerrymandering and primary-dominated congressional nominations. He suggests that the heightened partisanship in recent years stems in part from "the most closely contested control of Congress in half a century."[116] Perfect-tie politics is the premise for polarization and the "permanent campaign."[117] This may be true, though in the 1980s when House Republicans were so far down they could not see up, the presumption was that partisanship resulted from the lack of real competition for majority control. Having little hope of ever participating as part of the "government," "permanent minority" House Republicans turned to strategies of opposition out of frustration.

Can both perspectives be correct? Perhaps, though the insistence by Quirk and others that the partisan polarization is new and unprecedented is a bit ahistorical. Heightened partisanship is not limited to the past two decades. This presumption overlooks periods of American history when congressional parties were far more polarized. Quirk seems to suggest that partisanship dates to the late 1980s, but he is off by a good decade.[118] One could argue with justification that the partisan divisions began with the election of Tip O'Neill as Speaker. By downplaying the Democrats' tactics of the 1980s and early 1990s, Quirk and others exaggerate the changes that came with Republican control in the House.

Quirk clearly sees Republicans as the real culprit in the crime of sharpened partisanship. In this 2007 essay he offers as evidence of just how dysfunctional Congress has become the conservative policies engineered by George W. Bush:

> Congress has demonstrated significant weaknesses in policymaking. Although any assessment is subject to challenge, the Congresses of the first six years of the Bush presidency were widely criticized for enacting ideologically extreme measures, such as tax cuts—targeted toward wealthy taxpayers; for deferring to organized interest groups, mostly representing business, in areas such as energy, the environment, and prescription drugs; for catering to uninformed popular demands on Medicare, social security, and budget policy; for dramatically expanding appropriations earmarks and other district- and state-targeted spending, including by far the most expensive highway bill ever enacted; for failing to constrain constitutionally dubious administration policies on homeland security and surveillance; and, above all, for uncritically accepting a vague, unsubstantiated administration case for preemptive war in Iraq. In a word, there was considerable evidence of impaired performance in legislative policymaking.[119]

Was the broken branch broken because it was Republican? While Quirk clearly sharpens this line of attack, he also echoes common complaints among political scientists, including, for example, Hacker and Pierson in *Off Center*.[120] Mann and Ornstein sounded a similar note in their 2006 book when they acknowledged that to many readers the book "will sound particularly harsh on the Republicans. It is meant to be. They are the ones in charge" and "responsible."[121] Mann and Ornstein recognize Democratic complicity in the partisan rancor, but they conclude "Republican have far exceeded Democratic abuses of power."[122] How exactly does political science measure this GOP perfidy?

For decades House Rules Committee majority and minority staffers have rolled out dueling statistics on abusive closed rules engineered by the reigning majority party. Such endless jousting seems inconclusive at best, suffering as it does from the defects of "lies, damn lies, and statistics." No doubt there has been "procedural opportunism" by majority parties and harsh partisan rhetoric by minority parties when both Republicans and Democrats have been in the majority and minority. So how does political science stand in judgment of partisan politics without becoming partisan?

A three-hour "long count" held open by the majority party contrary to rules and practices is clearly an abuse, but so, too, is a one-hour "long count."[123] Newt Gingrich's "backbench bomb-throwing" rhetoric was at times outrageous, over the top, and often polarizing, partisan, pointed, and personal. And yet it was Tip O'Neill who had his words "taken down," an indignity never visited upon Gingrich. For political science, such partisan evaluations are a tar baby as little susceptible to resolution as the partisan finger pointing by Republicans and Democrats on the Hill. To his credit, Nelson Polsby's discussion of "how Congress evolves" dates the rising tide of polarization at least to the 1970s and underscores the complicity of both parties.[124] Political science cannot mediate effectively the ongoing partisan recriminations between the House majority and minority parties of the day, not least because our separation-of-powers system precludes simple and direct accountability.

At times one is left wondering if political-science trends just happen to coincide with partisan swings. Responsible parties were idealized by political science until Republicans were in control. Restrictive rules were a way to "manage uncertainty" and make the trains run on time, until they blocked Democratic amendments.[125] Until the early 1990s, political science routinely belittled the significance of gerrymandering. Suddenly during the twelve years of GOP House majority rule, redistricting became a grave problem even though the GOP may have gained less than Democrats. During the House Republican reign, we worried about majority tyranny in the majoritarian House. Was political science as solicitous of minority party concerns in the 1980s when Republicans were a "permanent minority"? Finally, is the broken branch no longer broken now that Democrats are back in the majority?[126]

A quick sampling of credible journalistic commentary during the 110th Congress following House Democratic ascension under Nancy Pelosi at least raises doubts about whether the newly majority Democrats improved upon purported House Republican majority misbehavior:

"Dems Bend Rules, Break Pledge," *Politico.com*, May 17, 2007

"In the Democratic Congress, Pork Still Gets Served," *Washington Post*, May 24, 2007

"The K Street Project, Part Blue," *Wall Street Journal*, July 25, 2008

"The Hammer's Back! This Time in the Form of a Democrat, Rep. John Murtha," *Washington Post*, May 27, 2007

And a *National Journal* special issue at the end of House Democrats' first year in the majority included "Bipolarization" by Brian Friel, "Us vs. Them" by Richard E. Cohen, and "More of the Same? Both Democrats and Republicans Doubt That the Level of Partisanship in Washington Will Be Significantly Reduced Anytime Soon" by James A. Barnes.

This sampling of commentary may or may not be representative; however, it does leave one wondering whether the more things change, the more they stay the same. Can political science answer the question: Are House Democrats really more virtuous than House Republicans? Or are Newt and Nancy "two peas in a pod"?[127]

As political scientists, we can compare polarization and partisanship longitudinally across decades. We can measure, for example, the emptying of the center in the House based on voting studies. Clearly, the House has become increasingly polarized over the past three decades, as Sarah Binder has documented, yet critics complained about harsh rhetoric and abusive floor tactics in the 1980s, 1990s, and 2000s—under Democratic and Republican majorities.

Apart from which party is in the majority or minority, and apart from trying to pin the tail on the donkey or elephant, perhaps Gingrich and Pelosi both deserve credit for leading their parties out of the minority wilderness by partisan means. Perhaps partisanship has a purpose.

One question worth exploring in this book: Are parties more polarized today, or are we more sensitive to partisan polarization? Is the problem today hyperpartisanship or hypersensitivity to partisanship?[128]

The answer may be both. The Anti-Federalists were uncomfortable with the jarring of adverse interests and "spirit of party" which informed Madison's new Constitution. Similarly, some Progressive reformers wanted to take the politics out of politics; for example, by turning governmental authority over to neutral civil-service experts.[129] For such reformers, "politics" sometimes meant the role of special interests and at other times it meant party competition, in other words, pluralism and party government. Either way, many Progressives did not seem to like politics.

Similarly, Quirk seems to admire elections that reflect national majorities rather than local majorities and intense pluralistic factions.[130] Like many, including Woodrow Wilson, Quirk appreciates the British parliamentary system, especially its reliance on a neutral civil service.[131] Like Wilson and others, Quirk laments limited government defined as limited legislative productivity; like so many commentators today, he dislikes gridlock. Unlike Wilson, however, Quirk is disdainful of sharpened partisanship.

Still, to his credit, Quirk acknowledges that "on some views . . . the partisan Congress represents only a different, not necessarily a worse, form of representative democracy—in a word, party government."[132] Perhaps both ends of the political pendulum, party government and pluralism, are constitutionally permissible?

It may be unfair or unnecessary to pigeonhole contemporary commentators like Quirk, Brownstein, and Mann and Ornstein as Progressive Wilsonians or traditional Madisonians, as Anti-Federalists or Federalists; though it is worth underscoring that contemporary discourse clearly echoes earlier debates.[133] These arguments are not new. For this reason alone, it is worth returning to the debate between the Federalists and Anti-Federalists, Madison and Wilson. Arguably, these great theorists and practitioners of American politics thought longer and harder about many of the questions we continue to debate today; their theory and practice continue to inform our politics today.

Over the past two decades, two House leaders, Newt Gingrich and Nancy Pelosi, effectively addressed the strategic dilemma confronting them, successfully leading their parties from minority to majority status. Chapter 2 looks at the ascent of Nancy Pelosi. Chapter 3 examines Newt Gingrich's echo of Anti-Federalist thought. Chapters 4, 5, and 6 respectively explore the ideas of Wilson, Tocqueville, and Madison. Alexis de Tocqueville provides a bridge between the Federalists and Anti-Federalists, between Madison and Wilson. In order to bring necessary historical and constitutional perspective to the subject, chapter 7 considers the Founders' practice of their principles. Likewise, chapter 8 considers case studies of legislative party strategy from recent decades. Finally, chapter 9 draws conclusions about the critical nexus between constitutional theory and contemporary political practice.

At the risk of getting too far ahead of the argument of this book, it is worth noting that a proper appreciation for institutional and constitutional context is critical to a more complete understanding and practice of contemporary legislative party politics. Institutional context matters. The Constitution shapes congressional behavior. To understand congressional party strategy we must take the Constitution seriously. The aim of this book is a better understanding of the theoretical and constitutional underpinnings of legislative party strategy as practiced in recent decades by leaders such as Bob Michel and Newt Gingrich, Dick Gephardt and Nancy Pelosi.

We need to see the strategic dilemma facing contemporary party leaders in constitutional terms. We need to understand the separation of powers more completely than those who would have us believe that Madison's Constitution allows only, or even primarily, for a politics of can't-we-all-get-along bipartisan compromise. Try as we might, we cannot take the politics out of politics, regardless of whether the politics we abjure entails the pluralism of competing "special interests" or the partisanship of "party government." Madisonian politics embraces both a pluralism of competing "factions" *and* the "spirit of party" or partisanship so often lamented today. The Constitution calls for compromise *and* confrontation. The Constitution as articulated in the *Federalist* requires congressional party leaders to be partisan and bipartisan according to circumstance and opportunity.

Today we seem hypersensitive to Madisonian politics defined either as pluralism or party government. At times Americans seemingly long to rise above politics defined as a pluralistic competition among jarring and adverse interests, just as they seem at times to renounce partisanship and party government. Our discussions of Fenno's "learning to govern," Ginsberg and Shefter's "politics by other means," Mann and Ornstein's "permanent campaign" and "broken branch," Brownstein's "second Civil War," and Quirk's concern about partisan polarization, have at least raised questions critical to understanding American politics today. In light of the studies above, let us return now to our initial discussion of legislative strategy during the House Democrats' post–2002 election leadership fight.

2

~

House Democrats:
The Wilderness Years

THE 2002 ELECTION AFTERMATH

To further define and refine the legislative strategy question, it is useful to examine at greater length the debate among congressional Democrats following their 2002 midterm setback. As they began to worry about becoming a "permanent minority" like the House GOP during the 1980s, would House Democrats adopt the "bomb-throwing" confrontational politics of opposition seemingly perfected by Newt Gingrich? Or would they strive to be responsible partners in governing, seeking compromise with majority Republicans? Would House Democrats increasingly resort to "politics by other means," embracing both "institutional combat" and "RIP" tactics? Or would they abjure the politics of personal destruction, focusing instead on policy? Finally, would House Democrats perpetuate the "permanent campaign," rather than contribute to governing as the "loyal opposition"? Before Democrats could adopt any stance toward Republicans, they first had to settle differences among themselves, as noted in chapter 1.

As one observer stated, the Democratic Party "boasts a big tent, but that tent doubles as a big boxing ring."[1] Therein lies one key to understanding the legislative party strategic dilemma: the fighting occurs *within* each party, factionalizing Democrats and Republicans alike. Following the 2002 election, congressional Democrats engaged in a round of intraparty bickering and infighting.

THE QUESTION PEOPLE WERE ASKING

Following the 2002 election, the *Wall Street Journal* reported that

> Democrats, inside and outside government, quickly began pointing fingers over their leaders' strategy. The most frequently voiced complaint: that Messrs. Gephardt and Daschle missed an opportunity to rally their party by not opposing Mr. Bush's requested authorization of military force against Iraq and by not seeking a rollback of his sweeping tax cuts.[2]

CQ Weekly raised a "fundamental question" for congressional Democrats: "Should the party steer itself back to its liberal roots which Pelosi represents, or should it modify but maintain its appeal to moderates and swing voters, the approach Frost advocated?"[3] *USA Today*, among others, explicitly spoke the language of "government" versus "opposition."[4]

Political analyst Michael Barone noted that congressional Democrats were confronted with a "hard choice," namely, whether to "reach out to the center" or "indulge the passions of its wingers." Barone opined that Democrats were likely to placate their "party base," thus providing Republicans with an opportunity to build a party majority from the center.[5] Barone compared Democrats' dilemma and their response to that confronting Republicans following the 1962 election. Finally, Peggy Noonan cast the Democrats' dilemma in even more consequential terms:

> The argument as many Democrats frame it so far is: should we tack left or should we fight it out in the center for the center? But that is essentially an argument about *how* to win. The bigger question . . . is this: what is the Democratic Party's reason for being?[6]

Clearly, Democrats were addressing the strategic dilemma question in their postmortems. Tom Oliphant, on *The NewsHour with Jim Lehrer*, on the other hand, offered a dissenting opinion about the significance of the strategic dilemma confronting congressional Democrats, specifically regarding the Pelosi vs. Frost race: "I haven't met a single person in the United States who cares at all about who wins this fight. . . . I'm not aware of anybody outside Washington who sees any stake for them in this. It is symbolic only."[7] Oliphant's dissent raises a legitimate question as to whether the Democrats' debate over legislative strategy and their struggles over party leadership matter. Is it really just so much inside-the-Beltway chatter and a political parlor game for pundits?

HOUSE DEMOCRAT LEADERSHIP STRATEGY IN THE 108TH CONGRESS

Just as House Republicans fought over leadership during their long "permanent minority" tenure, so, too, Democrats at the opening of the 108th Congress toppled one leader and fought over replacing him with another. The time and energy congressional Democrats invested in debating the question of legislative strategy in the context of this leadership fight, clearly indicates they think the question matters, Oliphant aside. Indeed, they acted as if the leadership fight might define the party's future direction.[8]

Immediately following the Democrats' midterm election setback, House Democratic leader Gephardt found himself on the defensive concerning his electoral and legislative strategy. "I do not know how I could have done more," he said.[9] He specifically defended his decision to discourage Democrats from discussing postponing or rolling back President Bush's tax cut along with his decision to work with President Bush on the Iraq War resolution, even though some in his party saw these two decisions as demoralizing the party's base.[10] Gephardt insisted Democrats would have lost even more seats in the midterm election if they had tried to nationalize the election.[11]

Minority Leader Gephardt rejected the notion that "his party had not laid out a strong ideological contrast to the Republicans," but he also acknowledged "his party needed to come up with ideas and themes to present to Americans in the coming years, suggesting that it was difficult for him to stake out distinct ground as long as he was viewed as speaking for the [House] Democratic caucus."[12] Shortly after stepping down as minority leader, Gephardt initiated his presidential bid, seemingly less encumbered by the responsibilities of leading House Democrats, including the need to reconcile competing interests within congressional Democrats' big tent.

After Gephardt announced he was stepping down, four candidates, offering different perspectives on legislative strategy, offered themselves to House Democrats for the position of minority leader: Nancy Pelosi (D-CA), Martin Frost (D-TX), Harold Ford, Jr. (D-TN), and Marcy Kaptur (D-OH). Each brought strengths and weaknesses to the race for House minority leader, and each brought a unique perspective on the question of legislative strategy. The latter seemed especially central to their public debate over leadership succession.

The two most serious contenders, Pelosi and Frost, each hailed from a large state delegation, respectively California and Texas—though Pelosi's state delegation within the Democratic caucus was almost twice as large as Frost's, giving her something of an advantage in the competition. The liberal Pelosi and moderate Frost also presented a stark contrast in personality, style, and temperament.[13] On the one hand, Pelosi was perceived as energetic, mediagenic, and even charismatic; while Frost was seen as steady, reserved, and probably less adept at public relations. On the other hand, Frost had extensive experience and skill as a backroom political tactician including years of service on the powerful House Rules Committee. In a word, Pelosi's strength may have been her "outside" game while Frost's "inside" skills were his *forte*. Pelosi's service on both the

Appropriations Committee and the House Select Intelligence Committee, however, suggested she had the ability to work across party lines. As chair of the Democratic Congressional Campaign Committee (DCCC), Frost had considerable electoral experience, while Pelosi was known for her fundraising prowess. Finally, as a woman, Pelosi had special appeal to women's groups and to those who wanted to see her advance higher than any woman in congressional history.

Clearly, Nancy Pelosi won the leadership fight for a variety of reasons, not just for her position on the legislative strategic dilemma confronting House Democrats. Regional, ideological, gender, and generational considerations played a role, along with assessments of her leadership skills, experience, and style. But it is just as clear—especially given the time, energy, and ink spent debating it—that legislative strategy was important to House Democrats. Where this *leader* would *lead* House Democrats and how she would organize them for victory mattered enormously. One indication Pelosi might be the best minority leader candidate Democrats had to offer could be seen in her nuanced answer to the legislative strategy challenge confronting minority Democrats.

> When a party selects a leader, they select someone who can lead them to victory. This isn't about going *right or left* on the political spectrum. It's about going into the future. . . . Perhaps people don't understand what it means to elect a leader. A leader is the person who rallies the troops, who develops the agenda to present a *vision* to the American people of what the Democratic Party stands for, expands the basis of knowledge of our issues so that our judgment is excellent and the best. And I've never voted for a leader since I've been in Congress 15 years on the basis of how many votes I have in common with them. It's all on the basis of how they can *organize us for victory*.[14]

In this NPR interview, Congresswoman Pelosi went on to define "victory" in both legislative and electoral terms. She noted that the Democratic Party is a *"giant tent"*; elsewhere she touted her ability to *"build coalitions* among the various sectors of our caucus."[15] As for the Republicans,

> We must *draw clear distinctions* between our vision of the future and the *extreme* policies put forward by the Republicans. We cannot allow Republicans to pretend they share our values and then legislate against those values without consequence.[16]

At the same time, Pelosi insisted, "I do think that we should have something to say that is *positive* and not just *oppose* what the president has to say."[17]

In sum, Pelosi argued that for House Democrats to become a majority party they must be a coalition-building, big-tent party embracing a broad ideological spectrum; though at the same time, Democrats need to draw clear distinctions between the visions of the two parties while remaining positive rather than merely oppositional. While it was not easy to pigeon-hole Pelosi on legislative strategy, her critics feared she might be inclined more toward learning to oppose than learning to govern, more toward perpetuating the "permanent campaign" and engaging in "institutional combat" than responsible governing. Nevertheless, the touchstone of Pelosi's leadership style and strategy was her oft-repeated mantra that Democrats must find common ground with Republicans, yet "[w]here we cannot find that common ground, we must stand our ground."[18] Demo-crats, Pelosi said, have a responsibility to work in a bipartisan fashion when possible; and yet Republicans—as the majority party in the House and Senate with a GOP president in the White House—are the "respon-sible" party and must "produce."[19]

The benchmark of Minority Leader Pelosi's leadership—to "find common ground" where possible, and yet "stand our ground" where necessary—of-fers a seemingly nuanced and potentially adroit solution to the minority party's strategic dilemma. Is this just a politician's empty rhetoric, or does she mean it and does it matter? Does Nancy Pelosi's formulation provide a good answer to the strategic dilemma confronting legislative parties? While we may never fully understand her true intentions, her articulate answer to the conundrum confronting legislative leaders is worth taking seriously, especially in light of her success in 2006. At a minimum, there is almost certainly an element of truth to her opinion on this question.

Of course, there may also have been an element of truth to Martin Frost's competing solution to the question of legislative strategy. Listen carefully to his words as well. As noted above, Frost argued that if House Democrats move to the left in an effort to be ideologically pure, they will become a "permanent minority." Interpreting the election results, Frost noted, "[The country] moved somewhat to the right. I believe our party must occupy the center if we are to be successful, if we're to come back to the majority, and not move further to the left."[20] As former chair of the DCCC, Frost insisted "the battleground is in moderate and conservative swing states."[21] He added: "If we're going to be a majority party, we have to have conservatives and moderates. We can't just have liberals. We have to be a broad-tent party, and I would hope that we would continue to be able to attract them."[22] Even when it looked like Nancy Pelosi had the nec-essary votes to become Democratic leader, Frost said he would "continue to be an outspoken advocate for the mainstream, centrist views that will lead us to the majority."[23]

In particular, on the subject of the Iraq War resolution, which he voted for while Pelosi voted against, Frost observed about the Democrats, "If you're seen by the country as not standing for a strong America, the coun-try will not listen to you on other issues."[24] Frost also saw a need for minor-ity House Democrats to compromise with the majority Republicans rather than always striving to sharpen the differences between the parties: "If it's a question of being pure all the time, just standing by certain fundamental beliefs and never compromising, we will be a minority party for the foreseeable future, and we will have less Democrats than we do today."[25] Frost felt the need, however, to defend himself against the charge that he would turn the House Democrats into a me-too, watered-down version of the Republican Party: "Nobody's talking about being 'Republican-lite.' We're talking about speaking to the vast center of this country, the people who determine elections in this country. I want us to be in the majority. I want the chance to pass things."[26] Martin Frost wanted Democrats to legislate, not just "wedgislate."

Unfortunately for Frost, his Democratic colleagues did not choose him to help them advance legislation and regain a majority. Democrats seemed to reject his brand of centrist politics involving compromise for the purpose of accomplishing policy change. Frost urged his party to be part of the government, not simply the opposition, to compromise rather than merely confront Republicans, to focus on policy as a way to win at politics, and to actively engage in governing rather than merely perpetuate the "permanent campaign." Surely, Frost's approach had some merit, as did Pelosi's. For that matter, so too, did those of Harold Ford and Marcy Kaptur.

When Frost's challenge to Pelosi faltered, Ford stepped forward in a last-ditch gambit. The thirty-two-year-old Ford pitched himself as a new generation of leadership, touting a third-way approach different from Gephardt and Pelosi. Ford had originally been a Frost supporter. While he ultimately lacked the votes Frost seemed able to muster, Ford offered a more complex answer to the legislative strategy question than Frost, rivaling the nuance of Pelosi's formulation. Ford's critique began thus: "It's obvious we need some fresh faces and some fresh leadership."[27] He even criticized Gephardt openly: "But much like a manager of a baseball team who really, really wants to win, is beloved by his players but simply can't win—sometimes it is time to move on."[28]

As evidence, perhaps, of his new approach, Ford announced his candidacy for Democratic leader on MSNBC's *Imus in the Morning* suggesting House Democrats cannot settle for "the same old, same old. . . . I think unfortunately and undeservedly that our party has become associated with the notion of *gridlock* and *obstructionism*."[29] Being "an *opposition* party will require a lot more than just a lot of yelling and screaming, and frankly, *unconstructive criticism*. If we're serious about being an opposition party and serious about doing what's in the *best interest of the nation* . . . [it] requires *working with the president* when his interest and, frankly, his position will benefit the nation."[30] As Democratic leader, Ford said he would "substantively *challenge the president* and support things in the best interest of the nation, but also . . . *navigate the amazing diversity* within our caucus—not racial diversity as much as ideological, gender, and geographical diversity."[31]

Ford followed the Imus interview with a *Washington Post* op-ed outlining his solution to the House Democrats' legislative strategy dilemma. "[O]ur party needs an infusion of new ideas and fresh leadership . . . [and] a real change in our party's direction."[32] Voters "told us they want *more than gridlock and obstruction*. They want candidates to articulate a *clear agenda for governing*." Democrats cannot afford to be *merely negative*: "Democrats spent too much time pointing out what Republicans are doing wrong and not enough time laying out what we would do differently." The party needs to accentuate the *positive*: "It is our responsibility to articulate a *coherent governing agenda*." After laying out some specifics on issues including President Bush's tax cuts and Iraq, Ford argued Democrats *cannot beat something with nothing*: "[O]ur problem . . . was that *we raised objections rather than offered solutions*." Ford offered to broaden the party's base with *"new ideas."* "I am not running for Democratic leader to move our party left or right, I want to move us forward," he insisted.

In an interview, a Democratic campaign consultant supporting Ford added further substance to the latter's third-way approach:

> I am actually in the (twenty-nine members strong in the House!) Harold Ford "not right or left, but forward" camp. I think Frost represents the Neville Chamberlain accommodationist approach, generally followed by Daschle and Gephardt this cycle, which was catastrophic. Pelosi makes up for the timidity critique, but I do not think the answer is a move to the left. The answer for the party, I think, is the radical, not mushy, center. Democrats got burned for a campaign that can best be summed up by "We're not them." You don't hold on to, and certainly don't regain, the leadership with that type of message. A bunch of Dems have asked me what did Newt do in 1994? My response is: the Contract With/On America. Like it or hate it, one could easily articulate what it meant to vote Republican. The critical mistake the Dems made was not nationalizing the election. They thought they could win it on the ground in each individual race through candidate recruitment and fund-raising. But the Rs have the White House and what Dem message there was got drowned out by the unified dispatch of the president and vice president in the last week of the campaign.[33]

In a nutshell, Ford's third way suggested Democrats could not afford merely to play opposition, obstructing, gridlocking, and criticizing majority Republicans; rather, Democrats needed to articulate a clear agenda for governing, working with President Bush where possible and challenging him where accommodation was not possible. Ford's approach rejected the purported appeasement of Frost, Gephardt, and Daschle, while insisting Democrats could not follow Pelosi into a liberal ditch on the left side of the road.[34] According to this argument, any new Democratic leadership needs to navigate the party's diversity, while rejecting the all-politics-is-local presumptive cure-all of candidate recruitment and fund-raising.

Rather, Ford seemed to argue House Democrats needed to nationalize elections by offering specific, concrete, creative issue-alternatives to GOP initiatives. The Ford supporter above even raised the specter of learning from Newt Gingrich's success with the 1994 Contract with America.

Did Ford in fact offer a third-way alternative, or was this just so much bluster and rhetoric on the part of an ambitious young politician? It is important to take seriously individuals' ideas and not assume they are merely acting out of their narrow political interest. Ford rejected the mere "bomb-throwing" confrontational politics of opposition, embracing instead the role of responsible partner-in-governing seeking compromise with Republicans. He seemed personally disinclined toward "politics by other means" or the "politics of personal destruction," choosing instead to meet Republicans on the field of policy.[35] Ford did not seem to want a "permanent campaign," rather he wanted to contribute to governing as the loyal opposition. Was this what House Democrats wanted? Apparently not, since they rejected Ford's third way and Frost's accommodationist approach—or at least they did not elect Ford or Frost.

Nor did House Democrats elect Marcy Kaptur. During her even shorter-lived candidacy she offered an explicit criticism of her party and contemporary American politics. Kaptur's candidacy largely served the purpose of allowing her to give a caucus speech warning Democrats about the dangers of becoming too beholden to powerful fund-raising special interests: "I don't believe it is a left-right contest. I think it should be about reform. And that means elevating the non-money wing of our party. . . . We need to clean out the Congress, give it back to the American people, put the fund-raising under strict spending limits."[36]

Like Common Cause, Ross Perot and John McCain before her, Kaptur offered a "reform paradigm" beyond liberal versus conservative. The contemporary "permanent campaign" critique of American politics includes the notion that members of Congress are captives of a perpetual money chase.[37] At bottom, Kaptur's "reform paradigm" detests the purported special-interest domination of our politics, longing instead for a politics ideally more immediately directed toward the public interest.[38] Kaptur worried powerful moneyed interests were corrupting congressional politics. Her Democratic colleagues listened politely to her speech, then elected Nancy Pelosi overwhelmingly, partly due to the latter's proven fund-raising skills, but presumably also partly due to Pelosi's solution to the House Democrats' legislative strategy dilemma.

HOUSE REPUBLICAN RESPONSES

Though the focus here is on the minority party's 2003 strategic dilemma, the House GOP's perspective on the Democrats' leadership struggle—in particular their choice of Nancy Pelosi—can inform our understanding of the strategic dilemma facing House Democrats. Deborah Pryce, the highest-ranking House Republican woman party leader, said, "Didn't the Democrats learn anything from the election? I think the American people want results, not roadblocks, and Nancy is a roadblock, that's her hallmark. She's a liberal in the true sense of the word."[39] Republicans quickly labeled Pelosi a "San Francisco liberal" as a not-so-subtle way of suggesting she was outside the political mainstream. One top Republican staffer volunteered to go "door to door" in support of Pelosi's candidacy on the assumption that she would provide a stark contrast and convenient foil for the GOP.[40] "She is very liberal," noted a high-ranking GOP staffer. "She opposed the president on tax cuts, on homeland security, Iraq, welfare reform."[41] CNN's Robert Novak intoned, "There's nobody more happy about Nancy Pelosi's rise than the Republicans."[42] One wonders if that remains true following the 2006 and 2008 elections.

Should House Republicans have been so gleeful that Democrats elected Pelosi, an articulate, mediagenic spokesperson seemingly inclined to sharpen partisan differences and advance a more confrontational strategy? Many House Democrats were similarly gleeful when the strident "bomb throwing" Newt Gingrich began successfully challenging the leadership of the more accommodating House GOP leader Bob Michel. In retrospect, Gingrich's strategy for winning a majority seems to have been effective in 1994 and Pelosi's in 2006. Pelosi, at least in her early pronouncements, set forth a thoughtful solution to House Democrats' minority dilemma. She argued Democrats should find common ground with Republicans where possible, yet stand their ground where necessary. Republicans also had evidence that Pelosi might have the combination of "insider" and "outsider" skills that seemed to elude Gingrich.

Perhaps newly elected Majority Leader Tom DeLay was right to see Pelosi as a "worthy opponent." Even in 2003 one might have recognized that the face-off between Majority Leader DeLay and Minority Leader Pelosi might not be an advantage for Republicans. The number two House Democratic leader, Steny Hoyer, emphasized Tom DeLay's own confrontational style: "He takes no prisoners and he has been the point man for the very hard-line, noncompromising, extreme wing of the party."[43] Some Democrats and Republicans appeared inclined to personalize and demonize the DeLay/Pelosi confrontation in what seemed like a continuation of the politics of personal destruction or "politics by other means."

On the other hand, there was growing evidence that House Republicans, having extended their majority for a decade at least, were "learning to govern." "We need to have learned from our experience in 1994 and try to get some things done," noted Dan Meyer, a lobbyist who was chief of staff to then–House Speaker Newt Gingrich, "We can't let the perfect be the enemy of the good."[44] Even DeLay said, "We learned our lesson. You can't turn this country around on a dime."[45]

L.A. Times reporter Janet Hook observed, "It remains to be seen how long Republicans maintain this circumspect tone. The new Congress will come under heavy pressure to tack to the right from key party constituencies that expect much from an all-GOP government."[46] Sure enough, *National Journal*'s Richard E. Cohen noted, early in the 108th Congress following the 2002 election, House Republicans—with their enlarged majority—were already beginning to experience "dissension" and "disarray" contrary to the extraordinary unity they had maintained in recent years.[47] From their many years as a "permanent majority," of course, House Democrats could tell Republicans that such dissension is inevitable as they grow their majority. It is much easier to stay united in opposition, including opposition to a president or Senate majority of the other party.

The 2002 election presented House Republicans with a new challenge beyond their extended majority. The election left Republicans in control of the House, Senate and White House; thus, they no longer had a Senate Democratic majority as a backstop for their actions. House Republicans could no longer pass sweeping legislation confident Senate Democrats would kill it, thereby allowing Republicans the luxury of blaming Democrats for gridlock.[48] Under the new partisan circumstances of the 108th Congress, House Republicans might understandably have greater difficulty passing some of the same bills they passed in the 107th Congress, specifically on issues such as prescription drugs, energy, taxes, and pensions where they had passed legislation in the 107th Congress secure in the knowledge Senate Democrats would kill it.

Finally, part of the strategic dilemma confronting House Republicans as they approached the 2004 election was whether to work to retain or augment their majority or to help President Bush get reelected in 2004. Once before House Republicans were given a choice between pursuing their own majority and getting another President Bush reelected. They chose then to lose the White House in order to win the House. Their gamble seemingly paid off—in part because it created unified Democratic control of the White House, House, and Senate during the 103rd Congress—but in so doing they underscored rather dramatically how pursuing majorities in Congress may not be compatible with winning the White House. Congressional Democrats, of course, had also crossed this bridge before.

OTHER MAJOR PLAYERS

The competition between House Democrats and Republicans, of course, does not take place in a vacuum. The Senate and White House loom particularly large in the external environment of House politics. As already noted, control of the Senate clearly affects the range of options open to House leaders. When Democrats lost the Senate in 2002, the House GOP could no longer pass legislation largely for show, confident in the knowledge that majority Senate Democrats would protect them. Similarly, a congressional majority party has less freedom to advance "veto bait" legislation, if a president of their own party occupies the White House. Partisan control of the presidency and the "other body" affects a legislative party's "politics or policy" calculus. The answer to the question "Do you want a law or an issue for the next election?" may depend on who controls the other chamber or the presidency. Let's examine, in order, the perspectives of Senate Democrats, Senate Republicans, and the White House.

Following their loss of the majority in the 2002 election, Senate Democratic leaders decided to sharpen distinctions between themselves and Republicans. "We can't just do the rope-a-dope," argued Assistant Democratic Leader Harry Reid.[49] Democratic Leader Tom Daschle said he found being in the minority "liberating," in part because marshalling unity is easier when a party is on defense and does not have the majority party's responsibility to advance an agenda.[50] Daschle said he would also proudly wear the "obstructionist" badge: "That's part of our role. Right now, I view as a major responsibility for our caucus being the brakes on inadvisable Bush policy, and we're going to do it proudly and aggressively."[51] He added: "If I hear one word that describes our Democratic mood right now, it's 'fight.' We really believe that we've got to fight for the things we believe in and fight against the things that we think undermine those dreams and those goals."[52]

Of course, Senator Daschle probably also felt somewhat liberated by the fact that, unlike his counterpart in the House Dick Gephardt, he survived the 2002 election debacle retaining his leadership position. Daschle probably also ultimately felt liberated by his decision not to run for president, unlike many of his fellow Senate Democrats. The final liberating influence for Leader Daschle might have been the growing sense among some that, like their fellow Democrats in the House, Senate Democrats might be facing their own "permanent"—meaning long term—minority status.[53] No longer bearing majority responsibility for the institution, Senate Democrats, like their House Democratic colleagues, might have been liberated to behave "irresponsibly." It depended in part on whether or not they perceived themselves as a "permanent minority." Either way, Senate Democrats' posture on the question of legislative strategy clearly influenced that of House Democrats. In Tom Daschle, did Nancy Pelosi find a soul mate?

Meanwhile, Senate Republicans once again had responsibility for keeping the trains running. Prior to his ouster as Senate GOP leader due to controversial comments he made at retiring senator Strom Thurmond's

100th birthday party, Trent Lott (R-MS) said, "I am willing to [work with Democrats], not because I necessarily prefer to, but because in the United States Senate you have no choice. This is a place that requires consultation, cooperation, and in many cases dirty, old bipartisanship."[54] The strategic dilemma confronting House and Senate parties may well be different given the extraordinary institutional differences between the two chambers. If Lott, a former House GOP party leader, is right in suggesting that a strategy of confrontation is less available to Senate party leaders, then that alone provides evidence institutions affect the behavior of individuals.

While we cannot here explore such institutional differences in the strategic dilemma facing House and Senate party leaders, for now it is worth noting this party leader acknowledged such constraints. Suffice it to say, the difference between the two chambers complicates the strategic calculus confronting legislative party leaders. House Democrats and House Republicans must regularly take into account the peculiar nature of the Senate in addressing their own legislative strategy challenges, including the fact that the highly individualistic Senate tends to be less party-oriented than the House.

Senate Republicans were also quick to acknowledge another constraint on their options, namely, their debt to President Bush. Lott's replacement as Senate GOP leader, Bill Frist (R-TN) chair of the Republican Senatorial Campaign Committee during the 2002 campaign, was the embodiment of a newly strengthened disposition among Senate Republicans. They were clearly in the mood to maximize cooperation with President Bush since conventional wisdom concluded they owed their 2002 election majority to his recruiting, fund-raising, and campaigning efforts—along with perhaps the White House's adroit political positioning during the 107th Congress on issues like taxes and Iraq.

Both conservative and moderate GOP senators seemed to appreciate President Bush's contribution to their new majority. Conservative senator Jon Kyl (R-AZ) argued Republicans need to expand and strengthen their base in 2004 by offering a bold and unified conservative agenda. President Bush, he said, saved Senate Republicans from their failure to unify behind a clear agenda in 2002: "If we didn't have George W. Bush and the strength of his popularity, we might have lost this one."[55] Moderate GOP senator Lincoln Chafee (R-RI) argued Senate Republicans' 108th agenda will not be as "aggressively conservative" as it had been because Senate Republicans will need to hold on to seats in key swing states in 2004, including Colorado, Missouri, Ohio, and Pennsylvania. Still, Chafee noted, newly elected moderate Senate Republicans like Lamar Alexander, Norm Coleman, Elizabeth Dole, and John Sununu will need to cooperate with Bush: "They're going to owe the president a huge debt of gratitude in all the help he gave."[56] The strategic dilemma confronting legislative party leaders in both chambers is, of course, complicated still further by the separation of powers and the constitutionally and institutionally independent presidency.

Conservative commentator William Kristol argued "the big test is 2004," for congressional Republicans because they "need to confirm . . . a midterm election with a presidential victory."[57] *CQ Weekly* editor David Rapp similarly said "the question" for congressional Republicans is "as simple as it is straightforward: What will a GOP House and a GOP Senate do to ensure that George W. Bush will be re-elected in 2004?"[58] Following the 1994 Republican "revolution" some insisted the congressional GOP should focus on winning the White House in 1996. Instead, House Republicans sought to foment their "revolution" from within Congress. According to Richard Fenno, they failed at "learning to govern," thereby enabling Democrat Bill Clinton to get reelected in 1996 by providing him a convenient foil. Apparently, so, too, did congressional Democrats in 2004.

Was it in fact in the collective interest of congressional Republicans to help Bush gain reelection in 2004? Is the congressional GOP's fate inevitably bound up with a president willing and able to act independently? Should they concentrate instead on retaining and expanding their own majorities? Or will they merely focus, as some congressional election theorists would have us believe, on their own individual and personal reelection?

And what about congressional Democrats—do they face a similar challenge? They must tackle their own more complex strategic dilemma thanks to the institutional independence of the executive. Again, Tom Daschle found his own decision not to run for president in 2004 liberating as did Daschle's Senate Democratic colleagues. Unfortunately, congressional Democrats in both the House and Senate found the presidential ambitions of some among them rather more debilitating than liberating. Senators Kerry, Edwards, and Lieberman along with Congressman Gephardt complicated the legislative strategizing by members of their own party, as witness the Iraq War resolution vote in 2002.

It is worth noting that in a separation-of-powers system presidential ambition affects legislative politics differently than does prime ministerial ambition in a parliamentary system. A parliamentary system rewards party leadership rather than personal candidacies. In our separation-of-powers system, the entrepreneurial efforts of presidential candidates clearly complicate the legislative calculus of congressional parties, again as witness the efforts of Gephardt, Kerry, Edwards, and Lieberman to position themselves on the Iraq vote during the 107th Congress. Following the 2002 election (though prior to Senator Daschle's decision not to run for president) *Chicago Sun-Times* editorialist Juan Andrade observed about the strategic dilemma facing congressional Democrats,

Bush is not smarter than Gephardt or Daschle, but he has just one job: being president. Gephardt and Daschle are congressional opposition leaders AND presidential wannabes, and that's the problem. Tuesday proved they can't be both. . . . Congressional Democrats need leaders who are single-minded about building majorities in their respective chambers, leaders who can craft a message, set an agenda and offer a vision for America that resonates with a majority of the people. Without such leadership, '02 will prove to be just a preview of what's coming in '04.[59]

Andrade called on Gephardt and Daschle to resign their leadership positions. Similarly, in the lead-up to the 1996 presidential contest Senate Republican leader Bob Dole ultimately concluded he could not juggle both jobs, thus he resigned his leadership post to run for president free from the complications of conflicting loyalties and responsibilities. The separation of powers complicates legislative strategy.

Congressional elections expert Charlie Cook went so far as to suggest Democrats will more likely be defined by their 2004 presidential standard bearer than by any efforts of House or Senate Democratic leaders.[60] Were congressional Democrats at the mercy of potential presidential candidates, and were they limited to following the lead of the eventual Democratic presidential nominee, John Kerry? Did congressional Democrats, under conditions of united GOP government, have a collective interest in following the lead of their presidential standard bearer? Or did they have an independent incentive to pursue their own majorities, or, again, pursue merely their own individual reelection interest?

In the lead-up to the 2002 midterm election, President Bush clearly displayed a keen interest in building congressional majorities in the House and Senate by his extraordinary efforts at recruiting, fund-raising, and campaigning. He clearly understood it to be in his political interest to promote and expand Republican majorities on Capitol Hill. Prior to the 2002 election, many commentators noted the political risk Bush took by participating in a high-profile effort to build larger GOP majorities in Congress. Some commentators were noticeably surprised when the president's vigorous efforts succeeded beyond their low expectations.[61] Yet President Bush's success, perhaps ironically, curtailed his own strategic options in running for reelection in 2004. Given GOP majorities in both the House and Senate, the president can not easily run against "obstructionist" Senate Democrats or against a "do-nothing Congress." Indeed, the confrontational "Truman strategy," recommended in 1948 by White House aide James Rowe in a famous memo and adopted by "give 'em Hell" Harry Truman, may not be an option for a president under conditions of united party government.[62]

Hotline's Chuck Todd concluded:

Needless to say, the president's re-election strategy will need to be dramatically different than his midterm strategy. While Bush doesn't have a filibuster-proof Senate majority, the public won't know that—so if Bush expects to be re-elected in 2004, he'll have to show the country proof of progress. There are no more of his "obstructionists" in the majority; so there won't be any running against a "do nothing" Congress.[63]

Was Democratic National Committee (DNC) chair Terry McAuliffe right following the 2002 election in insisting that Republicans were the responsible party and must produce or pay the price at the next election? In the British parliamentary system, the majority party is indeed the "government," yet it is not as clear the same is true even under conditions of united party government in our separation-of-powers system. Congressional Democrats even as the minority, especially in the Senate, clearly retain leverage and therefore, arguably, some responsibility. Senate Democrats' leverage, for example, on thwarting judicial nominations, can complicate the life of the Republican in the White House, but they may also complicate life for minority Democrats in the House. Congressional Democrats may not be able to afford to adopt with impunity a confrontational posture.

The discussion thus far has brought us full circle from the conundrum facing House Democrats in choosing a leader to considering briefly the differing perspectives of House Republicans, Senate Democrats, Senate Republicans, and the White House. We have not by any means exhausted the question of legislative party strategy facing House Democrats following the 2002 election as reflected in their leadership fight. The question is much more complex than first meets the eye. We turn now to consider the strategic challenge facing House Democrats as seen from the perspective of outside pundits, journalists, political consultants, election analysts, political scientists, and others.

TO GINGRICH OR NOT TO GINGRICH— THAT IS THE QUESTION

Hill Democrats and Republicans are not the only ones who speak the language of government and opposition, compromise and confrontation, policy and politics. Outside commentators do as well. The *Weekly Standard*'s David Brooks (now with the *New York Times*), employing his usual wit, commented following the 2002 election, "[I]f Democrats want to recover, they have to look in the mirror and say, 'I'm dumber than George Bush,' and they have to say that every day."[64] Brooks thought Republicans strategically outsmarted Democrats; but later, in discussing the remaining Senate campaign in Louisiana, Brooks articulated what he called "[t]he Democratic dilemma in short form: do you go for the base or do you try to widen the base?"[65] Even if targeting base versus swing voters is only one dimension of legislative strategy, perhaps congressional parties are confronted with a Hobson's choice.

The *Wall Street Journal*'s Al Hunt in a "Memo to Nancy Pelosi" insisted, "The argument over whether Democrats should be more accommodationist or more confrontational is a false choice for the congressional party."[66] Hunt then went on to argue for the politics of confrontation including personal contrast between Pelosi and the "reactionary" Tom DeLay. Hunt urged House Democrats not to become Republican-lite, adding, "[I]gnore those who claim all Democrats have to do is expand the base, the perpetual theme of political lost causes"; rather, "you need to both energize the base and win over more swing voters." Hunt urged House Democrats to "create serious alternatives" to GOP proposals on tax cuts and health care. He concluded, "You may lose on these issues in the House but win in public opinion." Al Hunt believes congressional Democrats do not have a stark choice between compromise and confrontation, policy and politics; by playing politics and advancing their own ambitions, House Democrats can promote good public policy. The strategic dilemma may not be a simple dichotomized choice.

Similarly, the *Washington Post*'s E. J. Dionne argued that the debate between liberal and centrist factions among Democrats is very much beside the point.

> The Democrats are a center-left party. If the party's moderate and liberal wings don't fly together, the old bird will crash into a tree every time. But the Republicans showed that a party can hold itself together and still stand up and fight. The Democrats lost because Bush was much tougher than they were, and much smarter in his choice of issues. The Democrats don't need to move left or right. They need to adjust to the new environment terrorism has created. They need to be less inward-looking and less intimidated. As one great Democrat has already put it, they have nothing to fear but fear itself.[67]

Bush understood the new political environment and effectively played "wedge politics," according to Dionne, with issues like homeland security when Democrats got hung up on protecting public-employee unions. Democrats also "resisted nationalizing the election" instead leaving that to Bush. So it is not simply left versus center, base versus swing voters, according to Dionne; rather, Democrats needed courage.

According to *Roll Call*'s Morton Kondracke, such courage included a willingness to challenge their base constituency. Kondracke seemed to think Democrats had gotten fat, dumb, and happy sitting in safe Democratic districts: "[T]hey don't seem to care whether they ever get back in the majority or not."[68] If Democrats were ever going to regain a House majority, he opined, they will need to live dangerously, take risks and actively pursue their majority; the old all-politics-is-local approach of House Democrats will not suffice now that they are *safely* mired in the minority.

Democratic consultants also urged courage and risk taking as well. "Part of the problem with Democrats is timidity," concluded James Carville.[69] Former Gore campaign manager, Donna Brazile, argued, "[W]ithout a bold vision of what America can be in the 21st century, my party will lose more elections. . . . In this new season of opportunity, the Democratic Party must become a real opposition party."[70] Brazile saw Congresswoman Pelosi as just about right for House Democrats: "What we need now is a bold strike—we have to come back fighting. . . . Nancy is our best answer: Someone who is willing to take a risk."[71]

Other Democratic consultants begged to differ. Tom Freedman and Bill Knapp, in "How Republicans Usurped the Center," urge Democrats to adopt "a compelling feasible and centrist approach to public policy."[72] Democrats must appeal, again, to both base and swing voters: "Candidates must do well both within their own party and among those who have little party allegiance." As for legislative strategy, "The only way forward for Democrats is to find effective ways to solve problems, working with Republicans where possible and repudiating their more extreme measures when necessary." Similarly, former Democratic congressman Tony Coelho, while applauding Pelosi's victory, argued, "It's very important to be the loyal opposition—meaning that you have opposing views when you disagree. But I also think it's important that you hug when you agree."[73] Coelho's balanced formulation echoed Pelosi's own. Again, there may not be a simple answer to the legislative strategy question. It may depend on circumstances.

Even respected election analysts disagreed on why Democrats lost the 2002 midterm election. Charlie Cook looked at the election from a seat-by-seat perspective and concluded, "This election was more about the triumph of individual candidates than about the triumph of an issue or an agenda."[74] Bill Schneider, on the other hand, concluded the election became a referendum on a popular president: "Democrats may try to console themselves by claiming that 'all politics is local,' but that is quite wrong. Republicans enjoyed a massive sweep across the country."[75] Local or national? Base or swing voters? Left or center? Compromise or confrontation? Play politics or seriously pursue policy? Courage or complacency? What's a party to do? Charlie Cook summarized the Democrats' dilemma:

> As Democrats attempt to regroup from their November 5 [2002] losses, they are trying to decide how to reposition their party. Should they move to the left, as some have suggested, to show that they "stand for something" and provide "a real choice," not just a "Republican-lite" alternative? Or should they move toward the middle? Or should they take the slightly different "New Democrat" approach advocated by the Democratic Leadership Council?[76]

Cook argued the 2004 Democratic presidential candidate is more likely than Democratic congressional leaders to determine the answer to these

questions for the party in much the same way Bill Clinton had done during the 1990s. "Bill Clinton found the true 'sweet spot' for his Democratic
Party—a carefully balanced nexus between policy and politics, vision and
realism," Cook concluded in an essay titled "Balance Will Become the
Democrats' New Mantra."[77]

Balance, however, is hard to achieve in the House these days given the
emptying of the center between the two parties. "In fact, the ascension of
Ms. Pelosi and Mr. DeLay reflects a long-running trend in Congress, particularly in the House. While presidential candidates race to the center,
congressional candidates often head the other way," given the growing
ideological polarization in the House in recent decades.[78] While the yawning chasm between the two parties makes it more difficult for congressional party leaders to resolve their strategic dilemma, the natural tension
between congressional parties and presidential candidates compounds
the problem still further. Again, the constitutional separation of powers
makes life difficult for legislative party leaders.

Think-tank Democrats echoed and elaborated some of the themes
above. Robert Borosage, director of the liberal-leaning Institute for
America's Future, maintained, "The lesson of 2002 is that the Democrats
have to be much bolder in laying out what they believe and an alternative agenda" consisting of "a combination of lunch-bucket issues and the
triumphant values of the 1960s—protecting the environment, civil rights,
and women's rights. There is a Democratic majority on these issues."[79]
Wendy Kaminer, formerly of the *American Prospect*, maintained:

> Democrats have to accept the fact that they're going to be reacting for the
> next two years. They have to embrace partisanship. There's nothing wrong
> with partisanship. That's why we have two parties. There are enough
> Republicans yessing the president. That's not the Democrats' job. And so
> they have to be able to stand up when the president accuses them of being
> obstructionists.[80]

The moderate Democratic Leadership Council's postelection analysis differed:

> We agree . . . the party needs a bigger, bolder, clearer agenda and message.
> But we disagree with those who are saying the party should achieve that
> clarity simply by moving to the left, creating partisan differentiation at any
> cost, and engaging in more negative campaigning against the president and
> Republicans in order to energize the Democratic base.[81]

Finally, one of the Democrats' most thoughtful intellectuals, Harvard's
Elaine Kamarck, in "Democrats Lost the Power of Ideas" concluded:

> As the Democrats deconstruct what went wrong on Tuesday, some will say
> the party should now turn right or left. But the real problem is not direction.

It is that in the 2002 campaign, the Democrats stopped thinking. One by one, they lost the big issues to the Republicans. In spite of its name, political opposition is not about doing the opposite of what the other party does. It is about creating real and better alternatives and seeing them through. The Democrats didn't do it, and they paid for it with control of the Senate.[82]

Kamarck detailed the specific issues Democrats mishandled, including corporate governance, creation of a Department of Homeland Security, and Iraq. Congressional Democrats lost the strategic fight with President Bush because they failed to exploit the corporate scandals effectively, kowtowed to their labor unions on Homeland Security and failed to offer a clear, creative alternative to the GOP position on Iraq.

Like journalists, Democratic consultants, and election analysts, these think-tank intellectuals argue over legislative strategy in terms of left versus center, partisan confrontation versus bipartisan compromise, reactive and negative versus creative and affirmative. All of these and more are dimensions of the strategic dilemma legislative political parties face. Not surprisingly, however, these intellectuals particularly emphasize the importance of ideas over interests. In criticizing Democrats for being captives of the unions on Homeland Security, for example, Kamarck concluded, "[W]e win when we're a party of ideas."[83] Her analysis is perhaps reminiscent of another professorial politician, Newt Gingrich, who premised his House GOP "revolution" on the notion that Democrats were the party of insiders and special interests, while insurgent Republicans were the party of outsiders and ideas.[84] Should House Democrats take their cue from their long-time nemesis, Newt Gingrich?

At least one Democrat strategist in 2002 was explicit about the need for Democrats to imitate Gingrich. Chris Lehane insisted, "Democrats need to disavow their politics of appeasement. Democrats ought to take a page out of the Gingrich approach. He had a guerilla warfare approach. He recognized we're in the minority and not responsible so they could pick and choose fights."[85] Other Democrats were not so sure. Congressman Anthony D. Weiner (D-NY), who had previously supported Nancy Pelosi's rise in his party's leadership ranks, now raised questions about the danger of this San Francisco Democrat providing an all-too-easy target for Republicans: "We have to be careful not to create a leadership figure that becomes so strident, so confrontational that they become Gingrichian."[86]

To Newt or not to Newt? Is that the question Democrats faced? Following their 2002 setback, were Democrats beginning to appreciate Newt's strategy? The longer House Democrats remained a "permanent minority," the more they seemed tempted by the siren song of Gingrich's politics of confrontation. Yet what exactly does it mean to be "Gingrichian"? It may include, as Chris Lehane implied, the recognition that the minority party is not responsible and therefore should adopt the confrontational tactics of "guerilla warfare." But as Congressman Weiner warned, the minority party really cannot afford to be simply irresponsible, engaging in "bomb-throwing," negative-attack politics—or worse. Alternatively, should House Democrats in the 108th Congress have embraced what Newt Gingrich called the "grand partisanship" of the politics of ideas, as Elaine Kamarck recommended?

Stated differently, as the minority party, did House Democrats need to "learn to govern" or should they play opposition? Should they embrace "permanent campaign" politics rather than pursuing policy as responsible partners in governing? Finally, should House Democrats have embraced the "politics by other means" seemingly favored by Gingrich? If so, would this be limited to "institutional combat," or would it also inevitably entail the politics of personal destruction and "RIP" tactics?[87] Under conditions of "united Republican government" following the 2002 election, were minority Democrats free to play the confrontational politics of opposition devoid of any responsibility for governing? Were Republicans, as Terry McAuliffe insisted, the responsible party and therefore saddled with the need to pursue policy and govern, while compromising with minority Democrats?

In the British parliamentary system, the two parties have a clear-cut choice between government and opposition, policy and politics, compromise and confrontation. Unfortunately, perhaps, for House Democrats and House Republicans alike, their choices are not that simple. For starters, unlike in the British parliamentary system, under our constitutional system, neither party by itself ever "forms a government." At all times, both major parties retain some responsibility for governing. Even at the height of Newt Gingrich's insurgency, there remained within GOP ranks, members of Congress who insisted Republicans should act like "responsible partners in governing."[88] During the 1980s, there may have been an element of truth to the perspectives of both the insurgents and their critics within the House Republican Conference.

Exploring the complexity of legislative party strategy first requires understanding the constitutional and institutional environment within which the two parties function. Given the complexity of legislative parties' strategic dilemma in the context of our separation-of-powers system, it is not at all surprising that partisans, pundits, political consultants, election analysts, and policy intellectuals often disagree over the right course for a legislative party. To say that the right answer to the conundrum of legislative strategy is difficult is not the same as assuming that we cannot answer the question at all. The fact that party politicians are more or less effective in addressing this question suggests there may be more or less correct answers to the question—unless, of course, the question does not really matter at all.

What about the political scientists? If, as some political scientists argue "exogenous variables" determine legislative outcomes and behavior, then the efforts of legislative party politicians are for naught. If the answer to the strategic dilemma confronting legislative party leaders does not matter, then a lot of politicians and political journalists are wasting a remarkable amount of effort, ink, and airtime debating a useless question. Political scientists might want to reconsider that presumption and instead take seriously what politicians and their closest observers take seriously. A good place to start is with the opinions of two political scientists close to the action.

Brookings Senior Fellow Thomas E. Mann urged the politics of "consensus" rather than "confrontation" on President Bush following the 2002 election: "If he takes some risks with his own [conservative] base, he can force the Democrats to legislate with him. . . . But if he plays the same game of words vs. deeds, rhetoric vs. policy, it could be pretty bloody."[89] "Pretty bloody" meant that Democrats could respond to Republicans' unwillingness to compromise by engaging in the confrontational politics of opposition, and perhaps even the "permanent campaign" or "politics by other means." Mann seemed to think the responsibility for choosing which course to follow rested squarely with majority Republicans.

Norman Ornstein at the American Enterprise Institute also commented on the parties' legislative strategy dilemma. Ornstein rightly noted the "perception," albeit perhaps not the reality, that Republicans under conditions of united GOP government had, as Terry McAuliffe insisted, the responsibility to govern. Democrats can exploit that "perception," Ornstein argued, in much the same way Gingrich-led Republicans did during the first two years of the Clinton presidency when Democrats had united control of the House, Senate, and White House. Because "you need 60 votes basically to make much happen in the Senate," Ornstein observed, "Democrats have some clout there now; in some respects, frankly . . . it may be a little greater." Having lost their Senate majority, Ornstein argued, Democrats may ironically have had greater leverage over Republicans, thanks in part to the perception that the GOP was now the "government." Democrats, perhaps, could play the politics of opposition with some impunity, while in fact retaining significant power and leverage in the government.

Ornstein went on to note the difficulty Senate Democrats had in maintaining unity while functioning as the majority. Again, ironically perhaps, it was easier for Democrats to maintain unity as a minority.

[N]ow they don't need the 51 that they needed then to try and get what they wanted done, they just need 40, and they will have 40 in many instances pulling them some to the left, but blocking things, which is a strategy that Republicans used *very successfully* in Bill Clinton's first two years—bedeviled him on his budget for months, they didn't give him a single vote to make anything happen, and then in the end of course on the health care plan.[90]

Ornstein made four crucial observations. First, legislative strategies can be more or less successful; presumably, therefore, legislative strategies matter. Second, Democrats may ironically be empowered by losing the Senate given the clout a minority party has in the Senate, thus raising the possibility that the minority party in our constitutional system retains some governing power. Third, it is easier to maintain party unity as a minority party playing opposition than it is for the majority party attempting to govern. And fourth, therefore, it may make sense for Democrats to embrace the politics of opposition given the, perhaps false, "perception" that Republicans *were* the government. Indeed, it may have been in the political interest of Democrats to promote and exploit that perception in order to adopt the obstructionist tactics Newt Gingrich used effectively in the early 1990s. Did House Democrats in the 108th Congress want to learn how to play opposition from Newt Gingrich?

In borrowing from the Gingrich playbook, House Democrats needed to decide whether they had any responsibility or desire to govern, whether politics must supersede policy, whether to perpetuate the "permanent campaign," and whether to embrace "politics by other means." To Newt or not to Newt—that is the question.

THE 2004 ELECTION

So how did House Democrats under the tutelage of Nancy Pelosi fare in the 2004 election? Did they understand adequately the complex institutional context and strategic calculus confronting them thanks to our constitutional separation of powers? To parse this last question, perhaps we need to clarify whether the test of successful legislative party strategizing is legislative or electoral victory, advancing the party's agenda or ambitions—or both. Presumably the two are connected. On the one hand, members often talk as if a legislative victory or loss may affect the next election. On the other hand, a party's electoral success—for example, gaining a majority or a large enough minority to have leverage—is necessary for effective legislating. Let's briefly examine the 108th Congress' legislative agenda first.

At a minimum, opposition House Democrats were able to make life difficult for the majority Republicans attempting to govern during the 108th Congress. At one point late in the 108th Congress, the *Washington Post* concluded that House Republicans had become practiced in the "art of one-vote victories." The *Post* story cited the votes on Head Start funding, D.C. school vouchers, and Medicare prescription drugs. The latter victory entailed the controversial late-night three-hour "long count" on the floor which angered House Democrats. In that instance, Minority Leader Nancy Pelosi proved remarkably effective in holding her troops in line—including David Wu (D-OR), albeit temporarily—thereby forcing House Republicans to round up votes from their side of the aisle.[91]

This 2003 House GOP long count was reminiscent of a similar outrage perpetrated on minority Republicans by Democratic Speaker Jim Wright in October 1987. The Republican 2003 long count lasted more than three times as long as the Democrats' in 1987. The Republican long count, however, did not entail, as Jim Wright had done, the Speaker announcing that all voting time had expired, and then reopening the vote to allow a fellow partisan to change his vote. Nor was the Republican 2003 long count preceded by the Speaker engaging in the legislative legerdemain of having the House adjourn only to reconvene for a new "legislative day" in order to allow a revote.[92] Still, Democrats were incensed. Some observers noted that House Democrats were now "united as never before."[93] Majority party victories sometimes come at a price.

According to *Roll Call*, in September 2003 Minority Leader Pelosi "launched her most aggressive broadside against" Republicans on the issue of the Iraq War, in particular against the $87 billion supplemental. Pelosi saw an opportunity to exploit politically GOP vulnerabilities on the war. Again, according to *Roll Call*, Pelosi was similarly aggressive in "playing politics" with the 9/11 Commission Report issued one day before the August recess.[94] Arguably, her "playing politics" may have contributed to advancing good public policy by forcing Republicans to address intelligence reform seriously in the closing days of the 108th Congress. Normally, such sweeping and significant legislation introduced late in a session would not stand a chance of passage, but House Democrats led by Pelosi took advantage of the opening created by the 9/11 Commission Report to pressure majority Republicans. Intelligence reform may be a good example of how elections and our separation-of-powers system *add* energy to the system, rather than—as is often assumed—merely subtracting energy by slowing or prohibiting policy change. Conceivably, Pelosi and House Democrats can claim some legislative success, or at least leverage and influence, in the 108th Congress.

Congressional Democrats can also take credit for making Republicans work for the increased majority the GOP enjoyed following the 2004 election. It is worth comparing and contrasting Senate and House Democratic leadership on this score.

Daschle and Reid

Senate Democratic leader Tom Daschle insisted the 2002 midterm election "liberated" him to fight enabling him to be proudly obstructionist. Prior to the 2004 election, however, the *Washington Post*'s Helen Dewar noted that Daschle's tight race in South Dakota constrained him as leader.[95] Daschle's loss in the 2004 election may have liberated him to pursue potential 2008 presidential ambitions, yet his defeat also sent a warning signal to Senate Democrats. "Daschle's loss," the *Washington Post*'s Charles Babington concluded, "is credited largely to Republican John Thune's portrayal of him as 'the chief obstructionist' to President Bush's agenda, a worrisome thought for Democrats seeking reelection in 2006."[96]

Senate Democrats turned to the ideologically more moderate Harry Reid (D-NV) as Daschle's replacement. "Reid's first challenge," Babington noted, "is to help his fellow Democrats assess the election results and decide whether to soften their opposition to GOP initiatives such as putting conservatives on the federal bench or drilling for oil in Alaskan wilderness."[97] Senate GOP Whip Mitch McConnell (R-KY) said Reid's "immediate challenge is to preside over an internal soul-searching debate [on] just how much to obstruct."[98]

Pelosi and Frost

Following the 2002 election, House Democratic leader Nancy Pelosi embraced conflict, intensifying partisanship in an effort to stall legislation and thwart Republicans. "She is turning out to be tougher and more confrontational than people thought," noted political scientist John J. Pitney, Jr. "In some ways she's a Newt Gingrich in a parallel universe."[99] During the summer of 2004 Pelosi denounced Republicans for heavy-handed procedural tactics while calling for a minority "Bill of Rights" in the House.[100] At the same time, she assailed a "do-nothing" Republican Congress.[101] Apparently for Pelosi, it was no more "Ms. Nice Guy."

Pelosi did not mince words. In a July 2004 story titled "Hard-Line Policy to Secure House Majority," the *Washington Post* dubbed Pelosi "the Lady Macbeth of politics" for her willingness to be frankly "hardheaded" and "hardhearted."

> We have to have the resources and then target them—this is going to sound harsh—in the most cold-blooded possible way. This is about winning the 11—and I want 22—seats that we need to win the House back. So it's not about being nice. I didn't come into this to win any popularity contests. I came in to win the election. So I have been brutally cold-blooded. When we make these decisions [about which candidates to support], no four-chambered creatures need come to the table. We want reptilian, cold-blooded creatures.[102]

Pelosi went on to link legislative strategy and message to recruitment, fund-raising, and get-out-the-vote (GOTV) efforts, critiquing her predecessor, Dick Gephardt, for his congressional strategy in 2002: "There was a decision not to have a message nationally. You can't mobilize without a message." Not surprisingly, House Democrats led by Pelosi rolled out their "New Partnership for America's Future" national message in September 2004. Democrats contrasted their document with Newt Gingrich's Contract with America by noting that their "New Partnership" "will not lay out specific legislative and policy proposals, but instead broadly define Democratic themes and present explanations for why voters should bump the minority into the majority."[103] Nevertheless, if imitation is the sincerest form of flattery, Newt Gingrich probably smiled upon hearing about House Democrats' new agenda.

2004 Election Aftermath

Nancy Pelosi survived the 2004 election, though her "New Partnership" national message apparently did not help Martin Frost and a few other moderate Texas House Democrats who lost their reelection bids. As noted earlier, Democrats in general were suffering from "postelection stress trauma" due to their loss of four seats in the House and four seats in the Senate, along with their failure to defeat President Bush. The day after the election ABC's *The Note* announced the "first Al From, Barbara Boxer, Bob Borsage, E. J. Dionne, Joe Klein, Carl Pope, etc., etc., etc., circular-firing squad, hand-wringing debate about 'what happens to the Democrats now?'"[104] House Democrats once again were mimicking the behavior of "permanent minority" House Republicans during the 1980s.

Meanwhile, the *Washington Post*'s Dana Milbank reraised the specter of a Halliburton scandal and the possible return to "politics by other means" over the next four years: "After last week's drubbing the president's opponents have begun to seek solace in scandal."[105] House Democrat Henry Waxman was already hard at work. The liberal *Salon* website predicted "[a]t some point in the next four years there will be a great scandal that will make Watergate look like a fraternity prank."[106]

In retrospect, did Hill Democrats adopt the right legislative party strategy following the 2002 election? Did they help or hurt themselves in the 2004 election with the tack they took following the 2002 election? For political scientists and politicians alike it is difficult at best to sort out the causes of congressional election success and failure. As noted earlier, the role of legislative party strategy must be understood in the context of other factors strongly influencing congressional elections, especially candidate quality. Such factors include retirement, recruitment, reapportionment, redistricting, fund-raising, GOTV, and the long-term building of farm teams in state legislatures. According to Nancy Pelosi, as noted above, these various factors are all tied into legislative party strategy. The minority cannot mobilize without a message, she insists.

Can minority party legislative strategy make a difference? Or are they damned if they do and damned if they don't? According to political scientist and long-time House Republican Ways and Means chairman

Bill Thomas, there is little that the minority party in the House can do in seeking majority status. As the minority party in the House, Thomas argued,

> You're going to lose either because you're too strident, demanding things people don't want or you're going to lose because you're too milquetoast and you're going along to get along. The point is when you're in the minority, you're going to lose no matter what tactic you take. Incumbents beat themselves. The majority beats itself. And the question is how long can you sustain the particular mix at the particular time to allow you to maintain the majority?[107]

If there is no right answer to this legislative strategy question, then why do minority parties continue to debate this conundrum? Even assuming there is nothing the minority party can do affirmatively, can they cause the majority party to falter, to overplay their hand, or commit costly errors? As we have seen, the majority party is sometimes very good at uniting the minority party. Moderate House Democratic Whip Steny Hoyer, for example, sounded a lot more like Nancy Pelosi following the Medicare prescription drug long-count vote.

Fortunately for the House minority party, the majority party also must confront the same, or at least a similar, conundrum. Commentator David Brooks notes "a paradox: the bigger GOP majorities will make it harder to establish one-party rule . . . the Republican win may actually mean less one-party dominance" following the 2004 election.[108] Republicans, Brooks predicts, will become even more discordant, assertive, and fractious. They may also become more arrogant and thus more likely to overplay their hand vis-à-vis the minority party, the Senate, and the White House. During the postelection intelligence reform debate some commentators accused them of precisely such arrogance.

On the other hand, the ability of House and Senate Republicans to maintain and expand their majority in 2004 while also contributing to the reelection of President Bush may stand as evidence that they had "learned to govern." Certainly, the 2004 Republican electoral victory would seem to imply that voters saw the GOP as having learned to govern; otherwise, why would voters entrust Republicans with continued control over the House, Senate, and White House? Of course, variables other than legislative strategy may explain Republicans success; for example, the Tom DeLay–inspired Texas redistricting or Senate Republican success in recruiting good candidates for open Democratic seats in the South. All these variables and others are important; nevertheless, the combined victory of Republicans in the House, Senate, and White House seemed to suggest that voters thought Republicans had learned to govern.

THE 2006 ELECTION

Republicans took a "thumping" in the 2006 elections. To understand why, we must start with election fundamentals beginning with the Constitution. The constitutional playing field presented Republicans in 2006 with the oft-dreaded six-year-itch election. Every two-term president since Teddy Roosevelt has suffered losses in his second midterm election.[109] When analysts predicted President Bush would be a drag on Republican candidates, they were, in part, acknowledging the *deus ex machina* of six-year-itch elections.[110] Coupled with the Iraq War, Bush's second midterm election was fated to harm Republicans. Every president at war since Abraham Lincoln has suffered midterm election losses. The six-year itch and Iraq War explain much about the 2006 Republican rout.

The economy, another election fundamental commonly cited by observers, seemed not to play a large role in this election; unless, of course, a sound economy provided a backstop to Republican fortunes. Democrats briefly flirted with talk of high gas prices and a housing slump, but neither seemed to capture the public's imagination, especially once gas prices plunged. Perhaps the economy mattered little because a more fundamental self-preservation issue—war—mattered a lot.

Democrats also sought throughout 2006 to make the "culture of corruption" charge stick to majority Republicans. The minority party had little success with corruption as an issue—in part because they too were implicated—until the Foley page scandal gift-wrapped the issue for Democrats. Election watcher Charlie Cook noted that Foley "took all the previous scandals that were totally unrelated obviously and then kind of put them in a box and put a big bow on it, and made them all sort of bigger than they had been before."[111] The charge of corruption, of course, is an accusation perennially available to either party in a Madisonian pluralist system premised on the unleashing of ambition, self-interest, and special-interest groups. This year it had a name: earmarks.

Typically, Americans seem to have a high level of patience with members of Congress doing favors for constituents and advancing their own reelection with pork; yet, from time to time, our suspicions about a special-interest-dominated politics reaches a critical mass. November 2006 represents one such instance when Woodrow Wilson's oft-echoed call for reform of Madisonian pluralism came home to roost.

As important as the six-year itch, Iraq, the economy, and corruption are as explanations, they still leave many questions unanswered. If such factors in fact created a *wave* of anti-Republican sentiment, how did it manage to breach the *wall* of structural advantages available to the incumbent majority party? How did the normally all-politics-is-local tenor of Madisonian congressional elections, suddenly give way to a clearly nationalized election wave?

Analysts of congressional elections commonly focus on certain additional fundamentals including reapportionment, redistricting, retirement, and recruitment. Along with fund-raising, these factors influence candidate quality for the majority and minority for incumbents and challengers alike.

Reapportionment and Redistricting

Constitutionally stipulated reapportionment has in recent decades shifted House seats into increasingly Republican-friendly parts of the country such as the Sunbelt, giving rise to GOP hopes of creating a "permanent majority" for House Republicans. GOP-controlled state legislatures have in turn (as have Democrats when they have had the chance) drawn redistricting lines amenable to party pickups. The Texas gerrymander is one infamous example. Why then did the Republican redistricting brick-in-the-wall not save them from the 2006 wave?

In part, it may in fact have saved them from a worse fate. Observers noted in 2006 that upwards of fifty to sixty House seats were in play, a clear increase over recent cycles; and yet, most House seats remained safe, incumbent redoubts, thereby almost certainly muting eventual turnover numbers. Redistricting remains an increasingly computer-driven science, rather than the art it once was. Still, the 2006 elections proved that redistricting lines can get old; indeed, the shifting-issue environment can render gerrymandered lines old before their time. Case in point: Iraq.

Retirement and Recruitment

In August 2006, *Congressional Quarterly* contrasted the 1994 Republican retirement and recruitment advantages with the more modest success of the 2006 Democrats: "Unlike the 1994 Democrats, the 2006 Republicans haven't seen a major incumbent exodus leaving a long list of vulnerable open seats," and the 2006 Democrats "haven't . . . matched the Republican recruiting success of 1994."[112] Perhaps this explains in part why Democrats did not pick up the fifty-two seats the Gingrich-led Republicans did in 1994. Certainly during the fall National Republican Congressional Committee (NRCC) chair Tom Reynolds did not miss an opportunity to tout the retirement and recruitment bricks in the GOP defensive perimeter. And yet immediately following the November 7th election, *Congressional Quarterly* noted a weakness in Republican recruiting: "In contrast [to the Democrats], the Republicans failed to recruit strong challengers to many House Democrats. Just five districts now held by Democrats were considered to be highly competitive."[113]

In other words, Republicans were playing defense in terms of retirement and recruitment. Why? The predictable six-year itch coupled with the unpopularity of President Bush and the Iraq War gave potential Republican candidates fair warning about the probable 2006 electoral environment. The limits of GOP success managing the challenges of candidate quality must be understood in the context of the six-year constitutional cycle coupled with war. The Constitution defines an institutional context that clearly influences retirement and recruitment decisions.

Fund-Raising and GOTV

The shrinking of any Republican fund-raising advantage in 2006 must also be understood in the same context. Political scientists such as Gary Jacobson sometimes measure candidate quality in terms of the capacity to raise money, though constitutional context almost certainly influences fund-raising success just as it does candidate retirement and recruitment decisions. In the months leading up to the election, the Republican political action committee (PAC) edge was eroding as K Street reevaluated the partisan odds. The Campaign Finance Institute noted that Democrats were financially more competitive in 2006 than in recent years. Democratic challengers sometimes outspent Republican incumbents, plus many more Democratic challengers had the requisite "enough" to be competitive against GOP incumbents.

A final structural advantage Republicans purportedly had was their vaunted Voter Vault and micro-targeting GOTV. Karl Rove and Ken Mehlman placed great stock in the GOTV edge that Republicans had in previous elections; indeed, in the days immediately preceding the election, the jaunty self-confidence exhibited by both seemed in large part premised on their faith in GOP GOTV. Was that faith misplaced, or did Republican GOTV efforts stem the Democrats' rising tide? Hard to say, though Heather Wilson's (R-NM) narrow victory, for example, clearly benefited from GOP GOTV.

Hurricane Flooding Breached GOP Levee?

Do structural advantages—the wall—matter less when there is a wave of discontent? In 2006, as in 1994, we once again learned that structural advantages are not impregnable. We also learned, once again, that there is no such thing as a permanent minority or permanent majority. And we learned, once again, that all politics is local except when it is national.[114] In 2006, somewhat ironically, the all-politics-is-local shoe was on the other foot. The NRCC's defensive Tom Reynolds preached the old-time Tip O'Neill gospel, while the DCCC's hard-charging Rahm Emanuel predicted correctly that a national wave was in the offing. There are limits to the advantage of incumbency; pent-up demand eventually breaks through.

DO CAMPAIGNS MATTER?

Campaigns matter at least at the margins—where, of course, many elections are won and lost—and in some years, campaigns matter more than merely at the margins. Campaigns begin, of course, with party leadership attention to redistricting, retirements, recruitment, fund-raising, and other fundamentals. Did Republicans fail to recruit strong challengers to many Democrats because potential GOP recruits recognized that a six-year-itch election during time of war did not provide a propitious electoral environment for the majority party? Potential candidates could read the writing on the wall so to speak. Did House Republicans lose because they ran a bad campaign, or did they run a bad campaign because they were going to lose?

To answer this question we must ask another: how did they govern? In the era of the "permanent campaign" there is an inextricable link between campaigning and governing. Why? There are many good explanations for the "permanent campaign," but for our purposes, three stand out.[115] First, journalists emphasize entertainment over enlightenment, conflict over compromise, opposition over governing—in other words, campaigning over governing. Second, political science has taught journalists that politicians act out of ambition and a desire for reelection, so why not conflate campaigning and governing? Third, the "permanent campaign" may not be entirely new; it may be premised on the Constitution's two-year House term treadmill. Therefore, in examining the House Republican campaign, we need to ask: how did they govern?

Again, campaigns are at least in part about character and issues. Character naturally looms larger in presidential elections than in congressional elections because the presidency is in the first instance a single individual, the president, while Congress is a complex institution made up of many individuals. Nevertheless, character counts even in congressional elections as witness those members who lost reelection due to scandal. Parties, too, may lose in part on character—call it a "culture of corruption." In the 109th Congress, the House GOP was in disarray on questions of ethics. They could not, for example, effectively address earmark reform. Nor were they able to manage the Foley fallout, in part because the leadership failed to bring both Democratic and Republican members of the page board into the equation.

The Governing Party?

House GOP disarray on ethics mirrored similar disarray on policy. As mentioned, the House Republicans fumbled earmark reform. Likewise, President Bush's Social Security reform effort seemed stillborn. Immigration reform found House Republicans fighting more with Senate Republicans and the White House than with Democrats. Thanks to the constitutional separation of powers and bicameralism, we have what Charles O. Jones calls a "government of parties," rather than party government. Furthermore, House Democrats' discipline and unity in opposition contributed to divisions among Republicans. For example, Nancy Pelosi's ability to have House Democrats hold the line on retaining Sensenbrenner's provision in the House immigration bill making illegal immigration a felony made political life more difficult for the House GOP. Congressional Republicans, of course, were also not in accord on the Iraq War, not least because war is an issue by its very nature that is difficult, not to say impossible, to manage. Wars never go according to plan including on the home front.

In the 109th Congress, congressional Republicans were in disarray—or more accurately, meltdown mode. Indeed, they looked a lot like Democrats in the lead-up to the 1994 election: policy disarray coupled with the politics of scandal, chaos, and factionalism within their ranks, and at odds with a president of their own party. Immigration reform in 2006 may have been the functional equivalent of Hillary's early 1990s health-care reform debacle. In 1994 and 2006 the majority party in Congress provided palpable, empirical evidence that they were in trouble and that they were going to lose their majorities. So how did they govern? They didn't. In 2006, the House Republicans in particular were clearly not the "governing" party. Like House Democrats in 1994, House Republicans in 2006 could not govern the country, could not govern Congress, and could not govern themselves. They were ineffective at campaigning because they were ineffective at governing. They ran a bad campaign because they were going to lose.

LEGISLATIVE PARTY STRATEGY

Government or opposition? Governing or campaigning? Pursuing policy or playing politics? Compromise or confrontation? This strategic dilemma is a true constant of legislative politics, factionalizing internally both parties. The dilemma may be a conundrum in the true sense of the word: there may be no right answer to the question, though the question clearly matters. The constancy of this conundrum suggests that the Constitution governs. Indeed, the Constitution governs in a way that neither party governs. Neither party in our separation-of-powers system is ever simply the government or the opposition. Instead, each party is constantly wracked on the horns of this dilemma.

The Constitution governs in the sense that each party is perpetually divided into internal party factions contending over the correct answer to this legislative party strategic dilemma. Certainly Republicans and Democrats constantly fight *between* themselves, but both parties just as constantly fight *among* themselves. There are various causes of intraparty factionalism, of course, yet one constant of intraparty warfare is the struggle over the correct answer to the "government or opposition" dilemma. In the British Parliament each party knows whether it is the government or the opposition. The U.S. Constitution denies the luxury of such clarity to our political parties.

Of course, in our separation-of-powers system politics and policy remain inextricably intertwined, consequently compromise and confrontation are both natural and desirable in American politics. This institutional contribution to the inevitable heterogeneity of our political parties is absent in the British parliamentary model. The constitutional separation of powers remains a strong determinant of congressional behavior as can be seen, for example, in Rahm Emanuel and Tom Reynolds debating whether the 2006 election was going to be "national" or "local."

Yet Democrats were also divided *among* themselves over the best strategy as well. The well-publicized 2006 clash between the DNC's Howard Dean and the DCCC's Emanuel provides concrete evidence of the Founders meddling in our politics. House Democrats have been internally divided for many years on questions of legislative party strategy. Hamlet-like, they debated "to Contract or not to Contract" throughout 2006, finally settling—sort of—on Six for '06. Similarly, Democrats were split between their liberal base and more moderate mainstream voters on the central question of the day: Iraq. They debated incessantly whether to adopt a high-profile confrontational strategy sharpening their differences with the White House, thus providing a choice and not an echo, or whether to play rope-a-dope on Iraq, criticizing Bush policy without clearly articulating an alternative policy. Jack Murtha seemingly settled that debate even if Minority Leader Pelosi only tepidly followed his lead.

Of course, 2006 did not provide House Democrats their first opportunity for internecine warfare; as already noted, they fought similarly in 2002 and 2004. Fortunately for the minority party, the majority party confronts the same conundrum; indeed, as noted above, David Brooks predicted in 2004 that Republicans would become even more discordant and fractious as their majority grew. They did. They also became more arrogant and more inclined to overplay their hand vis-à-vis the minority party, the Senate, and the White House. Arguably, they did all of the above in the 109th Congress. The irony that a majority party becomes more fractious as it becomes larger is built into the nature of our constitutional system. Minority parties might never win elections without the assistance of the majority party.

NEWT AND NANCY

Leadership fights are in part surrogates for factional struggles over legislative party strategy. The "young turk" Newt Gingrich challenged the "old guard" Bob Michel. Similarly, Nancy Pelosi rejected Dick Gephardt's less aggressive approach. The parallel is intriguing: to win her 2006 House majority did Pelosi finally succeed by becoming Gingrichian? In January 2005 the *Economist* wondered whether Democrats might become *insufficiently* Gingrichian, embracing "his passion for pugilism without embracing his passion for ideas." They went on to editorialize, "By all means let the Democrats learn from Newt the fighter; but if they want to recapture power they need to learn from Newt the thinker, too."[116] Did Nancy become enough like Newt?

She imitated Gingrich's Contract with her Six for '06. Along with Rahm Emanuel, she mimicked Gingrich's aggressive GOPAC recruiting efforts. Most importantly perhaps, she adopted a clearly confrontational legislative floor strategy sharpening differences with Republicans. She followed Jack Murtha's lead on Iraq. She held her troops in line on key floor votes such as on Medicare prescription drugs in the 108th Congress and immigration reform in the 109th Congress. On the former, she forced House Republicans into the now infamous three-hour long count, thanks to David Wu's loyalty, resulting in endless bad publicity for the majority. On the latter, she left Republicans squirming under Sensenbrenner's "felony" amendment. Was the 2006 Democratic victory Pelosi's reward for her Gingrichian efforts?

Fairly or not, Newt and Nancy are widely credited with their party victories in 1994 and 2006. Do minority parties win majorities, or do majority parties lose their majorities, as Ways and Means chair Bill Thomas insisted? Does the majority party beat itself?[117] Following the 2006 election, commentator Mark Shields concluded that the majority party indeed beat itself: "This was not a Democratic victory; it was a Republican defeat."[118] Similarly, Charlie Cook observed:

> Midterm elections are about punishing. They're driven by anger—anger and/or fear. And if Democrats see this as a mandate, I think they're crazy; if they see this as an opportunity, then I think they're smart. Because nobody voted for Democrats, they voted against Republicans.[119]

If the majority parties beat themselves in 1994 and 2006, they did so with the disarray brought on by internal party factionalism. Yet can the conventional wisdom crediting the minority party leadership of Newt and Nancy be completely wrong? Both leaders in opposition unified their parties behind a strategy of confrontation. Gingrich gained support from moderates like Bill Frenzel and Nancy Johnson and unified House Republicans behind the Contract. Pelosi did something similar. Perhaps the key to the strategic dilemma facing congressional parties—government or opposition? compromise or confrontation?—is found in successfully managing internal party factionalism. The split over legislative strategy is found *within* the two parties, more than *between* the two parties. Even if the majority party creates the wave, the minority party must be prepared to ride the wave. Some credit seems due both to Gingrich in 1994 and Pelosi in 2006. The challenge for the new majority party, of course, is to continue to manage the factionalism within their own party.

CONTROLLING THE MISCHIEFS OF FACTION

Following the 2006 election, a *Washington Post* headline captured that challenge perfectly: "Election Battles Are Over; Let the Infighting Begin."[120] In an inauspicious beginning that might not have surprised the Founders, the new majority party in the House found itself in disarray even before taking power. To the dismay of many in her party, Speaker-to-be Pelosi picked a fight with fellow Democratic leader Steny Hoyer by actively supporting Jack Murtha for majority leader against Hoyer. She lost, but not without first learning that it is easier to maintain party unity in the minority than in the majority. Being in the majority is tougher than playing minority opposition. Just ask former "backbench bomb-thrower" Newt Gingrich. If Democrats hoped to retain their majority following the 110th Congress, they would need to control the "mischiefs of faction" within their own ranks. If they failed to do so, they could provide Republicans the opportunity the GOP provided them in the 2006 elections.

Democrats won in 2006 in part by invading Republican turf and running more moderate candidates in Republican-leaning districts. As a consequence, of course, in the 110th Congress Pelosi needed to balance the interests of a newly enlarged Blue Dog faction with that of the "old bull" committee chairs, many of whom hail from the liberal wing of the party, and the Congressional Black Caucus, another bastion of largely liberal-leaning members. Democrats must satisfy their base without alienating mainstream voters. During the 110th Congress, Pelosi seemed sensitive, for example, to the need to rein in those like Judiciary Committee chair John Conyers who began to talk about impeaching President Bush.

Pelosi seemed to differ with Gingrich on one important particular. In 1992 Gingrich adopted a lose-the-White-House-to-win-the-House strategy. It worked. In winning Congress in 2006, Democrats may have made winning the White House in 2008 more difficult for their party. In fact some Democrats wanted to win all-but-a-majority in 2006, so they would not be the "responsible" party. Nevertheless, the unpopularity of the Iraq War and President Bush made it easier for congressional Democrats to balance retaining their majority and winning the White House in 2008. Though torn at times during the 110th Congress between competing institutional imperatives, for the most part House Democrats adopted an opposition posture toward President Bush. Still, if they hope to try governing the country or Congress, they first must govern themselves. Certainly the Constitution does not make that job easy.

In November 2006 the ever-insightful Charlie Cook said about Congress:

> [N]obody has been in control for the last two years, and I don't think anybody is going to be in complete control for the next two years. I mean . . . when you've got majorities that are this narrow, nobody is in control. You may have a majority, you may have some perks and some advantages, and you've got the gavel, you can schedule legislation, but you don't have control of the place. . . . Democrats can sort of steer things a little bit, but they're not in control.[121]

Cook is right. The majority party in Congress is not the government, nor is the minority party merely the opposition whether under conditions of divided government or even under conditions of so-called united party government. Neither Democrats nor Republicans govern; rather, the Constitution governs. Evidence for this proposition includes electoral challenges such as the six-year itch, but it also includes the strategic dilemma always confronting both Democrats and Republicans as they struggle to maintain party unity in order to gain or retain a legislative majority. In managing its own factions, each party faces a constitutional constant: the Scylla and Charybdis of government or opposition, compromise or confrontation, policy or politics.

CONCLUSION

The fact that the minority party in the House continues to debate legislative strategy election after election provides empirical evidence that legislative party strategy matters. Party leaders not only debate legislative party strategy; they act on it as well. The never-ending character of the debate over the strategic dilemma confronting legislative parties suggests that it presents party leaders with a conundrum. There certainly is no easy answer. There may not even be a generally applicable rule of thumb for addressing the "confrontation or compromise" quandary the minority party faces. Indeed, there may not be a simply right answer to the question.

Perhaps it all depends. Perhaps it depends on the issue at play, for example, Medicare prescription drugs or intelligence reform. Perhaps it depends on institutional time (including what Stephen Skowronek calls "political time"[122]), that is, on where we are in the separation of powers cycle. Individual party leaders must take into consideration competing interests or factions, and competing ideas or party principles. Above all, party leaders must understand the larger institutional context. Only then, perhaps, will party leaders "know when to hold them, and know when to fold them."

The very existence of this conundrum and the never-ending intraparty debate—a debate that sometimes has practical consequences in terms of leadership fights—stands as evidence that the strategic dilemma confronting legislative parties matters. The constitutional separation of powers creates the institutional context within which legislative party leaders operate. Institutional context in turn defines the strategic dilemma. Institutions affect behavior. Institutions count, as witness the way members fight endlessly over competing understandings of the rules of a political game defined by the constitutional separation of powers.

Understanding the institutional playing field and the rules of the game is important for congressional leaders. It is also important for political scientists to understand the institutional playing field and the rules of the game, if we hope to understand legislative behavior. Neither the standard pluralist nor party government paradigm fully captures the institutional dynamic of our separation of powers; although both contain important elements of truth. Our constitutional separation of powers invites compromise and confrontation, pursuing policy and playing politics, friction and fission. For the majority party, learning to govern is not reducible to compromise. Similarly, being an effective minority party means knowing when to confront and when to compromise. The minority party in the House is never simply the "opposition" anymore than the majority party is ever simply the "government."

To understand congressional politics, party leaders and political scientists need to understand fully the complexity of the constitutional separation of powers and how it molds legislative behavior. Presidency scholars understand that the constitutional separation of powers both humbles and empowers presidents.[123] Congress scholars need to understand how the separation of powers both humbles and empowers majority and minority legislative party leaders.

To more fully understand the practical consequences of constitutional structure on legislative party strategy we turn in the next four chapters to the ideas of the Anti-Federalists, Woodrow Wilson, Alexis de Tocqueville, and the Federalists on the nature of the American political system. Chapter 3 begins by comparing the ideas of Newt Gingrich and the Anti-Federalist critics of the Constitution.

3

~

House Republicans:
Newt the Anti-Federalist?

Newt Gingrich prides himself on being both a professor and a politician; he believes ideas count. During his first term as Speaker, Gingrich actively used the "bully pulpit" of the speakership to "set the intellectual framework" of political discourse in America. To understand the successes and failures of Newt Gingrich as Speaker, therefore, it may be useful to explore the roots of his thought. While the practical demands of politics may compromise theoretical consistency, certain clear themes resonate in Newt Gingrich's understanding of politics.

As with most of us, Gingrich's thought seems eclectic; he glides effortlessly, and perhaps glibly, from Tocqueville to Toffler, from traditional values to technology. In a 1995 *New Yorker* essay critical of Gingrich, Connie Bruck observed that his speeches and writings were "a simplistic, homiletic grab bag of notions and prescriptions," adding, the Speaker "seems to have no integral philosophy."[1] Michael Barone and Grant Ujifusa, on the other hand, observed in *The Almanac of American Politics* that over his long political career Gingrich "advocated steadily a coherent and consistent set of ideas."[2] Barone and Ujifusa perceived a healthy tension within the Speaker's thought: "Gingrich is . . . a believer in an energetic government that advances modern technology and promotes traditional values. . . . He is a cultural conservative who believes that liberal values are destroying the lives of the poor, a market capitalist who celebrates technological innovation."[3]

With his roots in Rockefeller Republicanism, Gingrich holds a peculiar place in the constellation of conservative thought. Gingrich is not a traditional conservative thinker; for example, he rarely quotes Hayek,

Friedman or Kirk.[4] Yet as witness the *Almanac* observation above, Gingrich seems to embody a tension within American conservative thought traceable at least to the "fusion" movement of the 1950s. In word and deed, Speaker Gingrich sought to bridge the gap between economic and cultural conservatives, thereby leaving him open to the charge by critics that he is intellectually inconsistent. This chapter explores what may be one central strain of Gingrich's thought as reflected in his words and actions.

Comparing and contrasting the ideas of Speaker Newt Gingrich and the Anti-Federalist critics of the Constitution may help us understand his practical successes and failures; he may share their virtues and defects. Furthermore, as we shall see, examining Alexis de Tocqueville's reconciliation of Federalist and Anti-Federalist ideas may provide a standard by which to judge the principles and policies of Gingrich and his fellow Republican "revolutionaries." Were House Republicans ever really able to become more than merely an opposition party?

NEWT AS ANTI-FEDERALIST?

In Newt Gingrich's thought one hears a clear echo of the Anti-Federalists' critique of the Federalist Constitution two hundred years ago. One finds this echo in the notion that the speakership rather than the presidency can be a "bully pulpit." The Anti-Federalists were suspicious of executive power; they were the legislative supremacists of their day. Following the 1994 GOP electoral "tsunami," Speaker Gingrich sought to promote "congressional government" with the "People's House" as the nucleus of the "revolution." Gingrich and his fellow House Republican "revolutionaries" were wary of presidential power, skeptical of what the Anti-Federalists saw as the aristocratic tendency of the Senate, and perhaps especially distrustful of "government by judiciary." Their "outsider" challenge to career politicians' inside-the-Beltway mentality reflected Anti-Federalist fears of opposition between court and country.[5]

The concept of a Contract with America echoed the Anti-Federalist call for accountability in government. The Speaker actively promoted what political scientists call "responsible party government" as evidenced by the phrase emblazoned on the *TV Guide* copy of the Contract: "If we break this contract, throw us out." Similarly, the Speaker's interest in term limits mirrored the Anti-Federalists' desire for "rotation" in office as a way of promoting "citizen legislators."[6] These new Anti-Federalists, like the old, wanted government closer to the people. To this end, on the first day of the 104th Congress, the new GOP majority passed the most sweeping internal congressional reforms in decades in an effort to make the House more open and democratic. Gingrich pitched the internal reforms as a populist attempt to overthrow the elite, oligarchic tendencies of forty years of "permanent majority" Democratic House rule.

Two hundred years ago, the Anti-Federalists were the true Federalists, critical of the idea of a strong, centralized national government.[7] Similarly, Newt Gingrich and his 1994 freshmen rejected one-size-fits-all national standards. They wanted to renew federalism, decentralize government and return power to state and local governments in order to curb an activist federal government. They wanted to devolve decision-making away from Washington, move the levers of power closer to the people and re-limit government to empower citizens and promote personal responsibility. Newt Gingrich spoke of volunteerism and spiritual renewal; he promoted Habitat for Humanity, for example. As his 1996 book title suggests, he wanted *To Renew America*.

Echoes of Anti-Federalist Thought Are Clear

In many ways, Gingrich is a fairly consistent Anti-Federalist. He distrusts a strong national government, he seeks to promote responsive government close to the people, and he favors decentralization of government and the devolution of power in order to inspire volunteerism, personal responsibility, and civic renewal. Gingrich, however, is not a consistent Anti-Federalist in all particulars. Exceptions exist. For example, the Anti-Federalists were suspicious of commerce, whereas Gingrich is a free marketeer. The Anti-Federalists were isolationists, while Gingrich refuses to join the "America First" faction within the GOP. The Anti-Federalists longed for a high level of autarky, or economic self-sufficiency, whereas Gingrich promoted passage of the North American Free Trade Agreement (NAFTA) in the 103rd Congress. Finally, reconciling Gingrich's Anti-Federalist proclivities with his fascination for Alvin Toffler's technological futurism may present the greatest challenge of all. Certainly, the Anti-Federalists would question whether cyberspace chats provide an adequate substitute for face-to-face civic participation and community. Of course, it is one thing to be intellectually consistent, and quite another challenge to be politically consistent.

As Speaker of the House, Gingrich's intellectual inconsistency or eclecticism may have been a political virtue, one that may, in part, explain his ability to survive the July 1997 coup attempt by party dissidents. Gingrich was comfortable with the cacophony within his own caucus. He understands better than most that majority party leadership in America necessarily involves "conflict management," not "conflict resolution."[8] In this, Gingrich may share more in common with Madison than with the Anti-Federalists.

Although one should not push the Gingrich-as-Anti-Federalist analogy too far, the Anti-Federalist echo is clearly present. A comparison of the thought of Gingrich and the Anti-Federalists will enable us to examine the tensions within his governing philosophy.

ANTI-FEDERALIST THOUGHT

In *What the Anti-Federalists Were For*, Herbert J. Storing examines the debate between the Federalists and Anti-Federalists over ratification of the Constitution.[9] Storing notes that the Anti-Federalists were a diverse lot defined largely in terms of their opposition to the Constitution, but he argues that their critique of the Constitution derived in part from "a positive political theory or set of political principles" often called the "small republic argument."[10] According to Storing, the Federalist/Anti-Federalist debate was a quarrel within a family. Both Federalists and Anti-Federalists were modern liberals who agreed that the end or purpose of government is the protection of individual liberty and that "the best instrument for this purpose is some form of limited, republican government."[11] They differed, however, on the proper scope and character of republican government.

The Anti-Federalists insisted rightly that history could provide no example of successful republican government on the scale the Federalists were proposing with their Constitution. The Anti-Federalist's small, agrarian republic ideal, therefore, stood in stark contrast to the large commercial republic of Madisonian pluralism outlined in the Constitution. Anti-Federalist critics of the Constitution sometimes cited the Swiss cantons as worthy exemplars of republican government. Anti-Federalists were also skeptical about the possibility of founding a healthy republican government on the unleashing of self-interest, ambition, and factionalism. They were wary of a system of institutional checks and balances premised on ambition counteracting ambition, interest counteracting interest. The Anti-Federalist author Centinel (Samuel Bryan's pen name), for example, decried a politics based on "an opposition of interests."[12] Centinel went on to ask, "[H]ow is the welfare and happiness of the community to be the result of such jarring adverse interests?"[13]

Madison's answer in Federalist No. 10 involves "the spirit of party and faction in the necessary and ordinary operations of government."[14] Hamilton in Federalist No. 70 adds:

> In the legislature, promptitude of decision is oftener an evil than a benefit. The differences of opinion, and the jarring of parties in that department of the government, though they may sometimes obstruct salutary plans, yet often promote deliberation and circumspection, and serve to check excesses in the majority.[15]

The Anti-Federalists argued instead that republican government presupposed republican virtue. Republican government required the conditions naturally found in small republics, namely, virtuous citizens and government close to the people. In the confines of a small agrarian republic with its simple way of life, one might best be able to find and promote the necessary public-spiritedness in a citizenry willing to balance a concern for rights with an acknowledgement of duties. Government close to the people also allowed citizens to hold their elected leaders accountable. Consequently, the Anti-Federalists seemed to conclude that, in practice, America might best remain a "confederacy of small, homogeneous, virtuous, religious republics" rather than become a large, pluralistic, commercial, continental nation.[16]

The Anti-Federalists were the conservatives of their day, the defenders of what is old, and the proponents of law and order.[17] They harkened back to the promise of the Declaration of Independence, seeing the Federalist Constitution as a fairly radical innovation. The Anti-Federalists were also the true Federalists. In the ratification debate, the proponents of the Constitution adopted the name "Federalists," as witness *The Federalist*, penned by Hamilton, Madison, and Jay. Yet the label "Federalist" was a misnomer; they were, in fact, nationalists who wanted to create a strong central government to replace the weak one under the Articles of Confederation. The Constitution's opponents were left with the awkward and inaccurate label of Anti-Federalists.[18] Nevertheless, the opponents of the Constitution were the true friends of federalism. They believed that most political problems, except defense and foreign policy, were best addressed at the levels of government closest to the people.

The Anti-Federalists were also the populists of their day and were more inclined toward simple, direct democracy. They were profoundly uncomfortable with the complexity of the Constitution. Centinel questioned the complex majority rule of the proposed Constitution with its separation of powers, checks and balances, and bicameralism. He noted, "[I]f you complicate the plan by various orders, the people will be perplexed and divided in their sentiments about the sources of abuses or misconduct."[19] The new constitutional structure, the Anti-Federalists argued, will preclude political accountability. To this day, this Anti-Federalist lament rings true. Neither party in our separation-of-powers system is ever simply the "government" or the "opposition." Both major parties at all times, including under conditions of "divided" and "united" party government, retain some governing responsibility. Both parties also can play opposition and legitimately blame the other party for the failings of government. The Anti-Federalists correctly identified this defect in our complex constitutional structure; indeed, the Federalists seem to concede the point.

The Anti-Federalists also strongly distrusted what they perceived as the aristocratic tendencies of the Constitution, especially in the Senate and the judiciary.[20] The Anti-Federalists generally supported "rotation" in office (i.e., term limits), and they were deeply distrustful of the federal courts' power of judicial review. "This power in the judicial [branch]," in the words of Anti-Federalist Robert Yates, "will enable them to mould the government into almost any shape they please."[21] As Brutus (Yates's pseudonym), Yates went on to say:

> There is no power above them to control any of their decisions. . . . They are independent of the people, of the legislature, and of every power under heaven. Men placed in this situation will generally soon feel themselves independent of heaven itself.[22]

The Anti-Federalists also feared the Hamiltonian presidency. Patrick Henry's speech against ratification included the famous warning "[This constitution] squints toward monarchy. . . . If your American chief be a man of ambition and abilities, how easy is it for him to render himself absolute."[23] Another Anti-Federalist, writing under the pen name Old Whig, argued that the constitutional presidency "is in reality to be a king, as much a king as the king of Great Britain, and a king too of the worst kind: an elective king."[24] Clearly, the Anti-Federalists did not agree with Hamilton's famous observation "Energy in the executive is a leading character in the definition of good government."[25] Again, the Anti-Federalists were the legislative supremacists of their day.

The heart of the Anti-Federalist critique of the Constitution, however, remained the "small republic argument." Storing summarizes the central tenets of this Anti-Federalist position:

> Only a small republic can enjoy a voluntary attachment of the people to the government and a voluntary obedience to the laws. Only a small republic can secure a genuine responsibility of the government to the people. Only a small republic can form the kind of citizens who will maintain republican government.[26]

The Anti-Federalists did not want a government far removed geographically or politically from the citizenry. They wanted simple, direct, accountable, democratic government, and virtuous citizens. Character formation was critical to the Anti-Federalist understanding of healthy republican government; above all, the small republic would be a "school of citizenship." In their view, the educative process necessarily begins with a relatively homogeneous citizenry, thus requiring immigration restrictions. Beyond that, they viewed "civil society as a teacher, as a molder of character, rather than as a regulator of conduct."[27] Finally, the Anti-Federalists saw a clear role for religion in the active promotion of civic virtue, and they denounced the perceived indifference of the Constitution to religion.[28] The Anti-Federalists recognized the fundamental importance of a healthy political culture to the maintenance of good government. The concern with character formation, of course, opened the Anti-Federalists to the charge that they were promoting an illiberal solution to the problem of founding liberal government. This was at once their strength and their weakness.

Ultimately, as we know, the Anti-Federalists lost the ratification battle, and the nation ratified the Federalist Constitution. Today we are, arguably, James Madison's America. The Anti-Federalists lost the debate for a reason. Storing explains why:

> The Anti-Federalists lost the debate over the Constitution not merely because they were less clever arguers or less skillful politicians but because they had the weaker argument. They were, as Publius said, trying to reconcile contradictions. There was no possibility of instituting the small republic in the United States, and the Anti-Federalists themselves were not willing to pay the price that such an attempt would have required.[29]

Unfortunately for the Anti-Federalists, the nation's unhappy experience under the Articles of Confederation made the status quo untenable. In a manner of speaking, the Anti-Federalists were in the untoward position of trying to beat something with nothing. More importantly, the Anti-Federalists lost the debate because they equivocated; ultimately, they "were committed to both union and the states; to both the great American republic and the small, self-governing community; to both commerce and civic virtue; to both private gain and public good."[30]

Although the Anti-Federalists may have lost the ratification debate, their legacy remains. American political history is replete with recurring reflections of Anti-Federalist arguments. Storing elaborates:

> If, however, the foundation of the American polity was laid by the Federalists, the Anti-Federalist reservations echo through American history; and it is in the dialogue, not merely in the Federalist victory, that the country's principles are to be discovered. The Anti-Federalists were easily able to show that the Constitution did not escape reliance on republican virtue.[31]

The Anti-Federalist critique points to the weakness of the Federalist Constitution. Indeed, the Anti-Federalists may have identified the essential defect of the American regime: republican government without republican virtue is impossible. "Will not the constitutional regime, the Anti-Federalists asked, with its emphasis on private, self-seeking, commercial activities, release and foster a certain type of human being who will be likely to destroy that very regime?"[32]

Republican government presupposes a civic-minded citizenry. The Anti-Federalists insisted that for a healthy republican government to endure, active character formation is imperative. We must, they argued, prevent the erosion of the moral foundation of the American Republic.

THE USE AND ABUSE OF ANTI-FEDERALIST THOUGHT

Speaker Gingrich's echo of Anti-Federalist thought had its advantages and disadvantages, virtues and defects. At times he may have been too much the Anti-Federalist, as for example with his populist, antibureaucratic rhetoric. At other times, Gingrich sounded more like Progressive Woodrow Wilson than an Anti-Federalist. For example, Gingrich and Wilson both embraced a politics of grand ideas and grand rhetoric that would be foreign to the Anti-Federalists. At still other times, Speaker Gingrich seemed to combine Federalist and Anti-Federalist thought, especially in his tendency to adopt Federalist means to Anti-Federalist ends. An example of the latter may be seen in the very notion of the speakership as a "bully pulpit." Finally, at times, Gingrich seemed to forget that the Federalists won the ratification debate. We will explore each of these limitations in his use and abuse of Anti-Federalist thought in turn.

Re-limiting Government versus Reinventing Government

Although the Anti-Federalists were defined in opposition to the Constitution, their opposition was informed by a positive set of principles. Similarly, many depicted the GOP under Gingrich as the "antigovernment" party. Yet most Republicans in the 1990s did not see themselves this way; rather, they understood themselves as opposing "big government" in favor of self-government. Their success in passing welfare reform in 1996 stands as a testament to their faith in limited government and in self-government.

Most Republicans did not want to "reinvent" government as did Vice President Gore; they preferred instead to "re-limit" government.[33] Republicans rejected "reinventing government" as a Progressive-style effort to promote more efficient and effective government, thereby providing the premise for "growing the government." Republicans feared that this 1990s variant of Progressive Era "good government" was little more than a liberal Trojan horse. Ironically, of course, when Republicans finally succeeded in attaining united Republican government under George W. Bush following the 2000 election, they passed initiatives such as the No Child Left Behind Act and the Medicare Prescription Drug, Improvement, and Modernization Act that seemed to increase, rather than limit, the responsibilities of the federal government.

In the 1990s, however, Republicans, including Newt Gingrich, preferred self-government to "good government." Indeed, for Republicans, self-government *was* good government. The GOP under Gingrich could best be described as favoring limited government. Generally speaking, the GOP sought to stem the sixty-year Democratic tide of growing the government; again, as witness the 1996 Welfare Reform Act. Republicans hoped to reverse the centralization of power in Washington embodied in New Deal and Great Society programs. Yet Republicans could rightly claim to be more than a merely oppositional party only if an affirmative alternate vision informed their opposition to big government. Speaker Newt Gingrich's positive formulation was to replace the liberal welfare state with a "conservative opportunity society." Contrary to his reputation, Speaker Gingrich may have been more than merely an iconoclast.

In his advance from "backbench bomb thrower" to leader of the House Republican "revolution," Newt Gingrich consistently railed against the House Democrats' seeming "permanent majority" as a corrupt, out-of-touch, elite establishment. He denounced the Democrats as the party of special interests, repeatedly stoked the nation's growing populist anti-Washington anger, and leveled withering verbal volleys at the inside-the-Beltway mentality of career politicians and bureaucrats. Such echoes of the Anti-Federalists are, of course, always available to the minority party in our Madisonian pluralist system. Gingrich held the bureaucratic handmaidens of the Democrats' liberal welfare state in special contempt. "In the welfare state," Gingrich argues in *To Renew America*, "power keeps slipping away to the bureaucrats and citizens feel defenseless."[34] Instead, he said, it is the responsibility of "elected officials to reassert the right of citizens to supervise their bureaucracy."[35]

This populist, antibureaucratic strain in Gingrich's thought clearly reflected the same tendency in Anti-Federalist thought. It was, after all, the Federalist Alexander Hamilton, not the Anti-Federalists, who sang the praises of administrative efficiency.[36] One sees a similar populist proclivity in Gingrich's attacks against the liberal "cultural elite" presumably found in Hollywood and New York or at the National Endowment for the Arts. Gingrich perceived precisely what the Anti-Federalists feared, namely, an entrenched and privileged elite establishment all too willing to serve its own interests.

But contemporary conservative theorists such as Harvey C. Mansfield, Jr., and Herbert Storing cautioned Gingrich about this populist, antibureaucratic echo of Anti-Federalist thought. "Conservative populism" may be an oxymoron. In a nation of three hundred million citizens living within the constitutional and institutional context bequeathed to us by James Madison, simple populism is untenable. Even the Internet does not enable us all to deliberate together under the old oak tree. In a 1995 essay, Mansfield urged small *r* republicanism upon Gingrich.[37] Similarly, Storing criticized conservatives for "their irresponsible and sometimes

violent attacks" on the federal bureaucracy, and their "doctrinaire commitment to . . . localism."[38] Smaller, local units of government often are
parochial and poorly administered; hence, a balance of national and state
responsibilities, relegating to each sphere its proper function, may offer
the best of both worlds. Following the crash of what Gingrich and Toffler
call the "third wave" on the shores of modernity, there may still be a role
for bureaucracy in promoting, according to Storing, rational government
and procedural fairness.[39] Gingrich's populist, antibureaucratic echo of
the Anti-Federalists may not have fully reflected the insights of Madison
and Hamilton.

Ideas versus Interests

As a "young turk" and as Speaker, Newt Gingrich wanted to replace a pluralist politics of competing interests with a politics of ideas; to the consternation of friend and foe alike, he often promoted a confrontational politics
of ideas rather than an accommodationist politics of interests. As a self-
proclaimed "revolutionary," Congressman Gingrich chafed at the incrementalism of pluralist politics. During the 105th Congress, pundits were
quick to conclude that a "chastened" Newt Gingrich had learned to accommodate himself to politics-as-usual. Nevertheless, like another professorial
politician before him, Woodrow Wilson, Gingrich seemed profoundly
dissatisfied with Madisonian pluralism, especially its self-interested and
parochial character.[40] In their dissatisfaction with Madisonian pluralism,
both Wilson and Gingrich echo the Anti-Federalists. In their solution to this
perceived defect in our constitutional order, however, they share more in
common with one another than with the Anti-Federalists.

The distinction between a politics of interests and a politics of ideas
reflects what political scientists call the "pluralist" versus "party government" schools of thought.[41] The former is commonly associated with
James Madison, while the latter typically traces its lineage to Wilson.[42]
The party government school might in turn legitimately trace its roots
to the Anti-Federalists who hoped for a more principled and ennobling
politics than the Federalist Constitution's tendency to pit jarring adverse
interests against one another. For party government reformers, principled
partisanship seems somehow more uplifting than the competition of parochial factions or special interests.

In explaining the House GOP's 1994 victory, Gingrich echoed this
distinction between what he called "petty partisanship" and "grand partisanship." While voters, he said, might be

> fed up with petty partisanship, I don't think they mind grand partisanship.
> . . . To have a profound disagreement over the direction of your country or
> over the principles by which your economy works or over the manner in

which your government should structure resources, that is legitimate, and the American people believe in that level of debate and relish it.[43]

Gingrich intended the Contract with America to be a classic example of principled or grand partisanship. Much earlier in his career, in 1980, Gingrich promoted among congressional Republicans a similar exercise, called "Governing Team Day." From the beginning of his legislative career, Gingrich espoused a nontraditional understanding of congressional leadership. What Gingrich dubbed "grand partisanship" some today bemoan as bitter partisan polarization. The outcome of the 1996 elections, of course, raised questions as to whether the public truly relished Gingrich's grand partisanship.

As Speaker, Gingrich rejected the Tip O'Neill (and Republican Leader Bob Michel) model of the Speaker as broker. Instead, he consciously embraced a Speaker-as-educator model. The Speaker as educator uses the "bully pulpit" of the speakership and a media-based "outsider" strategy to transform public discourse and to precipitate a partisan realignment. Gingrich outlined this model of Speaker as educator in a 1981 article in the *Futurist* magazine. Gingrich argued that in the decentralized "information age" politics of the postindustrial era, "the leader as learner" model would necessarily replace broker-style legislative leadership.[44] "In the postindustrial era, the legislator's job is beginning to change from an insider-fixer who solves personal problems for constituents, toward a student-teacher who works and educates to solve the nation's problems."[45] As Speaker, Gingrich repeatedly summarized this leadership model in four words: listen, learn, help, lead. In one sense, political leadership as education is quintessentially Anti-Federalist. Where the Anti-Federalists might part ways with Gingrich, however, is in the *means* he chooses to promote the *end* of political education. The Anti-Federalists were more likely to opt for the local church pulpit than the national "bully pulpit" of either Newt Gingrich's speakership or Woodrow Wilson's presidency.

The concept of political leadership as education can be seen in Speaker Gingrich's unprecedented 1995 post-Contract address to the nation. Even the manner of the speech was didactic. Professor Gingrich seemed at home speaking to the nation as a teacher, complete with pedagogic props like vacuum tubes. Similarly, Speaker Gingrich's media-saturated trip to New Hampshire during the summer of 1995 was an effort to educate the nation by setting the agenda for the 1996 presidential election. The *Washington Post* quoted Gingrich as saying rather expansively, "I'm trying to shape the entire language and ideas of the 1996 campaign. . . . If you are going to try to set the intellectual framework for the 1996 campaign, if you knew anything about politics, where would you go?"[46] Pointing to the huge press corps following him, Gingrich noted, "If I keep the door open, they'll show up. I can *teach*."[47]

Similarly, in a February 1995 CNN interview focusing on the Speaker's Reinhardt College course, Bob Franken had the following exchange with Gingrich:

> Bob Franken: Oftentimes people say that your political speeches are really Professor Newt lecturing to a larger audience.
>
> Speaker Gingrich: They are. They are. Very deliberately so. I am the most seriously professorial politician since Woodrow Wilson. I believe the purpose of my speeches is didactic. They're supposed to be educational.
>
> Bob Franken: So you're educating your peers, your political peers?
>
> Speaker Gingrich: The citizenry.[48]

Again, in one sense Gingrich articulated nicely the Anti-Federalist understanding of politics as education. Politics as education presupposes that debate over principles and programs can refine and ennoble the preferences of leaders and citizens. In this important sense, Gingrich's leadership as education challenged prevailing economic theories of political behavior. Newt Gingrich as a contemporary Anti-Federalist agreed with James Q. Wilson: "[W]hereas economics is based on the assumption that preferences are given, politics must take into account the efforts to change preferences."[49] The Anti-Federalists understood the importance of educating preferences to the maintenance of healthy republican government. Like the Anti-Federalists, Speaker Gingrich saw the polity as a "school of citizenship."

Again, however, where Gingrich and the Anti-Federalists differed is in the *means* chosen to the *end* of political education. For the Anti-Federalists, character formation or educating preferences naturally began with family, religion, and laws promoting self-restraint. Gingrich and Woodrow Wilson opted instead for a politics of grand ideas, grand rhetoric, grand partisanship, and grand political education. It is probably no accident that Gingrich borrowed Progressive Republican Teddy Roosevelt's well-known phrase "bully pulpit" in describing the speakership. Like Roosevelt and Wilson, Gingrich embraced what Progressive Era historian Herbert Croly understood to be "Hamiltonian" means to "Jeffersonian" ends.[50] For Speaker Gingrich, Congress and the speakership were important instruments in the political education of the nation. In this, Gingrich seemed to adopt the Federalist means of strong, national institutions to promote the Anti-Federalist end of educating the citizenry.

The Anti-Federalists might applaud the efforts in word and deed by Wilson and Gingrich to promote a principled, public-spirited participation in politics coupled with accountability; however, they most certainly would have been more reticent about the politics of grand ideas and grand rhetoric espoused by Wilson and Gingrich. In a true Anti-Federalist politics, Newt Gingrich's powerful speakership might not be necessary.

Congressional Government versus Presidential Government

In his "backbench bomb-throwing" days, Gingrich's critics denounced him as a Congress-basher intent on destroying the institution. For a while, the term *nihilist* came into vogue as a way of describing this rebel with a cause. Former Speaker Jim Wright, for example, compared Gingrich to the Nazis:

> At heart Gingrich is a nihilist. Throughout his career, he has been intent on destroying and demoralizing the existing order.... He is a bit like those who burned the Reichstag in Germany so they could blame it on the "Communists." Torpedoing Congress and blaming the Democrats has been Newt's route to power.[51]

His critics then must find it ironic that, under Speaker Gingrich, Congress arguably became more, not less, popular and powerful. Early in the 104th Congress and late in the 105th Congress, the institution enjoyed its highest poll ratings in history. Some commentators even suggested that in the 104th Congress, Gingrich constructed the most powerful speakership since "Czar" Cannon. More to the point, in the 104th Congress Gingrich sought to recreate congressional government. The Anti-Federalists, as legislative supremacists, would have applauded Gingrich.

Immediately following the 1994 election, Gingrich moved forcefully to recentralize power in the party leadership. He sought to replace decades of congressional "committee government" or "subcommittee government" (along with the attendant interest-group clientelism) with disciplined "party government." Among other changes, Gingrich brought the committee chairs to heel and curbed the legislative service organizations (LSOs). Borrowing a page from Woodrow Wilson's *Congressional Government*, Gingrich often used Republican-only ad hoc task forces to incubate policy, thereby executing an end run around the standing committees. In defunding the LSOs, Gingrich's true motives were generally overlooked by Washington journalists, who interpreted this action as an assault on the Congressional Black Caucus. Gingrich in fact sought to strengthen the hand of his party leadership by undercutting organizations like the well-staffed Republican Study Committee.

Strong, disciplined, party-oriented congressional government seemingly made Gingrich a veritable prime minister in 1995. Dan Balz and Ron Brownstein, in *Storming the Gates*, observe that even Gingrich was surprised at his newfound power:

> Throughout 1995, Gingrich often marveled privately at the power he had amassed as Speaker. In part, he knew it reflected the built-in powers of the Speaker bestowed by the Founding Fathers. Compared to Bob Dole in the Senate, he told friends, the Speaker had enormous power. But Gingrich

expanded his reach beyond anything the Founding Fathers had imagined, marrying the authority of the institution with a persistent strategy to speak to a larger audience through the power of television and a message that transcended the gritty legislative details of Capitol Hill. . . . In so doing, Gingrich created a political figure the country had not seen in generations: a congressional leader as powerful—and as polarizing—as a President.[52]

Consequently, Gingrich and his congressional Republican allies came to dominate the agenda-setting function in American politics. Balz and Brownstein conclude their 1996 book with the observation that "Republicans now define the terms of debate in American politics."[53] Despite subsequent GOP setbacks in the 104th Congress, Bill Clinton's 1996 State of the Union refrain, "the era of big government is over," seemed to acknowledge congressional Republicans' control of the political agenda.

At the peak of his power in the 104th Congress, Gingrich clearly acted as if the center of political gravity should reside in Congress. Yet an electronic "bully pulpit" speakership sounds less Anti-Federalist, and again more like "Federalist means to Anti-Federalist ends." Indeed, note the implicit suggestion of "Federalist means to Anti-Federalist ends" in the Balz and Brownstein observation above. Speaker Gingrich's ideology was complex and not readily reducible to any single strain; nevertheless, Gingrich's beliefs clearly reflected Anti-Federalist thought.

Like the Anti-Federalists, Speaker Gingrich was a legislative supremacist. Like the Woodrow Wilson of *Congressional Government*, Gingrich saw political energy as appropriately coming from Congress. In Gingrich's worldview, the 104th Congress returned our separation-of-powers system to its natural condition of congressional dominance after decades of presidentialism. In 1981, Gingrich predicted the devolution of power to state and national legislatures in the postindustrial era:

The legislative branch is about to explode in a renaissance of new energy, ideas and importance. For the past half-century the executive branch has dominated federal and state government. Educated and assisted by large and sophisticated professional staffs, presidents and governors proposed policies while legislative bodies reacted. . . . But now the post-industrial era is rapidly shifting power and influence away from the executive branch, toward the legislative branch. Increased rates of change combined with growing decentralization of society and an information explosion will put strains on all elected officials, but will put those *closest to the citizen*—the legislator—at an advantage.[54]

Decentralized government close to the people was a central Anti-Federalist theme that in part explains why they were legislative supremacists. By 1995, Newt Gingrich was arguing that the future is now and that his powerful new speakership "proves that you don't have to run for President to have an impact, that being Speaker of the House—oriented toward ideas and toward communications and spending probably a third of my time teaching—that you can have an enormous impact on the Capitol and you don't have to go to the White House."[55] Subsequently, of course, Gingrich appeared to have a change of heart as witness his widely reported interest in running for president in 2000, again in 2008, and perhaps in 2012. His faith in congressional government seemed to wane.

An Informed Citizenry

Congressional government and politics as education go hand-in-hand for Newt Gingrich as a contemporary Anti-Federalist. Again, republican government presupposes citizens capable of governing themselves. Thomas Jefferson once observed, "I know of no safe depository of the ultimate powers of society but the people themselves; and if we think them not enlightened enough to exercise their control with a wholesome discretion, the remedy is not to take it from them but to better inform their discretion."[56] Woodrow Wilson took Jefferson's argument a step further: "This informing function of Congress should be preferred to even its legislative function. Unless [the legislature informs the citizenry] the country must remain in embarrassing, crippling ignorance of the very affairs which it is most important that it should understand and direct."[57]

Speaker Gingrich's 1995 nationally televised address stands as a metaphor for the shift in the nation's political center of gravity, underscoring his emphasis on the "informing function" of Congress. Similarly, throughout his legislative career, Gingrich promoted and exploited the use of technology to bring Congress closer to the people. Examples include his innovative use of C-SPAN, his alliance with talk radio, the advent of the THOMAS website, and the use of the Internet to disseminate information to the nation. Coupled with electronic town-hall meetings and telecourses, such innovative political use of technology may highlight the potential contradiction in adopting Federalist means to Anti-Federalist ends. Electronic democracy may amplify the "informing function" of Congress, but an Anti-Federalist might wonder if it truly augments citizen participation in self-government. Nevertheless, Speaker Gingrich sought to increase such participation as witness his November 1994 rationale for online access to congressional documents:

> [W]e will change the rules of the House to require that all documents and all conference reports and all committee reports be filed electronically as well as in writing and that they cannot by filed until they are available to any citizen who wants to pull them up simultaneously so that information is available to every citizen in the country at the same moment that it is available to the highest paid Washington lobbyist. That will change over time the entire flow of information and the entire quality of knowledge in the country, and it will change the way people will try to play games in the legislative process.[58]

Gingrich worked assiduously to make Congress more accountable. Opening-day congressional reforms in the 104th Congress included the Congressional Accountability Act, which applied a variety of laws to members of Congress. Other innovations included term limits for the Speaker and committee chairs, a ban on proxy voting in committee, rules requiring that more committee meetings be open to the public, and a comprehensive audit of House books. Of course, all these reforms, and others, were part of the Contract with America effort to promote accountability. Even though the term limits constitutional amendment failed to gain the necessary two-thirds vote, it also represented an attempt to promote responsible government.

The Anti-Federalists would applaud such an effort to enforce "rotation" in office as a way of inspiring "citizen legislators" to advance self-government. Gingrich also saw term limits as a way to re-limit government: "The nationwide campaign for term limits was an outgrowth of the popular campaign against big government."[59] Truth be told, Gingrich opposed term limits until it became the consensus position within his party. In this instance, perhaps Gingrich was following, not leading, the growing Anti-Federalist sentiment in his party.

Never representing a purely consistent Anti-Federalism, Gingrich's opinions on party government and legislative supremacy may have evolved from the 104th to the 105th Congress in response to changing political circumstances. Between the 104th and 105th Congress, we witnessed a reassertion of committee leadership vis-à-vis party leadership and a reemergence of President Clinton in opposition to the GOP Congress. Gingrich's 1998 book, *Lessons Learned the Hard Way*, provided evidence of the evolution of his thought as circumstances changed.

ALAS, THE ERA OF CONGRESSIONAL
GOVERNMENT IS OVER

The Anti-Federalists may have been legislative supremacists but the Federalists were not. And the Federalists won the debate; their Constitution governs today. Our constitutional separation of powers does not provide for simple congressional government; though neither does it provide for pure presidential government. The president and Congress need one another; neither is supreme. By itself, moreover, the House of Representatives is not the government; the House needs the president and the Senate. The president and Congress are two halves of a whole; they fulfill two different, yet complementary, functions. The same is true of the House and Senate.

The failures of the Gingrich Republicans in the 104th Congress may have been due in part to an intellectual error rooted in their Anti-Federalist ideology. House Republicans failed to consummate their "revolution" because they misunderstood or ignored the constitutional separation of powers. House GOP members acted as if they could accomplish their "revolution" all by themselves with their take-it-or-leave-it budget strategy; they temporarily deluded themselves into thinking that the president and Senate were irrelevant, that the president and Senate would have to follow their lead. They ignored the independent constitutional authority of the president and Senate. They wrapped much of the "revolution" into their budget strategy and assumed the White House would cave. When the president did not give in, and when he acquiesced to shutting down the government, public opinion blamed the House GOP for this manufactured crisis. Gingrich had convinced the American people that they were witnessing congressional government in action; when the government failed to work, they held him responsible.

House Republicans may have been convinced that they had created congressional government, but congressional government inevitably failed within the constitutional context of Madison's separation of powers. Congress is not Parliament and wishing does not make it so. One can hardly imagine any more practical and palpable proof of the power of constitutional structures to govern the behavior of individuals than the defeat of the House GOP budget strategy.[60] Gingrich, like the original Anti-Federalists, failed to appreciate Madison's profound insight, namely, that institutions mold the behavior of individuals and groups. "The interest of the man must be connected with the constitutional rights of the place."[61] Arguably, James Madison, not Bill Clinton, tamed the House Republican "revolution." During the 1990s, James Madison governed America in ways Newt Gingrich and Bill Clinton could not.

In an interview with Elizabeth Drew during the 104th Congress, Gingrich argued,

> [W]hat we're doing is a cultural revolution with societal and political conse-
> quences that ultimately change the government. That is a vastly bigger agenda
> than has been set by any modern political system in this country.... We're not
> doing what people used to do. We don't resemble any previous system. There
> are no comparisons that make sense because you've never had an information-
> age, grassroots-focused, change-oriented structure.[62]

Gingrich was convinced that cultural and technological changes matter more than existing institutional structures; he, therefore, underestimated the tenacity of the White House: "The collision with the White House is a project, but it's a tiny part of what we're doing. I mean, we'll do that *en passant*. That will not be a major part of my planning operation."[63]

Unfortunately for Gingrich, the resilience of Madisonian institutions may have proven greater than any "third wave" paradigm shift. In

Lessons Learned the Hard Way, Gingrich concluded, "We had other lessons to learn as well. We had not only failed to take into account the ability of the Senate to delay us and obstruct us, but we had much too cavalierly underrated the power of the President. . . . How could we have forgotten that?"[64] He added, "A legislator and an executive are two very different things, and for a time we had allowed ourselves to confuse the two."[65] If Gingrich had been a more careful student of *The Federalist* he never would have confused the two.

Of course, our constitutional structure also may have proven more substantial than the president's tenacity. Gingrich and the House Republicans were not the only ones at the time to believe they were seeing congressional government in action. President Clinton suffered from the same illusion, as witness his almost plaintive insistence during a post-1994 election press conference that he was still "relevant."[66]

Again, during the second session of the 104th Congress we began to witness a reversal of fortunes for Gingrich and Clinton; nevertheless, opponents should not underestimate Gingrich simply because he was unable to accomplish in one term a political realignment the likes of which took FDR and Democrats decades to complete. Professor Gingrich continued to learn as seen in *Lessons Learned the Hard Way* and in his more measured approach during the 105th Congress. By the late 1990s, Gingrich recognized that the era of congressional government was over, yet he seemed confident that the era of big government was over as well.

DEVOLUTION REVOLUTION

In the 104th Congress, a group of House Republican freshmen called themselves the "New Federalists" not because they had any special affinity for Alexander Hamilton's strong, centralized national government; rather they favored a return to federalism, as seen for example in their support for the unfunded mandates plank in the Contract with America. Ironically, the New Federalists were in fact new Anti-Federalists; they reversed the ironic misnomers from the original Federalist/Anti-Federalist debate.

The mid-1990s Anti-Federalists, like their predecessors, opposed not just big government; they seemed to oppose "bigness" in everything. According to Speaker Gingrich, the "Third Wave Information Revolution" would promote decentralization across the board:

> [M]ore and more people are going to be operating *outside* corporate structures and hierarchies in the nooks and crannies that the Information Revolution creates. While the Industrial Revolution herded people into gigantic social institutions—big corporations, big unions, big government—the Information

Revolution is breaking up these giants and leading us back to something that is—strangely enough—much more like Tocqueville's 1830s America.[67]

The elimination of unfunded mandates and the revival of federalism were only the beginning. According to Gingrich,

> [O]ur ultimate goal is to move power even beyond the state capitals. . . . Republicans envision a decentralized America in which responsibility is returned to the individual. We believe in volunteerism and local leadership. We believe that a country with ten million local volunteer leaders is stronger than one with a thousand brilliant national leaders.[68]

Anti-Federalist firebrand Patrick Henry could not have said it better. Self-government is the essence of republican government.

Speaker Gingrich did not seek a return to federalism and decentralization for its own sake; rather, he wanted to promote self-government. Gingrich's commitment to volunteerism could be seen in his support for Habitat for Humanity or his Earning by Learning initiative. Bruck observed that Gingrich "has promoted Earning by Learning as a model of the kind of volunteerism that, in the cultural renaissance he means to bring about, will replace the assistance to the poor that is now dispensed by the government."[69] A cultural renaissance is precisely what Gingrich intended to promote, largely by empowering citizens.

> I wrote *To Renew America* because I believe that an aroused, informed, inspired American citizenry is the most powerful force on earth. I am convinced that if each of us does a little bit, we can remake the world. . . . No single person needs to be a hero. Everyone needs to be a little bit heroic.[70]

By "heroic" Gingrich meant, of course, what the Anti-Federalists called civic virtue.

Civic Virtue

Speaker Gingrich understood that self-government requires governing oneself: "[M]y challenge to the American people is real simple. You really want to dramatically reduce power in Washington? You have to be willing to take more responsibility back home."[71] The Anti-Federalists' idea of the polity as a school of citizenship implies that direct participation in self-government will be character-building. For Gingrich, replacing the liberal welfare state with a conservative opportunity society was a "moral imperative," one that required "reasserting the values of American civilization."[72] Gingrich cited, for example, Gertrude Himmelfarb who argued for reestablishing "shame as a means of enforcing proper behavior."[73]

As befits a 1990s Anti-Federalist, Gingrich wanted "a return to civic responsibility." It is worth quoting Gingrich at length:

> Now we must find a new path to replace the welfare state with an opportunity society. We must replace our centralized government approach with a dramatically, even radically, decentralized approach—one that relies on each citizen and each community to provide leadership and creativity. This requires a degree of evolving power out of Washington that virtually no one has thought through at this point. Furthermore, this devolution of power cannot just be to shift responsibility and resources between Washington and the state capitals. It is not enough just to return power to state and local governments. We must think through the process of returning power to local citizens, local voluntary associations, private businesses, and only then to the local, state and finally federal governments. . . . Yet a decentralized system that relies on citizen leadership and on voluntary activities actually requires a more thorough approach to developing principles, tools, habits, and values. A decentralized system has to have some core beliefs and core principles that are widely understood and agreed to if it is to be effective. . . . America will succeed by the renewal of civic responsibility, not by the centralized effort of government bureaucracies.[74]

CONCLUSION

Clearly, Newt Gingrich's worldview harkened back to the vision of the Anti-Federalists. Yet the Anti-Federalists were defined largely in opposition to ratification of the Constitution, and more importantly, the Anti-Federalists lost the debate two hundred years ago. They lost in part because they could not reconcile suspicion of governmental power with the insistence that government be responsible for nurturing personal responsibility and civic virtue. Today's fault line within the GOP between "economic" and "social" conservatives echoes this dilemma within Anti-Federalist thought. As Speaker, Newt Gingrich worked assiduously to bridge this gap, first by attempting to manage the factionalism within the House GOP Conference, striving, for example, to bring together the conservative Republican Study Committee with the moderate Wednesday Group, and Southern conservatives with moderates from the Northeast.

To move beyond the narrow confines of the Anti-Federalist perspective, Speaker Gingrich looked to a political theorist he often cited: Alexis de Tocqueville. In *Democracy in America*, Tocqueville concluded that by the 1830s America had forcibly reconciled the two irreconcilable traditions of the Federalists and the Anti-Federalists. America, he noted, had strong national political institutions, and it had a healthy state and local politics that invited citizen participation. Through participation in self-government primarily at the state and local level, Tocqueville observed,

Americans learn the "art of association," and they learn that peculiar American virtue Tocqueville dubbed "self-interest rightly understood."

If Speaker Gingrich was to make the transition from opposition to governing, then he would need, perhaps, to move beyond the Anti-Federalist critique of the Federalists to Tocqueville's synthesis of the two. From Tocqueville's perspective, the 1990s Republican "devolution revolution" could not afford to be merely a cynical excuse for cutbacks; rather it would need to be a well-grounded approach to domestic policy. At the 1992 Republican convention, Ronald Reagan challenged Americans "to invigorate democracy in your own neighborhoods."[75] Such language echoed Tocqueville's praise for America's administrative decentralization. Tocqueville understood that centralized bureaucracies strangle the voluntary associations needed for self-government. These associations—churches, charities, civic groups—help remedy the alienation of modern society, according to Tocqueville, by teaching citizens about their rights and responsibilities, and educating them in the art of self-government. Such mediating structures, Tocqueville argued, form our character as citizens capable of self-government. Gingrich Republicans believed that re-limiting government would reinvigorate those character-building and community-building institutions so crucial to our public life, especially voluntary associations.

Again, from Tocqueville's perspective, re-limiting government cannot be an end in itself; instead, it must be a way of empowering individuals and strengthening communities. Tocqueville criticized those among his contemporaries who claimed "that as citizens become weaker and more helpless, the government must become proportionately more skillful and active, so that society should do what is no longer possible for individuals."[76] Tocqueville thought that bureaucratic solutions would backfire: "The more government takes the place of associations, the more will individuals lose the idea of forming associations and need the government to come to their help. This is a vicious circle of cause and effect."[77] The danger is great, he thought:

> The morals and intelligence of a democratic people would be in as much danger as its commerce and industry if ever a government wholly usurped the place of private associations. Feelings and ideas are renewed, the heart enlarged, and the understanding developed only by the reciprocal action of men one upon another.[78]

Tocqueville understood that self-government begins with governing oneself, balancing rights and duties. Today, one sometimes wonders whether the free-market, libertarian wing of the GOP understands this insight of Tocqueville. On the other hand, one also wonders today whether the social-conservative wing understands why the Federalists won the ratification debate. Some Republicans argued in the 1990s that the GOP needed to strike a balance between their disparate factions."[79] Speaker Gingrich seemed to understand, thus he sought to mediate the internal party factionalism.

Tocqueville concluded in the 1830s that America had reconciled Federalist and Anti-Federalist principles so as to provide the necessary balance between rights and duties in a liberal regime. Had Speaker Gingrich's seemingly eclectic ideology adapted a "Tocquevillian" synthesis of Federalist and Anti-Federalist principles within the context of Madison's Constitution, then the Speaker might have had the makings of a philosophy of limited government that could have provided the GOP with more than a merely oppositional ideology. A healthy synthesis patterned after that of Tocqueville—rather than that of progressive thinkers—might have provided Republicans with the governing philosophy they needed to become more than simply an oppositional party. In the final analysis, what Richard Fenno calls "learning to govern" may involve more than merely learning to play you-scratch-my-back-I'll-scratch-your-back politics.[80] Successful compromise among competing interests, and the management of factions, whether between or within legislative parties, may need to rest on a principled understanding of the American constitutional context.

Eventually a scandal-tainted Newt Gingrich stepped down as Speaker in 1999, forced out by self-inflicted wounds, both personal and political, as well as the use by his critics of the same "politics of personal destruction" tactics he had wielded so effectively against House Democrats like Speaker Jim Wright. Live by the sword; die by the sword, perhaps. Republicans' unexpected 1998 seat loss sealed his fate. Gingrich's chosen successor, Bob Livingston, attempted briefly to take his place, only to be sidelined by his own personal scandal. Denny Hastert became Speaker with the aid of Whip Tom DeLay, aka "The Hammer," and the bloom was seemingly off the Republican rose.

The seeming idealism of the House Republican "revolution" during the early years of the Gingrich speakership, echoed in his words above, faded. The promise and the potential of those early days seems like ancient history today, and contrasts, in retrospect, with the purported pursuit of power for power's sake critics claim the Republican majority fell prey to in due time. Did the Republican majority "learn to govern" and in the process buy into the self-interested premise of a Madisonian pluralism epitomized by ambition counteracting ambition, interest against interest, faction against faction? Did ideas give way to interests, and idealism to ambition? Did the institutional constraints of the Federalist Constitution finally tame Newt Gingrich's Anti-Federalist infatuation?

Certainly Gingrich's experiment in congressional government was met by a reassertion of presidential power by Bill Clinton during the mid-1990s budget crisis, though perhaps more significantly by George W. Bush following September 11, 2001. Similarly, the committee barons, too, began to chafe under strong congressional party leadership and began to push back even during Gingrich's tenure. Still, in important ways, the pendulum of Speaker Gingrich's experiment has yet to swing all the way back. Gingrich's exercise in legislative party government has only partly given way to the pluralism of committee government. Certainly, under neither Speaker Hastert nor Speaker Pelosi has the "committee government" of the 1950s or "subcommittee government" of the 1970s returned with a vengeance.

At the same time, however, Newt Gingrich's early Anti-Federalist experiment and aspirations contrast with the politics-as-usual of the latter years of the House GOP majority scrambling to hang on to power prior to the 2006 election. The promise and the ideas of the early Gingrich speakership also seem to contrast with the ascent of Speaker Pelosi. Does Nancy really offer the same idealism as Newt?

Prior to House Democrats' 2006 victory, the *Economist* faulted Pelosi for adopting Gingrich's "passion for pugilism without embracing his passion for ideas." Has Nancy become enough like Newt? Just as her Six for '06 campaign agenda of 2006 seemed to be a pale reflection of the Contract with America, so, too, did Pelosi's speakership seem to pale in its promise. In the 110th Congress, "old bull" committee chairs like John Dingell, John Conyers, Henry Waxman, Charlie Rangel—all hangovers from the old "permanent majority" House Democratic years prior to the "revolution" did not seem to offer the ideas and the idealism of Newt Gingrich's House Republican "revolution." It is hard to think of Charlie Rangel as a revolutionary "young turk."

In the 110th Congress, House Democrats seemed to quickly fall prey to the trappings and temptations of power. Promises of a more open legislative process quickly gave way to the expediency of closed rules. And early ethical stumbles—including supporting John Murtha as majority leader—seemed to call into question Pelosi's 2006 campaign mantra promising the most ethical Congress ever. Perhaps forty years as a "permanent minority" gave House Republicans in 1994 a freshness and energy that House Democrats could not match after only twelve years in the minority wilderness. In retrospect, the refreshing idealism (and perhaps naïve Anti-Federalist aspirations?) of the early years of Speaker Gingrich contrasts with the self-interest, ambition, and power politics of Denny Hastert and Tom DeLay, especially during the death throes of the House GOP majority leading up to the 2006 election. Yet on the other side of the aisle, does Speaker Pelosi offer the ideas and idealism of Speaker Gingrich? With her supermajorities in the 111th Congress, Speaker Pelosi certainly sought significant policy change.

Newt Gingrich surrendered the dream of governing America from the "bully pulpit" of the speakership only to begin dreaming about the presidency in 2000. Given his low poll numbers, that ambition went nowhere.

And yet for Newt Gingrich hope seems to spring eternal. Once again, in 2008 he seemed to toy with presidential ambition. Even though his candidacy seemed far fetched given his unwillingness to actually organize like other contenders for presidential nominations, it is important to remember that pundits have underestimated Gingrich before—most notably when he was a "backbench bomb thrower" seemingly far removed from power. Consider the possibility that Professor Gingrich has higher aspirations. The mediagenic Gingrich may have hoped to use his faux candidacy and campaign to set the agenda for the 2008 election, albeit with limited success. Then again, there is another presidential election in 2012. Perhaps Professor Gingrich will, once again, be able to teach.

4

~

Woodrow Wilson's
Congressional Government

Former Speaker of the House Newt Gingrich once dubbed himself "the most seriously professorial politician since Woodrow Wilson."[1] Like Wilson, Gingrich was a man both of theory and practice, an intellectual and a politician. These two "professorial politicians" shared many ideas in common. Indeed, one need look no further than Newt Gingrich's 1990s House Republican "revolution" for evidence of the continuing relevance of Wilson's *Congressional Government*. Wilson's book almost reads like a field manual for Gingrich's experiment in congressional party government.[2] The parallels between the ideas of Wilson and Gingrich are remarkable; clearly, Woodrow Wilson's influence endures.

The Woodrow Wilson of *Congressional Government* and Speaker Newt Gingrich both admired the parliamentary ideal and tended to see Congress as central to our constitutional system with presidents as mere administrators.[3] Both men were critical of our separation-of-powers system, reducing it to the checks and balances.[4] Both Wilson and Gingrich disliked standing committee dominance of the legislative process and sought to elevate the role of legislative parties. They abhorred "committee government," preferring "party government."

Both Wilson and Gingrich favored an open legislative process. They preferred a politics of party platforms and principle, or "grand partisanship," to a "petty politics" of competing and compromising interests.[5] Both proposed the use of devices like Gingrich's 1994 Contract with America.[6] Both criticized the seeming corruption of Madisonian pluralism with its special-interest bargaining, lobbying, and logrolling.[7] Again, they preferred party government, with its confrontation of ideas, to pluralism, with its compromise among interests.

Both Wilson and Gingrich had limited appreciation for constitutional forms; individuals mattered more than institutions in their view.[8] Wilson saw that the public needed conspicuous leaders (perhaps like Gingrich?) to understand Congress. Both of these professorial politicians tended to conflate statesmanship and rhetoric; legislative leadership meant leadership by oratory.[9] Above all, both saw leadership as education. The purpose of principled party government was to promote serious public deliberation, thereby educating public opinion. Legislative leadership was to be government by discussion, advocacy, and persuasion.[10] The central function of Congress was to educate public opinion, with the informing function paramount to oversight and even legislating.[11] Woodrow Wilson might have appreciated Newt Gingrich's exercise of the "bully pulpit" of the speakership.

Ultimately, Wilson and Gingrich both emphasized the central importance of *Congress*, *parties*, and *ideas* in American politics; consequently, both professorial politicians were proponents of congressional party government. We can perhaps best understand the successes and failures, the strengths and limitations of experiments such as Gingrich's House GOP "revolution" by recognizing their roots in Wilson's *Congressional Government*.[12] Gingrich's exercise in congressional government provides an appropriate opportunity for reconsidering Woodrow Wilson's *Congressional Government*.

Professor Wilson's influence, of course, extends beyond politicians to the professorate. Wilson's powerful and seminal influence on twentieth-century political science is most evident in what is arguably the founding charter of the "responsible party school" of thought, namely, the report of the American Political Science Association Committee on Political Parties titled "Toward a More Responsible Two-Party System."[13] The report cites Wilson extensively. Wilson's influence can also be seen in E. E. Schattschneider's *Party Government* (1942), Austin Ranney's *The Doctrine of Responsible Party Government* (1962), James MacGregor Burn's *The Deadlock of Democracy* (1963), James Sundquist's *Constitutional Reform and Effective Government* (1986), and former Carter and Clinton White House counsel Lloyd Cutler's oft-cited *Foreign Affairs* article "To Form a Government" (1980). Some of these authors joined forces in the Committee on the Constitutional System to publish "A Bicentennial Analysis of the American Political Structure" (1987). The latter manifesto borrowed heavily from the thought of Woodrow Wilson, especially his early writings, including *Congressional Government*. In sum, Wilsonian thinkers and reformers abound to this day. Woodrow Wilson's *Congressional Government* remains highly relevant to the study and practice of American politics, not least because it provides a serious exploration of the role of Congress, political parties, and ideas.[14]

Of course, Wilson was himself part of a long intellectual tradition in American political thought traceable back to the Founding. In fact, he opens *Congressional Government* with a discussion of the original debate over ratification of the Constitution, making clear his own sympathies with the "opposition."[15] Indeed, the young Wilson seems intent on resurrecting serious opposition to the Federalist Constitution.[16] Wilson notes, "[W]e of the present generation are in the first season of free, outspoken, unrestrained constitutional criticism. We are the first Americans . . . to entertain any serious doubts about the superiority of our own institutions as compared with the systems of Europe."[17]

Wilson echoed Anti-Federalist "reservations" about the Constitution in many particulars.[18] Like that of the Anti-Federalists, Wilson's opposition to the Constitution stemmed, in large part, from a profound dissatisfaction with the unleashing of self-interest and factionalism in Madisonian pluralism. Like the Anti-Federalists, Wilson was wary of a system of institutional checks and balances inviting interest to counteract interest. The Anti-Federalist author Centinel, for example, was skeptical of a politics based on "an opposition of interests."[19] "How," he asked, "is the welfare and happiness of the community to be the result of such jarring adverse interests?"[20] Similarly, Wilson criticized "the conditions of public life which make the House of Representatives what it is, a disintegrate mass of jarring elements, and the Senate what it is, a small, select, and leisurely House of Representatives."[21]

Wilson shared Anti-Federalist disdain for the complexity of Madison's separation of powers, a complexity that precluded genuine responsibility and accountability of the politicians to the people.[22] Wilson and the Anti-Federalist Centinel were both clear on this point. Centinel noted, "[I]f you complicate the plan by various orders, the people will be perplexed and divided in their sentiments about the sources of abuses or misconduct."[23] Wilson concurred, "How is the schoolmaster, the nation, to know which boy needs the whipping?"[24]

Like the Anti-Federalists, Wilson correctly identified many of the defects of Madison's Constitution. Unlike many Anti-Federalists, however, Wilson did not embrace the "small republic" cure for these defects. Wilson, unlike the Anti-Federalists, was a nationalist who favored a strong central government. And of course Wilson was an internationalist, while many Anti-Federalists leaned toward autarky and isolationism.[25]

In searching for a cure to the perceived defects of Madison's Constitution, the young author of *Congressional Government* seemed more inclined to look abroad than back in time. Wilson was a serious comparative scholar who took the British parliamentary system as his ideal, borrowing explicitly from Walter Bagehot's *The English Constitution*.[26] Wilson, like Bagehot and many Anti-Federalists, embraced a simple, direct parliamentary ideal for democracy while rejecting Madison's separation of powers.[27] Like the Anti-Federalists and Bagehot, Wilson fundamentally challenged the American constitutional system. He provides a thoughtful and trenchant critique of the Founders' constitutional edifice; thus, we should take Wilson with the utmost seriousness. Woodrow Wilson in *Congressional Government* proves to be a worthy opponent of Madison and the Federalist Constitution.[28]

In Federalist No. 49, Madison famously argues in favor of "veneration" for the Constitution. In the conclusion to *Congressional Government*, on the other hand, Wilson insists "the Constitution is not honored by blind worship," calling instead for "fearless criticism of that system."[29] It may be that both men are right. We need to take seriously both the Founders' Constitution and Wilson's "fearless criticism" of the same, especially if our purpose is to understand the virtues and defects of that system. The centerpiece of Madison's Constitution and the centerpiece of Wilson's critique and challenge to the Constitution is the separation of powers. Arguably, Wilson's critique and challenge depends on his understanding of Madison's separation of powers.

WOODROW WILSON: POLITICAL SCIENTIST OR PROGRESSIVE REFORMER?

In *Congressional Government*, Wilson's challenge to the Founders' separation of powers takes the form of an indictment of congressional government. This classic study of the United States Congress is all the more impressive because a twenty-eight-year-old graduate student who had never visited Congress wrote it. Of course, this same young author would travel someday to Capitol Hill to deliver the State of the Union Address as president of the United States. Wilson's early reflections on American politics in *Congressional Government* are in some ways embryonic and incomplete; his thinking clearly evolved over time as witness his publication in 1905 of another book (originally a lecture series) titled *Constitutional Government*. In the latter book, Wilson turns from Congress to the presidency to find a cure for the perceived defects of our constitutional system. However, there remains an essential continuity between the two books; the shift to "Constitutional Government" is, arguably, tactical.[30] Wilson's thinking evolved, and yet he did not alter what he saw as the fundamental defect of our constitutional system, namely, the separation of powers.

In the original preface to *Congressional Government*, Wilson makes clear that his chief aim is to contrast "Congressional government" and "Parliamentary government."

> The most striking contrast in modern politics is not between presidential and monarchical governments, but between Congressional and Parliamentary

governments. Congressional government is Committee government; Parliamentary government is government by a responsible Cabinet Ministry.[31]

In this prefatory observation, Wilson merely alludes to his parliamentary reform ideal as a cure to the defects of the separation of powers. In two essays written prior to *Congressional Government*, Wilson directly espoused responsible party "Cabinet Government" reforms.[32] In "Cabinet Government in the United States" and "Committee or Cabinet Government?" Wilson recommends a "responsible Cabinet" fusion of the Founders' separated legislative and executive branches as the "remedy" for congressional government.[33] In *Congressional Government*, however, Wilson studiously avoids any explicit reform prescription. "I am pointing out facts—diagnosing, not prescribing remedies."[34] Yet, as Daniel D. Stid notes, Wilson confided to a friend soon after he published *Congressional Government* that the book's "mission" was to "set reform a-going."[35]

Was the author of *Congressional Government* a political scientist or a reformer at heart? Was he describing facts or prescribing change? Before becoming president of the United States, Wilson served as president of the American Political Science Association; thus, he was aware of the tension within political science between the imperatives of science and politics. In a letter to a friend following publication of *Congressional Government*, Wilson insists,

> It's the same old thing—Committee government—but it is worked up in a different form from that of the essay. . . . I leave out all advocacy of Cabinet Government—all advocacy, indeed, of *any* specific reform—and devote myself to a careful analysis of Congressional government. I have abandoned the evangelical for the exegetical—so to speak.[36]

Stid notes that Wilson compromised his reform advocacy in *Congressional Government* by abandoning the evangelical for the exegetical in order to gain a larger audience and greater currency for the book. Wilson's earlier polemical essay "Government by Debate" remained unpublished by Harper because the editors deemed it "too radical."[37] Did Wilson's advocacy, in turn, compromise his political science? Stid concludes that "Wilson saw himself as a statesman first; he was quite frank in professing that he was studying politics ultimately to bring about political changes."[38] James W. Ceaser argues that, as a Progressive reformer, Wilson always directed his concern to the political system's capacity for change and growth.[39] Did Wilson's desire for change color his perception of the separation of powers? Clearly, Wilson's Progressive impulse explains his dislike for "the too tight ligaments of a written fundamental law" such as the Constitution, along with his desire to explore the "living reality" of the nation's underlying constitution rather than any mere "literary theory."[40]

CONGRESSIONAL GOVERNMENT VERSUS
PARLIAMENTARY GOVERNMENT

Congressional Government is a paean to the virtues of parliamentary government, which, according to Wilson, promotes disciplined, responsible party government.[41] Borrowing from Bagehot, Wilson measures the American political system by the standard of the British parliamentary model: "The British system is perfected party government," Wilson proclaims.[42] Parliamentary party government promotes accountability of politicians to the people. According to Wilson, "*Power and strict accountability for its use* are the essential constituents of good government."[43] As he notes, "[S]omebody must be trusted," and that somebody must be held to the "highest responsibility."[44] Responsible party government allows for a concentration of authority, thereby engendering efficient and effective policymaking. The machinery of parliamentary government can avoid that "distressing paralysis" that, in Wilson's view, can all too readily afflict our separation-of-powers system.[45] Wilson probably would join today's neo-Wilsonian reformers in bemoaning the "divided government" that was common in Washington in the late twentieth century.[46] Finally, and perhaps most importantly for Woodrow Wilson, parliamentary party government promotes a *politics of ideas* rather than a *politics of interests*. Again, Wilson prefers party government to pluralism. The latter, he tells us, remains "a joust between antagonistic interests, not a contest of principles," and therefore cannot promote "the instruction and elevation of public opinion" that is the *sine qua non* of republican government.[47]

Wilson contrasts congressional government with parliamentary government, committee government with party government. "Congressional government is committee government," he laments.[48] Or as he observes ruefully in probably the most oft-quoted passage from *Congressional Government*, "Congress in session is Congress on public exhibition, whilst Congress in its committee-rooms is Congress at work."[49] Committee government makes Congress a "facile statute devising machine," but it renders the legislative process fragmented, incremental, inconsistent, and incapable of producing coherent legislation in the interest of the whole nation.[50]

Committee government also compounds another defect Wilson perceives in the separation of powers, namely, "the forcible and unnatural" divorce of legislation and administration.[51] Stid underscores the importance for Wilson of the unity of legislation and administration by citing a letter Wilson penned to James Bryce, the author of *The American Commonwealth*. Wilson argued, "[W]hat we need is the marriage of legislation and practical statesmanship—a responsible direction of those who make the laws by those who must carry them out and approve or damn themselves in the process."[52] Legislation must be grounded in detailed, practical responsibility for administering policy.[53] However, committee government as Wilson saw it reverses the appropriate relationship between legislation and administration. Congress meddles. Indeed, according to Wilson, under conditions of committee government, legislative oversight amounts to little more than meddling.[54]

The rise of committee government and concomitant legislative specialization during the first century of the American Republic, according to Wilson, deepened the divisions of the separation of powers and the disintegration of policymaking.[55] The rise of committee government rendered the legislature near absolute. Wilson complained that Congress tyrannized over the executive departments as their "real master."[56]

> Accordingly it has entered more and more into the details of administration, until it has virtually taken into its own hands all the substantial powers of government. It does not domineer over the President himself, but it makes the Secretaries its humble servants.[57]

Moreover, committee government precludes true accountability because much of the legislative process, at least in Wilson's day, occurred behind closed doors. And committee government enables special interests to dominate the legislative process: "[T]here can be no doubt that the power of the lobbyist consists in great part, if not altogether, in the facility afforded him by the Committee system."[58] Again, Wilson's critique of congressional government is, at bottom, a critique of pluralism with its unleashing of self-interest and factionalism.

Congressional government as committee government also fragments leadership. "Power is nowhere concentrated," Wilson notes.[59] Congressional government cannot provide unified leadership able to speak for the nation as a whole because of "this multiplicity of leaders, this many headed leadership."[60] In *Congressional Government*, Wilson declares the presidency "too silent and too inactive" for serious leadership.[61] On political leadership in general he concludes:

> In a country which governs itself by means of a public meeting, a Congress or a Parliament, a country whose political life is representative, the only real leadership in governmental affairs must be legislative leadership. . . . We have in this country, therefore, no real leadership; because no man is allowed to direct the course of Congress, and there is no way of governing the country save through Congress, which is supreme.[62]

Wilson argues further that "our system of government fails to attract better men by its prizes" because committee government "makes all the prizes of leadership small and nowhere gathers power into a few hands."[63] If committee government means small men working on petty details, then this may not attract ambitious men of high statesmanship, and the public may find it inherently uninteresting as well. Wilson argues

that a proper concentration of authority can attract and educate statesmen who will, in turn, elevate public opinion by enlightening debate.
Fragmented leadership limits the ability of congressional government to
enlighten public discourse and educate citizens. In sum, committee government precludes what Harry Clor calls "constructive statesmanship."[64]
Wilson thought republican government required leadership as education
for "the instruction and elevation of public opinion."[65] In this, too, Wilson
echoed the Anti-Federalists.

DELIBERATION

The greatest, and perhaps most impressive, contribution Wilson offers in
Congressional Government is his fundamental exploration of deliberation in
Congress and American politics. Indeed, Wilson's most successful challenge to Madison may be on the question of representative or republican
deliberation. Wilson offers a scathing critique of congressional deliberation in the context of committee government. Floor debate is "random,"
tends to "wander" and thus has "little coherency."[66] Wilson observes,
"[T]o attend to such discussions is uninteresting; to be instructed by them
is impossible."[67] When one hears "Beam me up, Mr. Speaker" uttered
from the well of the House, one is tempted to agree with Wilson's opinion
that deliberation in Congress is "government by declamation" rather than
government by discussion or deliberation.[68]

For Wilson, the problem is that members of Congress, especially in the
House of Representatives, bring their local and parochial perspectives
and specialized knowledge to bear on congressional deliberations when
what the nation needs is articulate and informative general deliberation.
Committee government augments the role of members as representatives
of narrow constituencies who are influenced by special-interest lobbyists. One consequence, Wilson concludes, is that "public opinion cannot
be instructed or elevated by the debates in Congress."[69] "In short," he
laments, "we lack in our political life the conditions most essential for
the formation of an active and effective public opinion," thus republican
government remains incomplete.[70]

Central to Wilson's concern for deliberation in *Congressional Government* is his desire to cure our politics of the excessive individualism that
he and the Anti-Federalists saw as the essential defect of the democratic
pluralism bequeathed to us by Madison. Wilson seeks to purify Madisonian pluralism of the surfeit of self-interest that informs our politics;
in *Congressional Government*, thorough legislative deliberation is the cure
for this defect. Like the Anti-Federalists before him, Wilson believed republican government required republican virtue among citizens. Herbert
Storing describes this virtue as including "an enlightened understanding

of the objects of government, a degree of public-spiritedness, [and] a participation in citizenship as distinct from a merely private life."[71] For Wilson, congressional deliberation is the panacea.

Thus, the major weakness of congressional government is that committee government undermines "the informing function" of Congress and instead elevates the oversight and legislative functions. Again, committee government promotes "facile" legislating and the tyranny of a legislative oversight divorced from governing responsibility. The aim of Congress, Wilson tells us, "is to have laws always a-making. Its temper is strenuously legislative."[72] Wilson ranks oversight as important as legislating, and enlightenment of the public as most important. "The informing function of Congress should be preferred even to its legislative function."[73] He urges, "Congress cannot be too diligent about such talking; whereas it may easily be too diligent in legislation."[74] Wilson notes that the term *parliament* refers to "talking" thereby implying that such talk is fundamental to a legislature.[75] In Wilson's view, government by discussion is imperative for a self-governing people. "It is natural that orators should be the leaders of a self-governing people."[76] Wilson has an abiding and almost unending faith in orators. He observes,

[M]en can scarcely be orators without that force of character, that readiness of resource, that clearness of vision, that grasp of intellect, that courage of conviction, that earnestness of purpose, and that instinct and capacity for leadership which are the eight horses that draw the triumphal chariot of every leader and ruler of free men.[77]

Wilson seems undeterred by the prospect of demagoguery, perhaps because he recognized in himself—as witness the rhetorical flourish above—the mentioned virtues of orators and leaders of free men.[78] Perhaps, too, Wilson was sanguine about the dangers of demagoguery in the context of congressional government because in legislative debate oratorical ambition can counteract oratorical ambition.

Were he alive today, Wilson probably would cheer the recommendation for instituting Oxford Union–style debates in Congress advanced by a group of political scientists as part of the Renewing Congress Project.[79] The authors of the project's reports, Thomas Mann and Norman Ornstein, echo Wilson in lamenting the "often lonely declamations" that pass for floor debate; they recommend "the use of Oxford Union–style debates as one means of encouraging deliberations on the House and Senate floor, forcing members to engage the *ideas* of the other *party* in a public setting and *educating* the American people on important issues facing the country."[80] This Wilsonian reform, along with C-SPAN and the Internet, might well improve the quality and educational value of floor deliberations. Such an experiment might also provide a useful test of Wilson's ideas in

Congressional Government. This would require, of course, a more sustained and thorough experiment and exercise in Oxford Union–style debates than the limited effort conducted in 1994.

Wilson's later book *Constitutional Government* completes his investigation of the central role deliberation plays in republican government, in particular with his discussion of "common counsel." A complete exploration of his thoughts on deliberation would require extended analysis of the later book, though that is not practicable here. Suffice it to note, however, that Wilson turns there to the presidency rather than legislative floor debate to promote "common counsel." This latter suggestion is, of course, of an entirely different order.

In *Congressional Government,* Wilson's views on deliberation differ from those of Madison. Madison sought "to refine and enlarge the public views by passing them through the medium of a chosen body of citizens, whose wisdom may best discern the true interest of their country."[81] Madison was concerned about the proper "institutional environment" for promoting deliberation; he famously observed, "Had every Athenian citizen been a Socrates, every Athenian assembly would still have been a mob."[82] Deliberation within the context of properly structured institutions would allow "the mild voice of reason" to be heard. Also, Madison was less concerned about the "informing function" of legislative deliberation as a means of educating public opinion; whereas for Wilson, the primary purpose of public deliberation is education and enlightenment of the citizenry.[83]

Madison grounds legislative deliberation in the local, parochial interests of members of Congress and in the pluralist struggle among contending interests. Elected representatives possessing knowledge of local, parochial concerns and particulars mediate the bargaining among competing factions or special interests.[84] Indeed, our Constitution even grounds presidential leadership in legislative bargaining. The president must deal with Congress. Wilson denounces this grounding of deliberation in legislative bargaining, and in doing so Wilson fundamentally rejects pluralism. As noted above, Wilson prefers instead to ground legislative deliberation in detailed, practical responsibility for administering policy. In principle, Wilson prefers the public deliberation of party government.

In sum, Madison tends to promote a pluralist politics of contending interests within representative institutions that can refine and enlarge the public views. Wilson prefers a politics of ideas premised on the principled competition between responsible parties. In the simplest terms, the choice Wilson casts seems to be between pluralism and party government, between a politics of interests and a politics of ideas, between interest accommodation and principled confrontation. Wilson's trenchant exploration of deliberation in *Congressional Government* challenges the Federalist authors of the Constitution by raising Anti-Federalist concerns about legislative deliberation in perhaps a more complete fashion than did the original opponents of the Constitution. Wilson raises fundamental questions about the adequacy of Madisonian pluralism, and he argues that the informing function of Congress is paramount and should serve the role of civic education for self-government.[85] The question remains, does Wilson—and do neo-Wilsonian scholars and reformers—provide a complete picture of Madison's constitutional system? Or, contrary to Wilson's sharp bifurcation between committee government and party government, is our separation-of-powers system in fact capable of promoting both a politics of interest and a politics of ideas, both pluralism and party government?

WILSON VERSUS MADISON:
THE SEPARATION OF POWERS

The heart of Woodrow Wilson's challenge to the Constitution is his critique of the separation of powers. This is altogether appropriate since the heart of Madison's Constitution is the separation of powers. Wilson's critique and challenge rises and falls, therefore, on the adequacy of his understanding of Madison's separation of powers. For Wilson, the separation of powers was a "radical defect" in our constitutional system.[86] Wilson sought to overcome the "friction" of the separation of powers, first in *Congressional Government* with disciplined, responsible legislative party leadership, and later in *Constitutional Government* with presidential leadership. Wilson concludes that the cure for the *friction* of the separation of powers can be found in the *fusion* of party government. Yet Wilson—to borrow another scientific metaphor—may have overlooked the potential in the separation of powers for *fission*.[87]

Beginning with *Congressional Government*, though continuing with *Constitutional Government*, Wilson reduces the separation of powers to the checks and balances.[88] Wilson tends to see the separation of powers in mechanistic terms. He suggests in *Constitutional Government* that the Founders constructed the Constitution upon "a sort of unconscious copy of the Newtonian theory of the universe."[89] And he concludes,

> The trouble with the theory is that government is not a machine, but a living thing. It falls, not under the theory of the universe, but under the theory of organic life. It is accountable to Darwin, not to Newton.[90]

But what if the separation of powers can add, rather than merely subtract, energy from the political process? Wilson, it seems, failed to appreciate the potential in the separation of powers for promoting Progressive change. The separation of powers both limits and empowers; it limits the abuse of power while also providing for the effective use of power. The separation of powers promotes effective change, in part, by creating a functional distinction between the three discrete branches, thereby promoting specialization. Jessica Korn concludes that Wilson premised his critique of the Founders' separation of powers on a crucial misunderstanding. The Founders created the separation-of-powers not only to check and balance the exercise of power "but also to produce a division of labor so that members of the different branches would develop specialized skills in pursuing the responsibilities of legislating, executing and judging."[91]

Martin Diamond argues that the Constitution's "functional parceling out of political power" promotes "not only free but effective government."[92] Our separation-of-powers system arguably promotes ambition counteracting ambition as well as ambition *vying* with ambition.[93] To return for a moment to Wilson's discussion of legislative leadership, does the fragmentation of the separation of powers, compounded by committee government, merely subtract from the energy and creativity of the legislative process? Or can the "multiplicity of leaders" he notes in fact promote a leavening of the legislative process? Many scholars have concluded, contrary to Wilson, that the separation of powers augments the system's dynamic potential for innovation. Nelson Polsby observes in *Political Innovation in America*, for example, that electoral and institutional competition encourages policy innovation. Polsby finds that there are "incentives to search for innovation" that are "incorporated into the constitutional routines of the American political process as they affect the ambition of politicians—routines associated with the electoral cycle and routines associated with the separation of powers."[94]

Careful case studies of major legislation also have provided concrete evidence of the separation of powers' potential for advancing, and not just retarding, change. Daniel J. Palazzolo, in his case study of the 1997 Budget Agreement, argues that contrary to the Wilsonian perspective, the separation-of-powers system is not destined to result in "inevitable gridlock," rather it can positively advance change. Palazzolo insists that "budget decisions are not easily explained by simple assumptions about how narrow, self-serving interests undermine general interests. Budget choices are based on a variety of political calculations, policy concerns, responsiveness to general public opinion, and basic principles."[95] Similarly, in their legislative case study of the landmark 1986 Tax Reform Act, political scientists Timothy Conlon, Margaret Wrightson, and David Beam argue that neither the modern political science "pluralist/incrementalist model" nor the "presidential/majoritarian" (read: party government) model fully captures the dynamics of the legislative process. They conclude that the political process invites "policy entrepreneurs" wielding new ideas to exercise creativity.[96]

Unfortunately, the dominant contemporary political-science understanding of Madisonian pluralism, perhaps taking its cue from Wilson, tends to reduce pluralism to mere interest-dominated incrementalism and reduce the separation of powers to the checks and balances.[97] To the contrary, scholars Martha Derthick and Paul J. Quirk in their case studies of *The Politics of Deregulation* underscore the importance of "the politics of ideas" in understanding policy change in America.[98] Similarly, James Q. Wilson emphasizes the importance of ideas and not just interests in American politics, and the continuing capacity of our constitutional system for promoting policy innovation.[99]

The separation of powers can promote policy change in part because the constitutional separation of powers is flexible, not static, in forming the policymaking process. Power oscillates between the president and Congress, and between party and committee leadership in Congress. Broadly speaking, the nineteenth-century era of congressional dominance, noted by Woodrow Wilson in *Congressional Government*, gave way to the rise of the "imperial presidency" from the 1930s to the 1970s. In *Constitutional Government*, Wilson himself saw the potential for a strong presidency, in part because of the examples of William McKinley and Theodore Roosevelt. Similarly, the 1990s witnessed a tug-of-war between Newt Gingrich's experiment in "congressional government" and the Clinton presidency. The same president who timidly asserted his own relevance in a press conference at the height of Gingrich's ascendancy later crushed the House Republican "revolution" with his veto pen during the government shutdown-showdown in 1995 and 1996. Also during the 1990s, power *within* Congress, especially in the House, oscillated between party leaders and committee leaders, arguably between what might loosely be called "party government" and "committee government."

James W. Ceaser explains how such shifts are possible given the flexibility of our constitutional order:

> The doctrine of the separation of powers . . . does not define fully—nor was it ever intended to define fully—the exact character of the policy-making process. The Constitution is not completely silent or neutral about the character of the policy-making process, but in the final analysis there is not one single constitutional model for the policy-making function but only constitutional limits within which models must be constructed.[100]

The separation of powers incorporates the potential for a strong Congress and a strong president, the potential for "congressional government" and "presidential government." The separation of powers mediates a healthy tension between pluralism and party government in Congress, between "committee government" and "party government." Congress is not just the politics of pluralist accommodation among contending interests, rather, it is also responsive to a principled politics of ideas. This is not to say, however, that our Madisonian system embodies the idealized party government that Wilson and neo-Wilsonian reformers prefer. Rather, our constitutional system can foster strong party leadership and a principled politics of ideas while grounding party and principle in a pluralist politics of contending parochial interests. In effect, the separation of powers maintains a healthy tension between these two halves of a whole. The organizational structure of Congress provides a case in point, as witness the "centripetal" and "centrifugal" influence of the "party principle" and "committee principle" respectively.[101]

Ironically, it may be precisely the flexibility of the constitutional separation of powers that explains why the power of Congress endures today, while the British Parliament, the source of Woodrow Wilson's *Congressional Government* ideal, succumbs to executive dominance.[102] Comparative legislative scholar Nicol C. Rae notes, for example, that "[t]he loss of power by legislatures has been a common feature of advanced industrial democracies."[103] Congress is, of course, the exception. The flexibility of the separation of powers may be a virtue and source of strength. David Nichols argues that contrary to the claims of neo-Wilsonian reformers, the parliamentary model, not our "presidential" model, may be the example of "arrested development."[104]

CONCLUSION

A complete appreciation for Woodrow Wilson's thought requires reading *Congressional Government* in tandem with *Constitutional Government*. While there is an essential continuity between the two books, the latter reflects Wilson's mature reflections. In *Constitutional Government* Wilson had second thoughts about the virtues of "congressional government," thoughts he articulated in his 1905 book. According to Stid, however, Wilson had what might be called "third" thoughts as president on the relative power between Congress and the president. As president, Wilson began to think that leadership perhaps really should come from Congress as he had originally suggested in *Congressional Government*.[105] Why this vacillation by a "literary politician" as brilliant as Wilson? Perhaps it is because both the president and Congress (and similarly party and committee leaders) are powerful in our constitutional system depending on circumstances such as the time, issues, and individuals involved.[106] Wilson had the perspicacity as a political scientist and a politician to see the weaknesses of our constitutional system, though not always the strengths residing simultaneously at both ends of Pennsylvania Avenue.

Congressional Government remains well worth reading over a century after its original publication because Woodrow Wilson's doctoral dissertation continues to influence political scientists and politicians. Even though this professorial politician may have met his match in the "combining mind" of James Madison, *Congressional Government* remains highly relevant for understanding the importance of Congress in American politics and for understanding American political science. Woodrow Wilson is a worthy opponent for the Father of our Constitution.

Ultimately, however, Wilson fundamentally misunderstood the constitutional separation of powers, which he assumed the Founders created simply to prevent the abuse of power. Consequently, he struggled to make an end run around the Constitution with his efforts in theory and practice to create responsible party government. As president, Wilson met with both success and failure, as seen, for example, in the New Freedom and the Versailles Treaty. Yet according to Stid, "The separation of powers, which Wilson had bridged with such drama and effect during the New Freedom, ultimately gave rise to a struggle that left his dearest policy, his presidency, and the man himself in ruins" following Senate rejection of the Versailles Treaty and the League of Nations.[107] Wilson's effort to create "responsible government under the Constitution" ultimately fell prey to "the countervailing and constitutionally entrenched logic of the Founders' separation of powers."[108] Reelected in 1916, Wilson and his party suffered repudiation in 1918 and 1920. In the end, one might argue, James Madison defeated Woodrow Wilson in both theory and practice. Constitutional reformers ever since *Congressional Government* have found themselves "confounded by the alternative logic of the separation of powers."[109] In this important sense, the Constitution governs and James Madison rules America.

In *Congressional Government*, Wilson raises trenchant questions about legislative deliberation, the separation of powers, and the nature of Congress and provides a remarkably serious exploration of the importance of ideas and parties within our constitutional system. Wilson, along with the Anti-Federalists, correctly identified a defect in our pluralist system, namely, a tendency to augment what Tocqueville called individualism or privatism, along with the role of special-interest groups in politics. But Wilson also explored and exploited the potential of our Madisonian system for promoting a politics of ideas and a politics of grand partisanship. While Wilson's pure party government ideal may not be practicable within our separation-of-powers system, it may be more feasible within the confines of the more majoritarian House of Representatives.

5

~

Alexis de Tocqueville's Congress

Alexis de Tocqueville's *Democracy in America* is once again popular among professors and politicians.[1] Some even urge greater attention to long-neglected sections of *Democracy in America*, such as the chapter titled "The Federal Constitution," which includes most of Tocqueville's explicit commentary on Congress.[2] Congress scholars, however, have given little thought to Tocqueville's observations on Congress. Perhaps this is not surprising since Tocqueville apparently slighted Congress. Still, we can learn much about Congress and about the study of Congress from a careful reading of *Democracy in America*.

According to one noted Tocqueville scholar, this Frenchman is "terse" on the subject.[3] Yet Tocqueville provides a useful link between two thinkers who have greatly influenced theorizing about Congress: James Madison and Woodrow Wilson. Congress scholars should take *Democracy in America* seriously because Tocqueville effectively mediates between Madison and Wilson. In *Democracy in America*, written in the 1830s, Tocqueville synthesizes the earlier debate between the Federalists and Anti-Federalists. In a similar manner, Tocqueville provides a bridge between Madison, a Federalist, and Wilson, arguably a latter-day Anti-Federalist. Wilson's 1885 *Congressional Government*, long popular among Congress scholars, echoes the Anti-Federalist critique of the Federalist Constitution, especially on the separation of powers and the role of self-interest. In important ways, *Democracy in America* stands between *The Federalist* and *Congressional Government*.

Why does Tocqueville write relatively little on Congress in a discussion of democracy in America? Tocqueville emphasizes that "mores do more than the laws" or institutions to maintain a democratic republic in the United States.[4] He slights formal constitutional institutions in general, and not just Congress, relative to informal, extra-constitutional voluntary associations and their role in educating democratic mores.[5]

In this, Tocqueville may share more in common with Wilson than Madison. While Madison famously discusses factions in nos. 10 and 51, *The Federalist* generally focuses on institutional structure. Wilson in *Congressional Government*, on the other hand, echoes the Anti-Federalists in emphasizing the importance of educating democratic mores. In *Democracy in America*, Tocqueville argues, in effect, that one cannot fully understand Congress without comprehending the democratic mores that provide the foundation for American political institutions. We cannot abstract our institutions from our interests and ideas.[6]

Understanding Congress requires appreciating the connection between constitutional structure and the culture of Congress. Congress scholars have much to learn from Tocqueville. At a minimum, he provides a useful corrective to our tendency to emphasize "rational choice" or self-interest alone in explaining congressional behavior. Tocqueville's insight into the link between laws and mores, institutions and culture can deepen the contemporary debate among political scientists over the nature of Congress.

Elevating Tocqueville as a commentator on Congress will encourage political scientists to take more seriously his thoughts on Congress along with his larger argument in *Democracy in America*. We can extend a Tocquevillian view of democracy in America more explicitly and clearly to the study of Congress. To accomplish this, however, we must go beyond Tocqueville's immediate and direct observations on Congress to a more general application of his larger argument to Congress.

To begin to appreciate Tocqueville on Congress, we need to consider not just *what* Tocqueville says about Congress but *how* he studies Congress. Tocqueville's "new political science" provides a useful starting point.

TOCQUEVILLE'S POLITICAL SCIENCE

In his introduction to *Democracy in America*, Tocqueville declares "[a] new political science is needed for a world itself quite new."[7] Tocqueville builds on Madison's political science with its emphasis on constitutional and institutional structures while anticipating Wilson's rejection of *The Federalist*'s "science of politics."[8] Tocqueville rarely mentions political science; though when he does he typically identifies institutional principles the Federalists embodied in their Constitution.[9] In Book One, for example, he cites bicameralism as an "axiom of political science."[10] Press pluralism is another "axiom of political science."[11] Similarly, the Constitution's new federalism is "a new theory that should be hailed as one of the great discoveries of political science in our age."[12]

Tocqueville's "new political science" builds on the "science of government" found in *The Federalist*.[13] Tocqueville knows of Madison's political science, yet he calls for a *new* political science. Tocqueville's new political science moves beyond a focus on constitutional structures to concentrate in greater detail than *The Federalist* on mores. In this, Tocqueville seems more Anti-Federalist than Federalist. As Wilson Carey McWilliams notes, "Fifty years after the ratification of the Constitution, Tocqueville refined and restated the Anti-Federalist case."[14]

In echoing the Anti-Federalist concern for something more than institutional solutions to political problems, Tocqueville anticipates Wilson's rejection of the political science of the Federalists. In *Constitutional Government*, Woodrow Wilson criticizes *The Federalist* as too mechanical: "The trouble with the theory is that government is not a machine, but a living thing. . . . It is accountable to Darwin, not to Newton."[15] Wilson's "living political constitutions" theory focuses more on changing mores.[16]

Tocqueville provides a bridge between Madison's focus on constitutions and institutions, and Wilson's Progressive behavioral demotion of the same. Herbert F. Weisberg, Eric Heberlig, and Lisa Campoli, in "The Study of Congress: Methodologies and the Pursuit of Theory," underscore the transformation within political science between the era of *The Federalist* and Wilson's *Congressional Government*: "The earliest approach to the study of legislatures was institutional . . . [and] focused on constitutions and legislative rules, as if reading such documents explained how legislatures functioned."[17] Madison's political science explicating the Constitution provides the archetype of the earlier approach, while Wilson's study of Congress provides a model of the later approach. Weisberg, Heberlig, and Campoli continue:

> Wilson went past the previous focus on legislative rules to examine how Congress actually worked in practice. His discovery of the importance of committees in the legislative process made it clear that legislative studies could not be limited to formal procedures and had to be more empirically based.[18]

An example of Tocqueville going beyond formal rules and institutions is his observation about what political scientists today call candidate emergence theory: "Although in democratic states all citizens can hold office, not all are disposed to seek it. It is the number and capacities of the candidates, not the qualifications for candidature, which there often limits the electors' choice."[19]

Physical Circumstances, Laws, and Mores

We see Tocqueville's explicit broadening of Madison's analysis in a famous chapter subheading: "The Laws Contribute More to the Maintenance of the Democratic Republic in the United States Than Do the Physi-

cal Circumstances of the Country, and Mores Do More Than the Laws."[20]
Tocqueville examines every facet of American politics through the lens of
this three-part framework incorporating *physical circumstances*, *laws*, and
mores.

An apt example appears toward the end of the chapter titled "The Fed-
eral Constitution." Opening a subchapter titled "Why the Federal System
Is Not within the Reach of All Nations and Why the Anglo-Americans
Have Been Able to Adopt It," Tocqueville observes:

> Sometimes after a thousand efforts, a lawmaker succeeds in exercising some
> indirect influence over the destiny of nations, and then his genius is praised,
> whereas it is often the geographical position of the country, over which he
> has no influence, a social state which has been created without his aid, mores
> and ideas whose origin he does not know, and a point of departure of which
> he is unaware that give to society impetuses of irresistible force against
> which he struggles in vain and which sweep him, too, along.[21]

Tocqueville summarizes this observation with a metaphor: "A lawgiver
is like a man steering his route over the sea. He, too, can control the ship
that bears him, but he cannot change its structure, create the winds, or
prevent the ocean stirring beneath him." Stated succinctly, Tocqueville
understands politics as *individuals* working within *institutions* to reconcile
competing *interest groups* and *ideas*.[22]

Tocqueville appreciates Madison's *Federalist* insight that institutions
affect the behavior of individuals and factions. Tocqueville, like Madison,
also appreciates the "autonomy of political things," as James Ceaser puts
it.[23] For Tocqueville, as for Madison, politics is neither epiphenomenal
nor—in the argot of our day—merely a dependent variable. Instead, for
both Tocqueville and Madison, politics is also not utterly *in*dependent of
the influence of competing factions. While taking politics seriously on its
own terms, Tocqueville and Madison both look above and below politics
to comprehend the role of ideas and interests. For both Tocqueville and
Madison, constitutions and institutions matter, individuals and interests
matter, and ideas count.

Tocqueville's political science looks at the *regime* as a whole, including both public and private realms. Echoing the most trenchant Anti-
Federalist critique, Tocqueville argues that public things affect the private
and vice versa. He notes "a human heart cannot really be divided in this
way."[24] Tocqueville is famous, of course, for focusing on the central role
of private voluntary associations. Whereas Book One of *Democracy in
America* looks at public institutions and political associations, Book Two
focuses more on essentially private concerns such as philosophy and
poetry, science and religion, art and literature, family and commerce.
Political and civil associations are central to the success of democracy in
America. Tocqueville insists we take seriously the grounding of politics
in mores: "If in the course of this book I have not succeeded in making

the reader feel the importance I attach to the practical experience of the Americans, to their habits, opinions, and, in a word, their mores, in maintaining their laws, I have failed in the main object of my work."[25]

The difference between Madison in *The Federalist* and Tocqueville in *Democracy in America* may be due, in part, to a difference in aim and emphasis. Madison sought to explicate constitutional provisions for the purpose of ratification. Tocqueville wanted to illuminate democracy in America more comprehensively. But Tocqueville also echoes the Anti-Federalist argument that constitutions and institutions are not enough; the regime whole predates the bifurcation of the parts into private and public. Mores provide the necessary foundation for political institutions.[26]

Tocqueville's three-part framework is central to his regime analysis. In *Democracy in America* he compares various regimes; he weighs the virtues and defects of democracy and aristocracy, France and America, North America and South America, and even the North and South within the United States. Tocqueville constantly evaluates various regimes, in effect implicitly asking what is the best practical regime under particular circumstances. Of necessity, then, Tocqueville's political science is both descriptive and prescriptive. Tocqueville insists, "I never, unless unconsciously, fitted the facts to opinion instead of subjecting opinions to the facts."[27] Yet, he freely shares his opinions on the advantages and disadvantages of democracy in America. Like Madison and Wilson, Tocqueville is a gadfly. All three are empirical *and* normative in their orientation.

Tocqueville's Methodology

Tocqueville spent nine months traveling in America, talking to a wide variety of Americans while observing democracy in action. He then returned to France and wrote an enduring classic. How did he accomplish this feat? Tocqueville's method may be key. His approach incorporates what is today called participant observation and interview-based research. He grounds his theorizing in concrete observation; a knowledge of particulars tempers his theoretical speculations. He works his way carefully from particulars to general conclusions.

Tocqueville's political science also mediates between theory and practice. In a famous observation from his *Recollections* Tocqueville notes:

> I have come across men of letters who have written history without taking part in public affairs, and politicians who have concerned themselves with producing events without thinking about them. I have observed that the first are always inclined to find general causes, whereas the second, living in the midst of disconnected daily facts, are prone to imagine that everything is attributable to particular incidents, and that the wires they pull are the same as those that move the world. It is to be presumed that both are equally deceived.[28]

Tocqueville recognizes that politicians and professors each know something the other does not. Consequently, Tocqueville's approach strives to encompass theory and practice, comprehending the forest *and* the trees. In Tocqueville's political science there is a warning for all political scientists: theory alone cannot complete the task of understanding politics. Experience counts for something. Marvin Zetterbaum notes:

> Tocqueville was in revolt against those of his predecessors who had looked on political things in an abstract way. To them, the political realm was like a geometrical system more or less deducible from a few simple axioms of human behavior. Hobbes and Locke had thought of civil society as developing, in accordance with these axioms, from a simple state of nature in which men possessed certain natural rights. However, Tocqueville (like Rousseau or Burke) placed equal stress on the influences of custom, tradition, historical continuity, religion, climate, and topography—in fine, on the situation of man in particular circumstances.[29]

Today, Tocqueville might be critical of political science as too abstract, mathematical, and simple. Congress scholars in the 1970s and 1980s turned to the rational-actor model borrowed from economics, just as Congress studies in the 1950s and 1960s borrowed heavily from group theory in sociology. Such efforts raise questions as to whether political science today has any subject matter or method of its own: does politics matter?

Tocqueville thought politics mattered, and he may have influential allies among political scientists today. David Mayhew's recent book *America's Congress: Actions in the Public Sphere, James Madison through Newt Gingrich* attempts to refurbish the study of Congress. Mayhew argues "members of Congress are capable of acting with a degree of autonomy" because "background political environments . . . ordinarily channel, influence or constrain moves by politicians—but they do not determine them."[30] Individual leaders in the public sphere can make a difference, in part, through persuasion.[31] Thus, individuals matter, and leadership is not merely followership.

The 1994 House Republican "revolution" was a wake-up call for political science, Mayhew argues, reminding us we need

> to take seriously the idea of congressional politicians acting in the public sphere with, arguably, consequence. This may seem an obvious idea to emphasize in studying congressional politics, but it is a recessive one in contemporary political science. There, in a deductively flavored kind of analysis, public officials are routinely cast as agents or instruments of societal interests or preferences—of interest groups, for example, or of opinion distributions residing in electorates—and, for the most part, that's that.[32]

Mayhew argues further that serious limitations exist to approaches that ignore "a world of politics that we experience in our lives, but, for some reason, tend to skirt in our scholarship."[33] Mayhew laments the loss of appreciation among Congress scholars for the independence of politicians acting within the public sphere.

> This may be a commonsense view, but it is not all that common within the boundaries of modern social science, where politics tends to be seen as driven or determined by exogenous forces such as classes, interest groups, interests, or otherwise pre-politically caused preferences.[34]

Mayhew insists, "I want to shake free from this idea of exogenous determination. Public affairs can matter; if so, it is worth focusing on."[35] Tocqueville, of course, would celebrate Mayhew's attempt to liberate and expand contemporary political science.

In a chapter titled "Some Characteristics Peculiar to Historians in Democratic Centuries," Tocqueville suggests that in democratic ages historians (read: political scientists?) will downplay the importance of individuals and look instead to "great general causes." "[A]n exaggerated belief in a system of general causes is wonderfully consoling for mediocre public men," Tocqueville intones, "while indulging their incapacity or laziness [it] gives them a reputation for profundity."[36] Tocqueville thinks such approaches surrender to "blind fatality" and deny "free will."[37]

Tocqueville also notes that Americans like to explain everything in terms of self-interest.[38] Contemporary political science may be a creature of our liberal-democratic regime with its tendency to look for general causes and explain everything in terms of self-interest. Do Congress scholars deny that individual leaders matter because any intimation of greatness offends our democratic sensibilities? Are we following the lead of Hobbes and Locke, as good modern liberals and devotees of individualism, when we explain everything in terms of self-interest?

Of course, not all Congress scholarship today is abstract, deductive, and general. Weisberg, Heberlig, and Campoli speak of a "golden era of Congress studies" in the late 1960s and 1970s that included the founding of the American Political Science Association Congressional Fellowship Program, along with classic studies by scholars such as Richard Fenno, Nelson Polsby, Charles O. Jones, and Randall Ripley.[39] Fenno in particular pioneered the use of participant observation and interview-based research. Fenno's "in-depth immersion into the life of a Member of Congress led to substantial insights," according to Weisberg, Heberlig, and Campoli, and "changed the way we perceive and study Congress."[40]

Fenno and Tocqueville have much in common. Participant observation, interview-based research, and case-study methods keep political science close to the subject. Ideally, such techniques offer an antidote to abstraction; participant observation helps bridge the gap between theory and practice. Tocqueville, too, used concrete, practical techniques, including

observing and talking to politicians, because he appreciated the importance of learning from practical experience. Again, practical experience
tempers and moderates the democratic taste for general ideas. He notes
in *Democracy in America* that "practical experience serves the Americans
even better than book-learning."[41] Tocqueville concludes, "True enlightenment is in the main born of experience."[42]

At the same time, this French social scientist maintains a discreet scholarly distance from democracy in America. He tells us his book is not a
"panegyric," nor is it partisan, and he claims "impartiality" for his work:
"[B]eing no enemy of democracy, I want to treat it with sincerity. Enemies
never tell men the truth, and it is seldom that their friends do so. That is
why I have done so."[43] Ultimately, the whole point of Tocqueville's political science is to educate democracy.[44] The importance of educating citizens to virtue is something the Anti-Federalists, Wilson, and Tocqueville
all appreciate.

Understanding Tocqueville's "new political science" provides a useful
point of departure for understanding his thoughts on Congress. What can
he teach us about Congress, and how does he mediate between Madison
and Wilson?

TOCQUEVILLE'S THOUGHTS ON CONGRESS

Tocqueville sprinkles some minor, albeit entertaining and enlightening,
observations about Congress throughout *Democracy in America*. For example, he praises the "natural demeanor" of democratic government; our
elected officials, he notes, are accessible, straightforward, attentive, and
civil: "American public officials blend with the mass of citizens; they have
neither palaces nor guards nor ceremonial clothes."[45] Later, he contradicts
himself slightly by poking fun at the "imagined capital" Americans were
building on the Potomac: "They have erected a magnificent palace for
Congress in the center of the city and given it the pompous name of the
Capitol."[46]

Tocqueville also notes in discussing state legislatures that lawyers are
naturally attracted to lawmaking, hence "their spirit penetrates the legislatures."[47] On balance, Tocqueville thinks that lawyers temper tyranny of
the majority: "[H]idden at the bottom of a lawyer's soul one finds some
of the tastes and habits of aristocracy. They share its instinctive preference
for order and its natural love of formalities; like it, they conceive a great
distaste for the behavior of the multitude and secretly scorn the government of the people."[48]

Such incidental observations, however, hardly constitute the heart of
Tocqueville's contribution on Congress. Tocqueville concentrates his
explicit commentary on Congress into a few chapters and pages; particu-

larly important is a chapter titled "The Federal Constitution" in Book One and another titled "Of Parliamentary Eloquence in the United States" in Book Two. As we shall see, combining Tocqueville's specific discussion of Congress with his larger argument in *Democracy in America* affords us even greater insight.

THE FEDERAL CONSTITUTION

While Tocqueville emphasizes mores in *Democracy in America*, "The Federal Constitution" provides ample evidence that he is aware of the importance of laws and institutions in influencing the behavior of individuals. Tocqueville follows Madison's lead in *The Federalist* in this regard. Institutional context and structure matter. The constitutional principles of bicameralism, federalism, separation of powers, and democracy define Congress' institutional context.

Bicameralism

Tocqueville's discussion of bicameralism represents a powerful example of his appreciation for Madison's institutional analysis. Tocqueville, like Madison, sees bicameralism in Congress as more than mere check and balance. The Constitution structures the House and Senate differently giving the two chambers distinct prerogatives and functions. Wilson, in *Congressional Government*, accepts the Constitution's bicameral structure, but from his perspective, the Senate essentially shares the same nature as the House. Wilson perceives the Senate as a useful, though modest and temporary, check on democratic sentiment. "The Senate commonly feels with the House, but it does not, so to say, feel so fast," Wilson concludes.[49]

Tocqueville, on the other hand, contrasts the true bicameralism of the federal Constitution with the illusory bicameralism of the state legislatures.[50] The U.S. House and Senate differ "in the principle of representation [as well as] the mode of election, length of the term of office, and diversity of prerogative."[51] While senators represent states, House seats are apportioned by population. Six-year rather than two-year terms, different chamber size, and generally different constituencies for Senate and House members all result in manifestly distinct legislative bodies filled with different sorts of legislators. If the House and Senate share the same nature, as Wilson supposed, why do they misunderstand and distrust one another? A hundred yards separates the two chambers, and yet to hear members talk they seem to operate in competing parallel universes.[52] The 2009 minuet between House and Senate Democrats on "cap and trade" and health-care reform legislation provides a case in point.

Tocqueville recognized the extraordinary differences between the House and Senate. In perhaps his most famous observation about Congress he notes:

> When one enters the House of Representatives at Washington, one is struck by the vulgar demeanor of that great assembly. One can often look in vain for a single famous man. . . . They are mostly village lawyers, tradesmen, or even men of the lowest classes. . . . A couple of paces away is the entrance to the Senate, whose narrow precincts contain a large proportion of the famous men of America. . . . They are eloquent advocates, distinguished generals, wise magistrates, and noted statesmen. Every word uttered in this assembly would add luster to the greatest parliamentary debates in Europe.[53]

"What is the reason for this bizarre contrast?" Tocqueville asks. He notes that election to the Senate is a two-stage process wherein state legislatures refine the popular will by electing each state's two senators.[54] The Seventeenth Amendment may in part render Tocqueville's distinction moot. Yet the House and Senate to this day provide serious bicameral differences due to the other enduring institutional distinctions Tocqueville cites above and the differing constitutional "functions" of the two chambers.[55] The House is purely legislative in its function, Tocqueville notes, whereas the Senate partakes of executive and judicial functions as well with its special responsibilities for ratifying treaties, confirming executive appointments, and trying impeachments.[56]

Tocqueville also notes that the *principled* bicameral distinction between the House and Senate is the result of a *practical* compromise between the Federalists and Anti-Federalists: "The spirit of conciliation caused diverse rules to be followed in the formation of each of these assemblies."[57] The Federalists, of course, sought a strong national government; the Anti-Federalists wanted a loose confederation. Arguably, each got half of what they wanted in the composition of the Senate and House: "The principle of state independence prevailed in the shaping of the Senate, the dogma of national sovereignty in the composition of the House of Representatives."[58] Tocqueville's observation that the Constitution's bicameral compromise "forcibly reconciled" the "theoretically irreconcilable" perspectives of the Federalists and Anti-Federalists comprises part of the larger argument Tocqueville makes about the Founders' new federalism.[59]

Federalism

Tocqueville's discussion of the Constitution's federalism places him between the Federalists and Anti-Federalists in the debate over large and small republics.

This constitution, which at first sight one is tempted to confuse with previous federal constitutions, in fact rests on an entirely new theory, a theory that should be hailed as one of the great discoveries of political science in our age. . . . Clearly here we have not a federal government but an incomplete national government. Hence a form of government has been found which is neither precisely national nor federal; but things have halted there, and the new word to express this new thing does not yet exist.[60]

Today, we have adapted the term "federalism" to designate the *new* federalism the Constitution created. A practical consequence of this "neither precisely national nor federal" (meaning *confederal*) constitutional structure is evident in the biennial debate over whether congressional elections are national or local. Following Tocqueville's insight, we can safely say congressional elections are neither and both. In the aftermath of the 1994 midterm election, for example, we now have the Gingrich corollary to Tip O'Neill's famous aphorism "All politics is local," namely, "Except when it is national."

According to Tocqueville, the Constitution's new federalism has additional important consequences. Like the Anti-Federalists, Tocqueville embraces "the small republic argument." He notes, "[A]t all times small nations have been the cradle of political liberty," hence he concludes "freedom is the natural condition of small societies."[61] Indeed, "history provides no example of a large nation long remaining a republic," therefore, "nothing is more inimical to human prosperity and freedom than great empires."[62] The primary reason, the Anti-Federalists argued and Tocqueville concurred, was that only a small republic can nurture among citizens the republican virtue necessary for republican government.

Yet, like the Federalists, Tocqueville understands the natural advantages of large nations in war and commerce. He seems convinced, again, that the Constitution reconciled the irreconcilable Federalist and Anti-Federalist perspectives by means of the new federalism: "The federal system was devised to combine the various advantages of large and small size for nations. A glance at the United States of America will show all the advantages derived from adopting that system."[63] In a nutshell, "[t]he Union is free and happy like a small nation, glorious and strong like a great one."[64]

Tocqueville is sympathetic to the argument of Madison and the Federalists in favor of a large republic with a strong central government. Yet he also agrees with the Anti-Federalists that republican government presupposes republican virtue among its citizens. The Constitution resolves this conundrum with its new federalism. Tocqueville opines, "Public spirit in the Union is, in a sense, only a summing up of provincial patriotism."[65] The Anti-Federalists accused the Federalists of taking for granted the requisite civic virtue among citizens of a republic.[66] Tocqueville argues, however, that the Constitution successfully copes with this dilemma by, among other things, maintaining with the new federalism a healthy, active state and local politics.

Wilson, in *Congressional Government*, resurrected the Anti-Federalist concern with promoting citizen virtue. Of course, by Wilson's time, the Civil War had largely settled the large- versus small-republic debate in favor of a large republic with strong national institutions. Wilson embraced the need for strong national-political institutions, but he united the large republic with the Anti-Federalist concern for republican virtue. Indeed, Wilson seemed to be promoting Federalist means to meet Anti-Federalist ends, as can be seen, for example, in his hope that the "informing function" of congressional deliberation could educate public opinion.[67] As we shall see, Tocqueville seems here to side with Madison.

Separation of Powers

Tocqueville also embraces Madison's understanding of the separation of powers, which is central to the debate between Madison and Wilson. In discussing bicameralism and federalism, Tocqueville notes the functional differences between the House and Senate and among the national, state and local governments.[68]

Similarly, Tocqueville, like Madison, understands the separation of powers as providing a clear functional differentiation among three distinct and independent branches. Congress, the president, and the judiciary are each independent and powerful within their own spheres while exercising their own functions. Our separation-of-powers system is in fact a separation of functions system with each branch organized and empowered to best fulfill its particular function and responsibility.[69] In this manner, our separation-of-powers system promotes both limited and effective government; our constitutional system promotes deliberation and energy. The separation of powers is not merely a system of checks and balances.

Unfortunately, Wilson and other Progressive theorists tend to reduce the separation of powers to the checks and balances. This may be understandable given the inclination among behavioral theorists to discount the importance of institutions in an effort to concentrate on individual and group behavior. But in reducing the separation of powers to the checks and balances, and in reducing Madison's argument to faction countering faction, ambition counteracting ambition, behavioral theorists lose sight of an important part of Madison's argument for the separation of powers.[70]

Tocqueville recognizes what Wilson seems to ignore in *Congressional Government*, namely, Madison's older, more complete understanding of the separation of powers. The separation of powers understood as a separation of functions reopens the possibility that our constitutional system can simultaneously produce deliberation and energy. In contemporary terms, the traditional understanding of the separation of powers articulated by Madison and Tocqueville may enable us to understand better Mayhew's discovery that divided government can be productive.[71] The separation of powers, even under divided government, does not necessarily produce gridlock.

Tocqueville notes:

> Democracies are naturally inclined to concentrate all the power of society in the hands of the legislative body. That being the authority which springs most directly from the people, it is also that which shares its all-embracing power most. Hence one notes its habitual tendency to gather every kind of authority into its hands.[72]

But the federal Constitution, unlike the state constitutions, provides an antidote to what Tocqueville sees as this dangerous democratic tendency. The federal Constitution makes the president and judiciary independent, strong, and free, each in its own "sphere." For example, Tocqueville notes, "The federal Constitution has concentrated all the rights of the executive and all its responsibilities in the hands of one man. . . . In a word, the Constitution, having carefully traced the sphere of the executive power, has striven to give it as strong and free a position within that sphere as possible."[73] Similarly, "the federal Constitution has been careful to separate the judicial power from all others. It has also made the judges independent by declaring their salary and their office irrevocable."[74]

Tocqueville knows that in a democracy, to borrow Madison's words, "the legislative authority necessarily predominates."[75] But Tocqueville, like Madison, sees an antidote to this potential danger in a properly structured separation of powers. Completing the argument begun above, Tocqueville concludes:

> Two main dangers threaten the existence of democracies: Complete subjection of the legislative power to the will of the electoral body. Concentration of all the other powers of government in the hands of the legislative power. The lawgivers of the states favored the growth of these dangers. The lawgivers of the Union did what they could to render them less formidable.[76]

Elsewhere in *Democracy in America*, Tocqueville notes how the American democratic experiment makes effective use of a functional division of labor he dubs "the great principle of political economy."[77] In an earlier discussion of public administration, Tocqueville notes the importance of specialization coupled with distinct spheres of responsibility: "[T]here is another way of diminishing the influence of authority without depriving society of some of its rights or paralyzing its efforts by dividing the use of its powers among several hands. Functions can be multiplied and each man given enough authority to carry out his particular duty."[78] The Constitution does the same for the Congress, presidency, and courts, as well as for the national and state governments. Tocqueville sees the same principle of political economy in the constitutional separation of powers.

Tocqueville's discussion of bicameralism, federalism, and the separation of powers focuses on the subtle effect of institutional and constitutional structure. The constitutional principles of bicameralism, federalism, and separation of powers combine to promote deliberation and energy; the same principles combine to make Congress both local and national. Andrew Busch, in *Horses in Midstream*, notes that midterm congressional elections often act as a "check" on presidents, but they also can serve as "a positive tool for innovation," thereby offering evidence that the separation of powers is more than mere checks and balances.[79] Examples include both the 1994 and 2006 elections.

In *Congressional Government*, Woodrow Wilson overlooks this dynamic quality of our constitutional structure, especially the separation of powers, because he fails to appreciate fully Madison's institutional analysis. The theoretical debate between Madison and Wilson has practical consequences. Constitutional structure defines the strategic dilemma our two parties face, namely, whether to be part of the *government* or part of the *opposition* in promoting policy and pursuing majorities.

In the British parliamentary system, Wilson's ideal, the majority party is the "government" while the minority party is the loyal "opposition." Our constitutional system muddles this calculus confronting legislative and executive party leaders, especially under conditions of divided government. The party best able to understand the institutional playing field, however, may be best positioned to capitalize on opportunities to advance its agenda and ambitions. Once again, Tocqueville stands between Madison and Wilson, and in doing so he leads us back to an appreciation of the potential for energy and innovation in our Madisonian system. Indeed, Tocqueville may recognize more than Madison the potential for democracy to introduce energy and innovation into politics.

Democracy

Like Madison and unlike Wilson, Tocqueville fears the "omnipotence of the majority" because of its potential for giving rise to "tyranny of the majority" including legislative despotism. In *Democracy in America*, Tocqueville discusses "what tempers the tyranny of the majority."

What is too often less well understood by commentators is Tocqueville's appreciation for the virtues of democracy in America. Contrary to those who understand the Founders as antidemocratic oligarchs, Tocqueville notes in 1835 "[t]he institutions are democratic not only in principle but also in all their developments."[80]

Tocqueville elaborates, making a distinction Madison well understood between merely democratic and fully popular government: "In the United States, as in all countries where the people reign, the majority rules in the name of the people."[81] Like the Federalists, Tocqueville fears the people less than he fears the potential for demagogues to corrupt democracy. Tocqueville preferred fully popular government, that is, government by the whole people, to mere majority rule, that is, government by a part. Too often today we lose sight of this distinction between democracy and popular government.

Tocqueville appreciates certain advantages of American democracy: "What strikes one most on arrival in the United States is the kind of tumultuous agitation in which one finds political society."[82] He adds, "The political activity prevailing in the United States is harder to conceive than the freedom and equality found there. The continual feverish activity of the legislatures is only an episode and an extension of a movement that is universal."[83] Tocqueville sees this energy in American politics, together with the mutability of our laws, as both virtue and defect.

He ties the mutability of laws to the frequency of elections. "When elections quickly follow one another, they keep society in feverish activity, with endless mutability in public affairs. . . . for democracy has a taste amounting to passion for variety. A strange mutability in their legislation is the result."[84] Tocqueville sees both the advantages and disadvantages.

> Democracy does not provide a people with the most skillful of governments, but it does that which the most skillful government often cannot do: it spreads throughout the body social a restless activity, superabundant force, and energy never found elsewhere, which, however little favored by circumstance, can do wonders. Those are its true advantages.[85]

Tocqueville seems less worried about the constant turmoil and churning in our politics than do today's critics of the "permanent campaign."[86]

Tocqueville is not concerned about legislative instability, in part, because in America this "passion for variety" does not reach the Constitution: "The Americans often change their laws, but the basis of the Constitution is respected."[87] Much later Tocqueville elaborates, "They love change, but they are afraid of revolutions. Although the Americans are constantly modifying or repealing some of their laws, they are far from showing any revolutionary passions."[88]

The constant agitation of American politics, including perhaps the "permanent campaign" quality of our politics, worries Tocqueville little because the federal Constitution can channel that energy.

For Tocqueville, what tempers majority tyranny includes, among other things, the decentralized character of our constitutional system, the constructive role lawyers can play (including lawyers as legislators, and the beneficial effect of the jury system on the character of the American people.[89] "Juries are wonderfully effective in shaping a nation's judgment and increasing its natural lights. That, in my view, is its greatest advantage. It should be regarded as a free school which is always open and in which each juror learns his rights."[90] Jury participation can educate citizens to the civic virtue Tocqueville and the Anti-Federalists saw as imperative to republican government.

Tocqueville, however, did not expect citizens to participate in legislative politics, especially at the national level. Wilson, to the contrary, was above all concerned with the "informing function" of legislative deliberation; the primary purpose of congressional deliberation, he suggests, is to educate citizens.[91] Madison understood congressional deliberation as a filter meant to "refine and enlarge the public views," empowering elected representatives to discern, articulate, and act upon the public interest.[92] Like Madison and unlike Wilson, Tocqueville did not expect congressional deliberations to educate citizens to virtue; indeed, Tocqueville exhibits little appreciation for what Wilson calls the "informing function." Congressional deliberations may educate members, but Tocqueville, unlike Wilson, hardly expected legislative debate to educate citizens in the most basic sense.[93]

Tocqueville seems closer to Madison than Wilson in his discussion of the federal Constitution, including his observations about bicameralism, federalism, separation of powers, and democracy. Yet Tocqueville anticipates Wilson's rejection of Madison's political science with his emphasis in *Democracy in America* on culture and mores over laws and institutions. Moreover, like Wilson, Tocqueville's analysis of American politics focuses on the political behavior of groups, including voluntary associations. Tocqueville, like the Anti-Federalists and Wilson, also appreciates the importance of educating citizens to republican virtue because Tocqueville, like the Anti-Federalists and Wilson, saw the essential defect of Madisonian pluralism as its tendency to augment selfishness rather than public spiritedness. Tocqueville synthesizes Federalist and Anti-Federalist thought.

PARLIAMENTARY ELOQUENCE

> To a foreigner almost all the Americans' domestic quarrels seem at the first glance either incomprehensible or puerile, and one does not know whether to pity a people that takes such wretched trifles seriously or to envy the luck enabling it to do so.[94]

Small parties, rife with petty partisanship, rather than great parties, dominate American politics, Tocqueville concludes. Small parties quibble over competing "material interests," unlike great parties, which contend over grand "principles."[95] Unlike Woodrow Wilson and neo-Wilsonian critics of the "permanent campaign" quality of our politics today, Tocqueville seems only mildly distressed by the, at times, "puerile" quality of political discourse; Tocqueville understands the democratic origins of our often petty partisanship. In an observation of enormous import, if accurate, Tocqueville notes "it is natural that democratic representatives think more about their *constituents* than about their party, while those of aristocracies think more of *party* than of constituents."[96]

Do congressional parties and representatives focus more on small, constituent interests, rather than the great questions of grand partisanship? Do our democratic parties advance material interests more than grand principles, a politics of interests rather than a politics of ideas, pluralism rather than "party government"?[97] Seemingly they do. On the other hand, does "politics" never give way to serious policymaking? Does campaigning invariably trump governing? Are American politicians addicted to the "permanent campaign"? Perhaps not. While our politics is often petty, puerile, and pluralistic, politics does *not* permanently crowd out the pursuit of policy on the Hill. Members are often attentive to sober policymaking, even though the legislative process is firmly grounded in factionalism and partisan concerns.[98]

At a minimum, our constitutional system blurs the strategic dilemma confronting legislative parties, namely, whether to be part of the "government" or part of the "opposition." Arguably, both parties at all times are both "government" and "opposition," even under united party government since Congress is not merely a majoritarian institution.

Just as our constitutional system is neither simply federal (in the older sense of the Articles of Confederation), nor simply national, so too, it may be neither simply pluralist, nor simply majoritarian. We have an incomplete pluralist and incomplete majoritarian system. Neither term nor tendency completely captures the "dual nature" of Congress, yet both contain an element of truth.[99] Congress is both local and national in its orientation, both pluralist and majoritarian. Congressional elections typically turn on local, parochial considerations, yet that certainly was not the full explanation for the 1994 congressional "tsunami" and its aftermath in the 104th Congress. The same can be said for the 2006 and 2008 elections. For legislative party leaders, learning to govern requires balancing compromise and confrontation along with attentiveness to both local concerns and national party principles.[100]

Woodrow Wilson lamented the dismal, even petty, quality of legislative debate and partisan competition in Congress. Without using the term, he lamented the "permanent campaign" quality of American politics. In our separation-of-powers system, we typically fail to fully distinguish one party as the "government" and the other party as the "opposition," hence "politics" remains perpetual, pervasive, and permanent.

Neo-Wilsonian reformers bemoan the tawdry quality of democratic discourse in America, longing instead for the purportedly more uplifting and enlightening qualities of "responsible party government." But if Tocqueville is correct in his observation above, the British "party government" ideal, rooted in the vestiges of an English aristocratic tradition, may not be transferable to the American political culture. Again, if Tocqueville is correct, the "permanent campaign" may be a permanent characteristic of *democracy* in America for both constitutional and cultural reasons.

The parochialism of congressional politics, often decried by party government reformers, is a function of our democratic Constitution and culture. Tocqueville notes the typical attitude of American voters and constituents:

> The electors see their representative not only as a legislator for the state but also as the natural protector of local interests in the legislature; indeed, they almost seem to think that he has a power of attorney to represent each constituent, and they trust him to be as eager in their private interests as in those of the country.[101]

Naturally, our democratic Constitution and culture affect legislative discourse. In a discussion of parliamentary eloquence worth quoting at length, Tocqueville notes:

> It follows that all laws making the deputy more dependent on his constituents affect not only the behavior of the legislators . . . but also their language. The influence is both on the substance of business and on the way it is discussed.[102]

Tocqueville elaborates in a passage that has echoes familiar to C-SPAN viewers today:

> There is hardly a congressman prepared to go home until he has at least one speech printed and sent to his constituents, and he won't let anybody interrupt his harangue until he has made all his useful suggestions about the twenty-four states of the Union, and especially the district he represents. So his audience has to listen to great general truths which he often does not understand himself and makes a muddle of exposing, and very minute particulars which he has not much chance of verifying or explaining. Consequently the debates of that great assembly are frequently vague and perplexed, seeming to be dragged, rather than to march, to the intended goal. Something of this sort must, I think, always happen in public democratic assemblies. Lucky circumstances and good laws might combine to provide a democratic legislature with much more remarkable men than those sent by the Americans to Congress. But nothing will ever stop the mediocrities who do get there from complacently airing all their views. I do not think this ill can be entirely cured, for it is not solely due to rules of procedure, but to *the constitution both of Congress and of the whole country.*[103]

Tocqueville's discussion of parliamentary eloquence in America offers little solace to Wilson who had high hopes for the "informing function" of Congress. Tocqueville sees little chance Congress will commonly promote grand legislative debates. Even if we were to institute Oxford Union–style debates in Congress, as some reformers wish, the nature of our constitutional democracy probably precludes regular recourse to a grand politics of ideas premised on party government. The failure of just such an experiment with Oxford Union–style debates in the mid-1990s underscores the limitations of party government in our constitutional context.

Though at times responsive to party principle and the role of ideas, congressional deliberations will typically remain local and parochial, focused on competing pluralist interests rather than grand ideological combat. Moreover, given our separation-of-powers system, we will always blend "government" and "opposition," governing and campaigning, policy and politics, ideas and interests.

In spite of the often "puerile" character of our politics, Tocqueville remains impressed with democracy in America. Indeed, he waxes eloquent when discussing the enormous potential for serious republican deliberation, even absent grand parliamentary eloquence. In a Book One subchapter titled "Concerning the Republican Institutions of the United States and Their Chances of Survival," Tocqueville remarks:

> What is meant by "republic" in the United States is the slow and quiet action of society upon itself. It is an orderly state really founded on the enlightened will of the people. It is a conciliatory government under which resolutions have time to ripen, being discussed with deliberation and executed only when mature.[104]

He continues:

> In the United States "republic" means the tranquil reign of the majority. The majority, when it has had time to examine itself and to prove its standing, is the common source of every power. But even then the majority is not all-powerful. Humanity, justice, and reason stand above it in the moral order; and in the world of politics, acquired rights take precedence over it.[105]

In the American democratic republic, Tocqueville concludes, majorities recognize their limits and respect rights. The democratic republic in America, founded on our Constitution and our culture, is, Tocqueville argues, beyond contention; it has become, he says, a *"consensus universalis."*[106]

While Tocqueville sees our legislative politics as largely consisting of competition among petty, local, pluralist interests, he remains optimistic in part because majority sentiment in America respects individual rights. America is a *liberal* democracy. Tocqueville is optimistic because he sees a role for reason and deliberation in American politics; the *enlightened* will of the people governs. Finally, Tocqueville is optimistic because he understands the dual nature of Congress as an institution responsive to both competing interests and competing ideas. Tocqueville sees Congress in both "Madisonian" and "Wilsonian" terms; once again, Tocqueville mediates between Madison and Wilson, combining the realism of one with the idealism of the other. To understand Tocqueville's optimism, we need to examine the relevance to Congress of the heart of Tocqueville's argument.

SELF-INTEREST PROPERLY UNDERSTOOD

The cornerstone of Tocqueville's political science, as noted above, is the idea that enlightenment flows from experience:

> The citizen of the United States has not obtained his practical knowledge and his positive notions from books; his literary education has prepared him to receive them but has not furnished them. It is by taking a share in legislation that the American learns to know the law; it is by governing that he becomes educated about the formalities of government. The great work of society is daily performed before his eyes, and so to say, under his hands.[107]

Tocqueville follows his chapter on parliamentary eloquence with a lengthy discussion of the beneficial effects of practical institutions on mores. According to Tocqueville, the practical experience of self-government teaches Americans the "art of association" and that peculiar American virtue he calls "self-interest properly understood."[108] Tocqueville reports that in America "the technique of association becomes the mother of every other technique; everyone studies and applies it."[109]

In the large American republic, most citizens cannot actively participate in politics in our nation's capital. Nevertheless, the federal system invites citizen participation at the state and local level.[110] The Constitution's administrative decentralization invites the creation of a plethora of voluntary associations within which this "nation of joiners" gains practical experience in self-government.[111] For Tocqueville, as for the Anti-Federalists, self-government begins with governing oneself. Republican government presupposes republican virtue, and for Tocqueville self-interest properly understood offers a serviceable substitute for civic virtue.

While the average American cannot—or at least does not—participate directly in our national politics beyond voting, we can readily apply to Congress the larger argument Tocqueville makes about political participation teaching the art of association and self-interest properly understood. Members of Congress clearly learn the art of association and self-interest properly understood while participating in the legislative process. Tocqueville has much to teach us about the mores and culture of Congress.

Tocqueville, like the Anti-Federalists and Wilson, criticized the tendency of Madisonian pluralism to augment individualism. Wilson, however, never looked seriously at Tocqueville; hence, he seems not to recognize the possibility of "self-interest *properly understood.*" Rather, Wilson seems to see only a stark choice between a self-interested and a public-spirited politics. Tocqueville offers a middle ground.

In a chapter titled "How Americans Combat the Effects of Individualism by Free Institutions," Tocqueville notes, "Citizens who are bound to take part in public affairs must turn from their private interests and occasionally take a look at something other than themselves.[112] In a passage applicable to members of Congress he says:

> Under a free government most public officials are elected, so men whose great gifts and aspirations are too closely circumscribed in private life daily feel that they cannot do without the people around them. It thus happens that ambition makes a man care for his fellows, and, in a sense, he often finds his self-interest in forgetting about himself. I know that one can point to all the intrigues caused by an election, the dishonorable means often used by candidates and the calumnies spread by their enemies. These do give rise to feelings of hatred, and the more frequent the elections, the worse they are. Those are great ills, no doubt, but passing ones, whereas the benefits that attend them remain.[113]

Tocqueville fears neither ambition nor the petty politics of the "permanent campaign."[114] This may sound ironic given Tocqueville's well-known distaste for majority tyranny, yet Tocqueville clearly believes the cure for the defects of democracy can be found in American practice: "The Americans have used liberty to combat the individualism born of equality, and they have won."[115] Federalism is a large part of that solution: "They thought it also right to give each part of the land its own political life so that there should be an infinite number of occasions for the citizens to act together and so that every day they should feel that they depended on one another. That was wise conduct."[116]

The administrative decentralization of the United States invites citizen participation primarily at the local level:

> It is difficult to force a man out of himself and get him to take an interest in the affairs of the whole state, for he has little understanding of the way in which the fate of the state can influence his own lot. But if it is a question of taking a road past his property, he sees at once that this small public matter has a bearing on his greatest private interests, and there is no need to point out to him the close connection between his private profit and the general interest. Thus, far more may be done by entrusting citizens with the management of minor affairs than by handing over control of great matters,

toward interesting them in the public welfare and convincing them that they constantly stand in need of one another in order to provide for it.[117]

Participating in politics educates individuals to a concern for something other than merely their own self-interest or ambition:

> The free institutions of the United States and the political rights enjoyed there provide a thousand continual reminders to every citizen that he lives in society. At every moment they bring his mind back to this idea that it is the duty as well as the interest of men to be useful to their fellows. Having no particular reason to hate others, since he is neither their slave nor their master, the American's heart easily inclines toward benevolence. At first it is of necessity that men attend to the public interest, afterward by choice. What had been calculation becomes instinct. By dint of working for the good of his fellow citizens, he in the end acquires a habit and taste for serving them.[118]

Members of Congress, as well as average citizens, can learn the art of association and self-interest properly understood by participating in politics: "Feelings and ideas are renewed, the heart enlarged, and the understanding developed only by the reciprocal action of men one upon another."[119] Although he applies his discussion of the "art of association" in these key chapters to the proliferation of voluntary political and civil associations, Tocqueville's larger argument, again, clearly applies to that assembly or "association" we call Congress and to the plethora of voluntary associations that spring up on and around Capitol Hill.

Washington is a magnet for, and an incubator of, associations. Within Congress we find an array of "voluntary" associations, formal and informal, permanent and ad hoc, including party organizations, caucuses, conferences, committees, and even social groupings. Are these not, in Tocqueville's words, "great free schools" in which members are "taught the general theory of association"?[120] From Tocqueville's perspective, the House and Senate are "great free schools" educating and enlightening members to a larger sense of duty and concern for the public interest—or at least a recognition that self-interest and the public interest cannot be so easily divided. Participation in Congress teaches members self-interest *properly understood.*

There is, for Tocqueville, a fundamental difference between self-interest and self-interest *properly understood.* As applied to Congress, self-interest properly understood means, at a minimum, learning you-scratch-my-back-I'll-scratch-your-back accommodation, more than the mere rational calculation of self-interest. For Tocqueville, self-interest properly understood as applied to Congress includes an attentiveness to the concerns of others and even to the public interest. Participation teaches a recognition of the necessary connection between rights and duty, self-interest and the public interest. Congress as an institution goes beyond mere checking and balancing or channeling of ambition and interest to the education and enlightenment of members. Congress is indeed attentive to ideas and principles, even if not in the idealized sense sought by Woodrow Wilson and neo-Wilsonian reformers.[121]

Again, Tocqueville, like Wilson, recognized the tendency of Madisonian pluralism to intensify self-interested participation in politics. Unlike Wilson, however, Tocqueville saw an antidote to this defect inherent in our constitutional system. Wilson and neo-Wilsonian reformers fail to appreciate Tocqueville's cure to this essential defect of pluralism.

Donald Matthews's discussion of congressional culture in his classic study of Senate folkways is useful in clarifying Tocqueville's point. Senators learn courtesy, reciprocity, and institutional patriotism, among other things, by participating in Senate politics and policymaking.[122] The importance of courtesy and comity is central to the effective functioning of Congress as a whole. Ross Baker, for example, cites the importance of "friendship" in the Senate.[123] Reciprocity includes the bargaining and trade-offs of Madisonian pluralism, in which one member's interests and ambitions are intimately bound up with those of others. Institutional patriotism underscores how the House and Senate as institutions elicit a larger attachment of the parts to the whole.

Members become part of a "team" inclined to defend the institutional prerogatives of their chamber against encroachments by "the other body" or the executive. Institutional patriotism entails a recasting of self-interest Madison would certainly understand and appreciate. Immediately following his observation in Federalist No. 51 that ambition must be made to counteract ambition, Madison adds, "The interest of the man must be connected with the constitutional rights of the place." Calculating self-interest is not easy; it requires a reasoned judgment as to what an individual's self-interest properly understood encompasses. It may well be in the *institutional* self-interest of members to defend the prerogatives of Congress, their chamber, their parties, and their committees. This alone carries them beyond a mere concern for their own *electoral* self-interest.

Participation in congressional politics educates members to the need for courtesy, comity, reciprocity, and institutional patriotism. Success as a legislator hinges, in part, on learning these norms. According to Matthews, participation in legislative life teaches other norms, including specialization, legislative work, and apprenticeship. While the culture of Congress may have changed since Matthews wrote "The Folkways of the Senate," Congress still values specialized expertise, and Congress often empowers knowledgeable individuals.[124]

Participation in the legislative process also teaches members to focus on the details and concrete particulars of legislation. Practical experience grounds the legislative process, promoting the inductive tendencies of practical politicians and deemphasizing ideology. The work in which members of Congress typically engage tends to focus their attention on local, parochial, material interests rather than on grand ideologies. Tocqueville argues:

> If, then, there is a subject concerning which a democracy is particularly liable to commit itself blindly and extravagantly to general ideas, the best possible corrective is to make the citizens pay daily, practical attention to it. That will force them to go into details and the details will show them the weak points in the theory. The remedy is often painful but always effective. That is how democratic institutions which make each citizen take a practical part in government moderate the excessive taste for general political theories which is prompted by equality.[125]

Certainly this applies to Congress. Members are above all practical. Congress can accommodate ideologues, yet they are often marginalized as "show horses" rather than "work horses."

The tendency of legislative politics to focus on concrete particulars is another reason Tocqueville remains optimistic. Participating in legislative politics also teaches members the need to compromise and accommodate the interests of others in order to advance their own interests and ambitions.

Institutions can educate citizens, including members of Congress, to virtue. Human beings are not *merely* self-interested. Today, politicians, journalists, and political scientists too often tend to explain Washington politics in the stark terms of self-interest. In so doing, they may be echoing the critique of Wilson and neo-Wilsonian reformers. Here again, Tocqueville's more nuanced and comprehensive understanding of politics and human nature provides a useful corrective:

> An American will attend to his private interest as if he were alone in the world; the moment afterward, he will be deep in public business as if he had forgotten his own. Sometimes he seems to be animated by the most selfish greed and sometimes by the most lively patriotism. *But a human heart cannot really be divided in this way.*[126]

Public and private interests are intertwined. Even during normal periods in our politics, self-interest cannot fully explain congressional behavior. A complete understanding of Congress and congressional behavior requires taking seriously Tocqueville's "properly understood" qualification. Often members properly understand and reason rightly about the connection between self-interest and the public interest. To suggest otherwise is to ignore the subtle, yet critical, dynamic of Congress as an institution and the culture it cultivates.

Congressional deliberation can educate and enlighten members of Congress, even if it does not educate ordinary citizens to virtue as Wilson wished. Participating in legislative politics, including both running for office and working on legislation, can teach members the art of association and self-interest properly understood. Such learning is an example of Madison's insight into how institutions affect behavior. Madison and Tocqueville both understood that institutions can go beyond mere channeling ambition to educating individuals. Participation in the legislative process—including floor deliberations—can educate members; the consequence can be more than mere compromise; it may entail real enlightenment.[127] Tocqueville understands the intimate link between institutions and mores, between our constitutional structure and our culture, between the Constitution and our constitution.

Our constitutional system maintains a healthy tension between pluralism and party government in Congress, as can be seen, for example, in the competition between committee and party leaders, between "committee government" and "party government." Perhaps Wilson recognized this potential within Madison's constitutional system, thus he sought to augment it in *Congressional Government*. Congress is not solely the politics of pluralist accommodation among contending interests, rather, Congress is also responsive to a principled politics of ideas. Note, for example, the evolution of the House from Speaker O'Neill's "All politics is local" 1980s to Speaker Gingrich's 1990s House Republican "revolution." Again, this is not to say our Madisonian system embodies the idealized party government Wilson and neo-Wilsonian reformers prefer. Rather, our constitutional system can foster strong party leadership and a principled politics of ideas, while grounding party and principle in a pluralist politics of contending parochial interests.

Madison might appreciate Tocqueville's middle ground, but Wilson seemed to ignore the possibility. Neo-Wilsonian good-government reformers and journalists tend to cast our politics in the sharp relief of a false dichotomy. They see a stark choice between a self-interested politics of interest aggregation, on the one hand, and an enlightened politics of public-spirited participation, on the other. American politics may not be that simple.

The separation of powers maintains a healthy tension between two halves of a whole. The dual organizational structure of Congress provides a case in point, as noted in the following passage from the leading text on Congress, *Congress and Its Members*, written by Roger Davidson and Walter Oleszek:

> As we have seen, the "party principle" organizes Congress. The "committee principle," however, shapes the measures Congress acts upon. These two principles are often in conflict. The first emphasizes aggregation, the second fragmentation. Party leaders struggle to manage an institution that disperses policy-making authority to numerous work groups. In short, leaders provide the *centripetal* force to offset committees' *centrifugal* influence.[128]

Understanding the dynamic of Congress requires comprehending the link between the constitutional structure and the culture of Congress. Political scientists, including Congress scholars, have much to learn from Tocqueville. Although he writes little about Congress, what little he writes provides profound insight and a useful corrective to our culturally induced tendency to emphasize self-interest alone. Tocqueville's insight into the link between institutions and culture, laws and mores, enables us to better understand the "dual nature" of Congress, combining the realism of Madison with the idealism of Wilson. Congress encompasses pluralism and party government, interests and ideas, politics and policy. Tocqueville mediates between Madison and Wilson.

6

~

The Federalist Revisited

To a remarkable extent essentials of the traditional regime are still intact. We live in a commercial republic, generating and accommodating a "multiplicity of interests" as the Madisonian system envisioned. We retain political institutions designed to register popular opinion and desire while allowing opportunity for the modifying effects of public deliberation and educative leadership. We are still committed (are we not?) to principles of liberty and civic order, liberty and equality, private rights and majority rule, despite the inevitable tensions among these goods.[1]

—Harry M. Clor

James Madison rules America. The Constitution governs. Institutions affect behavior. Our political parties are creatures of our constitutional system. The strategic dilemma confronting both parties in Congress, perhaps especially in the House, provides palpable evidence of how practically and concretely James Madison's Constitution governs the behavior of politicians and citizens to this day.

Of course, it is not just Madison's Constitution. While Madison is often called the Father of the Constitution, full credit belongs to the fifty-five delegates who attended the Constitutional Convention in the summer of 1787. According to Madison, *The Federalist*, penned by Hamilton, Madison, and Jay, stands as "the most authentic exposition" of the Constitution.[2] We might more properly argue, therefore, that Publius (Hamilton, Madison and Jay's pen name) rules America. The ideas and arguments of Madison and Hamilton, the two primary authors of *The Federalist*, provide the most authoritative insight into the workings of our constitutional system.

The Federalist, of course, was part of the larger ratification debate between the Federalists and Anti-Federalists. This debate taken as a whole provides even greater insight into how the Constitution governs as we noted in chapter 3. One cannot fully understand the Federalist Constitution without examining the arguments of its critics. Indeed, the Anti-Federalist critique of the Federalist Constitution accurately identifies the essential defects of the Constitution. Later critics, including Woodrow Wilson and contemporary neo-Wilsonians, echo the Anti-Federalist critique. Our political discourse and practice remain, in many ways, an enduring debate between the Constitution and its critics.[3] As Samuel Huntington noted in *American Politics: The Promise of Disharmony*, our politics consists of an abiding tension between our institutions and our ideals, between our Constitution and its critics. Our Constitution defines the institutional playing field of American politics.

To argue that James Madison, or Publius, or the Constitution governs is to suggest that constitutional institutions continue to influence and shape the understanding and behavior of politicians and citizens alike.[4] The well-known six-year itch in congressional midterm elections is an obvious example; our constitutional system presents a recurring midterm predicament for the party of the president. A second practical example of constitutional institutions concretely affecting the behavior of party politicians is the constant fight between, and perhaps especially within, the two parties in Congress over the best legislative strategy for advancing their ambitions and their agenda. One expression of this internal party factionalism, especially in the House, is evident in the enduring "two congresses" tension within congressional leadership ranks between party and committee leaders.[5] They fight on a playing field designed by the Federalists, again, perhaps especially Madison and Hamilton. *Our two political parties are creatures of our Constitution.*

In chapter 5 we observed that Alexis de Tocqueville in *Democracy in America* offers a healthy synthesis of Federalist and Anti-Federalist thought, a middle way between Madison and Wilson. While Tocqueville sees congressional politics as primarily consisting of competition among petty, local, pluralist interests, he also sees a role for republican institutions and majority sentiment in America, and in particular, a majority sentiment respectful of individual rights. America is a *liberal*-democratic republic. Tocqueville is an optimist about American politics—though not a naïve idealist—because he sees a role for reason and deliberation; the *enlightened* will of the people governs in the United States, he concludes. Constitutional institutions educate the people and the politicians alike to something like self-interest rightly understood. Tocqueville understands the dual nature of Congress as an institution responsive to both competing interests and competing ideas. Tocqueville mediates between the realism of Madison and the idealism of Wilson.

This is not to say that our Madisonian system embodies the idealized party government that Wilson and neo-Wilsonian reformers prefer. Rather, in Tocqueville's eyes, our constitutional system can foster strong party leadership and a principled politics of ideas, while simultaneously grounding party and principle in a pluralist politics of contending parochial interests. Tocqueville offers then a useful corrective to our tendency today to emphasize self-interest alone; he understands how Congress combines interests and ideas. Tocqueville offers a healthy synthesis of Federalist and Anti-Federalist thought. His *self-interest rightly understood* formulation is perhaps the best articulation of Tocqueville's appreciation for the role of interests and ideas, special interests and party principle in American politics.

DO TAKE A CLOSER LOOK

Tocqueville's synthesis invites us to take a closer look at *The Federalist*. Viewed from the Federalist perspective, contemporary political science has developed a narrow conception of the separation-of-powers system, a criticism largely premised on the arguments of the Anti-Federalists and Wilson.[6] Some today have embraced more the arguments of the critics than the drafters of the Constitution.[7] To anticipate the argument of this chapter, the constitutional separation of powers provides for *neither* and *both* the contemporary "party government" and "pluralist" models of the policy process. Neither model is complete; indeed, the contemporary notion of simplified modeling may be part of the problem. The Constitution is neither and both because it provides for a policy process that is more complex, more nuanced, and more complete than either the contemporary "party government" or "pluralist" perspective.

Charles O. Jones helps us understand the limits of the "party government" perspective while James Q. Wilson assists us in understanding the limits of the modern "pluralist" perspective.

PICTURES IN OUR HEADS

Charles O. Jones argues that politicians, pundits, and political scientists act and understand politics according to certain "pictures in our heads" because "people commonly reach for simple explanations" to explain complex phenomena.[8] One such picture in our heads, according to Jones, is the "party government" perspective, a prominent, albeit narrow and incomplete, conception of our constitutional system. In place of the "party government" model, Jones offers his "government of parties" perspective. The "government of parties" argument provides a constructive bridge to a more complete understanding of our separation-of-powers system.

Like Jones, Roger Davidson and Walter Oleszek observe that political journalists are often enthralled by a cynical "cartoonish stereotype" of Congress.[9] This entertaining, simple, and sharply critical "picture in our heads" tends to reflect the views of party government theorists. While there may be a large element of truth to party government criticisms— namely, that Congress obscures accountability, promotes gridlock, and is prone to special-interest domination—the party government perspective demonstrates how critics of the Constitution, influenced by the Anti-Federalists and Wilson, may have eclipsed the Federalists today.[10] Yet to fully understand Congress today, we need to begin with *The Federalist* and its response to the above criticisms. Taking Publius seriously will enable us to move beyond the modern Wilsonian reduction of our constitutional separation-of-powers system.[11]

Jones notes the "impressive creativity and flexibility" of our separation-of-powers system. He describes it as "an extraordinarily mature process, with a seemingly infinite number of mutations that are bound to challenge the analyst and the reformer."[12] Our separation-of-powers system is complex, constantly changing, flexible, and perhaps even protean in character.[13] It is hardly the static Newtonian machine described by Wilson and neo-Wilsonian critics and reformers. The party government perspective fails to fully capture the complexity and energy of our institutional structure.

Jones explains that such simplified pictures influence how we interpret elections and legislative policy debates. The party government picture in our head heightens expectations of election "mandates" and legislative productivity. We assume at times that the majority party has a mandate to govern; indeed, we assume that the majority party *is* the government! This assumption allows us easily to affix blame for failures. This clearly constitutes an overly simple explanation of a complex system. Similarly, we criticize a "do nothing" Congress that fails to live up to the standards of the New Deal or the Great Society as if such extraordinary legislative activity represents the norm rather than the exception.

It is worth noting that such pictures in our head also influence our understanding of party leadership battles including the Gingrich/Michel struggle outlined in chapter 1 and the Pelosi/Frost fight discussed in chapter 2. The party government picture may heighten our expectations as to what a minority party leader can do to gain a majority; when in fact, the fate of minority parties in Congress may be more in the hands of James Madison and the six-year-itch constitutional window of opportunity, for example, than in strategic decisions by embattled party leaders.

House GOP Ways and Means Committee chair—and former political scientist—Bill Thomas may be in part right when he insists there is little or nothing the minority party can do in seeking to gain a majority other than wait for the majority to stumble.[14] Meanwhile, James Madison may be constitutionally pushing the party of the president out the congressional door due to midterm losses. Even a minority party with a president of their party in the White House can feel Madison's push, as Bill Thomas's House Republicans understood all-too-well during the 1980s. One can see clear evidence of Madison's influence, for example, in the Gingrich-led Republicans' willingness to adopt a lose-the-White-House-to-win-the-House strategy leading up to the 1992 election.[15]

In short, the separation of powers, along with factors such as reapportionment, redistricting, retirements, and recruitment, constitutes one of the *fundamentals* of election analysis.[16] The separation of powers may matter even more than the role of money in politics to which journalists too often reduce electoral analysis. The fixation of the popular press on campaign finance provides a simple shorthand for neo-Wilsonian analysis, premised on the notion that special interests dominate politics. Certainly special interests and their money matter in politics. But is that all that matters?

Jones concludes that ours is a "government of parties" not "party government." The constitutional system promotes a plurality of parties, as witness, for example the plethora of acronymic party organizations on Capitol Hill: DNC, DSCC, DCCC, RNC, NRSC, and NRCC—not to mention the state party organizations. The parties organize themselves in accord with our constitutional structure. According to Tocqueville, America is teeming with many small parties.[17] Given the plurality of parties, is it any wonder that neither party ever truly governs? Even under conditions of united party government, neither party *is* the government—neither party *governs*. Did Carter and the Democrats really govern in the late 1970s? Did Clinton and the Democrats govern in the 103rd Congress—especially toward the end? Did George W. Bush and majority Republicans, for example, govern in the summer of 2006? In all these instances, the majority party had trouble governing itself, never mind the country. House Democrats approaching the 1994 election and House Republicans approaching the 2006 election had enough trouble governing the House. Given their internal party factional chaos, they certainly did not seem to be governing America. One might usefully ask: Do we have a plurality of parties or a plurality of governments? Neither the president nor Congress governs. Neither Republicans nor Democrats govern. The Constitution more often governs all of the above.

Robert Dahl and Charles Lindblom famously explained the effects of the Constitution's staggered election terms and diverse electoral bases:

> The strategic consequence of this arrangement, as the Constitutional Convention evidently intended, has been that *no unified, cohesive, acknowledged, and legitimate representative-leaders of the "national majority" exist* in the United States. Often the President claims to represent one national majority, and

Congress (or a majority of both houses) another. The convention did its work so well that even when a Congressional majority is nominally of the same party as the President, ordinarily they do not speak with the same voice.[18]

"[N]ominally of the same party" suggests that no one governs. The cacophony of voices within each party is an example of Madisonian pluralism at work.

Jones argues that it is not fair to evaluate the presidency by the criteria of "party government" because this is a test that it will fail; such "lofty expectations" are a burden for presidents.[19] Perhaps, then, it is equally unfair to evaluate the majority party in Congress by the criteria of "government" as well, for this, too, is a test that it will fail. In their 2006 book *Off Center*, political scientists Jacob S. Hacker and Paul Pierson frequently touted Republican "control" of the government. Control of the government or control of Congress may in fact never really rest with either party, especially given the individualist nature of the Senate. Whether voiced by political scientists, the press or politicians like Nancy Pelosi in the 109th Congress, the suggestion that the majority party "controls" the government or Congress condemns the majority to failure. This applies to either party in the majority. The observation may be as much partisan ploy as perceptive analysis. Congress controls the majority party at least as much as the majority party controls Congress.

Jones takes on another canard flowing from "party government" analysis: gridlock. Two points are worth emphasizing. First, gridlock may be good. Second, gridlock may not in fact reduce legislative productivity as is often assumed.

The Constitution provides for limited government in order to promote liberty. Democrats and Republicans can find common ground on this observation as witness the cultural libertarians among Democrats and the economic libertarians among Republicans. Jones posits, what if gridlock is a form of governing? The "prevention of legislation may also represent effective governance."[20] At times, the status quo may be preferable to legislative change. Who has not agreed with this observation at one time or another? Limited government, as opposed to activist government, may at times be desirable. Or as the humorist noted, "No man's life, liberty or property are safe while the legislature is in session."[21]

Humor aside, the separation of powers may not in fact limit legislative productivity. Jones addresses James MacGregor Burns's "deadlock of democracy," Sundquist's "stalemate," and Woodrow Wilson's belief that "you cannot compound a successful government out of antagonisms."[22] He might also have added the Anti-Federalist lament about "jarring and adverse interests."[23] Jones further cites David Mayhew's *Divided We Govern*, which raises doubts about the presumption that our constitutional system inevitably limits productivity.[24] The notion that the separation of

powers is reducible to the checks and balances and inevitably produces
gridlock is, at a minimum, incomplete, if not simply inaccurate. Congress
brings energy to the legislative process precisely because power is fragmented and decentralized.[25] Let a thousand flowers bloom, one might say.
"Federalism, separation of powers, and jurisdictional overlaps are opportunities for change as much as inhibitors of change."[26] Multiple veto points
may in fact be multiple access points in our complex legislative process.

Finally, Jones concludes that "competition" and not just compromise
may be good and may facilitate good government. Institutional and
partisan conflict may be necessary and healthy.[27] Confrontation—including partisan confrontation—is a natural part of the legislative process,
harnessing what Publius called the "spirit of party."[28] Jeremy Waldron
articulates another major purpose of lawmaking in a democracy, namely,
that of airing disagreement: "Legislation is the product of a complex deliberative process that takes disagreement seriously and that claims its
authority without attempting to conceal the contention and division that
surrounds its enactment."[29] Jones elaborates: "Legislatures are organized
precisely to invite disagreement, publicly identify alternative views of
an issue, and provide means for reaching an accommodation."[30] In fact,
according to Daniel Palazzolo in *Done Deal*? disagreement may be a necessary predicate to accommodation, as seen in the way the 1997 budget
accord followed the 1994–1995 budget showdown/shutdown.

Jones's "government of parties" perspective offers a useful corrective to
the incomplete "party government" perspective rooted in the thought of
Woodrow Wilson. Common critiques of our political system today—that
it precludes accountability and promotes gridlock—also find early articulation in the thought of Woodrow Wilson. Still, the party government
model fails to fully capture the complexity of our separation-of-powers
system. Jones's critique of the "party government" picture in our heads
provides a useful bridge to a more complete understanding of our constitutional system.

In a similar fashion, James Q. Wilson's trenchant criticism of the modern pluralist perspective also provides an important building block in
developing a more comprehensive understanding of our separation-of-
powers system. Both Charles O. Jones and James Q. Wilson enable us to
move beyond the modern reduction of the separation of powers. Their
arguments naturally lead us back to the Federalists.

INTERESTS AND IDEAS, INTERESTS AND DELIBERATION

In his 1990 American Political Science Association James Madison Lecture
titled "Interests and Deliberation in the American Republic," James Q.

Wilson suggests that Madison's two central essays, Federalist No. 10 and No. 51, contain all of contemporary political science.[31] Madison synthesizes the "two approaches to political science" dominant today, "one that emphasizes *norms and deliberation* and another that draws attention to *interests and calculation*."[32] Wilson argues that Federalist No. 51 focuses on the role of interests while Federalist No. 10 focuses on deliberation. Madison, it seems, thought longer and deeper about the nature of politics than we do today: "That Madison was able to combine both views into a larger synthesis and that we seem unable to do so is one measure of Madison's superior greatness."[33]

Today, normative political scientists often talk about the role of ideas, opinions, and deliberation representing majority sentiment in republican institutions. Empirical political scientists—modern pluralists and rational choice theorists—focus on the role of special interests, ambition, and self-interested calculation. Rationalists view normativists as naive, while normativists view rationalists as cynical.[34] While both schools can find support in Madison's thought, James Q. Wilson reserves special criticism for the pluralist and rational choice perspective since they may represent the dominant paradigm in the discipline. Madison, he suggests, was neither naive nor cynical but rather a realist in his more comprehensive perspective: "man is good enough to make republican government possible and bad enough to make it necessary."[35] Madison's larger view combines democratic pluralism with republican institutions; thus, majorities, intense minorities (special interests or factions), and representative institutions all matter. Politics is not reducible to one dimension.

The Anti-Federalists, Woodrow Wilson and Robert Dahl—whose *A Preface to Democratic Theory* is a cornerstone of modern pluralist thought—tend to reduce Madison's thought to interest-group competition or pluralism. Similarly, ambition theory reduces Madison's perspective to self-interest, and rational choice reduces republicanism to principal-agent theory. Yet pluralism is only half of Madison's argument, James Q. Wilson insists. Madison focuses on interests *and* deliberation as opposed to a reductionist modern pluralism, which reduces the constitutional system to interests alone.[36] One can readily see this in Madison's famous formula for good government at the end of Federalist No. 10: "In the *extent and proper structure* of the Union, therefore, we behold a republican remedy for the diseases most incident to republican government."[37] The "extent" of the republic encompasses so many diverse interests checking and balancing one another that majorities will inevitably be coalitional, yet the "proper structure" of our republican institutions allows for the effect of thoughtful and discerning debate and deliberation among competing opinions and principles. Intense minorities, complex majorities and "reflection and choice" all play a role in our politics. For Madison, interests matter, ideas matter, and institutions matter.

THE CONSTITUTION: LEGISLATIVE
OR EXECUTIVE SUPREMACY?

In *Congressional Government*, Woodrow Wilson laments the weakness of the separation of powers, and seeks to strengthen Congress. In *Constitutional Government*, Wilson again laments the weakness of the separation of powers, and seeks to strengthen the presidency. In a similar fashion, scholars today are of two minds about Congress and the president in the separation of powers. In their book *The Broken Branch*, Congress scholars Thomas Mann and Norman Ornstein lament a weakened contemporary Congress, arguing that Congress is the "First Branch of government."[38] On the other hand, presidency scholars Thomas Cronin and Michael Genovese in *The Paradoxes of the American Presidency* conversely bemoan the weakness of the president relative to an overweening Congress.[39]

Both perspectives, however, may be premised on a zero sum, static checks-and-balances view of the separation of powers with only modest appreciation for the dynamic quality of the separation of powers. Yet "legislative-executive struggles are not necessarily zero-sum games."[40] In fact, the president and Congress are both powerful within their respective spheres depending on the timing and the issue at hand.

Thus, both perspectives above contain an element of truth. Perhaps the two Woodrow Wilsons of *Congressional Government* and *Constitutional Government* together are right while either one alone is wrong. Wilson seemed to see the potential in each branch at different times, yet he failed to appreciate the fact that the separation of powers is inherently dynamic, energetic, and not reducible to a static checks and balances. Wilson saw the Founders' constitutional system as Newtonian; if, instead, we take the Wilson of both *Congressional Government* and *Constitutional Government* together, we may see the potential for a strong legislature and strong executive. The Federalists sought to create neither a legislative nor an executive supremacy system; while at the same time, they sought to create a powerful Congress and powerful presidency. Our separation of powers may include the potential for both an approximation of "congressional government" and "presidential government." Neither branch "permanently dominant"; both granted an invitation to struggle.[41] The system is less Newtonian than Wilson recognized; more dynamic, flexible, and protean than he understood.

The Founders clearly did not intend to create legislative supremacy, as witness how quickly separation of powers realities brought Newt Gingrich's short-lived experiment in congressional party government to heel. Gingrich and Woodrow Wilson, however, are not the only ones infatuated with the idea of legislative supremacy. Congress scholars often cite the famous Federalist No. 51 line: "In republican government, the legislative authority necessarily predominates."[42] They just as frequently ignore Madison's very next sentence:

> The remedy for this inconveniency is to divide the legislature into different branches; and to render them, by different modes of election and different principles of action, as little connected with each other as the nature of their common functions and their common dependence on the society will admit.[43]

The Federalist Constitution created bicameral competition within Congress to curb the legislature's institutional appetite.

During the Constitutional Convention, the Framers had before them two models of legislative supremacy: the Articles of Confederation and the British Parliament. They rejected both, choosing instead "a government limited . . . by the authority of a paramount Constitution."[44] In Federalist No. 48, Madison warns against the dangers of the legislative "vortex," adding, "[I]t is against the enterprising ambition of this department that the people ought to indulge all their jealousy and exhaust all their precautions."[45] At the Constitutional Convention, the Federalists sought to correct the defects of the Articles of Confederation by strengthening the executive and judiciary, creating a powerful presidency and powerful judiciary. For example, Madison (not Hamilton, as one might expect) argued: "As the weight of the legislative authority requires that it should be thus divided, the weakness of the executive may require on the other hand, that it should be fortified."[46] Again, the Founders clearly did not intend to create a legislative supremacy system, yet neither did they intend to create a presidency-dominated system. Rather, the Federalist separation of powers is flexible, at all times containing the potential for a powerful legislature, executive, and judiciary.[47] Each branch is potentially powerful, especially within its own sphere; therein resides the heart of an argument too often little understood.

THE SEPARATION OF POWERS

The innovative understanding of the separation of powers found in the Federalist Constitution is more complete than that articulated by the most thoughtful critics of the Constitution, including the Anti-Federalists and Wilson. In *The Federalist*, one finds a more complete understanding of the separation of powers than exists even in the thought of Tocqueville. In fact, one can find much of Tocqueville's synthesis or balance of Federalist and Anti-Federalist thought on the subject in the Constitution and *The Federalist*, properly understood.

One finds in *The Federalist* a more complete understanding of the separation of powers than one can find even in the writings of the most noteworthy political philosophers on the subject, including Locke, Montesquieu, and Hume.[48] To take the argument one step further, our separation of powers represents the modern invention of practical politicians at the Constitutional Convention.[49] Theory and practice need one another, and the separation of powers provides a classic example of practice completing theory. Intellectual challenges from politicians can often be as incisive, acute, and productive as those offered by theorists. The "combining mind" of James Madison, when confronted with the cauldron of practical politics, advanced our understanding of separation of powers theory beyond the understanding of Locke, Montesquieu, and Hume. The crucible of political conflict focused the mind of Madison, Hamilton, and other Federalists, producing a more comprehensive understanding of the separation of powers than found anywhere else. Unfortunately, today we have in large part lost sight of this more complete conception.

Since the separation of powers constitutes the heart of our political system, the separation of powers emerges as the key to understanding Congress. Publius understood this; but so, too, did Woodrow Wilson, which is why the latter targeted the separation of powers for special opprobrium. The difference between Publius and Wilson, however, is that Publius understood the modern separation of powers in all its fullness, whereas Wilson reduced the separation of powers to the checks and balances and inveighed against it at every turn. The separation of powers is not merely the Anti-Federalists' "jarring" adverse interests or Woodrow Wilson's checks and balances promoting gridlock—though certainly it is capable of promoting slow, incremental change, and even gridlock. The constitutional separation of powers cannot be reduced to mere incremental pluralism; rather, it contains as well the potential energy hoped for by party government theorists and reformers.[50] *The separation of powers simultaneously limits the abuse of power, while providing for the effective use of power.* Properly understood, it contains an approximation of both the pluralist and party government models.[51] Again, the Constitution provides for neither and both pluralism and party government.

Two simple observations help us understand Congress in the context of our separation-of-powers system: First, Congress is not Parliament. Second, Congress is not the president. The contrasts are instructive. Congress is not Parliament, as Newt Gingrich learned the hard way; yet Congress remains the most powerful legislature in the world, even though it is not the electoral chamber for the executive, as is, for example, the British Parliament.[52] What other legislative body can declare the executive's budget—arguably the single most important and complex piece of legislation in any given year—dead on arrival? What other legislature has the institutional capacity to then write its own budget? Congress is powerful; yet, Congress is not all powerful, as Speaker Gingrich learned. Congress alone is not the government.

Congress is also not the president. In examining congressional leadership, for example, we should not look for executive-style leadership; congressional leaders cannot command their troops; nor is Congress adept at executive action. Congress talks; the executive acts. In these simple observations, one begins to see a fundamental functional difference distinguishing the separate branches.

One additional observation is also instructive: Roger Davidson and Walter Oleszek note that Congress is actually "two congresses."[53] Congress displays a "dual nature." As an institution, Congress has two different organizing principles: the party principle and the committee principle—and they conflict! Congress has two sets of leaders—party leaders and committee leaders—hence, Congress often appears leaderless. What other large, important institution purposely organizes along two conflicting lines? Congress is not leaderless; rather, it may simply have *too many* leaders; thus, making it appear chaotic and leaderless. Yet such chaos may be creative. Party leaders and committee leaders often clash; though both are crucial to the effective functioning of Congress.

This dual nature of Congress derives directly from the separation of powers and the independence of the legislature from the executive. "The committee system," for example, "originally grew out of Congress' desire to assert its independence of the executive branch."[54] Far from being an impediment to congressional action, the pluralistic committee system makes Congress more independent and effective: "The United States is virtually alone among modern nations in that it has an independent and influential legislative branch."[55] Congress originates, initiates, and innovates. Contrary to those who see all energy as coming from the executive, our separation of powers cannot be reduced to the simple nostrum "The president proposes and Congress disposes." Congress, too, promotes innovation.[56] Congress remains powerful precisely because of—not in spite of—the separation of powers. Woodrow Wilson never seemed to fully appreciate this central feature of the separation of powers.

Yet how else can one explain the following insight by noted comparative legislatures scholar Nicol Rae?

> In the United States, with a strict separation of powers and a weak party system, Congress has survived as a much more powerful legislative body than in other democracies, with more independent control over the bureaucracy and a greater ability to thwart the will of the executive. Congress is probably better informed, better staffed, and gives more power to the individual member than any other legislature in the Western world.[57]

According to Michael Malbin, "Congress remains by far the world's most important national legislature."[58] Except when judged by the false standard of legislative supremacy, Congress remains powerful.

The separation of powers gives Congress its dual nature making Congress better at representing, deliberating, and legislating. The committee principle tends to promote a slow, deliberate politics of compromise among parochial interests, or in other words, incremental pluralism. Think, for example, of the Appropriations committees. The party principle tends to promote energy and innovation, with competing sets of party principles or ideas attempting to appeal to broad-based, often national majorities; in other words, something like party government. Still, committees and parties both contribute to making Congress deliberate and energetic; Congress is capable of "friction" and "fission."[59] At times, Congress approximates "committee government"; at other times, it approximates "party government." Never is it simply one or the other; both are constants of Congress—and constantly in tension. At various times Congress seems more one than the other, but at all times, both characteristics remain latent and continually define congressional behavior.

Likewise, Davidson and Oleszek note that members of Congress, unlike members of Parliament, tend to be local in their orientation, while Congress as an institution necessarily has national responsibilities. Is Congress in essence local or national? Both. The 1980s gave us Tip O'Neill's "All politics is local." The 1990s gave us the Gingrich corollary to Tip O' Neill's famous aphorism, namely, "Except when it is national." The 1994 and 2006 elections, of course, gave us a mix of both national and local influences. Congress is protean in its potential to encompass both tendencies in a healthy tension.

GOVERNMENT OR OPPOSITION?

This healthy tension within Congress helps define the strategic dilemma congressional party leaders constantly face: Do they want a law or an issue? Do they want to pursue policy and accomplish legislation, or do they want to play politics in order to have an issue they can take to the voters in the next election? Do they want compromise or confrontation? Do they want to be part of the government or part of the opposition? This is the central dynamic of Congress as an institution and the strategic dilemma confronting leaders and members at all times. This strategic dilemma accounts for a great divide within each party in the House.

Popular analysis sometimes translates this divide within each party in the House into ideological terms, for example, party "moderates" or "centrists," on the one hand, versus the party's ideological wing or base, on the other hand. While the division sometimes corresponds to such ideological differences, it cannot be reduced to the same. One can see this

cleavage within each party in the House as the division between prag-
matic committee-oriented members—for example, appropriators—and
more ideological, party-oriented members. As we saw with the competition between Bob Michel and Newt Gingrich, this great divide sometimes hinges on the establishment faction versus the "bomb-throwing"
revolutionary faction, the "old guard" versus the "young turks," or the
all-politics-is-local versus except-when-it-is-national factions.[60] All these
dimensions, and more, make sense. Congressional parties, especially in
the House, are rent by factional differences of ideology, style, generation,
and institutional orientation. Regional differences, too, play a role since
the ideological base of the two parties sometimes correlates roughly with,
for example, Northeast vs. South, East and West coasts vs. the Midwest
and West, or urban vs. rural.

While there is certainly no simple direct correlation across all these
factional cleavages, the great divide within the two congressional parties
turns in part on the question of legislative party strategy: to advance the
party's legislative agenda and electoral ambitions, should the party play
the politics of compromise or confrontation, be part of the government or
part of the opposition? This factional cleavage within the two parties has
its roots in our constitutional separation of powers. Again, in the British
Parliament, the majority and minority parties know whether they are part
of the government or part of the opposition. Our two parties, however,
are constantly stymied by precisely that conundrum. A key source of factionalism within the two congressional parties is this legislative dilemma
rooted in the constitutional separation of powers. Factions within each
party constantly fight over whether they are part of the government or
part of the opposition.[61] This intraparty factionalism proves that neither
party is ever simply government or simply opposition. In order to understand this strategic dilemma as a critical dynamic of Congress, one must
first understand the separation of powers as Publius understood it.

Madison's separation of powers is more than merely the mechanical
systems of checks and balances, described by Woodrow Wilson as "a
copy of the Newtonian theory of the universe."[62] The separation of pow-

Table 6.1.   Dimensions of Congressional Party Factionalism

Moderates and Centrists	Ideological Wing and Base
Pragmatists	Ideologues
Establishment	Revolutionaries
Old Guard	Young Turks
Committee-Oriented Members	Party-Oriented Members
Local	National
Compromise	Confrontation
Government	Opposition

ers is a separation of functions, dividing power and focusing authority. As Jessica Korn notes,

> By institutionally separating executive, legislative, and judicial powers, the Framers intended not only to encourage members of each branch to check the powers of the other branches, but also to produce a division of labor so that the members of the different branches would develop special skills.[63]

Premised on the idea that different institutions do different things, the separation of powers prevents the abuse of power, while providing for the effective use of power. It simultaneously limits *and* empowers government. This functional differentiation is critical to free *and* effective government.[64]

FREE AND EFFECTIVE GOVERNMENT

Responding to the defects of the Articles of Confederation, the Constitutional Convention sought to strengthen government, in particular providing for three strong and independent branches. The ineffective legislative supremacy of the Articles of Confederation gave way to three coequal branches, including a strong executive, strong judiciary, *and* strong legislature—each powerful within its own sphere. In Federalist No. 22 Hamilton outlined the dangers of an overly weak government with its "tedious delays," "contemptible compromises," "inaction," "weakness," and the "mischiefs that may be occasioned by obstructing the progress of government."[65] The Framers had enough of the weakness of the Articles of Confederation: "[W]e forget how much good may be prevented, and how much ill may be produced, by the power of hindering the doing that which it is necessary to do."[66] With the new Constitution, the Federalists sought more effective and energetic government. In a word, they sought to empower government, rather than weaken it as has so often been presumed ever since Woodrow Wilson's critique of the Constitution. As Marvin Meyers notes, Madison "never forgot that it was a twofold process: arresting the abuse of power and promoting the use of power for the public interest; cancellation and summation."[67]

The constitutional separation of powers consists of more than the checks and balances designed to limit the abuse of power. With the differentiation of three separate, independent branches each designed to best exercise its peculiar function, the Framers sought to simultaneously provide for the capable use of power by three separated branches each within its own sphere. Again, they sought free and effective government.

As Madison noted, they wanted "energy" *and* "stability" in government.[68] The key to promoting energy and stability simultaneously lay with the creation of a separation of functions system. As Madison noted:

> In order to lay a due foundation for that separate and distinct exercise of the different powers of government, which to a certain extent is admitted on all hands to be essential to the preservation of liberty, it is evident that each department [i.e., branch] should have a will of its own.[69]

Hamilton, too, suggested that the new "science of politics" had advanced: "The efficacy of various principles is now well understood, which were either not known at all, or imperfectly known to the ancients," including "[t]he regular distribution of power into distinct departments" and "the introduction of legislative balances and checks."[70] Note that checks and balances, according to Hamilton, are not simply the same as the separation of powers. The separation of powers and checks and balances represent flipsides of the same coin, but they are not identical. To reduce the separation of powers to the checks and balances, as Woodrow Wilson does, is to fundamentally misunderstand the nature of the separation of powers.

Indeed, the checks and balances exist in part precisely to maintain the principled separation of powers. Hamilton observed, "Unless these departments be so far connected and blended as to give to each a constitutional control over the others, the degree of separation which the maxim requires, as essential to a free government, can never in practice be duly maintained."[71]

> It will not be denied, that power is of an encroaching nature, and that it ought to be effactually restrained from passing the limits assigned to it. After discriminating, therefore, in theory, the several classes of power, as they may in their nature be legislative, executive, or judiciary, the next and most difficult task is to provide some practical security for each, against the invasion of the others.[72]

Note that political power is by nature of three distinct kinds—legislative, executive, and judicial—corresponding to the three separate branches of government each designed to best exercise its peculiar function. The function of the legislature is to legislate, the function of the executive is to execute and the function of the judiciary is to judge.

The Constitution organizes Congress to best exercise its legislative function. To effectively legislate, our democratic legislature must be broadly representative and deliberative. Five hundred and thirty-five members divided into two chambers redundantly represent (every citizen is represented by three members of Congress) and redundantly deliberate.[73] Congress is good at talking. The executive is good at acting, that is, good at taking executive action. A unitary, rather than a plural, executive promotes the energy, secrecy, and dispatch needed in the presidency.[74] In a similar manner, the Constitution effectively organizes the federal judiciary to exercise a dispassionate judgment removed, for example, from the direct pressures of democratic elections. Publius provides one of the best articulations of the principled, functional differentiation of the three branches in Hamilton's famous discussion of the judiciary as the least dangerous branch:

> Whoever attentively considers the different departments of power must perceive, that, in a government in which they are separated from each other, the judiciary, from the nature of its functions, will always be the least dangerous to the political rights of the Constitution; because it will be least in a capacity to annoy or injure them. The Executive not only dispenses the honors, but holds the sword of the community. The legislature not only commands the purse, but prescribes the rules by which the duties and rights of every citizen are to be regulated. The judiciary, on the contrary, has no influence over either the sword or the purse; no direction either of the strength or of the wealth of the society; and can take no active resolution whatever. It may truly be said to have neither FORCE, nor WILL, but merely judgment; and must ultimately depend upon the aid of the executive arm for the efficacious exercise of this faculty.[75]

Sword and *purse, force* and *will,* represent executive and legislative functions respectively. Judgment—applying general principles or laws to particular cases—is an inherently judicial function; therefore, the Constitution organizes the courts to best exercise that particular function. Similarly the "formation of the legislature" in the Constitution promotes "deliberation and circumspection."[76]

Congress is democratic, pluralistic, and deliberative. The pluralistic "jarring of parties" promotes deliberation while checking the excesses of majority sentiment. In sum, the Constitution's separation of powers is in truth a separation of functions designed to promote the successful exercise of legislative, executive, and judicial functions while simultaneously curbing the misuse of power by each branch.

SEPARATION OF POWERS, FEDERALISM, AND BICAMERALISM

The Federalist separation of powers perspective is more complete than that of its Anti-Federalist or Wilsonian critics, especially if we understand it as including the principles of federalism and bicameralism. One cannot understand the complexity of the separation of powers apart from federalism and bicameralism; the latter two principles inform—that is, contribute to forming—our separation-of-powers system. Congressional elections, for example, are national *and* local in orientation because of our peculiar federal system. Similarly, the bicameral Congress incorporates this same federal tension. Generally speaking, the Senate tends to be more national in its orientation, while the House tends to be more local and parochial.

In Federalist No. 39, Madison argued that the Constitution is "in strictness, neither a national nor a federal Constitution," but a composition of both.[77] The American federal system is neither and both a federal—meaning confederal—and a national system. It is neither a confederacy of independent states that have ceded authority to the central government, nor is it strictly national. Rather, it is a compound republic, an ever-fluctuating tension or balance between state and national sovereignty. The state and national governments are each sovereign within their own spheres, though the line demarcating their functions is ambiguous and in constant flux. In the twentieth century, the national government stole a march on the states, and yet Gingrich's Republican "revolution" was in part meant to rebalance state and national responsibilities, as witness the 1996 Welfare Reform Act. Like the separation of powers, the Constitution's "new federalism" both humbles and empowers. In principle, the national and state governments are each powerful within their sphere when exercising their designated functions.[78]

Arguably, we still have an incomplete national and incomplete federal system. In the 1830s, Tocqueville concluded that the American constitutional system is "neither exactly national nor exactly federal; but the new word which ought to express this novel thing does not yet exist."[79] The "new" word today, of course, is *federal*, meaning a mix between the old confederal and national systems. The Constitution, Tocqueville argued, has "forcibly reconciled" the irreconcilable, creating a compound republic encompassing, for example, congressional elections that are both national and local depending on the circumstances and the cycle. Perhaps Madison agrees with both Tip O'Neill *and* Newt Gingrich: all politics is local except when it is national. While congressional elections generally tend to be local in orientation, the 1994 "tsunami" and the 2006 "wave" elections were clearly national. Congress is more complex as an institution because of the federal character of our Constitution. Members of Congress, for example, must constantly tend to both national and local concerns.

In a similar fashion, bicameralism assures that Congress is more than the sum of its parts. Conference committees as the "third house" of Congress demonstrate this fact. Even though bicameralism is arguably the first "rule" of Congress, according to Walter Oleszek, "many accounts of legislative activity overlook bicameralism as a *force* in influencing member behavior and policy outcomes."[80] Like the separation of powers, bicameralism ensures institutional loyalty and conflict, thereby simultaneously promoting slow, deliberate change and energizing the process by inviting competition and innovation. Bicameralism provides both multiple veto and multiple access points for those who wish to retard or advance legislation; therefore, Congress is more deliberative and more dynamic. Bicameralism also augments opportunities for individual entrepreneurial ambition. In *House and Senate*, Ross Baker concludes that bicameralism promotes greater "vitality" in Congress.[81]

Like the separation of powers, bicameralism divides power and focuses authority. Broadly speaking, the Senate specializes more in foreign policy while the House specializes in tax policy. Consequently, the Senate Foreign Relations and House Ways and Means committees are more prestigious than their bicameral counterparts. House and Senate committees generally operate differently. House committees, sometimes called the "work shops of Congress," are filled with specialists, while senators tend to be committee generalists given the lack of a germaneness rule for floor amendments. The legislative process is more committee-driven in the House, and more floor-driven in the Senate.[82] Even though the Senate has experienced a "transformation" in recent decades, becoming, according to some, more like the House, bicameralism still makes for two very different chambers.[83] Contrary to Woodrow Wilson, the Senate is not "a small, select, and leisurely House of Representatives."[84]

Even though the legislative process evolves constantly within each chamber, certain broad differences endure. Generally speaking, the House is governed by majority rule while the Senate is more respectful of the individual rights of members. The House is more prone to partisanship and conflict while the Senate, operating by "unanimous consent," strives for comity and consensus. The House is more efficient and autocratic, and the Senate is more deliberative and at times chaotic. The House is more responsive, given two-year terms, and the Senate is more responsible, given six-year terms. According to Ross Baker, the two chambers represent two different articulations of democracy: adversary democracy and consensual democracy.[85] Bicameralism as a component of the separation of powers exemplifies the "confrontation or compromise" legislative party strategic dilemma in institutional form. Again, the House tends toward partisan confrontation, while the Senate tends more toward compromise and accommodation; *though at all times both chambers invite confrontation and compromise*. Still, bicameral differences provide an example of how institutional structure encourages different approaches to legislative strategy.

COMPLEX MAJORITY RULE

The institutional separation of powers, federalism, and bicameralism demonstrate that the Framers did not want merely democratic government or simple majority rule. They wanted what Madison called "popular" government or government by the whole, not a part, even if that part constitutes a majority. They designed republican institutions defined by the separation of powers, federalism, and bicameralism for the purpose of promoting the complex majority rule of a balanced republic. Complex majority rule means mere democratic majorities are not the "government." Majorities, including majority parties in Congress, do not govern pure and simple in either the House or Senate. Instead, the legislative process requires constant pluralistic coalition building, even within a majority party, in order to build temporary legislative majorities. In turn, these majorities will commonly differ as between the House and Senate.

Our constitutional system promotes democratic pluralism—majority rule coupled with competition among intense minority factions—an approximation of pluralism and party government. The three models of Timothy Conlon, Margaret Wrightson, and David Beam in *Taxing Choices*—pluralist/incrementalism, presidential/majoritarian, and individual/entrepreneurial—each capture part of the whole. Our liberal-democratic republic, they argue, encompasses pluralism, majority party government, *plus*. Our system empowers intense minorities, partisan majorities, and individual policy entrepreneurs.[86]

In Federalist No. 10 and No. 51, Madison outlines the republican, democratic, and pluralist character of the regime in words that echo familiar. "Enlightened statesmen will not always be at the helm," he tells us, and yet he expects these elected advocates to "refine and enlarge the public view" through deliberation.[87] The "principal task of modern legislation" is the regulation of "various and interfering interests," which "involves the spirit of party and faction in the necessary and ordinary operations of government."[88] In spite of, or perhaps because of, the "multiplicity of interests," Madison is sanguine about his balanced republic:

> In the extended republic of the United States, and among the great variety of interests, parties, and sects which it embraces, a coalition of a majority of the whole society could seldom take place upon any other principles than those of justice and the general good.[89]

Madison is confident because of the constitutional separation of powers, federalism, and bicameralism, coupled with the multiplicity of interests. Again, he summarizes succinctly his formula for good government: "In the extent and proper structure of the Union . . . we behold a republican remedy for the diseases most incident to republican government."[90]

The "diseases most incident to republican government" are factionalism and majority tyranny, or in other words, the excesses of pluralism and party government. Parties in our system are an approximation of majority factions. These majority factions are tamed by their inherent pluralist, coalitional character, and the "proper structure" of institutions defined by the separation of powers, federalism, and bicameralism. The

Founders designed the Constitution to cure the excesses of both pluralism and party government. An example might include the natural tension
within congressional majority parties. A majority party that seeks to govern by a partisan "majority of the majority" (perhaps an approximation of
majority tyranny?) may be in danger of rendering itself an ideologically
pure *minority* party. The 2006 House GOP provides an instructive example, as does the 1994 House Democratic Party. Congressional majority
parties that attempt to govern by themselves and arrogantly abrogate all
prerogatives for themselves will run athwart a constitutional system designed to preclude majority tyranny.

Finally, in Federalist No. 10 and No. 51 Madison makes clear that the
republican, or representative principle, by promoting deliberation, will
also guard against the dangers of both factionalism and majority tyranny,
the excesses of both pluralism and party government. Our constitutional
system is not merely pluralist, as Robert Dahl would have us believe, nor
does it provide for parliamentary party government as some responsible
party theorists and neo-Wilsonian reformers wish. Republican deliberation will help curb the excesses of factionalism and majority tyranny,
pluralism and party government. Madison is indeed sanguine for all the
reasons Harry Clor outlines in the quotation at the opening of this chapter
not least of which are the "effects of public deliberation and educative
leadership."

CONSTITUTIONAL REALISM VERSUS RATIONAL CHOICE

The Federalists were realists about human nature. They created a constitutional system of ambition counteracting ambition, interest counteracting interest. They assumed that most people most of the time pursue their
own self-interest. Yet our political system cannot be reduced to a mere
mechanical checking and balancing of faction against faction, ambition
against ambition. Madison cannot be reduced to the narrow, minimalist
conception of pluralism that Charles Beard and Robert Dahl imagine.[91]
According to Michael Malbin, coalition building and accommodation are
important in our constitutional system, and yet "large republics do more
than produce multiple factions and the Constitution provides for something more than a pluralistic politics of compromise and coalition."[92]

Immediately following Madison's famous observation "Ambition must
be made to counteract ambition" in Federalist No. 51 comes a sentence
too often overlooked by political scientists: "The interest of the man must
be connected with the constitutional rights of the place." This may be
the single most important sentence in *The Federalist* in that it raises the
idea that an individual's self-interest can be redefined by attaching it to a
larger institutional responsibility. Institutions affect behavior. Institutional

responsibility or institutional loyalty redefines an individual's—and a group's—self-interest.[93] Institutional loyalty can, for example, educate members of Congress to a larger sense of responsibility, thus changing their self-interest and educating their ambition. Following the 1994 and 2006 elections, for example, it became the institutional interest of the new majority party to defend the prerogatives of Congress vis-à-vis a president of the other party. Newt Gingrich's attempt at creating "congressional government" is a classic example.

The Federalists were realists, but they also recognized the potential for the "cool and deliberate sense" of the people to prevail.[94] Republican government presupposed the possibility of thoughtful deliberation: "The republican principle demands that the deliberate sense of the community should govern the conduct" of elected representatives.[95] The Federalists were convinced that the "mild voice of reason" could be heard above the cacophony of competing factions, and that government by "reflection and choice" and not just "accident and force" was possible.[96] "Enlightened statesmen may not always be at the helm" means, by definition, that sometimes enlightened statesmen are at the helm even if only rarely.

The Federalists thought deliberation required persuasion, the crucial link between inclinations and decisions. They thought it possible to distinguish between wants and needs and to prioritize the same because they were confident reason could arbitrate among the passions: "[I]t is the reason, alone, of the public that ought to control and regulate the government. The passions ought to be controlled and regulated by the government."[97] Politics was about both "interests and deliberation," or as James Q. Wilson observed, "[W]hereas economics is based on the assumption that preferences are given, politics must take into account the efforts to change preferences."[98] Legislative deliberation can change minds.

Deliberation matters because human beings are capable of self-government and are not merely self-interested. The Enlightenment theorist David Hume argued that people act not on their interests but on their opinions of their interests.[99] Publius took this a step further. In Federalist No. 55, Madison famously concludes:

> As there is a degree of depravity in mankind which requires a certain degree of circumspection and distrust, so there are other qualities in human nature which justify a certain portion of esteem and confidence. Republican government presupposes the existence of these qualities in a higher degree than any other form. Were the pictures which have been drawn by the political jealousy of some among us faithful likenesses of the human character, the inference would be, that there is not sufficient virtue among men for self-government; and that nothing less than the chains of despotism can restrain them from destroying and devouring one another.[100]

Madison was not as cynical about human nature as his Anti-Federalist critics, nor was he as cynical about human nature as today's good-government reformers and journalists who assume that all politicians all the time are merely self-interested and ambitious. Not even Alexander Hamilton was as cynical as some today:

> The supposition of universal venality in human nature is little less an error in political reasoning than that of universal rectitude. The institution of delegated power implies, that there is a portion of virtue and honor among mankind, which may be a reasonable foundation of confidence; and experience justifies the theory.[101]

"Virtue and honor" make self-government possible. Indeed, by the lights of Madison and Hamilton, self-government begins with governing oneself. Hamilton is defending the representative principle inherent in republican government, while Madison is making the point that "if men were angels" no government would be necessary—but we are not angels, hence, government is necessary—and possible. Or as James Q. Wilson noted, "[M]an is good enough to make republican government possible and bad enough to make it necessary."[102] Unfortunately, many political scientists today seem convinced that ambition and self-interest explain everything about politics. The Federalists, on the other hand, "saw self-interest as anything but a monolithic passion."[103] Human beings pursue, for example, wealth, honor, and fame as noted in Federalist nos. 57, 25, and 71. The Federalists also thought there was "sufficient virtue among men for self-government."

Ambition theory today is sometimes too narrowly focused on reelection. Richard Fenno, however, suggests that members of Congress seek power, prestige, and policy; their ambition begins, but does not end, with the desire for reelection. Perhaps ambition needs to include personal, partisan, and policy ambition. Certainly members seek reelection, though not always as an end in itself. Some members some of the time seek, for example, the collective good of their party. Members want to be in the majority. Some policy entrepreneurs have legitimate, albeit often contending, policy ambitions; oftentimes they wish to advance the principles of their party.

RATIONAL CHOICE AND ITS LIMITS

For a while in the 1950s and 1960s modern pluralism, as defined by Dahl, Lindblom, Truman, and others, threatened to become the dominant paradigm in political science.[104] Today, rational choice or principal-agent theory seems to have emerged as the successor to that honor.[105] Rational choice is a powerful tool for making sense of political behavior; moreover, we find in *The Federalist* "ample Madisonian support for a rational choice model of politics."[106] Rational choice has even become popularized in the media. Political journalists, borrowing from political science, have taught generations of Americans that all politicians are self-interested. Each year, for example, when I bring my Washington Term students to D.C. for internships, they all typically begin with the ready assumption that all members of Congress at all times are single-minded seekers of reelection. The students ardently believe this even before they have read Mayhew's *Congress: The Electoral Connection!* What explains the popularity of this assumption?

Tocqueville noted in the 1830s that Americans like to explain everything in terms of self-interest.[107] As creatures of a liberal regime, perhaps we are culturally conditioned to assume self-interest lies at the root of all. Charles O. Jones's explanation, which he applies to the party government model, might also apply here: we all look for simple explanations to explain complex phenomenon. A possible explanation for the popularity of rational choice theory among political scientists might be our passion for science. In many instances, principal-agent theory provides empirically verifiable models of legislative behavior. What's not to like?

But is rational choice *enough*? Can it fully comprehend and explain legislative politics? My interns begin with a ready presumption, and yet they typically come away from their participant-observation experience with a very different take on our politics. Often they come to see their member of Congress as a statesman motivated by higher motives including reputation, honor, love of the Senate or House, concern for the common good, patriotism, and even veneration for the Constitution. Curiously enough, the exceptions to this rule often are those students who intern with the press, in which case they often become even more cynical than when they began. Why do most of my interns begin with the self-interest assumption, and why do they then change? Perhaps it is because they have "gone native" and been co-opted by their offices; perhaps they have become politicians rather than political scientists. But, perhaps, too, they have seen up close and personal that self-interest alone is inadequate as an explanation.

"Politics is not physics," James Q. Wilson argues; hence, he concludes, rational choice is not so much wrong as incomplete.[108] Rational choice, like pluralism, tends to reduce Congress to "interests," ignoring "deliberation." Again, James Q. Wilson recommends a Madisonian synthesis. So, too, does David Mayhew in his 2000 book *America's Congress: Actions in the Public Sphere*. Pluralism and rational choice theory make "good sense," he says, but "I do not see any need in this book to cling to the theoretical purism of the electoral incentive."[109] In part, this is because "values" are not necessarily a fixed standard, and "[l]earning can occur."[110] Opinion expression and opinion formation both matter: "Members of Congress . . . can occasionally shape the views of their colleagues."[111]

Opinions and not just interests form the foundation of politics, and for that reason interests and deliberation matter.[112] Interests *and* ideas count. Madison argues in Federalist No. 10 that the latent causes of faction sown into the nature of man include differences of interest, opinion, and passion—in other words, not just self-interest. Opinions for Madison are not epiphenomenal, and sometimes human beings act out of passion divorced from self-interest. Reducing Madison to rational choice theory does not do justice to his thought. Politicians sometimes act out of motives above and below self-interest.

The Constitution creates a republican Congress that transcends the minimalism of rational choice, in part, by virtue of the "second half" of the separation of powers argument. The separation of powers is a separation of functions that promotes limited and effective government.

The *representative* principle means Congress can, for example, go beyond mere aggregation of preferences to "refine and enlarge the public views."[113] Congressional *deliberation* allows the "mild voice of reason" to be heard. Furthermore, because Congress is independent and powerful it can at times *legislate* in response to motives higher than self-interest, for example, duty, gratitude, and honor.[114]

In refining and enlarging the public views Congress can go beyond mere reflecting and aggregating of preferences. Congress can choose among and even educate preferences. From the perspective of rational choice, preferences are givens. Yet the "extent" of the republic, including, for example, the size of member constituencies, often means that there are so many diverse factions that members of Congress are forced or enabled to choose among them. The "extent" of the republic creates "slack" for members, who are empowered to choose among competing factional interests. The "proper structure" of the Union includes the republican character of our political institutions. The republican character of the system (fixed terms, six-year Senate terms, for example) allows more than mere "shirking" by rational members, it enables the exercise of a discretion informed by member motives both higher and lower, including a concern for the common good.[115]

As a young Congressional Fellow traveling in Wyoming with then-congressman Dick Cheney, I once witnessed him tame a room full of ranchers furious that the Defense Department was about to take some of their land by eminent domain. Far from acceding to the adamant demands of these irate landowners, Cheney listened, and then—a bit to my surprise as a Congress scholar—said no. He carefully and earnestly explained the important national security interests at stake. He also made clear he was not going to change his mind. By the end of the meeting, again, a bit to my surprise, he had calmed the waters. It was abundantly clear that these ranchers respected his stand on principle and even his courage in disagreeing. Afterward I said, "You're not behaving like a single-minded seeker of reelection." He responded, "I don't want to be reelected if it means I cannot do what I think is right on what I consider most important—national security." He also noted, probably correctly, that most of the individuals in that room would more than likely vote for him in the future. The republican character of Congress creates "slack," at a minimum allowing members to "shirk." Yet it also enables members to exercise a discretion informed by something more than electoral self-interest; at times, a republican Congress empowers members to do what they think is right, rather than what is merely politically expedient.[116]

Again, according to James Q. Wilson, rational choice is not incorrect, but it is incomplete. Joseph Bessette in *The Mild Voice of Reason* concludes similarly that the self-interest model (which he dubs the "political explanation") is incomplete.[117] Both *political* and *deliberative* explanations are necessary and useful for understanding Congress, Bessette argues.[118] Martha Derthick and Paul Quirk in *The Politics of Deregulation* argue in a similar fashion that interests are less powerful than assumed and ideas more important.[119] Likewise, Randall Strahan concludes that we need to consider both lower and higher motives in understanding legislative behavior. Ambition, interest, and passion are important, Strahan argues, but so, too, are reputation or honor, enlightened self-interest, and a concern for the common good.[120] The arguments of Bessette, Derthick and Quirk, and Strahan can best be understood in the context of Madison's argument that institutions can affect behavior. The institutional incentives of our constitutional structure are complex and changeable, capable of channeling and educating ambition, and even teaching self-interest properly understood. As Arthur Maass argues, Congress as an institution matters because it can redefine a member's self-interest.

According to Bessette, the Framers' republican institutions were an attempt to create "deliberative democracy." Deliberation, or "reasoning on the merits of public policy," involves collective reasoning about common concerns.[121] From Bessette's perspective, our elected representatives stand midway between Edmund Burke's "delegates" and "trustees," whereas rational choice theorists tend to reduce representatives to mere delegates or agents of the voters.

Bessette argues that the Founders hoped to institutionalize in our constitutional system the qualities essential to sound deliberation. The Constitution does this, he concludes, by solving four problems. First, it defuses majority faction by means of Madison's "extent and proper structure" formula. Second, it defines and delimits the reach of the legislative power through the principled separation of powers. Third, the Constitution fashions selection mechanisms calculated to attract into our national political life responsible and knowledgeable leaders (by means of large districts for example). And, fourth, it creates representative bodies that promote informed and reasoned decision making.[122] The institutional environment promotes deliberation by means, for example, of small chamber size and long terms. "Had every Athenian citizen been a Socrates, every Athenian assembly would still have been a mob," Publius notes.[123] The Framers understood that institutions, including institutional size, matter.

In *Congress and the Common Good*, Arthur Maass asks what is a member's self-interest? Like Bessette, Maass maintains that institutional structures confront members of Congress with the "problem of dominant loyalties."[124] In Madison's terms, the interests of the man are connected with the constitutional rights of the place, thus constantly presenting members of Congress with a problem of overlapping loyalties and transforming their self-interest. Preferences are not fixed. Maass's "discussion model," like Bessette's "deliberative democracy," suggests that deliberation matters because the institution refines members' "breadth of view." The whole controls the parts. The whole House, for example, controls the committees, since committee legislation must pass on the floor. The same is true of individual members. Their individual self-interest alone does not determine the operation of the institution; the institution also influences their behavior by redefining their self-interest.[125] A member interested in prestige or reputation within Congress is perforce going to be attentive to the interests of other members. Advancement within the party or committee leadership systems will require members to attach their self-interest to the interests of others, whether party leaders or rank-and-file members.

In *The Politics of Deregulation*, Derthick and Quirk ground their theorizing in a series of empirical case studies. They reject economic theories of politics, suggesting politics matters as well as economics. Particularistic views, including the reelection incentive, iron triangles, and capture theories, all fall short because single-cause theories cannot adequately explain the complexity of Congress and the policy process. Both ambition and conviction motivate politicians. Plus, the role of majoritarian influences, expert analysis, and policy entrepreneurs as idea vetters also helps explain complex policymaking.[126]

Paul Quirk notes,

> [M]embers of Congress do not pursue re-election exclusively. Contrary to the self-interest assumption, many act on judgments about the merits of policy issues or, more generally, conceptions of the public interest. They do so because to act in that manner is one of the major satisfactions of holding office and because, under many circumstances, it causes very slight additional risk of electoral defeat.[127]

Quirk also argues that politics includes the love of honor. Party and committee leaders, for example, desire prestige and reputation. Leadership positions foster a sense of responsibility to ends larger than mere private advantage.[128] In a similar vein, Steven Kelman adds that Congress as an institution promotes public spiritedness (a form of virtue) among its members, especially leaders with their love of honor. As in Tocqueville's "little schools of democracy," members of Congress learn the art of associating and self-interest properly understood.[129] Self-interest differs from self-interest *properly understood*, according to Tocqueville. In this sense, rational choice theory tends to be incomplete.[130]

Randall Strahan in "Personal Motives, Constitutional Forms, and the Public Good: Madison on Political Leadership" also recognizes "the more public spirited motivation of reasoned attachment to the broader public good."[131] Like James Q. Wilson, Bessette, Maass, and Derthick and Quirk, Strahan concludes that one cannot reduce Madison to rational choice theory. Madison understood rational choice, though he understood more. Madison's political science is more complex than game theory, rational choice, and principal-agent theory because it includes an appreciation for the role of enlightened statesmen, along with institutions that allow the "mild voice of reason" to be heard, and a willingness to discuss the common good.

On this last point, the willingness of the Federalists to talk frankly about justice and the common good, Strahan and the scholars discussed above, part company with much of contemporary political science, which finds such discussions of justice and the common good unscientific and conclusory. Robert Dahl, for example, in "James Madison: Republican or Democrat?" says about the Father of our Constitution, "[T]oday his contention that the public good can be definitely known by elected representatives would scarcely be debated."[132] Dahl is right in suggesting that the conventional wisdom among political scientists today sides with him, rather than Madison, on the "public good"—including the need to place such terms in quotation marks. Yet Strahan takes the Federalists seriously when they suggest that the common good is knowable and attainable.

Strahan asks, what do the Founders mean by the "public good"?[133] He concludes they mean the good of the whole, not the parts. They mean the long-term, not short-term good of the whole. They mean the ends of government. What are the ends of government? Throughout *The Federalist*, Publius speaks as if the ends of government are knowable and attainable; indeed, the authors of *The Federalist* echoed the conventional wisdom of *their* day in assuming the ends of government are attainable and knowable. They were good modern liberals who took for granted certain "self-evident" truths as articulated most famously by Thomas Jefferson in the Declaration of Independence.

In the Declaration, Jefferson tells us that the end of government is the protection of rights—liberty. The best means to this end is government by consent of the governed, or what we call democracy, though the Founders called it popular government. Among the rights that liberal-democratic government is meant to secure are "life, liberty, and the pursuit of happiness," Jefferson's reformulation of John Locke's life, liberty, and property. The public good, then, is the protection of individual liberty and the provision of the security and prosperity, or peace and prosperity, necessary for citizens to exercise their rights. Security includes domestic tranquility and national security.

Is this really so exceptional or objectionable today? Or is Harry Clor right in observing, as he does at the opening of this chapter, that the "essentials of the traditional regime are still intact"? Are we not still committed to "principles of liberty and civic order, liberty and equality, private rights and majority rule, despite the inevitable tensions among these goods"? We may differ as to our particular definitions of these terms and the particular means to these ends, but surely, our political system remains dedicated to these propositions. Indeed, we constantly debate little else as a nation. This is not to gainsay the difficulty of translating principles into practice or theory into practice. Yet after two centuries, we still find ourselves debating and deciding these questions of the common good by means of the republican institutions created by the Constitution.

In this sense, the public interest is knowable and attainable. Rational choice theorists, of course, tend to think the public interest is neither knowable nor even exists. Yet on balance, after two hundred years, the American experiment in constitutional government seems reasonably successful, albeit imperfect. The conventional wisdom among Americans today, including political scientists, is certainly not in favor of embracing some radically different political system. We remain in large part liberal-democratic republicans, having learned our principles and practice from Founders such as Jefferson, Madison, and Hamilton. Our constitutional faith remains secure.

The Constitution creates institutions, including Congress, designed to promote the public good defined in terms of liberty, security, and prosperity. According to Strahan, the Founders designed their political institutions to increase the likelihood of selecting public-spirited leaders and then encouraging them to advance the public good.[134] Members of Congress can "refine preferences" and "deliberate" rather than simply reflect and aggregate preferences.[135] Congress is designed to attract and even educate leaders. The Founders' constitutional system is more than mere mechanical checking and balancing of interests.

The Framers designed our constitutional institutions, Strahan explains, to increase the *probability* that enlightened statesmen will be at the helm.[136] Election from large districts increases the probability of selecting better legislators and public-spirited leaders.[137] The Founders expected Congress to be filled with more eminent and more talented representatives than our state legislatures.[138] Strahan notes, however, that Madison's analysis of constitutional forms or institutions serves two larger purposes.

First, our constitutional institutions channel and control lower motives. Second, they encourage and reinforce higher motives. The Constitution provides for limited but effective government.

The lower motives Madison hoped to channel include ambition ("the pursuit of power for its own sake") interest and passion.[139] The latter motive, passion, including for example religious passion, is potentially more dangerous than mere self-interest or ambition. The Founders were not unmindful of the particular danger of religious passion in politics.[140] With the First Amendment separation of church and state, they sought to limit the role of religious passion in our politics. Passion might also include an attachment to a particular leader or an ideology (arguably a form of secular religion). Unlike Madison, rational choice cannot account for motives more dangerous than mere self-interest, for example, the religious passion behind the 9/11 attacks.[141] It clearly can not be in one's self-interest, narrowly defined, to die for a cause. Ironically, rational choice may suffer from a limited conception of reason and rationality; rational choice may be in danger of ignoring man's irrationality. Far from being too cynical, rational choice may be naive.

Strahan also observes that Madison sought to encourage and reinforce higher motives, including a reasoned attachment to the common good, enlightened self-interest, and reputation. In other words, Madison thought elected representatives were capable of a reasoned concern for the common good and the adoption of a long-term perspective, and were susceptible to the love of honor. Madison, Strahan comments, saw ambition itself as governed by duty, gratitude, and pride.[142] Clearly, the category of "self-interest" is complex.

What, for example, is partisanship from the perspective of Strahan's higher and lower motives? At its best, partisanship or party affiliation may reflect a concern for the common good of the whole. Both the party principles of the Democrats and Republicans articulate, albeit perhaps incompletely, visions of the public interest or the good of the whole. Partisanship can just as often reflect lower motives such as the economic interest of rich versus poor or business versus labor or one industry against another. Partisanship can also represent lower passions such as an ugly, ideologically driven, blind hatred of the other side. This can be found in either party, especially perhaps at the ideological extremes. Partisanship may also reflect a blind attachment to a candidate or blind hatred, for example, of a sitting president. One thinks of the vitriol and anger directed at both Bill Clinton and George W. Bush—clearly a passion beyond any reasonable definition of self-interest. Rational choice may be in danger of ignoring the basest of motives.

Madison was not merely Hobbesian. He did not see ambition as an end in itself, nor did he believe the desire to be reelected was all that motivated politicians. Political leaders have reasons for their ambition.

Though Madison saw ambition and self-interest as prevalent, he thought politicians sometimes act on higher motives such as reason and enlightened self-interest or lower motives such as passion. Honor, too, plays a prominent role in the thought of the Framers. Hamilton calls "love of fame the ruling passion of the noblest minds."[143] Strahan observes that senators are sometimes motivated by a concern for reputation—their own, the Senate's and the nation's, along with a reasoned attachment to the broader public good.[144]

The Federalists also understood that majority sentiment may not always reflect the interest of the whole. Majorities can be tyrannical. The Constitution, therefore, creates "slack" so that leaders may discern and advance the public interest. The Constitution builds "slack" into the institutional structure of Congress (for example, six-year terms) not so members will "shirk" the interest of their principals, but rather so they might better "refine and enlarge" the public view.[145] Again, Congress is capable of promoting deliberation that is central to the role of Congress as a legislature designed to represent broad and diverse interests, and yet to legislate in the good of the whole. In fact, according to Hamilton, the diversity of factions—the cacophony of competing interests—can contribute to promoting deliberation:

> In the legislature, promptitude of decision is oftener an evil than a benefit. The differences of opinion, and the jarring of parties in that department of the government, though they may sometimes obstruct salutary plans, yet often promote deliberation and circumspection, and serve to check excesses in the majority.[146]

Political scientists including James Q. Wilson, Bessette, Maass, Derthick, Quirk, and Strahan underscore the limits of the pluralist paradigm and rational choice theory. So, too, do Madison and Hamilton in *The Federalist* as noted above. Other political scientists, including Morris Fiorina, for example, have shown, on the other hand, how useful rational choice theory can be in illuminating congressional behavior. Fiorina's *Congress: Keystone of the Washington Establishment* makes productive use of Mayhew's reelection incentive to explain the growth of government.

By any reckoning, Fiorina's *Keystone* is a major contribution to legislative studies. Yet Fiorina may be pushing his argument about the particularism and clientelism of American politics to an extreme when he says, for example, that the "main theme of this book is that . . . congressmen rarely vote the general interest," or "[p]ublic policy emerges from the system almost as an afterthought."[147] To his credit, Fiorina qualifies these sweeping conclusions using terms like "rarely" and "almost." He even speaks of the "general interest of the United States" and the "public interest" which presumably are knowable, and perhaps even attainable.[148]

In the second edition of this successful book, however, Fiorina responds defensively to those who dare to disagree with rational choice theory. He accuses others of making a straw man of his argument; yet he, in turn, is in danger of making a straw man of those who differ.

"This book is not immoral," he insists even though it is not at all clear that those who disagree with rational choice make such an accusation.[149] Nor are Fiorina's critics arguing "the primacy of public spirit over self-interest."[150] Fiorina seems in danger of caricaturizing the argument of those who emphasize "deliberation" and not just "interest" in Congress. Moreover, Fiorina seems to underplay key elements in the Federalist argument, for example, the difference between interest, opinion, and passion, or the ambiguity and complexity behind the term "interest." Is one's self-interest what one wants or what one needs? In concluding that public policy is almost an afterthought, Fiorina seems to be calling into question the very notions of self-government and republican government as understood by the Founders.[151] By the reckoning of Madison and Hamilton, government by "reflection and choice" and not just "accident and force" is possible. Again, the Founders took seriously deliberation and persuasion. They also understood that structure has purpose and that institutions can govern the behavior of individuals.

Ultimately, Fiorina's *Keystone* analysis of the rise of the Washington establishment in the 1970s and 1980s is powerful and insightful: "The problem with Congress is that congressmen conscientiously, openly, and as a matter of electoral survival assiduously service the special interests of their districts."[152] He laments the excesses of pluralism: "In the absence of the coordinating forces of strong parties or presidential leadership, the general interest of the United States gets lost in the shuffle."[153] Fiorina's solution to the narrow parochialism of Congress seems to echo the party government perspective of theorists like E. E. Schattschneider and Woodrow Wilson. Strong parties and strong presidents provide an antidote to the defects of pluralism. The solution to narrow particularism is to broaden the scope of conflict as Schattschneider recommended.

Fiorina's solution to the excesses of pluralism and the rise of the Washington establishment makes sense. He sees a need to balance pluralism and party government. He seems to be calling for the sort of balanced republic *The Federalist* created—a republic that balances majorities, factional minorities, and the rights of individuals. In his second edition Fiorina laments the decline of parties, the rise of the "personal vote," incumbency advantage, candidate-centered elections, and member staffs supplanting local parties.[154] He argues that the personal vote and clientelism seem to trump partisan concerns and national needs. Fiorina's laments reintroduce considerations of justice and the common good into the political equation.

JUSTICE AND THE COMMON GOOD

For the Federalists, however, there is no need to reintroduce concern for the common good. For Madison the common good is a staple of politics and political analysis; one cannot speak intelligently or completely about politics without discussing questions of justice and the common good. Ideas and opinions about justice and the common good, and not just interests, are the essence of politics. Moreover, spiritedness, including love of honor, the passion for justice, partisanship, and public spiritedness, is inevitably part of politics. Madison's republic balances pluralism and party government. Our separation of powers incorporates both perspectives in a healthy synthesis more completely reflecting the complexity of our constitutional system than either perspective alone.

Rational choice, pluralism, and party government are all examples of Charles O. Jones's "pictures in our heads." Each provides a paradigm or model of our complex policy process. Modeling by its very nature produces incomplete pictures. James Q. Wilson is right when he says that Madison's synthesis presents a more comprehensive view of our constitutional system. Madison understood rational choice, pluralism, and party government, but Madison understood more. The Constitution creates a Congress that transcends the minimalism of rational choice, pluralism, and party government by virtue of the "second half" of the separation of powers argument. The separation of powers is more than the checks and balances, more than the mere pitting of interest against interest. The separation of powers humbles and empowers factions, majorities, and even individual politicians.

The more complete Federalist understanding of the constitutional separation of powers precludes and includes pluralism and party government. Our constitutional system does not allow for party government yet cannot be reduced to pluralism. At the same time, pluralism is only half of Madison's argument. The constitutional system may not allow for pure party government yet it is not reducible to the mere pluralism of Robert Dahl. Rational choice is powerful yet incomplete. Interests *and* deliberation both matter.

Politicians, political scientists, and political journalists are constantly torn between the twin temptations of the separation of powers. As noted in chapter 2, the perspectives of Nancy Pelosi and Martin Frost both contain an element of truth even though they understand legislative politics in very different terms. In chapters 1 and 3, we saw a similar tension in the perspectives of Newt Gingrich and Bob Michel. Both are right *and* wrong. For example, our politics is local *and* national. Sometimes our politics seems more responsive to local, parochial interests; other times, national majority "waves" topple politics-as-usual, providing a wake-up call to those who see our politics merely in terms of the accommodation of competing interests. Our politics needs and has, for example, both "old guard" and "young turk" factions. As noted in chapter 1, the late congressman Barber Conable once observed:

> Old as I am, I recall being a "young turk" at one point and participating noisily in a successful effort to change House rules which the Establishment found adequate. I learned a lot about the institution from the effort, vented my frustrations, and gradually became part of the Establishment myself. Youth presses age, provides a good deal of the dynamic and the dialogue, and eventually ages. Partisans may not like the tranquility of my view of these recent histories, but I find reassurance in the cycle of renewal.[155]

The cycle Conable mentions is natural to all organizations, but it is also part of the dynamic character of our constitutional system and a function of the healthy tension built into that system. Congressional politics is a constant tension between the "establishment" and the "revolutionaries" as long-time House GOP leadership aid Bill Gavin noted:

> It's like good jazz: In the midst of his improvisatory explorations, a jazz soloist has to be willing to take musical risks because it is in spontaneous risk-taking that great things happen in jazz. But in order to succeed, the risk-taker needs a reliable, steady accompaniment that sets the formal structure within which the creative leap takes place. The underlying chord structure and rock-solid beat provide security and order: the soaring improvisation provides freedom and spontaneity. Combine both and you have the great synergism called art.
>
> The same is true in House politics. The rock-solid political establishmen-tarian, setting the formal "rules of the game," and the soaring political revo-lutionary, guided, but not dominated, by the limits, need each other. If the establishment dominates the party, it becomes paralyzed and disintegrates; if the revolutionaries dominate, the party becomes wild and explodes. A great leader uses both elements, without letting either dominate for any length of time.[156]

Politicians, political scientists, and political journalists all fall prey to the twin temptations of our separation of powers. A full understanding of our constitutional system recognizes that our politics contains elements of both party government—with its ideological, principled combat offering a choice—and pluralism, with its coalitional accommodation of competing interests. The twin temptation is a constant of our separation-of-powers system. Yet even these two dominant paradigms cannot do full justice to Madison's perspective. Even taken together, they still miss part of the whole.

The separation of powers empowers both the majority and minority parties in ways the British parliamentary system does not. Thanks to the decentralization of the separation of powers, "leverage" accrues to both parties at all times. The separation of powers also empowers individual members of Congress apart from party to shape debate in ways inconceivable in a parliamentary system of strict party discipline. One cannot imagine, for example, a one-person filibuster tying down the House of Commons. Mr. Smith could never go to Westminster. One of the many ways our constitutional structure introduces energy into the policy process is by encouraging entrepreneurial legislative leadership by individuals outside formal party and committee leadership positions.

As noted earlier, in *Taxing Choices*, political scientists Conlon, Wrightson, and Beam offer a triumvirate of productive perspectives, each providing insight into the complex workings of the policy process. Call it pluralism and party government, *plus*. Conlon, Wrightson, and Beam's three models—pluralist/incrementalism, presidential/majoritarian, and individual/entrepreneurial—each capture part of the whole. Our liberal-democratic republic, they conclude, encompasses pluralism, majority party government, *plus*; it empowers intense minorities, partisan majorities, and individual policy entrepreneurs.[157]

PRACTICAL CONSEQUENCE OF CONSTITUTIONAL PRINCIPLE

The most common criticisms of our political system provide practical evidence that our constitutional system incorporates elements of pluralism, party government, *plus*. Critics of our constitutional systems from the Anti-Federalists and Woodrow Wilson to contemporary commentators frequently complain that (1) special interests dominate our politics, (2) partisan gridlock limits needed policy change, and (3) neither party can ever be held responsible or accountable. The constancy of these complaints suggests—at a minimum—that they must contain an element of truth.

Of course, it is not merely theorists or commentators who level these criticisms. Practical politicians, including both Democrats and Republicans, regularly make use of these criticisms in denouncing one another. In our Madisonian system, either party, though perhaps especially the minority party, constantly has available to it various critiques of the other party premised on the systemic defects correctly identified originally by the Anti-Federalists and later reiterated by Woodrow Wilson. Special interests do often dominate our politics, sometimes producing at least the appearance of a "culture of corruption" on Capitol Hill. Partisan gridlock, whether in the form of a "do nothing" Congress or minority party "obstructionism," often seems to plague our politics. The system is prone to the excesses of pluralism and partisanship.

The system also seems to suffer from a third defect correctly identified by the Anti-Federalists and Woodrow Wilson, namely a lack of accountability and a lack of party responsibility. Either party can legitimately level this charge, blaming one another, because both parties at all times bear responsibility and retain leverage; thus, neither party is ever wholly responsible. All three criticisms above at all times contain an element of truth when leveled by and at either party. The Anti-Federalists and Woodrow Wilson correctly identify the essential defects of our constitutional system; hence, these criticisms are constantly available to the minority and majority party.

But that is only half the story. Special-interest pluralism often dominates, yet our politics is also responsive to majority sentiment, for example, the legislative activism following 9/11. Moreover, deliberation within republican institutions can "refine and enlarge" the interests and opinions of intense minorities and overbearing majorities. Gridlock frequently plagues our politics, until a sudden breakthrough results in significant change. Sometimes these breakthroughs take the form of partisan electoral victories followed by a flurry of legislative activity such as in 1994 and 2006, or even more dramatically in 1932, 1964, and 1980. Other times breakthroughs take the form of bipartisan compromises, such as the 1986 Tax Reform Act or the 1997 Budget Accord. Gridlock may even be a necessary predicate to energetic change.

The third common criticism, too, remains constantly valid, yet rarely seems to give way to ready resolution. Our separation of powers precludes party accountability or responsibility. Party accountability is virtually impossible because both parties at all times are constantly part of the government and part of the opposition. Neo-Wilsonian Lloyd Cutler is right when he complains that, unlike the British parliamentary system, we invariably fail to "form a government" in our separation-of-powers system.[158] At all times both parties remain part of the government and part of the opposition. Nowhere is this more true, perhaps, than in the Senate. Still, on occasion the "opposition" party is able to pin the tail on the Donkey or Elephant. Voters held Nixon and the GOP accountable in 1974, Carter and the Democrats in 1980, Democrats again in 1994, and Republicans in 2006 and 2008. Perhaps assigning blame is easiest under conditions of so-called united party government, but even then the majority party can sometimes shift blame to minority obstructionism.

Nevertheless, our separation-of-powers system introduces a different kind of party accountability in the form of internal party factions holding one another's feet to the fire. One example is the September 2006 fight over intelligence tactics and detainee interrogation between the Bush White House and Senators McCain, Graham, and Warner. Another example is House and Senate Republican disagreement over immigration reform in 2006. In both instances, factions within the "majority" party vied for the role of government or opposition, rather than the two parties doing so. Party mavericks and dissenting party factions (again, internal party factions) provide a plethora of constant accountability and openness, without the clear-cut party accountability that party government theorists desire. Examples include mavericks like Senator John McCain or critics of earmarks like House Republican leader John Boehner.

This intraparty factionalism proves that neither party is the "government" or the "opposition" simply. Indeed, internal party factions constantly contend over whether their party is part of the government or part of the opposition. The "government or opposition" dilemma confronts both parties at all times, promotes factionalism within both parties and proves that neither party "controls" Congress. The term "control" again clearly overstates, for example, Republican hegemony prior to the 2006 election. Both parties retain leverage at all times.

Just as our constitutional system produces a surfeit of leadership, rather than the lack of leadership that presidency and Congress scholars sometimes lament, so, too, does our separation-of-powers system produce a surfeit of responsibility, accountability, and openness in the form of internal party factionalism. Both parties are constantly held accountable by internal party factions and *intra*party differences, including disagreements between the party in the White House and the party on the Hill, or between the party in the House and the party in the Senate. In this sense, the separation of powers precludes *and* includes accountability. Neither party is strictly speaking the government or the opposition, yet both are held accountable by their copartisans. Even when the press criticizes the majority party for a failure to hold effective oversight hearings, such as in 2006, the party on the Hill is still holding the party in the White House accountable, as we saw in 2006 with the intelligence reform and immigration reform debates. It may be a different kind of accountability than provided in the British Parliament, but it still is accountability. The 2006 election results prove the point. The Republican Party could not govern itself, never mind the Congress or the country, and the GOP paid the price, as did Democrats in 1994.

The Federalists' constitutional separation of powers concretely affects contemporary legislative party strategy by failing to produce a clear choice between the party of government and the party of opposition. Since neither party ever effectively "forms a government," the practical consequence of this constitutional principle may be the "permanent campaign" many lament today. Similarly, though perhaps at different times, our constitutional system produces the excesses of both partisanship and pluralism. Sharpened partisan confrontation may be endemic to our politics. So, too, might the excesses of pluralism be endemic to our constitutional system, including at times a politics dominated by special-interest collaboration, deal making, and pork. Finally, as Tocqueville notes, American politics is marked by individualism or privatism. The excess here may be the ugliness of the "politics by other means" or "politics of personal destruction" many lament. Given the independence and prominence of individuals in our politics, is it any wonder that their opponents attack them personally? Madison may be responsible for heightened partisan confrontation, the "permanent campaign," and the politics of personal destruction. Madison is certainly responsible for the strategic dilemma bedeviling both legislative parties at all times.

The legislative party strategic dilemma has its roots in the constitutional structure of our institutions. The Constitution governs in the commonplace sense that ours is a "government of laws not men." No one person governs. Neither the president nor the Congress simply governs, and certainly neither political party is ever wholly the government. Indeed, even majorities do not govern; our republican institutions temper even super majorities. The Federalists made certain that neither party is ever simply government or opposition. Neither party governs. Rather, the Constitution governs. Our parties are creatures of our constitutional structure. Party competition between and factionalism within the two parties is played according to constitutional rules written over two hundred years ago.

The proof of these constitutional propositions can be found in the Founders' own practice of their principles as partisans in the 1790s.

7

~

Practical Consequences of Constitutional Principle: The 1790s

A zeal for different opinions concerning religion, concerning government, and many other points, as well as speculation as of practice; an attachment to different leaders ambitiously contending for pre-eminence and power; or to persons of other descriptions whose fortunes have been interesting to the human passions, have, in turn, divided mankind into parties, inflamed them with mutual animosity, and rendered them more disposed to vex and oppress each other than to co-operate for their common good.

—Federalist No. 10

A DECADE-LONG SHOUTING MATCH

We have come to think of the Founders as statesmen, and James Madison, in particular, as a soft-spoken gentleman inclined toward the politics of compromise and reconciliation presumably embodied in Madisonian pluralism. Yet these statesmen were also politicians and ardent partisans; indeed, Madison was a particularly effective legislative party strategist, dubbed "Jemmy the Knife" by friend and foe alike.[1] Historian Joseph Ellis described the 1790s as "a decade-long shouting match" unparalleled in American history.[2] Partisans were quick to label their opponents "Jacobins" or "Monarchists" as they tussled over contentious issues including the assumption of state debt, the Bank Bill, Washington's Proclamation of Neutrality, and later the Alien and Sedition Acts, just to name a few. Gordon Wood observed, "The 1790s became one of the most passionate and divisive decades in American history . . . partisan feelings ran very high."[3] By the end of the decade, Wood concluded, "Party spirit . . . ruled all."[4]

Temperamentally, Madison may have been a balancer and reconciler, "the master committeeman" interested in promoting comity and civility.[5] Yet Madison did not try to take the politics or "spirit of party" out of politics; nor did he share Jefferson's pretense to rising above party. Madison understood clearly that the "spirit of party" factionalism was fated to be a constant in free governments, even if factionalism did not always take the form of two ideologically distinct party coalitions. Partisan and personal differences in the 1790s were sharp, significant, and often rooted in competing constitutional interpretations. Arguably, the two increasingly polarized parties evolving in the 1790s even perpetuated a "permanent campaign" premised on a fundamental tension built into our Constitution, a tension rooted in two central constitutional principles: the separation of powers and federalism.

Clearly Madison and Hamilton were, in retrospect, statesmen, though they also were successful statesmen in part because they were *party* statesmen. Allied with one another against the critics of the Constitution during the ratification debate, these two men found themselves increasingly at odds during the early years of the republic. In many ways, the 1790s were like today. Just as Federalist majorities eventually gave way to the Republicans and to Jefferson's "Second Revolution," so, too, the "permanent majority" House Democrats succumbed to the House Republican "revolution" in 1994, with House Republicans, in turn, losing their own extended majority to the Democrats in the bitter partisan warfare leading up to the 2006 election. Newt Gingrich and Nancy Pelosi may not be the statesmen we rightly understand Madison and Hamilton to be, but the latter two Founders were certainly part and parcel of the politics, partisanship, polarization, and "permanent campaign" of the early years of the American Republic. One lesson all four leaders learned in their time: majorities fall, but Congress and the Constitution stand.

THE FOUNDERS DID IT, TOO

Ellis's description of the 1790s sounds like the polarizing partisanship and "politics of personal destruction" so oft lamented by critics of today's politics:

> The politics of the 1790s was a truly cacophonous affair. Previous historians have labeled it "the Age of Passion" for good reason, for in terms of shrill accusatory rhetoric, flamboyant displays of ideological intransigence, intense personal rivalries, and hyperbolic claims of imminent catastrophe, it has no equal in American history. The political dialogue within the highest echelon of the revolutionary generation was a decade-long shouting match.[6]

Madison and Hamilton were part of that cacophony. While Madison was wary of the mischief of faction and "suspicious of political parties," in Federalist No. 10 he also invited the proliferation of factions and the "spirit of party" as cures for the defects of the same.[7] As a theorist and practitioner, Madison is famous for his "combining mind"; according to Robert Goldwin, Madison had a "penetrating intellect" coupled with "a talent for political tactics and the legislative temperament suited to dealing with practical politicians."[8] Garry Wills saw Madison as "a supremely great legislator" whose "backstage tactics" and "parliamentary deftness" provided his "strength as a legislative reconciler."[9] Indeed, Madison's skill as a legislative craftsman capable of balancing competing interests and perspectives, whether in Congress or at the Constitutional Convention in 1787, contributed to what we know today as the Madison Question.

Gary Rosen, for example, asks whether Madison ultimately was a liberal, like Hamilton, or a republican, like Jefferson, a nationalist or states righter, a Federalist or an Anti-Federalist.[10] Madison's subtle, deft mind, complex thought, and practical skill as a legislator make it difficult to fit him neatly into such categories and boxes. Yet there was no doubt where America's philosopher-king stood in the party wars of the 1790s. Clinton Rossiter identifies Madison as "the skillful architect of the opposition party in Congress," the Republicans.[11] Rossiter notes, "[T]he Republicans were a tendency in the country from the beginning, an identifiable group in Congress in 1792, a governmental party in 1795, an election fighting alliance in 1796, and an organization functioning on a national scale in 1800."[12]

> While the new Federalists of the 1790s (as distinguished from the old Federalists of 1788 and the even older ones of the mid-1780s) behaved more and more like a party while insisting they were nothing of the sort, the men around Jefferson slowly forged an instrument, the Democratic-Republican party, for winning control of the government peacefully and then exercising it purposefully.[13]

Certainly, Rossiter concludes, the Democratic-Republicans "were a party in every meaningful sense of the word" by 1800, as were their opponents, although the "gratuitous feud" between Hamilton and Adams severely factionalized the Federalists. The Federalists were in the process of becoming a minority party in part because of the Republicans' success as the opposition, but also because the Federalists failed to manage successfully their own internal party factionalism. The Federalists provided their partisan opponents with the opening the Republicans needed to become the majority party in 1800, just as House Democrats did in 1994 and House Republicans did in 2006.

BITTER PARTISANSHIP

In *The Mind of the Founder*, Marvin Meyers details the bitter partisanship of the 1790s:

> Republicans as well as Federalists found it difficult to conceive of a legitimate party competition for control of government: each commonly portrayed the other as enemies of the constitutional regime, and after the wars of the French Revolution began, as agents of a foreign power.[14]

In Madison's 1792 essay titled "A Candid State of Parties," the Founder outlined the history of parties in the early republic beginning with the revolution, eventual ratification of the Constitution, and finally the establishment and early administration of the federal government in 1788. The latter, according to Madison, gave rise to a third division of parties he deemed "natural to most political societies," and therefore likely to endure.[15] Madison's "A Candid State of Parties" reads like a political-science history of the evolving party system, and yet it also served as an opposition editorial critical of the Federalists led by Hamilton.[16]

Today, we might call this third division of parties Hamiltonian versus Jeffersonian, though Madison saw the division as between an anti-republican party and a pro-republican party. The "anti-republican" party, Madison argued, is "more partial to the opulent . . . having debauched themselves into a persuasion that mankind are incapable of governing themselves."[17] This party is inclined "less to the interests of the many than the few," and marked by an affinity toward "rank," "money," "military force," and hereditary power.[18] "The Republican party, as it may be termed" in Madison's first recorded use of the formal name, believes in "the doctrine that mankind are capable of governing themselves."[19] The Republican Party, "hating hereditary power" as an "insult to reason" and an "outrage to the rights of man," is naturally more inclined toward the "general interest of the community" and more "conducive to the preservation of republican government."[20]

"This being the real state of parties among us," Madison insisted, the Republican Party was aligned with the "mass of the people" and inclined toward "promoting a general harmony."[21] The Republican Party's "superiority of numbers is so great" that it represented the "common cause," "common sentiment," and "common interest" of "the great body of the people."[22] Nevertheless, this silent majority in 1792, according to Madison, was temporarily outmaneuvered by "the anti-republican party," which while "fewer in number" was "moneyed" and adept at "strategy" and "taking advantage of prejudices."[23] The "rival party," Madison lamented, capitalized on the fact that "in politics as in war, stratagem is often an overmatch for numbers."[24]

Ron Peters similarly outlines and elaborates on the differences between the Federalists (dubbed the "the anti-republican" party by Madison) and Republicans:

> Federalists were more suspicious of democracy and more oriented toward an industrial expansion guided by the hand of capital. Republicans, while no less devoted to private property, were inclined to fear the power of the federal government and gave a far more egalitarian interpretation to the idea of the rights of man.[25]

Federalists, Hamilton in particular, favored a strong, assertive executive, while Republicans, with their base in Congress, were more suspicious of executive authority, thereby giving rise to the caricature each party drew of the other. "To the Federalists, Republicans were Jacobins in disguise; to the Republicans, Federalists were undisguised monarchists."[26] By the end of the 1790s, partisan rancor in Congress was so great Republican legislators "refused to join in the vote of thanks from the House" for Federalist Speaker Theodore Sedgwick.[27]

Historian Joseph Ellis's description of partisan animosity in the 1790s makes it sound very much like the polarized politics of today, complete with an empty political center. Amid a "sea of mutual accusations and partisan interpretations . . . the center could not hold because it did not exist."[28] Political rhetoric matched the polarized politics. Jefferson saw the Federalists under Adams as seditious and treasonable.[29] John Adams, responding in kind, "wallowed in the muck. His supporters tarred his opponent, Thomas Jefferson, as 'an atheist, anarchist, demagogue, coward, mountebank, trickster, and Francomaniac.'"[30]

Ellis underscores the hypocrisy behind Jefferson's oft-quoted declamation against political parties: "[I]f I could not go to heaven but with a party, I would not go there at all."[31] Jefferson was behind scandalmonger James Thomson Callender's libels against Adams, with Abigail Adams responding in kind and labeling Jefferson a villain, traitor, and scoundrel.[32] The bitter partisanship of the 1790s further erupted into scandals and what we today call "the politics of personal destruction." The growing division between Adams and Jefferson found its parallel in a similar growing split between former collaborators Hamilton and Madison. At the same time, personal disagreements between Adams and Hamilton weakened the Federalist party. The partisan division also became personal.

In his meticulously reconstructed historical novel *Scandalmonger*, the late *New York Times* journalist William Safire carefully recreates authentic dialogue to underscore just how rife the 1790s were with polarizing partisanship and "politics by other means."[33] The book includes a famous 1798 cartoon depicting "congressional pugilists" literally fighting in the well of the House, along with ample samplings of the hot rhetoric of the day, including "turncoat," "poltroon [coward]," "hoary-headed incendiary," and more.[34] Safire's scandalmongers dredge up Hamilton's Maria Reynolds affair and Jefferson's Sally Hemmings liaison, along with Jefferson's purported atheism and the charge that Treasury Secretary Hamilton speculated in currency.

Safire makes the case that the "politics by other means" of the 1790s was fueled by "polluted" (Jefferson's word) newspapers and a licentious press.[35] At one point, a colleague criticizes Callender thus: "You scandalmongers make a mockery of your liberty of the press, and by so doing endanger it. You're drawn to all this tittle-tattle only to sell your newspapers."[36] Safire clearly understands the parallels between the 1790s and today, and he has Hamilton defending the free press with its inevitable license and propensity for promoting the politics of scandal.[37] This sounds all-too-familiar today.[38]

Clearly, our First Amendment freedom of the press and freedom of association allow and even invite the abuses of licentiousness and excessive partisanship, but what is the alternative? Negotiating the slippery slope of regulating First Amendment freedoms is no more desirable than attempting the impossible task of taking the politics out of politics. In Federalist No. 10, Madison observes,

> Liberty is to faction what air is to fire, an aliment without which it instantly expires. But it could not be less folly to abolish liberty, which is essential to political life, because it nourishes faction, than it would be to wish the annihilation of air, which is essential to animal life, because it imparts to fire its destructive agency.[39]

In a free society, politics is ubiquitous. Those, who like Humphrey Bogart in *Casablanca* (falsely as it turns out) declare, "There will be no politics in my place," may be wishing for what never was, nor ever will be in a liberal regime. One is reminded of the old nostrum "A man who says he is not interested in politics is like a drowning man who says he is not interested in water." Not only is politics ubiquitous in a free society, it is also permanent.

Historian Michael Kazin traces today's "permanent campaign," which some lament, all the way back to the 1830s. Nostalgia for the good old days of short campaigns is fatuous, Kazin opines: "Like most evocations of a golden age, this is a myth. In fact, the nearly "permanent campaign" has been a feature of American politics since before the Civil War."[40] Just as presidency scholar David K. Nichols traces the "modern presidency" back to George Washington, so, too, might we trace the "permanent campaign" to the 1790s. Rossiter, Meyers, Ellis, Peters, and other scholars document the polarizing partisanship of the early republic. Today's perpetrators of a polarized politics and the politics of scandal have not really improved upon the 1790s; bitter partisanship is hardly new in American politics.

ISSUES OF CONTENTION

Over the course of the early years of the American Republic, certain issues stand out as particular points of contention between the competing factions. Legislative fights particularly worth highlighting include the Bill of Rights amendments passed in the First Congress, slavery, the Assumption [of state debt] Bill in tandem with the Residence [of the District of Columbia] Bill, the Bank Bill, the Proclamation of Neutrality, the Jay Treaty, and the Alien and Sedition Acts.

The Bill of Rights

James Madison was first elected to the House of Representatives on the "campaign promise" that he would introduce what later came to be called the Bill of Rights amendments to the Constitution.[41] In principle, Madison opposed amending the new Constitution; yet he favored a bill of rights because it was, in his words, "highly politic."[42] In this, he acted contrary to the wishes of leading Federalists with whom he had worked to gain ratification of the Constitution. The brilliance of Madison as a political strategist, however, became readily evident in the First Congress in the fight over a bill of rights.

Madison saw popular demand for a bill of rights as both a problem and a solution; or rather, he took a problem and turned it into a solution.[43] Robert Goldwin concludes: "By proposing his amendments, which in the end did not change one word in the text of the Constitution, Madison blocked the adoption of all the structural amendments of the Anti-Federalists."[44] Moreover, Madison used the Bill of Rights fight to secure majority sentiment behind the new Constitution. Madison agreed with Hamilton that the Constitution was itself a bill of rights.[45] Yet Madison seized the initiative from the Anti-Federalists and, by means of a brilliant legislative stratagem, gained the people's "devoted allegiance" to the Constitution by adding a bill of rights that changed not a word of the Constitution.[46]

Madison sought, as he stated, to "satisfy the public mind that their liberties will be perpetual, and this without endangering any part of the Constitution."[47] In this instance and others, Madison proved to be the master legislative craftsman of the early Congress. Yet Madison was not merely accommodating and compromising with his Anti-Federalist opponents; rather, he engaged in what we today call "wedgislating." Herbert Storing observes:

> Madison knew that his amendments would not satisfy the hard-core Anti-Federalists. His strategy was rather to isolate them from the large group of common people whose opposition did rest, not on fundamental hostility

to the basic design of the Constitution, but on a broad fear that individual liberties were not sufficiently protected. By conciliatory amendments, he told Jefferson, he hoped "to extinguish opposition to the system, or at least break the force of it by detaching the deluded opponents from the designing leaders."[48]

Madison thereby "neatly boxed in" his opponents, the Anti-Federalist leaders.[49] This Founding statesman and crafty legislative politician proved adroit at simultaneously playing politics and promoting principle. In one of the most consequential legislative fights in the nation's history, Madison effectively demonstrated that good politics is good policy.

The Slavery Compromise

Madison did compromise on principle during the First Congress, however, on the subject of slavery. Ellis tells us that on the issue of slavery Madison was caught between the North and the Deep South, as well as between his conscience and his constituents; hence, he adopted the "Virginia straddle."[50] Madison opted for interest accommodation over principled confrontation given the enormity of the issue and the impossibility of the challenge. Yet here, too, Madison's legislative prowess was evident according to Ellis: "In parliamentary maneuvering of this sort, Madison had no peer."[51] He "lived in the details," showed "deft tactical proficiency," and employed "masterful circumlocutions" and "indirection."[52] Nevertheless, his legislative strategy failed.

Madison concluded that the effort to end slavery at this time was "premature, politically impractical, and counterproductive" to the establishment and maintenance of the fledgling republic.[53] It was impossible to end slavery at this time, so Congress finessed the issue just as the Constitutional Convention had done. Ultimately, Madison chose prudence over principle; slavery proved to be the intractable problem the revolutionary generation was unable to solve either at the Constitutional Convention or during the First Congress.[54] The issue of slavery, as we know, promoted a factional divide, in part pitting northern states against southern states, which ultimately resulted in the Civil War, the most serious political crisis in American history.

The Dinner and Beyond

Madison further engaged in the politics of accommodation at a dinner Jefferson arranged in June 1790 between Hamilton and Madison. The dinner sorely challenged the friendship between the two former *Federalist* collaborators. Madison and Hamilton struck a bargain on the federal assumption of state debt and the location of the future capital on the banks of the

Potomac. Some argue that the friendship between Madison and Hamilton ended with this dinner, though what is known for certain is that in July 1790 the Assumption Bill and Residence Bill both passed Congress with the able assistance of that master legislative craftsman, James Madison.[55] In historic retrospect, one is tempted to conclude that Hamilton got the better of the deal by gaining a cornerstone of his economic program, but in the process he may have lost a friend and ally.

Gary Rosen argues that Madison adopted a balancing role between Hamilton and Jefferson, and that Madison's differences with Hamilton turned partisan only with the Bank Bill in 1791.[56] Jack Rakove concludes, "Manageable differences over policy began to develop into more volatile disagreements over principle" with the Bank Bill.[57] Madison was a strict constructionist in interpreting constitutional provisions, while Hamilton was more willing to adopt a loose construction. In the fight over the Bank Bill, Madison began to see an "aristocratic plot" with Hamilton at its center.[58] "Madison's opposition, which had previously centered on the particular measures of Hamilton's program, turned to the administration itself," Rosen avers. "The republican cause was transformed into the Republican Party with the political demise of Hamilton and his principles as its end."[59] The new party system centered on a debate over constitutional interpretation, as seen with the Bank Bill; but these constitutional conflicts between Madison and Hamilton, between the Jeffersonians and Hamiltonians, between the Republicans and Federalists, extended to further questions of constitutional interpretation regarding the conduct of foreign policy as well as First Amendment freedoms.[60]

Foreign and Domestic Quarrels

The next flashpoint between Hamilton and Madison was President Washington's 1793 Proclamation of Neutrality in the war between Great Britain and France. Hamilton and Jefferson clashed openly in Washington's cabinet over whether such a proclamation was properly an executive or legislative function. Hamilton and Madison, who previously had collaborated in writing under the pseudonym Publius in defense of the constitutional separation of powers, next took up pens as Pacificus and Helvidius to engage in what Clinton Rossiter called a "violent disagreement."[61] Madison branded Hamilton's constitutional interpretation "vicious in theory."[62] Historian Rossiter later concluded: "Interpretation of the Constitution was to be the juiciest bone of contention in American politics for generations to come."[63]

In fact, questions of constitutional interpretation have been "perpetually arising," to borrow Chief Justice John Marshall's felicitous phrase, ever since.[64] Similar debates over constitutional interpretation have provided partisan flashpoints as recently as the struggle between the president and Congress over executive prerogative and the Iraq War in 2006–2007. It is worth noting that the Helvidius and Pacificus letters, not unlike *The Federalist*, were simultaneously partisan diatribe and serious constitutional analysis. Politics and policy often go hand in hand.

The French Revolution by itself provided the premise for acrimonious partisan debate in America, debate filled with "bitter invective, manipulation of facts and knee-jerk dogmatism."[65] According to Lloyd S. Kramer, "the French Revolution transformed the new nation's first decade into one of the most divisive and ideologically charged periods in all of American history."[66] Federalists labeled the pro-French Republicans "anarchists" and "incendiaries," while Republicans returned the favor, branding the Federalists "Anglomen" and "monarchists."[67] Conor Cruise O'Brien notes that Jefferson dismissed as "British lies" any reports that reflected badly on the French Revolution.[68]

The mid-decade Jay Treaty between the United States and Great Britain further provided the premise for partisan conflict. Madison himself proved capable of sharp partisan rhetoric when he blamed his defeat on the treaty in the House to "the exertions and influence of Aristocracy, Anglicism, and mercantilism" advanced by "the Banks, the British Merchts., the insurance Comps."[69] Although the treaty was widely unpopular from the start, and Madison began the debate with a solid legislative majority, George Washington's prestige ultimately carried the day, handing the Republicans a defeat. Jefferson was even less politic than Madison when, in a letter to the latter, he applied to Washington a line from Joseph Addison's play *Cato*: "a curse on his virtues, they've undone his country."[70]

The Alien and Sedition Acts

Under President Adams, partisan relations worsened. On July 4, 1798, Federalists frightened by the "specter of French intrigue" and "Jacobin" subversion, passed the Alien and Sedition Acts. "Jefferson and Madison saw at once a deadly threat to liberty and *a priceless political opportunity*," observed Marvin Meyers.[71] These Republican leaders exploited this opening to pave the way for their partisan electoral success in 1800. Jefferson talked of secession and "the reign of witches," drafting the Kentucky Resolution while Madison drafted the more moderate Virginia Resolution in response to the Federalist assault on precious First Amendment freedoms.[72]

By this time, Meyers notes, Madison and Jefferson "were up to their necks in a demi-loyal opposition movement" against Hamilton's system of finance, the Jay Treaty, Adam's quasi-war with revolutionary France, and other real or perceived Federalist excesses.[73] Madison and Jefferson were at the center of a "rising anti-Administration party."[74] Madison's

"Report of 1800," written after his election to the Virginia legislature, was an attempt to defend the sharp political criticism embodied in his earlier Virginia Resolutions. Such vituperative criticism was essential to "exciting reflection" among the public, Madison argued, in response to the threat posed by the Alien and Sedition Acts.[75]

By 1800, America had two clear ideologically polarized political parties; Republicans were offering a choice rather than an echo of the Federalists, so much so that Jefferson's election in 1800 came to be called the "Second Revolution." This "revolution" was at least as great a challenge to the existing order as would be Newt Gingrich's House Republican "revolution" in 1994 or Nancy Pelosi's victory in 2006. All three partisan victories were marked by sharp rhetoric and bitter conflict. In many ways, the decade of the 1790s seemed, like today's politics, to be a long "permanent campaign" between two warring parties. The partisan polarization even partook of the "politics of personal destruction" and "politics by other means" fomented by an increasingly partisan and petty press. One key partisan leader, Alexander Hamilton, eventually lost his life in a duel premised on the polarized politics of the era. Ironically, the proximate cause of the duel with Burr was Hamilton's accommodation with his partisan foe, Jefferson, and Hamilton's willingness to throw his support in a famous letter behind the election of Jefferson in 1800. Needless to say, political-science ambition theory and rational choice theory today would be hard pressed to explain the willingness of Hamilton to die for a cause in defense of his honor. Politics involves more than mere self-interest narrowly construed.

The Second Revolution

Following the Republican victory in 1800, partisanship did not disappear even though the Federalists were in decline. "Partisanship was not something that faded after 1800, not even after the drastic fall of Federalist influence during Jefferson's first term. The Republicans split into factions, which soon became more difficult to handle than the Federalists had been."[76] The Republicans had been united in opposition to the Federalists. "When they tried to govern, they discovered that the regional cleavages of the new republic caused divisions within their own ranks."[77] The Republican majority learned a lesson every congressional majority party would learn over the next two centuries: it is easier to maintain party discipline in opposition, and attempting to govern as a majority party is difficult at best. Partisan leadership necessarily involves managing factionalism.

In a liberal regime, partisanship is ever present; the "spirit of party" and faction cannot be extinguished. Partisanship exists even if it does not always take the form of two ideologically polarized parties. Both John Adams and Thomas Jefferson eventually had to accept that the Washington ideal of a nonpartisan presidential statesmanship was history.[78] The American presidency necessarily includes the role of head of party. A similar observation could be made about congressional leadership. By 1800, there was a recognition that the speakership, for example, was inevitably, in part, a partisan office.[79]

President James Madison had to manage factionalism within his own party or be managed by that same factionalism. The first strong Speaker, Republican Henry Clay, came to power during Madison's presidency. Tensions built between the Republicans and the Federalists, and between the president and Congress, including and especially over the War of 1812. Partisanship did not end at the water's edge during Madison's presidency, nor did intraparty factionalism. "The vote in both houses was purely partisan," Garry Wills observed, "no Federalist voting for the war, several . . . Republicans voting against it."[80] Indeed, Washington, D.C., was a "gloomy place" during much of the War of 1812; Congress was rife with obstructionism and New England Federalists flirted with secession.[81]

In many ways, the domestic politics of the War of 1812 resembled the partisan and factional divisiveness of the Iraq War during the presidency of George W. Bush. Then suddenly, in February 1815, the good news of Andrew Jackson's victory in New Orleans and the conclusion of the Treaty of Ghent gave rise to exhilaration in the nation's capital. During Madison's last year in office the swell of popular nationalism mollified obstructionism in Congress. The election of James Monroe brought the dawn of the "Era of Good Feeling," a period of muted partisanship not unlike the aftermath of World War II. George W. Bush was not so fortunate.

TAKING THE POLITICS OUT OF POLITICS

Periods of muted partisanship in American politics are noteworthy because they are more the exception than the rule. Even in the "Era of Good Feeling" and the Ozzie and Harriet 1950s, partisan and factional tensions existed, as evident for example, in the dissension over the Missouri Compromise and McCarthyism. Partisanship has, in fact, been a constant of American politics since the ratification of the Constitution.

James Madison understood that partisanship was concomitant with American constitutionalism. He did not seek to take the politics or "spirit of party" out of politics; he did not share Jefferson's infatuation with a nonpartisan politics, nor the latter's pretense to rising above partisanship. As noted above, Jefferson apparently was willing to forego heaven if his only option was to go there with a party. Instead, according to Ellis, Jefferson preferred to think of his "lofty principles" as "uncontaminated by the kind of infighting that Madison and Hamilton had perfected to an art."[82] In fact, Jefferson temperamentally did not like argument and conflict, unlike Madison who was willing to stand his ground in debate at the Constitutional Convention and later in Congress. Madison was also willing, including at Jefferson's behest, to engage his keen intellect and sharp pen in political combat, writing for example as Publius and later as Helvidius.

Madison did not share Jefferson's nonpartisan pretense, nor did he share the intellectual vanity of his friend's grand principles purportedly unsullied by politics. Indeed, Madison's "matchless political savvy" was combined with his superior understanding of constitutionalism and the Constitution.[83] "In every political society, parties are unavoidable," Madison clearly understood; in fact, he later concluded parties "must always be expected in a government as free as ours."[84] Madison recognized that American politics and partisanship are rooted in constitutionalism and the Constitution. Mere partisanship is possible precisely because of limited constitutional government; the Constitution governs parties more than parties govern the Constitution. Political parties can be more partial and more partisan precisely because parties do not govern; rather, the Constitution governs. Tocqueville notes, "In America the Constitution rules both legislators and simple citizens."[85]

Our constitutional concrete is sufficient to withstand partisan warfare today, just as it did in the 1790s, because of the "veneration" for the Constitution that Madison sought beginning with the ratification debate. In Federalist No. 49, Madison argues explicitly against Jefferson's call for generational constitutional conventions meant to reexamine first principles. Madison understood how critical veneration for the Constitution would be as a firm foundation for the regime.[86] Veneration for the Constitution would limit the few and the many, the politicians and the people.[87] In fact, a shared veneration for the Constitution is a necessary prerequisite for the creation of a loyal, legitimate opposition party. Both partisan compromise and confrontation are permissible because our partisan differences are part of a "quarrel within a family."[88]

Madison, unlike Jefferson, did not see partisan opposition as illegitimate. Madison did not want to take the politics out of politics. To do so would run contrary to the Constitution and our liberal experiment. Freedom of speech, freedom of the press, freedom of association, and the right to petition government all invite the formation and exercise of factions, parties, and a partisan press.

Partisanship is rooted in the Constitution because of what we today call First Amendment freedoms, yet partisanship is also rooted in the Constitution in another fundamental way. Throughout our history, beginning in the 1790s, partisanship has been premised on the fault lines of constitutional debate and interpretation of the central principles of separation of powers and federalism. Beginning with the debates in the 1790s between Federalists and Republicans, Americans have had constant recourse to debates over the meaning of the Constitution. Tocqueville noted in the 1830s, for example, that in America most political questions eventually become constitutional questions. Clinton Rossiter concludes that beginning with the disagreements between Madison and Hamilton in the 1790s, "interpretation of the Constitution was to be the juiciest bone of contention in American politics for generations to come."[89] Differences over constitutional interpretation continue to provide fodder for our political, including partisan, debates. Herbert Storing takes this a step further, concluding that American politics consists of an ongoing and ever-deepening debate between the principles of the Federalists and Anti-Federalists.[90]

Partisanship in the highly charged and polarized decade of the 1790s focused on the relationship between the Congress and the president, and the relationship between the national government and the states. The two central principles of the Constitution, the separation of powers and federalism, provided the premise for partisan differences in the 1790s, just as they do today. Ron Peters notes:

> The partisan tendencies manifested during the First Congress became more accentuated during the remainder of the eighteenth century. The Federalists were, for the most part, the majority party of the decade, although their majorities were never overwhelming, and party identification itself was ill-defined. From the skirmishes between Federalists and Republicans of the Federalist decade emerged the contours of the first American party system as it was to develop after 1800. Likewise, the struggle between Hamilton and Madison defined two of the principal constitutional issues of American history: the relationship between the federal and state governments and that between the executive and legislative branches of the federal government.[91]

In simple terms, "Hamilton trod upon the prerogatives of the states as well as those of Congress," consequently Republicans felt compelled to fight back. Madison fought against Hamilton's intrusions into congressional affairs. The American party system was born from the adversarial relationship between Congress and the president.[92] Similarly, competition between Republicans and Federalists provided the stimulus behind the embryonic committee system in Congress.[93] Michael Malbin concludes that the separation of powers provided the impetus behind the congressional committee system: "The committee system . . . originally grew out of Congress' desire to assert its independence of the executive branch."[94] In brief, the institutional structure of Congress, including its "dual nature" defined by the "party principle" and the "committee principle," has its roots in fundamental constitutional structure.[95] Congress and our political parties are creatures of the constitutional separation of powers and federalism. Partisanship has its roots in the Constitution.

Similarly, the "permanent campaign" is permanent because of the perpetual tension built into the Constitution between the president and Congress and between the national government and the states. Hamiltonians and Jeffersonians interpreted and debated the proper balance of the separation of powers and federalism. Both sides had "legitimate claims on historical truth" according to Ellis, and "neither side completely triumphed"; consequently, "taking sides in this debate is like choosing between the words and the music of the American Revolution."[96] Arguably, each side had half the whole: "The Constitution did not resolve these questions; it only provided an orderly framework within which the arguments could continue."[97]

The orderly framework provided involved political parties: "the revolutionary generation found a way to contain the explosive energies of the debate in the form of an ongoing argument or dialogue that was eventually institutionalized and rendered safe by the creation of political parties."[98] Democrats and Republicans continue the "ongoing and ever-deepening" debate today although there is clearly no simple correlation between the parties of the 1790s and party divisions today. Still, the debate continues to involve struggles between competing perspectives: a strong, effective executive versus legislative supremacy, and a strong, centralized national government versus the states. This constitutional tension or "contradiction" created by the Founders has given rise to the disharmony and the cacophonous partisan competition that is American politics.[99] We have oscillated between the two perspectives throughout our entire history. Again, the "permanent campaign" is permanent because it has its origins in the Constitution.

Harvey Mansfield contends that "politics is essentially partisan."[100] James Madison concurs: "no free Country has ever been without parties, which are a natural offspring of Freedom."[101] Mansfield concludes, "In America, party was begun by a Founder, Thomas Jefferson . . . in opposition to other Founders."[102] The concept of loyal or legitimate partisan opposition is intrinsic to our politics even when we are inclined to question the motives and good faith of our partisan opponents. We cannot take the politics, including partisanship, out of politics. Nor should we want to try. Compromise and confrontation are both inherent in American politics.

CONCLUSION

Having explored the partisan polarization of the 1790s, including the break between *The Federalist* collaborators Alexander Hamilton and James Madison, we can safely conclude that the bitter polarization within the Founding generation during the 1790s was at least as great as partisanship today. Alexander Hamilton, who like Madison was a brilliant political and legislative strategist, lost his life due to the bitterness of politics in the early years of the republic. William Safire's carefully researched historical novel *Scandalmonger* provides evidence that the politics of scandal and the "politics of personal destruction" loomed as large in the early years of the United States as it does today.

Proof that compromise and confrontation, including partisan confrontation, are both constitutionally permissible legislative strategies for party leaders may be found in the fact that during the 1790s our supposedly anti-party Founders engaged in rather sharp elbowed partisanship—indeed, in rather bitter, polarizing, and personal partisanship. Again, the Founders may have been statesmen, but they were also politicians. Madison and Hamilton understood—as evidenced by their words and actions—that *politics is good.*[103] To judge by their words and actions, both partisan politics and partisan polarization are positive aspects of our political system. Again, the "spirit of party" informed their words and actions, both when they were allied against the Anti-Federalists in the 1780s and then arrayed against one another—for example, as Helvidius and Pacificus—as was increasingly the case in the 1790s. Arguably, the Federalists ultimately became a minority because they failed to manage their own internal party factionalism.

The Founders understood that politics, partisanship, and polarization are good in part because our constitutional concrete can withstand a contentious and confrontational politics. The Constitution will not collapse, though its mettle was sorely tested during the early years of the American Republic. In the modern era, partisan guerilla Newt Gingrich found himself accused of trying to "destroy" Congress in order to save it, but shortly after he became the leader of the new majority party, Congress found itself enjoying the highest approval ratings in memory. Ironically perhaps, few such accusations were hurled at Nancy Pelosi by journalists and political scientists during her effort to upset the longstanding Republican majority leading up to November 2006 even though her rhetoric was similar in style and substance to that of Gingrich.

Ultimately, the Constitution is not likely to collapse under the strain of polarizing partisanship, whether fomented by Newt or Nancy; it has in fact survived the rise and demise of various political parties over two hundred years. Civil wars are rare in American history; so, too, are *literal* floor fights in the House and Senate. Canings on the floor and duels between members are also rare. Does anyone today really expect Nancy or Newt to lose their lives in a duel to the death? Even if politicians, political journalists, and political scientists regularly take refuge in war metaphors to depict partisan conflict, our constitutional institutions seem to survive even when the latest generation of harsh partisan critics go on the attack.[104] Majorities may fall, but Congress and the Constitution remain intact.

Even when seemingly "permanent majorities" fall, Congress still survives. As Jack Pitney and I noted in our book, *Congress' Permanent Minor-*

ity? some Congress scholars and journalists in the 1980s and early 1990s began to identify Congress with the majority House Democrats. Such commentators often criticized Newt Gingrich and House Republicans for attacking "Congress" and the "government," as if the House Republicans were not part of the government. These critics charged House Republicans with being "antigovernment," when in fact the House GOP was bent on becoming a majority and a more influential part of the government. Similarly, in the lead-up to the 2006 election, some saw the House and Senate GOP majorities as part of a "broken branch," in part because of heightened partisan polarization on the Hill.[105] Partisan polarization may not necessarily mean Congress is broken.

In the United States, politics is not in fact war by other means. As Tocqueville noted, in America there are few revolutionaries and many reformers; differences in American politics are often mere differences of "hue."[106] Hence, the compromising incrementalism of pluralism constitutes a critical component in the character of our constitutional system, while the closest we get to revolutions are party realignments like the rise of New Deal Democrats—or in other words, an approximation of party government. But such strident partisan competition is just as critical a component of our constitutional system as compromise, at least if we are to judge by history. In his theory and practice of politics, James Madison cannot be reduced to compromise and comity.

Politics, partisanship, and polarization are good and integral to our political system. So, too, is the "permanent campaign" so often lamented by modern-day Cassandras. The sky is not falling. We need to step back, take a deep breath and gain some historical perspective on our current travails. The "permanent campaign" may be a permanent feature of our constitutional system, especially given the two-year treadmill of House elections. Again, only in the British parliamentary ideal favored by neo-Wilsonian reformers is one party the "government" and the other party neatly the "opposition." In the British system, such reformers like to note, campaigns are short relative to American campaigns. Once British elections settle a campaign fight, one party adopts the posture of the government, while the other becomes the loyal opposition. No "permanent campaign."[107] Yet today's "permanent campaign" lament might just as well trace its roots and origin to the partisan intrigue of the 1790s, as witness Joseph Ellis's *Founding Brothers* and William Safire's excruciatingly detailed and careful historical novel *Scandalmonger*.

Indeed, the "permanent campaign" may be traceable farther back to the Federalist/Anti-Federalist fight over ratification of the Constitution. American politics may be continuing a conflict rooted in the ratification battle. The tension between our two parties even today may be an attempt to—as Tocqueville put it—"forcibly reconcile" the irreconcilable perspectives of the Federalists and Anti-Federalists. The "permanent campaign" may be an intrinsic feature of our Constitution, and part of what Samuel Huntington identifies as "the promise of disharmony" rooted in the Founding and the Constitution.

Politics, partisanship, polarization, and the "permanent campaign" are natural, necessary, and, therefore, good.

8

~

Practical Consequences of Constitutional Principle: The 1980s and 1990s

The reality is that a president gets judged by whether he runs Congress, or Congress runs him. Voters assume Congress is beastly. They hire a president to tame the beast—to overcome the legislative obstacles and rein in Congressional prima donnas and parochialists.[1]

—Norman J. Ornstein

The "Era of Good Feeling" during the Monroe presidency did not last, of course, and American politics returned to the norm of, well, politics, including polarizing partisan politics and the politics of personal destruction. Monroe's overwhelming victory in 1816 and reelection sans opposition in 1820 were followed by the rancorous election of 1824, including the purported "corrupt bargain" between John Quincy Adams and Henry Clay, which laid the foundation for Andrew Jackson's defeat of Adams in 1828. Charges of adultery and murder marred the 1828 election, although the election in fact turned on the critical National Bank issue. On the same issue, Jackson won an overwhelming reelection victory over Henry Clay in 1832, marking what some consider a critical partisan realigning election.

Historians of the period are quick to remind us that partisan politics is nothing new. Paul Johnson notes wryly, "The Monroe Presidency has been described, at the time and since, as the 'Era of Good Feeling,' the last time in American history when the government of the country was not envenomed by party politics."[2] But Johnson also comments on the seemingly endemic corruption coterminous with the "Era of Good Feeling," and the "permanent campaign" (or "endless campaign") for Jackson's election in

207

1828 that began in earnest in the spring of 1825 following Adams's inauguration.[3] "A huge political fissure opened between the administration and the Jacksonites. From that point, opposition in Congress became systematic" and the modern two-party system came of age, in large part thanks to Tammany Hall boss Martin Van Buren, who would himself become president in 1836.[4]

Paul Johnson concludes, "Those who believe present-day American politics are becoming a dirty game cannot have read the history of the 1828 election."[5] The "politics by other means" of the period included all sorts of scurrilous charges against Jackson, as documented in detail by many, including Alexis de Tocqueville in *Democracy in America*. For example, Jackson was called a "heartless despot. . . . Ambition is his crime. . . . Intrigue is his vocation. . . . He governs by corruption" and is "a gambler without shame."[6] Opponents readily resorted to the politics of personal destruction, slandering not only Jackson, but even his wife and mother. Jackson, who blamed prominent opponents, reportedly on his deathbed regretted that "I did not hang Calhoun and shoot Clay."[7] Henry Clay, of course, was in fact involved in a duel on the Potomac, though he did not share Alexander Hamilton's fate.

POLITICS TODAY

The politics of the early republic provides ample evidence that polarizing partisan politics is nothing new and certainly not limited to the present day. Even so, critics of our purportedly bitter partisanship today sometimes sound like they believe it all began during the George W. Bush presidency or during the 1990s Republican ascendancy in Congress. The Clinton years were marked by partisan strife, as were the Reagan years, with plenty of bipartisan blame for the partisanship shared on both sides of the aisle. Even George H. W. Bush's efforts to promote a "kinder, gentler" politics were rebuffed by Senate majority leader George Mitchell, dubbed "the meanest man in the U.S. Senate" by a widely respected former GOP congressman.[8] President Jimmy Carter was plagued by factionalism within his own party on Capitol Hill, and the presidencies of Johnson, Nixon, and Ford, marked by Vietnam and Watergate, were certainly not part of an "Era of Good Feeling." So when did partisanship and the partisan era begin? As noted in the last chapter, polarizing partisanship began in the beginning, during the early days of the American Republic. Partisanship is endemic or even natural to our constitutional system. The question, of course, is whether the mischief of partisan faction is good or bad. Is it corrosive of good politics and policy or conducive to good politics and policy? The answer is potentially both as we shall see in the following case studies from the 1980s and 1990s.

THE 1986 TAX REFORM ACT

One of political scientists' favorite legislative case studies, the 1986 Tax Reform Act (TRA), provides a useful starting point for examining the partisanship of the present period and whether it is productive or destructive. While any single case study is in some important senses merely anecdotal, the 1986 TRA, as it came to be called, offers powerful insight into the nature of the legislative process, including party competition, as detailed by Timothy Conlon, Margaret Wrightson, and David Beam in their book *Taxing Choices*, a perennial favorite among fellow political scientists. The authors summarize their own argument by citing an observation by former representative John Brademas that "any bill passed by Congress is a tapestry woven from strands of intellectual effort, political opportunity, institutional rivalry, and personal ambition."[9] To understand congressional politics, in other words, we need to consider the role of ideas, interests (including partisan interests), institutions, and individuals.[10]

The 1986 TRA was anything but incremental change; indeed, by common consensus it marked the most significant restructuring of the federal tax code in fifty years. The authors of *Taxing Choices* set out to examine how such fundamental reform ever came about in a constitutional context some presumed marked by gridlock, incrementalism, and a bias against change. It was, perhaps, all that much more surprising—especially from the perspective of neo-Wilsonian reformers like Lloyd Cutler who perennially lament the plodding pluralism of our politics—that the 1986 TRA passed under conditions of divided government, the *bête noir* of policy change according to some critics of our Constitution. Among other things, Conlon, Wrightson, and Beam conclude that ideas count; opinions about the principles of good public policy influence politics, and vice versa. Politics for these authors is neither epiphenomenal nor detrimental to the formation of good public policy.

For the purposes of examining their chosen case study, the authors offer three models of the policy process, beginning with the traditional two: (1) pluralist/incrementalist, and (2) presidential/majoritarian (often tied to party government theory). Noting that neither of these two common models fully captures the complexity of the legislative process, Conlon, Wrightson, and Beam offer a third, which they call the "new politics of reform" focusing on the role of ideas, experts, and policy entrepreneurs.[11] What is especially interesting to note is that these three models correspond to the three key mediating institutions in American politics: interest groups, parties, and the media. The authors conclude that all three models taken together best explain our complex policy process. In other words, the legislative process is rooted in bargaining among competing interest groups and is responsive to a majority sentiment often galvanized by parties and presidents; it even sometimes soars to the heights of policy entrepreneurs' passion for justice premised on the role of experts' ideas. The latter element in this particular case study is represented by ardent tax reformers Congressman Jack Kemp and Senator Bill Bradley. Rational choice theory narrowly conceived cannot capture the fullness of this case study, the authors opine.[12] Again, the role of ideas, interests (including partisan interests), institutions, and individuals must be taken into consideration.

In *The Politics of Regulation*, James Q. Wilson advances an argument critical to understanding the role of ideas in the "new politics of reform": "a complete theory of politics . . . requires that attention be paid to beliefs as well as interests."[13] Martha Derthick and Paul Quirk make a similar argument in *The Politics of Deregulation*. "Unlike traditional pluralism," Conlon, Wrightson, and Beam argue, "the new politics of reform must take into consideration ideas as an independent creative force in the political process."[14] They echo Deborah Stone's contention that "ideas are the very stuff of politics," and they cite John Kingdon to the effect that ideas are not "mere smokescreens or rationalizations."[15] Finally, they quote Gary Orren:

> People [in politics] do not act solely on the basis of their perceived self-interest, without regard to the aggregate consequences of their actions. They are also motivated by values, purposes, goals and commitments that transcend self-interest or group interest. . . . At times, in effect, people act as they feel they *should* act.[16]

Both the "politics of interests" and the "politics of ideas" must be taken into consideration in attempting to fully understand the legislative process. Modern pluralism and rational choice theory narrowly conceived are incomplete.

One premise of modern pluralist theory seems to be the assumption that our separation-of-powers system suffers from a gridlock-inviting bias against change; the presumption being that divided government, in particular, further precludes significant policy change. The 1986 TRA suggests the opposite may sometimes be true; the tax reformers' success may in fact have been premised on divided government, with Republicans controlling the White House and Senate while Democrats reigned as a "permanent majority" in the House. The authors conclude that "partisan competition" propelled the tax-reform bill forward: "Blame avoidance simply replaced credit claiming as a motive force. Neither party, and neither chamber of Congress, wanted the proverbial dead cat on its doorstep."[17] Both sides feared future voter reaction. In short, rather than ambition counteracting ambition, we may have witnessed ambition vying with ambition, thereby augmenting energy in the process rather than subtracting energy as is so often presumed. Playing partisan politics promoted policy reform in the case of the 1986 TRA.

Similarly, members' institutional loyalty to Congress, the House or Senate, or even a particular committee can promote change via ambition vying with ambition. House Ways and Means Committee chair Dan Rostenkowski and his committee members felt compelled "to prove their committee could meet its responsibilities and produce a bill."[18] Competition between the Democratic House and Republican Senate also seemed to increase the energy in a "dynamic" legislative process that included members "hungry for action proposals."[19] Our constitutional routines, Nelson Polsby notes, invite innovation rather than, as is so often presumed, subtract energy from the system.[20] The separation of powers and bicameralism provide multiple access points as well as multiple veto points; in part, because our constitutional system is flexible.[21] In sum, the constitutional system is more than the sum of its institutional parts; it has a life of its own. Institutions affect behavior, molding, channeling, and educating the actions of politicians.

Conlon, Wrightson, and Beam also underscore the importance of individuals in the passage of the 1986 TRA, including policy entrepreneurs such as Kemp and Bradley, administration heavyweights like James Baker and Dick Darmen, and congressional leaders such as Senate Finance Committee chair Bob Packwood and House Ways and Means Committee chair Dan Rostenkowski. The "personal ambition" of Chairman Rostenkowski may have been critical:

> Rostenkowski did far more than stand aside for a popular president. Though no reformer by background or temperament, he came to view tax reform as good policy and good politics—a historic opportunity to secure his reputation and protect his party's interests. To this end, he compelled his reluctant committee to go where it preferred not to tread, crafting legislation uniquely designed to pass the House. By doing so, Rostenkowski stoked the partisan engine of tax reform, placing enormous pressure on the Republican-controlled Senate to respond in kind or face the political fallout.[22]

The partisan and powerful Ways and Means Committee chairman (in those days the word "powerful" seemed permanently grafted to Chairman Rostenkowski's name) fully understood the essential partisan dynamic of Congress, and he clearly understood the necessary nexus between politics and policy. This man who had come of age in the ward-healing politics of Boss Richard Daly's Chicago did not think "politics" was a dirty word. He apparently also had a softer side to complement his rough, tough exterior persona. During a Ways and Means Committee retreat designed to consider tax reform, the normally gruff Rosty famously, albeit briefly, got downright sentimental in rallying his troops. His reputation and honor, along with that of his committee, party, chamber, and Congress were at stake. James Madison certainly would understand

Rostenkowski's sentiment, incentive, and motivation.[23] It is not clear if rational choice theory can accommodate such a broad definition of self-interest without vacating its essential premise.

Politics, including and perhaps especially the politics of the legislative process, is too complex to be explained in terms of single-cause theories such as reelection, clientelism or interest-group capture theories; thus, Conlon, Wrightson, and Beam are right to rely on three different models and levels of analysis to fully comprehend the 1986 TRA. For similar reasons, Jack Pitney and I turned to the Rubik's Cube analysis encompassing the independent roles of ideas, interests (including partisan interests), institutions, and individuals. The sheer complexity of the game cube also at least feigns in the direction of the sort of complexity underlying legislative politics. *Taxing Choices* also underscores the fact that politics—including the politics of ambition and partisanship—is good, and that politics and policy in our system inevitably go hand in hand. Conlon, Wrightson, and Beam understand the dual nature of the "two congresses" outlined by Roger Davidson and Walter Oleszek. They also seem to appreciate the fact that the 1986 TRA occurred in the context of a Washington dominated by two old, powerful, partisan Irish-American politicians: Tip O'Neill and Ronald Reagan.[24]

Taxing Choices authors comprehend the latent potential of our separation-of-powers system to accommodate all three of their models: pluralism/incrementalism, presidential/majoritarian, and the ideational/entrepreneurial "new politics of reform." Yet what the authors describe is not really new. Each of the three models makes sense and contains an element of truth because the Constitution embodies all three. The principled flexibility of our separation of powers invites energy and innovation rather than the stasis and stagnation presumed in the modern pluralist model. As argued earlier in this book, James Madison understood and incorporated all of the above in his constitutional separation of powers system. Our constitutional system encompasses the paradigms of pluralism, party government, *plus*.

James W. Ceaser, in an earlier discussion of the separation-of-powers, provides some insight into the flexibility of our constitutional order:

> The doctrine of separation of powers . . . does not define fully—nor was it ever intended to define fully—the exact character of the policy-making process. The Constitution is not completely silent or neutral about the character of the policy-making process, but in the final analysis there is not one single constitutional model for the policy-making function but only constitutional limits within which models must be constructed.[25]

Ceaser argues that the flexibility of the separation of powers explains how the same constitutional order can provide for the era of congressional dominance in the nineteenth century and the rise of the imperial presidency in the period from the 1930s to the 1970s. The flexible and dynamic quality of the separation of powers might also explain the simultaneous existence of different "systems of power" as the authors of *Taxing Choices* call their three models. The constitutional separation of powers means that the American political system potentially and simultaneously is all three, depending on timing, issues, and participants. Power floats, depending on institutional cycles and institutional time.[26] Divided government and partisan combat can be productive, promoting fission as well as friction. David Mayhew's books *Divided Government* and *America's Congress* underscore how the separation of powers can produce energy rather than just subtract it from the overall innovative energy in the political system.

Jemmy the Knife might have been right at home with the likes of Ronald Reagan, Tip O'Neill, James Baker, and Danny Rostenkowski in 1986. The competition between Republicans and Democrats over the 1986 TRA provides a good example of politics energizing public deliberation. Ambitious individuals operating within constitutional institutions that enhance competition and conflict—and surrounded by a demanding environment—make for a dynamic politics that is a far cry from the conventional Wilsonian image of Congress as suffering from gridlock and a bias against change. Like the capitalist free markets described by economists—complete with creative destruction—a pluralist free market channeled and broadened by institutional structures augments the energy and creativity that goes into policymaking. Politicians, beginning in a self-interested quest for reelection, search for compelling ideas and the support of competing interests, and sometimes ideally end by serving the public interest. The full understanding of the separation of powers found in *The Federalist* provides a more complete explanation for the 1986 TRA success than the conventional Wilsonian perspective so commonplace today.

THE 1995–1996 BUDGET SHOWDOWN/SHUTDOWN AND THE 1997 BALANCED BUDGET ACT

The titanic 1995–1996 budget showdown between Newt Gingrich and Bill Clinton and the resulting government shutdowns are often cited as classic examples of the inevitable gridlock built into divided government in times of bitter partisanship. As Congress scholar Richard Fenno noted, Speaker Gingrich had much to learn about governing. Among other things, Speaker Gingrich learned that parliamentary party government, pure and simple, is not possible in the context of our separation of powers; his experiment in congressional party government backfired—or at least in part it backfired.

Yet the lesson we also learn from the 1990s budget battles is not that our political system is simply prone to partisan gridlock and utterly adverse to needed change. The lesson is not that the only way to bring about meaningful policy change is by means of the compromise of pluralist accommodation seemingly favored by some critics of our polarized politics today. Finally, the lesson is not that politics and partisan competition are bad; indeed, the partisan conflict of the 1990s proved productive and even promoted the kind of accountability that critics of our separation of powers sometimes insist our constitutional system precludes.

One might argue that House Republicans lost the budget battle in 1995–1996, only to win the war in the Balanced Budget Act of 1997. The breadth and depth of budget discipline in the 1997 Balanced Budget Act would not have been possible without both sides—Congress and the president, Republicans and Democrats—first experiencing the heightened institutional and partisan confrontation of 1995–1996. These two case studies must be understood as one. Out of the ashes of the earlier battle came the phoenix of the latter accord. In this instance, as in so many others in our legislative process, confrontation provided the premise for compromise. As the *Promises* candy-wrapper aphorism states, "there is a time for compromise . . . later." In the case of the 1995–1996 showdown/shutdown, "later" came in 1997.

Confrontation and compromise are in fact two sides of the same coin. This is the real lesson of the 1990s budget battles, which in retrospect proved highly productive, thanks in large part to two talented partisan warriors, Newt Gingrich and Bill Clinton. The 1996 election also provided accountability for the two parties and their leaders. Newt Gingrich in effect helped reelect Bill Clinton; yet voters also refrained from rewarding Clinton and the Democrats with majorities in Congress. Congressional Republican majorities went on to win reelection in 1996 and 1998. Voters seemed content in the 1990s to perpetuate divided government.[27] Again, the backfiring of Gingrich's overly ambitious, overreaching exercise in congressional party government does not mean that our political system is ultimately reducible to the mere interest-accommodating incrementalism and compromise of modern pluralist theory.

Rather, Madison's pluralism is more robust and potentially constructive, embracing as it does the energy and "spirit of party." In a word, partisanship can be productive. Ron Haskins's insider account of the successful 1996 welfare-reform effort provides a similarly useful case study, supporting the argument that partisanship can be productive, though for our purposes here we focus only on the 1990s budget wars.[28]

With his 1994 ascension to majority status, Gingrich, ever the Wilsonian, adopted Woodrow Wilson's *Congressional Government* aspiration for our political system. Speaker Gingrich thought he had created parliamentary government with himself as prime minister. His short-lived experiment in congressional government provides useful insights into the limits of party leadership in our separation-of-powers system. In *Learning to Govern*, Richard Fenno criticizes Gingrich's House Republican "revolution," arguing that the separation of powers requires compromise—which no doubt it does. Fenno, however, seems in danger of suggesting that the separation of powers provides *only* for the politics of accommodation.

Ironically, Fenno too, like Gingrich, seems overly Wilsonian in his perspective. Whereas Gingrich adopted Wilson's aspiration for our constitutional system, Fenno, like other political scientists critical of the Gingrich "revolution," seems to adopt the Wilsonian critique of our constitutional system.[29] As witness the 1990s budget battles, Madison's constitutional system in practice limits Wilsonian aspirations such as Gingrich's. Yet it also calls into question the Wilsonian critique of our separation of powers so commonplace among political scientists today. Our constitutional separation of powers does not inevitably promote gridlock, prevent needed change, preclude party accountability or guarantee that special interests always trump broad-based interests.

In the battle between the Gingrich Republicans and Clinton Democrats, one can easily argue Republicans lost the battle, yet won the war. The 1995–1996 showdown/shutdown provided the necessary predicate for the historic 1997 budget accord between congressional Republicans and the Clinton White House. Again, confrontation can lead to compromise. Evidence to this effect can be found in various accounts of the 1990s budget wars, including those offered by Elizabeth Drew, Nicol Rae, and Daniel Palazzolo.

Newt and Woodrow

The failures of the Gingrich Republicans in the 104th Congress were due in part to an intellectual error rooted in Gingrich's Wilsonian misunderstanding of the separation of powers. Gingrich and Wilson both tended to downplay, not to say ignore, the importance of institutional and constitutional structure. For example, during Governing Team Day, a 1980 forerunner of the Contract with America, Gingrich said in a floor speech, "This is the first step toward a *de facto* constitutional amendment that will give us accountable party government by giving us accountable party campaigns and accountable party government." In point of fact, neither Governing Team Day nor the Contract With America were de facto constitutional amendments; to the contrary, constitutional structure constrained both exercises. In *Storming the Gates*, an early book about the House Republican revival, journalists Dan Balz and Ron Brownstein concluded "Gingrich expanded his reach beyond anything the Founding Fathers had imagined."[30] In retrospect, it is clear Gingrich did no such thing.

House Republicans failed to consummate their "revolution" in part because they misunderstood or ignored the constitutional separation of powers and bicameralism. House GOP members acted as if they could achieve their "revolution" all by themselves with their take-it-or-leave-it budget strategy; they temporarily deluded themselves into believing that the president and Senate were irrelevant, that the president and Senate would have to follow their lead. They ignored the independent constitutional authority of the president and Senate. They wrapped much of the "revolution" into their budget strategy and assumed the White House would cave. When the president did not give in, and when he acquiesced to shutting down the government, public opinion blamed the House GOP for this manufactured crisis. Gingrich had convinced the American people that they were witnessing "congressional party government" in action; thus when the government failed to work, they held him accountable.

House Republicans may have been convinced that they had created congressional government, but congressional government inevitably failed within the constitutional confines of Madison's separation of powers. Congress is not Parliament and wishing does not make it so. The defeat of the House GOP budget strategy in 1995–1996 provides practical and palpable proof of the power of constitutional structure to govern the behavior of individuals. Gingrich overlooked one of Madison's central insights, namely, that institutions mold individual and group behavior. James Madison, not Bill Clinton, tamed the House Republican "revolution." Conceivably even greater practical proof of the limits of Gingrich's experiment in "congressional government" might be the failure of the congressional Republican effort to impeach and remove Bill Clinton from the presidency. In his heart of hearts, did Gingrich think of impeachment as the congressional equivalent of a parliamentary vote of no confidence?

Gingrich's Wilsonian perspective was evident in an interview with journalist Elizabeth Drew during the 104th Congress. As noted in chapter 3, Gingrich observed rather expansively,

> [W]hat we're doing is a cultural revolution with societal and political consequences that ultimately change the government. That is a vastly bigger agenda than has been set by any modern political system in this country . . . we're not doing what people used to do. We don't resemble any previous system. There are no comparisons that make sense because you've never had an information-age, grassroots-focused, change-oriented structure.[31]

Democrats are the "establishment," he insisted, while Republicans are the "revolution."[32] Gingrich was convinced that cultural and technological changes matter more than existing institutional structures, thereby causing him to underestimate White House tenacity: "The collision with the White House is a project, but it's a tiny part of what we're doing. I mean, we'll do that *en passant*. That will not be a major part of my planning operation"[33] Gingrich, as we know in retrospect, did not bring about a revolution.

To Gingrich's credit, he tends to see politics as fundamentally about principles and ideas; like Woodrow Wilson he is not content with a politics of competing special interests. His "cultural revolution" recognizes, along with political scientists such as Ron Peters and Eric Uslaner, the cultural and philosophical differences between our two political parties.[34] As Drew noted in *Showdown*, the politics of the 104th Congress was "a contest over large questions about the role and direction of government."[35] The stakes were significant and the parties stood on principle.

With his typical hubris, however, Gingrich pushed his revolutionary perspective too far, insisting politics is a clash between two different worldviews.[36] For Newt, perhaps Republicans are from Mars and Democrats are from Venus. While American politics often entails a clash between competing ideas, transcending mere accommodation among interests, to see our politics in terms of a "cultural revolution" seems something of a stretch.[37] Certainly politics is about ideas, though Gingrich would have done well to pay greater heed to James Madison's ideas about the role of institutional and constitutional structure, including the separation of powers and bicameralism.

Unfortunately for Speaker Gingrich, the resilience of Madisonian institutions proved greater than any "third wave" paradigm shift he hoped to foment. In chapter 3 we saw that Gingrich concluded in *Lessons Learned the Hard Way*, "We had other lessons to learn as well. We had not only failed to take into account the ability of the Senate to delay us and obstruct us, but we had much too cavalierly underrated the power of the President. . . . How could we have forgotten that?"[38] He added, "A legislator and an executive are two very different things, and for a time we had allowed ourselves to confuse the two."[39] Had Gingrich been a more careful student of *The Federalist* he never would have confused the two. Central to Madison's understanding of the separation of powers is the recognition that different institutions do different things; the separation of powers is in fact a separation of functions. The separation of powers empowers each independent institution within its own sphere.

During the showdown/shutdown, our constitutional structure also proved more robust than President Clinton's tenacity. It appears Gingrich was not the only one at the time to believe he was seeing congressional party government in action. President Clinton suffered the same illusion, as noted earlier, witness his infamous seemingly plaintive insistence that he was still "relevant" during a post-1994 election press conference.[40]

The second session of the 104th Congress began to witness a reversal of fortunes for Gingrich and Clinton; nevertheless, Gingrich critics should not underestimate him simply because he was unable to accomplish in one term a revolution or even a political realignment the likes of which took FDR and Democrats decades to complete. Gingrich should not be judged by the exaggerated expectations he fomented. Professor Gingrich continued to learn as seen, for example, in his *Lessons Learned the Hard Way* and in his more measured approach during the 105th Congress. By the late 1990s, Gingrich recognized that the era of congressional government was over, yet he remained confident that the era of big government was over as well, as evidenced by welfare reform, for example. While revolutions may not be feasible within our constitutional context, party realignments surely are possible. History has given us repeated examples of the latter.[41] Significant policy change—even significant change in policy direction—is possible in the American political system. Gridlock, stasis, and "demosclerosis" are not always and inevitably the order of the day.

FENNO'S *LEARNING TO GOVERN*

In *Learning to Govern*, Richard Fenno concludes that forty years as a "permanent minority" left House Republicans unprepared to govern during the 104th Congress, in part because their lack of experience in the majority led them to over-interpret their election victory. House Republicans "missed their golden governing opportunity," thereby reviving the Clinton presidency.[42] Gingrich Republicans, Fenno argues, failed to make the transition from opposition to government; they engaged in the politics of confrontation with President Clinton when they should have embraced a more sensible politics of compromise.[43] During the 104th Congress, Fenno concludes, House Republicans finally started learning to govern, first by recognizing they could not govern from the House alone. Fenno is correct in underscoring Gingrich's failure to appreciate the limits of Congress within our constitutional order. *Learning to Govern* makes an important argument about the nature of the legislative process and the separation of powers. Yet if Gingrich overestimated the potential of Congress, one wonders if Fenno underestimates the institution's potential.

In large part, Fenno's analysis and argument in *Learning to Govern* are accurate, and his articulation of that argument is compelling. His understanding of the constitutional separation of powers remains incomplete, however, raising questions about Fenno's larger argument. Fenno's incomplete understanding of the separation of powers provides an opening for expanding on his analysis of the defects of Newt Gingrich's House Republican "revolution." A more complete understanding of the separation of powers necessitates taking into consideration both the actions of Newt Gingrich and the analysis of Richard Fenno. Gingrich and Fenno may each have, so to speak, half the whole when it comes to understanding in theory and practice the central principle of the Constitution.[44]

Fenno concludes that Gingrich in the 104th Congress failed to fully appreciate the "very different requirements of insurgency and governance."[45] House Republicans failed to make the transition from campaigning to governing. Fenno quotes Charles Krauthammer to the effect that "Republicans seem unable to realize they are no longer the party of protest, but the party of governance."[46] For Fenno, the distinction between insurgency and governance, campaigning and governing, and ultimately between opposition and government, is critical.

Learning to govern, according to Fenno and as noted in chapter 1, requires an appreciation of the "inevitable incrementalism, trade-offs, compromises, negotiations, and public resonances" of the legislative process.[47] Successful legislating involves

> a practical grasp of lawmaking as a lengthy, incremental, multilevel, coalition-building process. And it involves a seasoned strategic sense in matters such as establishing priorities, negotiating outcomes across the *separated institutions of government*, and calculating feasibilities, trade-offs, and timing at every decision-making juncture.[48]

Fundamentally, learning to govern means learning to compromise, according to Fenno, and the House Republican revolutionaries were in no mood to compromise. House Republicans, Fenno concludes, made a fundamental error in using the Contract with America—an *electioneering* document—as a *legislative agenda* during the forced march of their first one hundred days.[49] The Contract strategy merely focused on action in the House. "It took no account of the broader legislative context that lay beyond, a context of *separated institutions sharing responsibility and power*."[50] Such a context of institutions sharing power by its very nature requires compromise. Yet the question is this: Does the Constitution in fact provide for separate institutions sharing power?

Fenno is, of course, right in criticizing Speaker Gingrich and House Republicans for seemingly forgetting about the Senate and president, and for assuming that in some fundamental sense they *were* the government pure and simple. In *Lessons Learned the Hard Way*, Gingrich appropriately acknowledges this failing as noted above. But is Fenno correct in reducing the legislative process to incrementalism and compromise? Certainly the legislative process is not conducive to revolution, but is Congress really incapable of sweeping political and policy change? FDR's first one hundred days suggests otherwise, as does the *success*, as opposed to the *failure*, of the House Republican "revolution."

During the 104th Congress, House Republicans kept the legislative trains running, which in itself is surprising from Fenno's perspective given their lack of experience after forty years in the "permanent minority" wilderness. Their first one hundred days were little short of a tour de force in this regard, including the fact that they fundamentally reformed legislative procedures in a manner that even won the praise of experienced "old bull" Democrats like Dan Rostenkowski. Yet, Fenno insists, such success is not to be mistaken for governing. The "extraordinary diligence and discipline" of the House GOP's first one hundred days is not sufficient for governing: "Not only had they not understood the difference between passing the Contract and governing the country, but what was worse, they had mistaken one for the other."[51] Again, Fenno argues, governing requires compromise between the House and Senate, between Congress and the president, and between the two political parties.

Governing requires compromise, Fenno concludes, because our Constitution gives us "separated institutions, sharing responsibility and power." But what if our Constitution gives us no such thing? What if our Constitution instead gives us three separate, independent, and powerful branches, and two independent and powerful legislative chambers? Congress and the president, the House and the Senate are each independent and powerful *within their sphere*. Neither chamber nor branch by itself is the government. Neither chamber nor branch governs. Indeed, even the House, Senate, and president together do not govern; rather, the Constitution governs each chamber and branch. Compromise certainly is crucial at times in the legislative process, but vetoes, veto overrides, filibusters, and each branch or chamber digging in its heels and refusing to compromise are also part of the legislative process. Confrontation *and* compromise together comprise the legislative process. Even stalemate is at times a necessary and productive part of the legislative process, especially if it halts bad legislation.[52]

Gingrich's independence and confrontational stance were not the problem; rather, his mistake was the presumption that the House by itself was the government. He forgot (if that is even possible) about the "cooling saucer" of the Senate and the president's veto pen. The only way Gingrich could "forget" this is if he blinded himself, as he seemed to do, to the true nature of the separation of powers. He assumed ours was a House-centered parliamentary system, and he forgot about the independence and power of the Senate and the executive. Similarly, Fenno assumes that compromise is the essence of both the legislative process and governing because our separated branches purportedly share power. They all need to get along, and they all need to work together. Fenno is in danger of overlooking the independence of the president and Congress, the House and Senate.

Fenno echoes the commonplace perspective on the separation of powers found in the writings of Richard Neustadt and Woodrow Wilson, namely, that our system is one of separate institutions sharing power. Fenno, Neustadt, Wilson, and a host of other political scientists all seem to reduce the separation of powers to the checks and balances. Certainly the checks and balances are a concomitant of the constitutional separation of powers; for example, according to Madison and Hamilton, the checks and balances help keep the branches separate.[53] But the checks and balances are not the sum and substance of the separation of powers; rather, institutional independence and vigor—not stasis—are the heart of our separation-of-powers system. Congress, for example, remains powerful, unlike legislatures in other advanced liberal democracies, because ours is a complete separation-of-powers system unlike the incomplete separation of powers one finds, say, in the British parliamentary system. The independence and power of Congress, of course, are also why it is "the most popularly despised legislative body in the Western world," another lesson Newt Gingrich learned.[54] The separation-of-powers provides for limited, yet effective government. Woodrow Wilson never seemed to understand or appreciate this feature of the separation of powers even though it is clearly articulated in *The Federalist*.

Similarly, Fenno assumes Congress and the president must work in concert, rather than at loggerheads. Fenno suggests, for example, that House Republicans should have bided their time and worked to get a Republican president elected in 1996 rather than impatiently attempting to consummate their "revolution" all by themselves in the 104th Congress:

> If, as I think was the case, the party's most important long-run goal was to bring about a *unified Republican government*, the Republicans should have interpreted the election as an invitation to take some carefully selected first steps toward the accomplishment of that goal.[55]

This may be wise advice for a party, but institutional incentives, including electoral incentives, do not promote such a long-term and other-institution-regarding perspective by either the majority or minority party in the House. Where are the institutional incentives designed to inspire this foresight among House members? Where in our constitutional system are the institutional incentives to inspire foresight beyond two years in House members, especially foresight focused on advancing party ambitions in the "other body" or another branch?

The recommendation that House Republicans in the 104th Congress should have worked toward attaining "unified Republican government" ignores the institutional incentives of our separation of powers, which preclude, or at least do not promote, a long-term presidency-targeting perspective among members of Congress. Members of Congress are elected independently of the executive and for two- or six-year terms rather than the president's four-year term. The impatience of House members should come as no surprise since it is predicated on their two-year terms. Their unwillingness to advance the ambitions of presidents or presidential candidates of their own party is, of course, matched historically by the willingness of presidents and presidential candidates to "orphan" their fellow party members serving in or running for Congress.

The natural institutional tendency of members of the House or Senate is to look out for their own electoral interests and to defend the prerogatives of their institution; the executive acts similarly. It may be miracle enough that the institution of Congress educates members to a larger sense of institutional responsibility, attaching the "interest of the man" to "the constitutional rights of the place."[56] It may be the case that other-regarding behavior springs from a natural human tendency, but experience suggests that members of Congress and presidents are naturally going to first serve their own electoral self-interest and defend the institutional prerogatives of their home institution before turning their attention elsewhere.

Examples abound. House Republicans were endlessly frustrated by President Reagan's pursuit of a forty-nine state victory in 1984, just as House Democrats were angered by President Clinton's inattention to their electoral plight in 1996.[57] House Republicans returned the favor with Newt Gingrich's lose-the-White-House-to-win-the-House strategy undercutting President George H. W. Bush in 1992, while House Democrats in 2007 seemed more intent upon advancing their legislative agenda than the ambitions of their party's presidential contenders for 2008.[58] There are, of course, countervailing examples. When it was clear to Bob Dole that he was going to lose in 1996, he sought to shore up congressional Republicans in various races. Once a senator, always a senator, perhaps. Similarly, George W. Bush famously stumped tirelessly in the 2002 midterm election to advance his party's prospects in Hill elections. At the other end of Pennsylvania Avenue one also finds within both Hill parties "presidential loyalists" willing to support a president of their own party, and even subordinate the interest of the party on the Hill to the party leader in the White House.[59] Still, on balance, the institutional incentives built into the separation of powers promote conflict between the chambers and branches at least as much if not more than they promote cooperation. Again, Madison's separation of powers precludes pure party government, though not necessarily party loyalty.

Fenno argues in *Learning to Govern* that House Republicans should have worked to bring about "unified Republican government." Yet bringing about a unified Republican or Democratic government is not possible in our separation-of-powers system. Even when elections produce what we sometimes call unified Republican or Democratic government—where one party controls the White House and at the same time has majorities in the House and the Senate—the fact remains that neither party is ever, by itself, the government, just as neither party is ever simply the opposition. Such may be the case in a parliamentary system but never in our separation-of-powers system. The closest approximation of such unified party government can be seen, for example, when the party in the White House enjoys supermajorities in Congress, such as happened with Democrats following the 1932 and 1964 elections. Such periods may be party realignments, but they are not in fact periods of unified party government. Again, party government is not possible in our separation-of-powers system, though party loyalty is possible.

Ironically, Fenno's view that the House GOP ideally should have worked toward "unified Republican government" in 1996 runs contrary to his belief that they should have learned to govern. Should they have been *governing* or *campaigning*, pursuing policy or playing politics during the 104th Congress? Working toward unified Republican government in the next election would seem to mean using their position in government to advance party ambition in the next election cycle, thereby conflating governing and campaigning. Should House Republicans have learned to govern or learned to campaign better? Are campaigning and governing the same?

Fenno rightly notes that House Republicans revived the Clinton presidency. The House GOP helped reelect Bill Clinton to a second term.[60] Yet, if James Ceaser and Andrew Busch are right in *Losing to Win*, this result may have been almost inevitable in the 1990s. Ceaser and Busch argue neither Democrats nor Republicans had a positive governing majority during that decade. Rather, both had, at best, negative majorities, that is, majorities premised on a rejection by voters of the other party.[61] As a consequence, the decade was marked by "the politics of repulsion"—not between the two parties but between the presidential and congressional wings of the same party. "The success of one [wing] positively hurts the other," as seen for example in the fate of GOP presidential candidate Bob Dole in 1996 following Newt Gingrich's electoral success in 1994, or as seen in the fate of House Democrats following Bill Clinton's election victory in 1992 winning 43 percent of the vote. This losing-to-win phenomenon, however, may not be limited to the 1990s; it may be part of the irony of the constitutional separation of powers. The irony can be seen most readily in midterm elections, especially six-year-itch elections when the party in the White House commonly loses seats in congressional elections. The politics of repulsion, where the success of one party wing positively hurts the other wing is in part hardwired into our separation-of-powers system.

Fenno criticizes House Republicans for helping to reelect Clinton in 1996 by their overreaching in the 104th Congress. One is tempted to ask, When was the last time prior to 1995–1996 that a party engaged in legislative overreaching that redounded to its disadvantage in the next election? Answer: Democrats in the 103rd Congress with Hillary Clinton's health-care reform initiative. Arguably, President Clinton and congressional Democrats made the same mistake in the 103rd Congress that Fenno cites Republicans for in the 104th Congress; namely, they tried to govern with what Ceaser and Busch call a negative majority—or what others might call an absence of consensus. The Clinton health-care debacle in the 103rd

Congress rivals the House GOP's showdown/shutdown fiasco in the 104th Congress. The first helped elect the House Republican majority in 1994, and the second helped elect Bill Clinton to a second term in 1996. Experienced House Democrats contributed to the first, while inexperienced House Republicans contributed to the second.

Fenno's criticism of House Republicans for overreaching is legitimate, but it needs to be placed in context. The "permanent majority" House Democrats, with four decades of experience, may have made the same mistake Fenno accuses Republicans of making as a new and inexperienced majority. Furthermore, it is worth noting that while House Republicans may have helped reelect Bill Clinton, they also retained Congress. Was the glass half empty or half full? Were the inexperienced, overreaching, and mandate-over-interpreting House Republicans to blame? Or was their eventual fate in part tied to the constitutional context and the irony of the separation of powers where party success sometimes breeds party failure? Remember, one reason House Republicans remained mired for decades in their "permanent minority" was their party's success at winning the presidency in the 1970s and 1980s. The Madisonian separation of powers precludes, or at least limits, long-term unified party government. As we shall see, however, it does not preclude significant policy change or doom us to deadlock and stasis.

IMITATION AS FLATTERY

Fenno concludes House Republicans' "late-term conversion to compromise" saved their majority in the 1996 elections.[62] Speaker Gingrich, Fenno argues, recognized his "radical party centralization plan" had failed.[63] Fenno quotes Gingrich in support of his *Learning to Govern* thesis:

> We need a slower, broader participatory structure to move toward solving our problems. There will be a tremendous amount of implementation in this Congress and much less confrontation. And so I think that this kind of open leadership activity will work better than the centralized system.[64]

Gingrich's "prime-ministership adventure had ended," Fenno observes, "a victim of experience."[65] Newt's Wilsonian congressional government experiment, complete with party centralization and political confrontation was over. Presumably, then, the pendulum should swing back to decentralized committee government and the politics of compromise. But did it?

As of 2010, neither House Republicans nor House Democrats had simply returned to the good old days of committee government and accommodation, nor had they returned to the bad old days of subcommittee government. Following the 1994 election, the new minority House Democrats quickly *un*learned the lessons of governing as a "permanent majority"; instead they immediately began emulating the supposedly irresponsible confrontational behavior of House Republicans when they were in the minority prior to 1994. Furthermore, House Democrats quickly found themselves frustrated by President Clinton's tendency to "orphan" them just as Republican presidents had done to the House GOP; consequently, they broke with their president. James Barnes and Richard Cohen observed about House Democrats, "While the lawmakers took a partisan line in hopes of regaining their majority, Clinton focused more on consensus and the demands of governing."[66] Congressional Democrats felt particularly sold out by Clinton on the 1997 Balanced Budget Act.[67] Such party divisions owe more to the institutional separation of powers than the individual, strategic predilections of party politicians.

Eventually, House Democrats became "bomb throwers" like the early Gingrich, rejecting the accommodating tendencies of Minority Leader Dick Gephardt and embracing the Gingrich-imitating strategy of Nancy Pelosi. In many ways, House Democrats, in spite of their years of experience as the majority party, behaved similarly to House Republicans under Gingrich both before and after the 1994 election. In the minority, House Democrats adopted a confrontational approach, complete with the "politics by other means" tactics of attacking the "culture of corruption" in Congress. Were they trying to destroy the institution, as Gingrich was accused of doing as a backbench "bomb thrower"? Or were they merely attempting to capture majority control of the chamber as Gingrich insisted he was doing prior to 1994?

Minority House Democrats tried various Contract-like experiments in campaigns prior to their Six for '06 platform in 2006 when they toppled the Republican majority after twelve years. Moreover, like Gingrich, and contrary to Fenno's judgment, Pelosi chose to use her Six for '06 campaign platform as a governing document and legislative agenda during her first-one-hundred-hours echo of the House Republicans' 104th opening. Nancy's one hundred hours also echoes Newt's one hundred days, but from Fenno's learning-to-govern perspective, this pell-mell rush to legislate Six for '06 would seem to exacerbate the defects of Newt's use of the Contract with America. The Pelosi Democrats similarly reformed congressional procedures in the early days of their majority, just as the Gingrich revolutionaries had done in 1995.[68] Whether as a minority prior to the 2006 election, or as a majority since, House Democrats mimicked the behavior of House Republicans during the 1990s, including a hostile posture toward the White House. If imitation is the sincerest form of flattery, then Gingrich Republicans could not have been all wrong, at least if judged by the practice of House Democrats.

House Democrats under Nancy Pelosi, both while serving in the minority and while serving as the majority, seem to perceive Newt Gingrich's earlier confrontational strategy as effective; otherwise, why emulate him? Are House Democrats not learning to govern? To borrow Fenno's earlier observation, House Democrats may be missing "their golden governing opportunity."[69] Perhaps in the 110th Congress, they should have worked diligently at finding areas of agreement with President Bush and advancing legislation. After all, the senior ranks of House Democrats, especially among committee chairs, were filled with wizened, experienced former committee chairs from the days when Democrats were last in the majority. Yet senior chairs such as Waxman and Conyers instead adopted the same confrontational tactics Gingrich purportedly pioneered. Were they failing to govern? Were they compromising as the governing party and working toward winning the White House for their party in 2008 as Fenno would presumably recommend?

Oversight may in fact be part of their contribution to governing under our separation-of-powers system. If governing means producing legislation signed by the president, then the first Congress of the new House Democratic majority provided more gridlock than governing. Yet the idea that governing means legislative productivity may reflect a Progressive perspective. For Woodrow Wilson, who feared that our constitutional separation-of-powers was not up to the task facing a great nation in the twentieth century, good government meant activist government. On the other hand, as noted in an earlier chapter, James Madison and Charles O. Jones seem willing to make the case that governing may include halting legislative productivity. House Democrats, for example, may have been accomplishing something by limiting President Bush's legislative initiatives. A confrontational partisan strategy may make sense depending on your perspective. House Democrats in the 110th Congress opted for a strategy of playing "opposition" rather than "government" but that may make sense in our separation-of-powers system. Their success may have depended on limiting Republicans' success.

Gridlock may be good. Pelosi Democrats may have been doing what they should be doing by limiting, for example, George W. Bush's efforts at Social Security reform, just as Gingrich Republicans may have been doing what they should have been doing when they limited Clinton's health-care initiative. Newt and Nancy are alike in many ways. Her imitation of Gingrich's strategy raises questions about Fenno's analysis.

Of course, some Republican critics—though not including Fenno—among political scientists and journalists can and have simply shifted the blame for our confrontational politics to Republicans regardless of whether the House GOP is in the majority or minority.[70] At a minimum, it would be ironic if such critics were partisan in their denunciation of partisanship. Did these same critics celebrate House Republican success in passing bipartisan legislation, including Foreign Intelligence Surveillance Act (FISA) reform in summer 2008?

HOUSE REPUBLICAN SUCCESS

Newt's "revolution" failed. Yet House Republicans can claim some success in terms of advancing their politics and policy, their ambitions and agenda. Fenno credits Gingrich's confrontational minority-insurgency strategy as winning the House for Republicans in 1994.[71] House Republicans held on to that majority for twelve years, one of the longest such runs of partisan success in congressional history.

Evidence that the budget showdown/shutdown was not an unmitigated disaster for the House GOP can be found in the fact that House Democrats gained only nine seats in 1996, failing to match House Republicans' own paltry pickup of fifteen seats in 1984, the last previous comparable election in which a president sought and gained reelection. The meager nine-seat pickup is especially surprising in light of the fifty-two seats won in 1994 by House Republicans; traditionally, first-term members provide inviting targets for the opposition party.

Fenno argues Republicans maintained their majority in 1996 because in the end they compromised with Clinton, which is intuitively plausible.[72] The politics of compromise aids a congressional party in appealing to middle-of-the-road swing voters. Just as plausible, however, is the argument that House Republicans maintained their base by standing on principle. Political parties in the House are caught between a rock and a hard place. They typically must appeal to their base *and* to swing voters; thus, they must constantly play the politics of confrontational principle *and* the politics of interest accommodation, depending in part, of course, on whether they are facing a midterm election or presidential election year. Republicans maintained their majority again in 1998; and in both the 2000 and 2004 elections Republicans won "unified Republican government."[73] Only in the 2006 six-year-itch election did House Republicans relinquish their majority. In 2006, minority Democrats successfully tarred Republicans with their "culture of corruption" charge (once again echoing Newt), while at the same time an increasingly unpopular President Bush was defending an increasingly unpopular Iraq War. A twelve-year run as the majority is no small accomplishment, especially when it includes gaining the Senate and White House as well.

In terms of policy success, Fenno sees the passage of the Contract with America agenda as a "remarkable achievement."[74] In *Showdown* Elizabeth Drew remarked, "Going into the celebrations of the Hundred Days, Gingrich could rightly claim success" even if there were "some clouds" on the horizon.[75] Much of the Contract eventually became law, including the

Congressional Accountability Act, the item veto, and sweeping welfare reform. Democratic Senatorial Campaign Committee chair Bob Kerrey said at the time, "Congress is relevant again because of the House Republicans who promised to do ten things [in their Contract with America], many of which I disagree with, but they did them all, and that has increased confidence in our democracy."[76] If popularity in polls is a measure of success, it is worth noting that Congress soared to record levels of public esteem in 1995.

Charles O. Jones concluded in his study of legislative productivity that 1996 was the third most productive year of major legislation in fifty years. Fenno argues "party-wide learning" and a "late-term conversion to compromise" explains House Republican success, citing legislative accomplishments including health-care portability, a minimum-wage increase, drinking water legislation, and welfare reform.[77] The latter is sometimes seen as a Clinton success story, yet congressional Republicans confronted Democrat Clinton three times with serious welfare-reform bills before he signed legislation. If the 1996 Welfare Reform Act was a Democratic success story, why did Representative Henry Waxman specifically cite welfare reform in condemning President Clinton?

> The combination of last year's welfare reform bill and the [proposed] cap on Medicaid will mean more harm will have been done by President Clinton to poor people than by President Reagan and President Bush. It's unworthy of a Democratic president.[78]

In two years, Congress went from the failed health-care reform attempt to grow the government to a successful effort to limit government and devolve policy responsibility to state governments with welfare reform. Arguably, House Republicans had learned to govern.

Regarding the budget impasse, Fenno noted:

> In the end, Republican pressure did cause the president to submit a balanced budget, make large reductions in Medicare, set a seven-year timetable, and permit Congressional Budget Office participation. And when the government reopened, the president offered a budget that had moved closer to the Republicans than anyone thought possible.[79]

In his 1996 State of the Union Address, Democrat Clinton acknowledged "the era of big government is over," only to be greeted by thunderous applause from congressional Republicans. Shortly thereafter, emblazoned across the front of the conservative *Weekly Standard* magazine was the headline "WE WIN."

And that was before the 1997 Balanced Budget Act.

If the best evidence of the failure of the Gingrich "revolution" is the budget showdown/shutdown debacle, the best evidence of House Republican success may be the 1997 budget agreement. The landmark Balanced Budget Act included several Contract with America items, including a five-hundred-dollars-per-child tax cut, American Dream savings accounts, and a capital gains tax reduction. Even if House Republicans were neither graceful nor altogether sensible in ongoing budget negotiations, the fact is they had taken significant steps toward limiting government, including welfare reform and the 1997 Balanced Budget Act. In the process, Democrats had been converted to the green eyeshade party, a mantle they continued to wear for some time thereafter; this was no small revolution in its own right. In sum, Gingrich's failures must be understood in the context of his successes.

LOSING THE BATTLE, WINNING THE WAR

In *Conservative Reformers: The Republican Freshmen and the Lessons of the 104th Congress,* Nicol Rae comments that House Republicans proved capable of working the legislative process, keeping the legislative trains running on time, and passing legislation in the House even if they did not always reckon successfully with the Senate or president.[80] Moreover, Republican freshmen had two primary goals, institutional reform and a balanced budget, both of which they ultimately attained.[81] The freshmen, including Senate freshmen, believed that "although they might have lost the budget battle as a result of bad strategy and tactics, they had won the wider battle for the political direction of the country."[82] As E. E. Schattschneider might appreciate, broadening the scope of conflict and setting the political agenda is no mean feat.

Rae agrees with Fenno, in part, when he remarks that Senate compromises "probably salvaged" GOP majorities in both Houses in 1996.[83] House Republican revolutionaries ultimately learned their limits, "learned to be politicians," and fell back on the perquisites of incumbency to save their majority.[84] They also learned that James Madison rules America in the sense that "the whole design of the American governmental system is intended to preclude short-term ideological majorities from getting their way," and "the system does not lend itself to radical change."[85] This, of course, was the lesson Newt Gingrich learned the hard way.

President Clinton was, according to Rae, able to use "the stature and visibility of his office" along with "a ruthlessly efficient political operation . . . to best a discordant, divided, quarrelsome Congress."[86] Congress is at an institutional disadvantage in competing with the executive. Ultimately, Congress "cannot lead," or at least cannot lead for long, because it is "a divided, discordant, and pluralistic legislative branch."[87] This, too, is a lesson Gingrich learned—or should have learned—from James Madison. Congress is at a natural disadvantage competing with the presidency given the differing natures of the two institutions, given, for example, that the nature of the one institution is to be, in the first instance, a single individual, namely the president, while the other institution, Congress, is by its very nature "beastly."

As indicated in this chapter's epigraph, Norman Ornstein once observed "the reality is that a president gets judged by whether he runs Congress, or Congress runs him. Voters assume Congress is beastly. They hire a president to tame the beast—to overcome the legislative obstacles and rein in Congressional prima donnas and parochialists."[88] It is in the very nature of a legislature to differ from an executive; it is also in the very nature of the House to differ from the Senate. This, too, is a lesson Newt Gingrich could have learned from a closer reading of James Madison's *The Federalist*. Different institutions do different things. Congress and the president, the House and the Senate, each have their own structures, functions, and virtues. This is not a lesson Gingrich could have learned from Woodrow Wilson's *Congressional Government*, where Wilson expected leadership from Congress and where he assumed the Senate was "a small, select, and leisurely House of Representatives."[89] Ultimately, the question is whether Clinton tamed Congress or Madison tamed Congress.

DONE DEAL?

In *Done Deal? The Politics of the 1997 Budget Agreement*, Daniel Palazzolo provides the most authoritative account of the 1997 budget accord. He concludes "the 1997 bipartisan budget agreement could not have come together without the partisan battles that preceded it. It would be no exaggeration to say that the glow of bipartisanship emerged from the ashes of partisan stalemate."[90] Confrontation was the necessary predicate for compromise. Playing politics sometimes advances policy.[91] Palazzolo also challenges the conventional wisdom that "all politics is local" in Congress, concluding "all politics is local—sometimes."[92]

Done Deal? details in dramatic fashion the penultimate battle of the 1997 budget accord when Budget Committee chair John Kasich had to fend off on the House floor five substitute amendments to his budget resolution H.Con.Res. 84, the most threatening of which was the Shuster-Oberstar politics-as-usual, all-politics-is-local, pork-laden alternative. The floor fight pitted Kasich, representing the House GOP party leadership, against Bud Shuster and Jim Oberstar, the chair and ranking member of the House Transportation and Infrastructure Committee. Party leadership against committee leadership. The somewhat abstract principled reform of a balanced budget—very much at the heart of the House Republican "revolution"—versus the, literally, concrete temptations of committee pork projects dangled before most members. Kasich and party leaders ultimately prevailed, following a late-night impassioned floor debate, by convincing enough members to "rise above district interests."[93] "In the end, after a vigorous effort by Republican leaders, the House rose above local politics and supported the budget resolution with its dramatic shifting of budget priorities."[94]

Palazzolo further concludes from his careful case study that there is no "neat, simple model" that alone explains the legislative process: "Theories of policymaking that rely solely on interest-group power or reelection motives cannot explain why the House defeated Shuster-Oberstar," and "budget decisions are not easily explained by simple assumptions about how narrow, self-serving interests undermine general interests."[95] The simple, modern pluralist model alone cannot capture the complete legislative process. Instead, principle (including party principle) along with politics, rational policy analysis, and responsiveness to public opinion (including majority sentiment) all taken together best explain the legislative process.[96] Principle and ideas matter. Public opinion and majority sentiment matter. And party leaders matter. Like the authors of *Taxing Choices*, Palazzolo concludes that no simple single-cause model explains the complexity of the legislative process. Pluralism, party government, *plus* may all be needed to fully comprehend Congress.

CONCLUSION

Politicians and political scientists can learn a great deal about both campaigning and governing from the experience of House Republicans during the 1990s. Indeed, a century from now, scholars will still be studying the Gingrich speakership, much as today we study the reigns of Czars Reed and Cannon. The enduring legacy of Speaker Gingrich for Congress, political parties, and political science will be his exploration in theory and practice of the limits of congressional party government. Gingrich learned the limits of insurgency and the possibilities of governing, the limitations of revolution in an institutional structure inclined toward incrementalism, and the potential for change and policy innovation even under conditions of divided government. We can learn from Newt's successes and failures, virtues and defects.

Early in his House Republican "revolution," Gingrich contrasted the Democrats and Republicans: "[T]hey're an organized establishment. We are a disorganized revolution."[97] While probably right about "disorganized," Gingrich is mistaken in adopting the sociological language of "establishment" and "revolution." Our political system, thanks to Madison, is neither dominated by an establishment nor readily susceptible to revolution; it does, however, combine an approximation of both pluralism and party government, carefully balancing stability and innovation. Our separation of powers system constrains *and* empowers parties and leaders who must, at all times, appeal to both their base and the political center if they wish to be successful in advancing their ambitions and their agenda. Ultimately, there is an element of truth to the perspectives of both Richard Fenno and Newt Gingrich; but, either perspective alone is incomplete.

Fenno's definition of governing seems to echo Sam Rayburn's "go along to get along" and Tip O'Neill's "All politics is local." Gingrich's approach to campaigning entailed verbal "bomb throwing" and nationalizing elections. It would be difficult to quarrel too much with the skills and success of Rayburn, O'Neill or Gingrich though, of course, all three were fallible. Perhaps each was appropriate to his time and party—at least for a while. Congressional politics is not reducible to the approach of any one of these three Speakers.

Political scientists Ron Peters and Doug Koopman suggest that party leadership must be understood in terms of differing party cultures.[98] Similarly, journalists Mark Halperin and John Harris in *The Way to Win* distinguish between "Clinton Politics" in the 1990s and "Bush Politics" in the first decade of the twenty-first century. Halperin and Harris contrast the purportedly compromising third-way politics of Bill Clinton and the allegedly confrontational base politics of George W. Bush.[99] Without settling the questions raised by Peters and Koopman or Halperin and Harris, their arguments at least raise the possibility that there is an element of truth to both perspectives and approaches; both approaches have their merits and demerits. Compromise and confrontation, at different times and on different issues perhaps, are each valid legislative strategies. Party leaders need to know when to hold them and when to fold them, whether in the executive or legislative branch, House or Senate, majority or minority. Learning to govern entails learning to campaign. And learning to campaign entails learning to govern.

Out of the ashes of the 1995–1996 budget showdown/shutdown rose the phoenix of the 1997 budget accord. The breadth and depth of the 1997 budget accord would not have been possible without the stridency and controversy of the 1995–1996 budget discord. Confrontation is often the premise for compromise; they are two sides of the same coin.

9

～

James Madison Rules America: Just Ask Newt and Nancy

Who governs? Who rules America? Political scientists have been asking and attempting to answer this question at least since Robert Dahl's classic *Who Governs?* While the pluralist, party government and rational choice paradigms all give different answers to the question, no one has ever conclusively resolved this debate within political science— and for good reason: each perspective may be partial and incomplete. A more complete answer, at least more complete than any of the contemporary contenders for the honor of dominant paradigm, may be "all of the above." Each perspective may contain an element of truth, though none of the paradigms within political science today seems to capture the whole.

An even more complete answer to the question may be "James Madison rules America." This answer is more complete since it encompasses many of the insights found in the above paradigms. As James Q. Wilson argued in his 1990 APSA James Madison Lecture, Federalist No. 10 and No. 51 contain all of contemporary political science in a "larger synthesis" that is "one measure of Madison's superior greatness."[1] Furthermore, as Harry Clor notes in the epigraph opening chapter 6, the American regime still operates as Madison intended. The Constitution is still intact and we remain a liberal-democratic, pluralist, constitutional republic. Our republican institutions balance the ambitions of individuals, the pluralism of intense minorities, and the majoritarianism of party government, maintaining an equilibrium among the interests and ideas of the one, the few, and the many. In this fundamental sense, James Madison rules America. In what other ways can we further justify this seemingly outlandish claim?

To say that James Madison rules America is to say that the Constitution governs. Our written Constitution remains the supreme law of the land, promoting the rule of law. As Tocqueville notes, "the Constitution rules both legislators and simple citizens."[2] The long-settled dispute over the power of judicial review provides evidence that the Constitution governs. Defending judicial review in Federalist No. 78, Alexander Hamilton notes the importance of a written constitution: "the Constitution ought to be preferred to the statute, the intention of the people to the intention of their agents."[3] He concludes, "[J]udges ought to be governed" by the Constitution; thus, the Constitution governs both the Congress and the Court. Chief Justice John Marshall in *Marbury v. Madison* makes the same argument.

In an even more fundamental sense, James Madison rules Congress, the Court, and presidents by means of his central insight in *The Federalist*— institutions affect behavior—summarized in the famous passage "Ambition must be made to counteract ambition. The interest of the man must be connected with the constitutional rights of the place."[4] Constitutional structure has purpose and promotes institutional responsibility by redefining the interests of individuals and groups, drawing them out of their narrow self-interest and ambition. How members of Congress act and what they think is tied to where they sit; differences between the House and Senate provide an obvious example. Thus, "location, location, location" in our constitutional constellation is essential to understanding the actions of all three branches.

Daniel Stid labels the Constitution "one of the foremost independent variables in American politics."[5] In this sense, too, James Madison rules America. Constitutional analysis is critical to understanding political behavior. The Constitution shapes and informs congressional behavior, for example, by channeling and constraining the behavior of members, leaders, factions, and parties. The influence of the Constitution—and James Madison—on legislative practice and congressional behavior should not be underestimated.

The Constitution also governs by empowering and humbling Congress, presidents, and the Court as necessary. At various times in our history, including the present, we have debated whether we have an "imperial or imperiled" Congress, presidency, or Supreme Court. Although perceptions shift, the authority of the Congress, president, or Court remains intact even when they are not popular. The foundation for the authority of each branch is the Constitution, not popular opinion, and that constitutional authority is solid, as seen, for example, in the ability of President George W. Bush to advance his "surge" strategy for U.S. forces in Iraq at the nadir of his popularity following the 2006 election. The Democratic Congress was not able to stop him even though they believed they had a clear mandate from the 2006 election to do so; so-called mandates matter less than fundamental constitutional authority.

At the same time that the Constitution upholds the rule of law, it also recognizes the limits of the rule of law, embracing, for example, executive prerogative, and enabling presidents to act beyond the law in emergencies if necessary to protect the Constitution, as President Lincoln argued in his famous letter to A. G. Hodges.[6] Following 9/11, George W. Bush notably sought to extend executive prerogative to fight the war on terrorism. At first, Congress went along, for example, passing the Patriot Act; but before long, Congress naturally began to push back. Even here—or perhaps especially here—James Madison rules America. The history of the separation of powers consists of frequent pendulum swings between the executive and legislative branch. The Supreme Court has, of course, played a role in curbing the abuses of one branch or the other; yet the checks and balances between the Congress and the president entail political and institutional regulation more than legal regulation. Institutional conflict between Congress and the president is at least as important in curbing our powerful and independent political branches as any ruling by the Court. As Edwin Corwin famously noted, the Constitution is an "invitation to struggle." The limits of executive authority, for example, depend in large part on the willingness of Congress to assert itself, as we saw following the 1994 and 2006 elections.

Yet another practical example of how James Madison rules America can be seen in the rhythm and equilibrium of elections. Midterm election losses for the party in the White House are a Madisonian constant, especially six-year-itch elections. Recent exceptions to this rule in 1998 and 2002, if anything underscore the constancy of this historical law of congressional elections. A related truism is the observation that were it not for Republicans, Democrats would never win an election, and were it not for Democrats, Republicans would never win an election. Minority parties in Congress often need majority parties to provide the opening for electoral advance, and majority parties frequently comply. Just ask Newt Gingrich and Nancy Pelosi in 1994 and 2006. Each leader deserves credit for leading their party out of the minority wilderness, but the majority party in both instances provided the opening.

Still another palpable example of James Madison ruling America can be seen in congressional election strategy and analysis. Does a wall of structural incumbency-advantages for the majority party determine elections, or can a wave of national sentiment sometimes breach that wall? Is all politics local, except when it is national? The endless debate among politicians and political scientists over this question is a measure of Madison's ongoing influence. There is no simply correct answer to this question. Structural advantages do matter, except when they are overcome by national sentiment. All politics is local, except when it is national. Again, just ask Newt and Nancy. As minority party leaders and as Speakers, each has at different times adopted either strategy.

Another example of James Madison ruling America—or at least ruling Congress—is the constant struggle within each congressional party, especially in the House, between party and committee leaders as noted in earlier chapters. There is no similar sharp conflict in the British House of Commons, for example, where legislative committees are clearly subordinate to party leadership. The "dual nature" of Congress—a function of the separation of powers—can be seen in the fact that decades of apparent "committee government" finally gave way to conditional "party government" in the House over the past twenty years. At the opening of the 111th Congress, though, Nancy Pelosi, perhaps secure in her speakership, eliminated term limits for committee chairs, thereby possibly signaling the future resurgence of strong committee chairs in the House. Indeed, her reliance on the "Three Tenors," chairmen Waxman, Miller, and Rangel, while working on health-care reform during summer 2009 underscores the fact that strong speakers and strong committee chairs never completely eclipse one another.

Among Congress scholars, the tug-of-war between party and committee leadership translates into an unending debate over whether Congress is leaderless and whether "leadership is followership."[7] Arguably, Congress does not lack leaders; rather, it has a surfeit of leaders, and therefore appears chaotic and leaderless, as witness the infighting among party and committee leaders. Party and committee leaders do not govern Congress. James Madison governs Congress, in part, by sometimes pitting party and committee leaders against one another. Madison keeps Congress balanced on the razor's edge of its own dual nature. Congress is not in fact leaderless; Madison leads Congress today, just as he did rather adroitly in person in the 1790s.

Finally, and perhaps most importantly for our purposes in this study, James Madison rules America because our constitutional structure constantly confronts members of Congress and congressional parties with the conundrum at the heart of this book: Government or opposition? Pursue policy or play politics? Compromise or confrontation? Bipartisanship or partisanship?

Our two political parties continually face these choices. The "government or opposition" strategic dilemma is a true *constant* of legislative politics. This conundrum divides internally both Republicans and Democrats, both the majority and minority parties in Congress. The dilemma may in fact be a conundrum in the strict sense of the word; there may be no right answer to the question, though the question clearly matters. Party politicians, political journalists, and political scientists frequently raise the question and disagree endlessly over the answer.

The constancy of this conundrum confirms the Constitution governs. Indeed, the Constitution governs in a way neither party governs. Neither party in our separation-of-powers system is ever simply the government or the opposition; instead, each party is constantly wracked on the horns of this dilemma. The Constitution governs in the sense that each party is perpetually divided into internal party factions contending over the correct answer to this legislative party strategic dilemma. Certainly, Republicans and Democrats constantly fight *between* themselves, but both parties just as commonly fight *among* themselves. There are various causes of intraparty factionalism, of course, yet one significant constant of *intra-party* warfare is the struggle over the correct answer to the "government or opposition" dilemma. In managing its own factions, each party faces this constitutional constant. The summer 2009 health-care tussle between Blue Dog and Progressive House Democrats is only one example; one faction wanted bipartisan cover, while the other faction would have happily advanced partisan reform.

Madison stirs constant infighting *within* the two parties in Congress by foisting this strategic dilemma on congressional parties. The Constitution precludes the formation of a "government" or an "opposition." At any given time neither the president nor Congress governs; neither branch alone is the government. At any given time, neither Democrats nor Republicans are the government pure and simple; indeed, at all times both parties are both government and opposition. Consequently, bipartisan compromise and partisan confrontation are both appropriate legislative strategies. The Constitution governs because no one else governs.

Politicians are not the only ones plagued by this dilemma. Political scientists, too, contend over competing "pictures in our heads" or paradigms. Within political science, unlike economics, there is no dominant paradigm that fully captures the true nature of our political system. There is no dominant paradigm in part because of the complexity of our constitutional system. Indeed, this complexity does not lend itself to simple, clear-cut explanations borrowed from other, simpler political systems, such as the British parliamentary system.

In the British system, one party is the government, while the other party is the opposition. No such luck in America. Our parties are constantly perplexed by what role they should play. Perhaps this is just as the Federalists intended, but it is not what Woodrow Wilson wished. Wilson wanted "party government" for America, both in *Congressional Government* and *Constitutional Government*, though we never quite seem to attain this Wilsonian ideal. The fact that we at best approximate from time to time something resembling Wilsonian "party government" confounds party reformers and some political scientists. Again, even if the party government school of thought aspires to be the dominant perspective, within political science no one paradigm ever attains that distinction. Madisonian pluralism, party government, *plus* may be the most complete description of our politics.

But, again, it is not only political scientists who are constantly tempted by the twin sirens of pluralism and party government; indeed, politicians find themselves tempted, too, by the Scylla and Charybdis of pluralism and party government. Can party politicians assume that the essential nature of our political system is pluralist and thus call for incremental accommodation and compromise among competing interests? Or can they operate on the assumption that our political system invites party government, and therefore adopt a confrontational politics of contending principles and ideas? Perhaps both, though at different times and under different circumstances. Does the struggle among interest groups comprise or corrupt our politics?[8] Both. Does the confrontation between parties comprise or corrupt our politics? Both.

Politicians and political scientists both are torn between pluralism and party government because of one central truth about our separation-of-powers system that is too often misunderstood. Our separation of powers limits the abuse of power *and* provides for the effective use of power. The separation of powers *humbles* and *empowers* both majority and minority legislative parties. It often humbles the party that purports to be the government and empowers the party that sees itself as the opposition; it can also do the opposite. But at no time is either party simply the government or the opposition, even if each often pretends to be one or the other. Our constitutional system invites—indeed it foists upon the two parties—the "government or opposition" dilemma. Should a party pursue policy or play politics? Choose compromise or confrontation? Provide a choice or an echo? Both options are constitutionally permissible. The Constitution governs parties more than parties govern the country.

Some say "bipartisanship" and "compromise" are in the eye of the beholder. House Republican revolutionaries rejected Bob Michel's spirit of bipartisan compromise in the early 1990s. Would they have remained in the "permanent minority" wilderness with Michel at the helm? Similarly, congressional Democrats rejected Dick Gephardt's bipartisan approach in 2003 and Joseph Lieberman's bipartisan style in 2006. Would they have wallowed in the minority doldrums otherwise? As for legislative compromise, the House GOP's August 2006 "trifecta" legislation combining a minimum-wage increase with estate-tax relief—something for Democrats and something for Republicans—found itself roundly denounced as a mere ploy even though it gained bipartisan majorities in the House and Senate. Nevertheless, this broadly bipartisan legislation was ultimately defeated due to the Senate's supermajority filibuster requirement. Was the defeat unduly confrontational partisanship or principled partisanship?

Similarly, in 1999 Democrat John Dingell and 45 House Democrats voted with 173 Republicans on a gun-control measure, yet "there was negligible praise for the spirit of comity that saw so many Democrats crossing the aisle" according to the conservative *Weekly Standard*: "Apparently 'real' bipartisanship is when House Republicans join the 'Democratic' side, not when Democrats cross over," they concluded.[9] In the same way, presidents often get little credit for bipartisanship. Bill Clinton and George W. Bush both ran for president as conciliators seeking to overcome personal and partisan differences. As presidents they became polarizing figures—at least to their partisan critics, who, of course, used polarizing and partisan tactics to advance their own perspectives. The early optimism about Barack Obama's "post-partisan" presidency seemed to quickly fade in 2009. More to the point, is partisanship always bad?

The perennial objection that our politics suffers from a "permanent campaign" provides further evidence that the Constitution governs. The "permanent campaign" and gridlock—sometimes dubbed a "failure to govern"—can be beneficial and even productive. As Charles O. Jones notes, sometimes not to act is to act.[10] After all, one purpose of the Constitution was to limit government—including legislative activism. A gridlocked majority or obstructionist minority may be serving a useful purpose by preventing harmful legislation. House Republicans thought so in the 103rd Congress. House Democrats thought so in the 109th Congress. This, too, is James Madison ruling America.

Our constitutional system includes, perhaps at different times, an approximation of Jones's "government of parties" and Schattschneider's "party government" because the Constitution includes elements of both pluralism and majoritarianism. As Harry Clor observed, our republican government embraces intense minorities as well as majority sentiment. The latter often takes the form of popular support for one of our two great parties.

The Democrats and Republicans are the closest approximation we have to majority factions. Yet factionalism within the two parties renders polarization less dangerous. Toward the end of Federalist No. 51, Madison seems sanguine about the dangers of majority faction:

> In the extended republic of the United States, and among the great variety of interests, parties, and sects which it embraces, a coalition of a majority of the whole society could seldom take place on any other principles than those of justice and the general good.[11]

How can Madison be so sure? He is confident because he has internally factionalized our two congressional parties; both must at all times control the "mischiefs of faction" within their own coalition if they wish to succeed in advancing their ambition or agenda. If they aspire to govern America, they must first govern Congress; if they hope to govern Congress, they must first govern themselves. This is not an easy task as Newt Gingrich and Nancy Pelosi both have learned.

Partisanship, therefore, is not as dangerous as some believe precisely because partisan majorities naturally tend to fall apart. The fracturing of the Federalists in the 1790s provides one example. The collapse of Democrats in the 103rd Congress and Republicans in the 109th Congress offer two other examples. Majority parties also may fall apart when they become too large, too dominant or too homogeneous. One reason House Democrats remained a "permanent majority" from 1954–1994 may be that they were often constrained—saved from themselves so to speak—by the "conservative coalition" tracked by *Congressional Quarterly* for decades. Another reason is that they managed to lose the White House so frequently in the later years. Majority factions are naturally tamed by their inherent pluralistic, coalitional character—and their own constant infighting, including and especially over legislative strategy. Yet when they overreach, they may pay a price.

Finally, James Madison rules America, as witness the enduring debate between the Federalists and Anti-Federalists, echoed to this day among both politicians and political scientists.[12] The debate resonates in what Samuel Huntington dubs the perennial American "institutions" versus "ideals" debate. As argued in chapters 3 and 4, our institutions today remain Federalist, while our ideals are increasingly Anti-Federalist. As noted earlier, minority party politicians and political reformers always have available the criticisms of Madison's constitutional system articulated by the Anti-Federalists and later Woodrow Wilson. Our politics often is in fact characterized by the "jarring" of adverse special-interest factions; it is frequently prone to gridlock; and it often precludes accountability. Similarly, political scientists echo the Federalist/Anti-Federalist debate among themselves in the never-ending debates over contending paradigms noted above and in chapter 6. James Madison and Woodrow Wilson continue their powerful sway over the discipline of political science.

JAMES MADISON DOES *NOT* RULE AMERICA?

In what way does Madison not rule America? Conceivably, the Constitution is no longer simply Madison's since there have been twenty-seven amendments. Although given the provenance of the Bill of Rights in Madison's early congressional efforts, perhaps we should say seventeen amendments.[13] Still, those seventeen amendments include significant changes to our constitutional order, including institutional changes; for example, the Seventeenth Amendment (direct election of senators) and the Twenty-Second Amendment (two terms for presidents), which clearly have altered the institutional dynamics. One might also argue that Madison does not rule America given that we are a different country than we were two hundred years ago. New circumstances—the growth of government, the increasing centralization of government in Washington, technological innovation, and our greater international responsibilities as a superpower—may suggest we are no longer Madison's America. In practice, are we still the same regime Madison founded?

If Harry Clor, in the epigraph opening chapter 6, is to be believed, the essentials of the regime are still intact, and Madison still rules in practice. Yet are we still Madison's America in our *understanding* of politics? Our institutions are Madison's, but are our ideals still his? Perhaps instead of Madison, the Anti-Federalists rule America given Jefferson's "Second Revolution," or given the prevalence of the Anti-Federalist critique of our constitutional system today. Perhaps the Wilsonian and Progressive heirs of the Anti-Federalists rule? Certainly Wilsonian and Progressive influence on our theory and practice of politics is palpable today. The rise of the Wilsonian and Progressive perspective is an explicit challenge to Madison's predominance. Is the Progressive perspective supreme today?

The constant complaints today among reformers about gridlock, accountability, special interests, and jarring partisanship all echo Progressive thought, including Woodrow Wilson's. Democratic congressional reformers in the early 1970s and Gingrich-led Republican reformers in the 1990s both echoed Progressive thought. While reformers purport to be nonpartisan, often their criticisms coincide with the interest of a party—or personal ambition as in the case of Ross Perot. Perhaps enlightened statesmen are not always at the helm. Reforms designed to make Congress more open, democratic, and responsive to majority sentiment echo Wilson. So do reforms of the presidential and congressional selection processes, along with "good government" reforms like the McCain-Feingold campaign-finance reform. Our political practice is naturally informed by our understanding of politics. At times today that understanding seems to be governed by Woodrow Wilson more than Madison, perhaps particularly among political scientists.

James Madison also does not rule America if we take for granted Wilson's reduction of Madison's separation of powers to a static "Newtonian" system of checks and balances or if we embrace Wilson's "Darwinian," "living constitution" perspective. The Constitution does not govern if institutions do not matter, if the constitutional system "does not remain fixed," and if "institutions are the creatures of opinion" as Wilson opined.[14] Wilson viewed the Constitution as essentially irrelevant to congressional behavior. Similarly, if we assume that leadership is mere followership then Madison no longer governs American political science. Principal-agent theory has its roots in Wilson's thought, as Donald Wolfensberger notes in quoting Wilson's observation from *Constitutional Government*: "He [the Speaker] is the instrument, as well as the leader, of the majority in controlling the processes of the House. He is obeyed because the majority chooses to be governed thus."[15] If we change "he" to "she," does this really apply to Nancy Pelosi today? Did it really apply to Newt Gingrich? Nevertheless, as political scientists and citizens, perhaps our faith in science and our passion for democracy naturally leads us to embrace Wilson's perspective.[16]

Another example of Wilson rather than Madison ruling America today may be our desire for compromise, civility, and bipartisanship, which has its roots in Wilson's call for "the synthesis of power in government" and for politics as an "organic unity," rather than the jarring of adverse interests.[17] According to Wilson, "synthesis, not antagonism, is the whole art of power. I cannot imagine power as a thing negative, and not positive."[18] Madison, of course, could understand power as both negative and positive; the separation of powers limits and energizes, promotes friction and fission. Unfortunately, Wilson's Whig-like reduction of the separation of powers has blinded us to the full potential in the constitutional separation of powers. Again, the separation of powers restrains and empowers individuals and institutions—providing limited, yet effective government— though Tocqueville today might conclude that our democratic passion for change as citizens makes us impatient with limited government and leaves us longing for activist Progressive government ideally fueled by bipartisan majority sentiment.

Still, James Madison may rule if, as Donald Wolfensberger concludes, the dynamics of Congress are "more cyclical than longitudinal," thereby suggesting that perhaps James Madison's Constitution, rather than Woodrow Wilson's "living constitution," governs.[19] What if constitutional structure does constrain and empower? What if institutions do matter? What if there is a reason the pendulum swings back and forth in our theory and practice of politics between pluralism and party government? And what if even those two perspectives, too, remain incomplete in capturing the whole of our politics? The fact that popular and scholarly opinion continues to oscillate between the Constitution's embrace of "energy" and "stability"—that is, the Constitution's creation of effective, yet limited government—suggests that Madison still rules the theory and practice of politics.

To suggest that James Madison rules means that Madison governs us more than his single most worthy opponent Woodrow Wilson. *The Federalist* and the Constitution it outlines govern us more than even Woodrow Wilson's very popular and influential critiques in *Congressional Government* and *Constitutional Government*. Wilson as the pretender to America's philosopher-king throne has powerfully influenced the thinking of politicians, journalists, and political scientists about politics, including on the subject of legislative party strategy.[20] The "pictures in our heads" that many adopt today are often those colored by Woodrow Wilson. Yet those pictures of how our constitutional system works—or should work—are inaccurate or at least incomplete. Madison provides a more accurate and complete understanding of our constitutional system. Again, in our separation of powers, bicameral, federal system, neither party is ever simply government or opposition. The institutional structures of our constitutional playing field, the rules of the game, so to speak, govern party politicians. No party ever governs.

Nor does any school of thought within political science ever govern; no paradigm ever attains hegemony. In the final analysis, perhaps James Madison rules the American Political Science Association (APSA) more than former APSA president Woodrow Wilson. Proof of this proposition is the way Madison has political scientists endlessly asking, "Who governs?" Even as brilliant a political scientist as Woodrow Wilson had second—or third—thoughts as professor and president.

CRITICS' CRITICISMS STILL STAND?

If James Madison's Constitution still governs, then his critics' criticisms also abide. As argued in chapter 3, the Anti-Federalists correctly identified many of the defects of Madison's constitutional system. Madison acknowledged many of those defects, including, for example, the danger of factionalism and the difficulty of providing accountability in such a complex system. Ultimately, however, the Anti-Federalists lost the ratification debate, not because they were wrong about the defects of the Federalist Constitution but because their solution to the problem of liberal government was found wanting. They lost the debate because they had the weaker argument.[21] Even so, the Anti-Federalist criticisms of the Constitution contain an element of truth.

Later critics, including Wilson and the Progressives, echo the Anti-Federalist criticisms in identifying the defects of Madison's system. Indeed, the Anti-Federalist and Wilsonian critique has become commonplace today. Some have embraced more the arguments of the critics than the arguments of the drafters of the Constitution; the critics of the Constitution, influenced by the Anti-Federalists and Woodrow Wilson, may have eclipsed the Federalists today. Have we sacrificed our Federalist principles for our Anti-Federalist hopes, abandoned Madison's realism for Wilson's aspiration?[22]

At times today our reigning aspiration seems to be for a politics of consensus, civility, compromise, and bipartisanship. We dislike special-interest politics and partisanship. We disdain the excesses of pluralism and party government. We seem to want to take the politics out of politics. Too often this aspiration becomes a presumption—a Progressive presumption.

Wilson believed "you cannot compound a successful government out of antagonisms," echoing the Anti-Federalist complaint about "jarring and adverse interests." Wilson saw the separation of powers as a "radical defect." Neo-Progressive theorists today denounce the "deadlock of democracy" and complain of "stalemate." In the 1990s, presidential candidate Ross Perot wanted us to rise above the squabbling of politics; in this decade, *Washington Post* columnist David Broder scorns the "stench of partisanship."[23] The commonplace Progressive presumption prefers compromise to confrontation and bipartisanship to partisanship, abjuring a politics infused with factionalism and the "spirit of party." As political scientist Marc Hetherington has observed, "It is not socially desirable for people to tell you that they think bipartisanship is a bad thing."[24]

The latest manifestations of the Progressive presumption are today's longing for "post-partisanship," the denunciation of the "permanent campaign" and the desire to take the politics out of politics. As Jonathan Rauch recently noted in the *Atlantic*, "The idea of a politics that rises above partisanship dates back at least to the Progressive movement of a century ago, and the term 'post-partisan' surfaced as far back as the 1970s."[25] Similarly, Donald Wolfensberger traces the "permanent campaign" to Woodrow Wilson.[26] And Thomas Patterson traces the "anti-politics" perspective of many journalists to Progressivism.[27]

The Progressive presumption favors politically correct can't-we-all-get-along civility, compromise, and bipartisanship; it tends to demonize disagreement and debate. The Progressive presumption looks askance at ambition counteracting ambition, faction against faction, special-interest group against special-interest group, party against party. In seeking an end to the "permanent campaign," critics sometimes seem to want an end to politics, embracing the anti-politics perspective of early Progressive reformers. Such critics today scorn the Madisonian politics of both pluralism and party government. Perhaps like early Progressive reformers, they assume a consensus on the big questions, hoping to reduce politics to administration. If it is "just that simple," as Ross Perot insisted, we can "get under the hood," turn everything over to experts and take the politics out of politics.[28]

Yet politics is not that simple, nor can we take the politics out of politics. Sidney Milkis suggests "partisan rancor" is intrinsic to our democratic republic, and he warns us about "the alluring false hope that politics can be reduced to administration."[29] In a similar vein, Herbert Storing argues that the Founders had a greater appreciation for the "problematic character of democracy" than we do today given Wilson's influence on our understanding of politics.[30] The Progressive presumption to the contrary, Storing suggests, we cannot reduce politics to simple majority rule and the administration of things. Channeling Alexis de Tocqueville, David Brooks takes the argument a step further. As a democratic people, he argues in *Bobos in Paradise*, we long for consensus, dislike conflict, deride partisan contentiousness.[31] Our disdain for partisan gridlock today may reflect what Tocqueville saw as the impatience and avidity for change of a democratic people; a democratic people can be impatient with those who dare to disagree with seeming majority sentiment.[32]

A CURE WORSE THAN THE DISEASE?

While the Anti-Federalists, Wilson, and critics today may have correctly identified the defects of our constitutional system, what alternative or solution to these defects do they offer? Is it a cure worse than the disease?

In Federalist No. 10, Madison tells us that the diseases most incident to republican government are factionalism and majority tyranny, that is, the excesses of pluralism and party government. The cure to the "mischiefs of faction" requires either removing the causes or controlling the effects. Removing the causes requires either destroying liberty or giving everyone the same opinions, passions, and interests. The first is a cure "worse than the disease" and the second is impracticable. Thus, Madison concludes, we are left with controlling the effects of faction by means of the "extent and proper structure of the Union." The appropriate solution is pluralism coupled with republican institutions defined by the separation of powers, checks and balances, federalism, and bicameralism. Regulation of these interests "involves the spirit of party and faction in the necessary and ordinary operations of government."[33] Madison's institutional regulation of these interests involves constitutional structures that invite, and perhaps even promote, competition and confrontation.

Too often, however, contemporary critics and reformers seem bent on curing the "mischiefs of faction" by removing the causes, either by curbing liberty or promoting a stifling conformism. Campaign-finance reform and its endless Supreme Court–orchestrated minuet with the First Amendment may be an example of the former.[34] The insistence on the politics of civility, consensus, and bipartisanship may be an example of the latter.

So-called good-government reforms such as ethics and lobbying legislation may run the danger of criminalizing Madisonian pluralism in an effort to curb self-interest, ambition, faction, and partisanship in politics. If "the latent causes of faction are sown in the nature of man" we will never eliminate special interests and partisanship in politics. We will never take the politics out of politics; the attempt may be a cure "worse than the disease."[35] On the other hand, giving everyone the same opinions, passions, and interests, while impracticable, does not hinder some politicians, journalists, and political scientists from trying. In this, they may be echoing Anti-Federalist desires for a homogeneous and public-spirited citizenry, much as Ralph Nader today calls on all of us to be "public citizens." They also seem to want enlightened public-spirited statesmen who are above the "spirit of party" and factionalism.

While calls for a more temperate civil discourse and greater bipartisanship are certainly legitimate, efforts to delegitimize partisanship may be unwarranted. Transcending partisanship in a post-partisan era may be an idle dream, an intellectual conceit, a disingenuous partisan ploy or all of the above. At best, such calls may simply be a desire to tone down the rhetoric, but can we really turn off FOX and CNN and silence the bloggers? Journalists who denounce partisanship and pluralism, may want to first consider the role of the media in setting the tone of our politics.

Political scientists may also benefit from self-reflection. Is it possible to take the politics out of political science? Applying the scientific method to the study of politics certainly has produced learning and insight, but as James Q. Wilson argued, both normative and empirical political science have their place in the discipline. Can we exile consideration of "values," ideas, and principles from political science given that differences of interest, passion, and opinion are the very stuff of politics? According to Harvey Mansfield, "Politics means taking sides; it is *partisan*."[36] For political science, however,

> The question of what view to take of partisan debate is still an issue today; some people relish their partisanship, some—perhaps a growing number— feel uncomfortable with loud arguments and deplore partisan attitudes. In recent decades the political science profession has been subject to successive new theories such as behavioralism and rational choice, each of which promises to put an end to the old debate over values . . . bringing consensus and doing away with debate.[37]

Yet debate is the essence of politics. There are important principled differences between Democrats and Republicans over enduring questions about the role of government, markets, and the military in securing liberty, prosperity, and security. Experienced politicians understand this. James Baker says "politics and policy cannot be separated" in a democracy.[38] Leon Panetta insists policy goes nowhere without politics.[39] Dick Cheney concludes one cannot separate campaigning and governing.[40]

Why then do some bemoan the "permanent campaign" and partisanship today? Perhaps our Anti-Federalist ideals and democratic instincts explain in part our sensitivity to politics. Is the problem today hyperpartisanship or hypersensitivity to partisanship?

POLITICS IS PARTISAN. TODAY IT IS VERY PARTISAN.

As noted in chapter 1, the evidence is fairly clear that our politics today is more polarized, partisan, and confrontational. Marc Hetherington, for example, observes: "Perhaps the most important development in American politics in the last two decades has been the marked ideological polarization of the two major parties, especially in Congress."[41] As also noted in chapter 1, political scientists cite a raft of causes for this heightened polarization and partisanship, including, for example, the growth of government and the increased stakes in our politics.[42] But the Democratic and Republican parties are not solely responsible for the polarizing partisanship today. The other two key mediating institutions, interest groups and the media, are also complicit.

Ironically, one might argue that the *decline* of parties, and the rise of a more interest group- and media-dominated politics has contributed to partisan polarization. An excess of "party" and "partisanship" may not be the problem. The explosion in the formation of new interest groups, as the agenda of government has grown and technology has made organizing easier, has contributed to cacophony in our politics. Hyperpluralism, or "demosclerosis," as Jonathan Rauch calls it, has made our politics more competitive and discordant.[43]

Similarly, the decentralization and fragmentation of the "new media," as the hegemony of the "old media" erodes, may also have contributed to the confrontational quality of our politics. Groeling and Kernell note, "The media prefer conflict and controversy to cooperation and conflict."[44] "In the permanent campaign, parties are weak," Sidney Blumenthal argues, while "the media is strong."[45] Barbara Sinclair cites "a more intrusive, confrontational, and consequential news media" armed with "a voracious appetite for conflict and for stories that [are] simple, negative, and sensational" as compounding polarization.[46] The new-media environment invites outsider strategies of "going public" as mediagenic leaders such as Speakers Gingrich and Pelosi seek to broaden the scope of conflict.[47]

In *Party Wars,* her classic study of partisanship, Sinclair concludes, "Partisan polarization cannot be blamed for many of the features of contemporary politics that we do not like, such as ugly politics."[48] According to Roger Davidson and Walter Oleszek, press norms exacerbate the media's tendency to augment polarization:

> Journalistic hit-and-run specialists . . . perpetuate a cartoonish stereotype: an irresponsible and somewhat sleazy gang approximating Woodrow Wilson's caustic description of the House as "a disintegrated mass of jarring elements."[49]

The press's Progressive presumption, a sort of "journalistic Naderism," including the media's disdain for political parties, has contributed to the polarization of our politics as much if not more than Democrats and Republicans.[50] "Even though the media is not partisan, the media drums up conflict," according to former congresswoman Connie Morella (R-MD).[51] Ironically, a more media-dominated politics has vilified parties and interest groups while making our politics more polarized. The alternative to strong parties and partisanship is not a politics devoid of politics, rather, it is a politics dominated by either or both of the other key mediating institutions: special-interest groups and the media.

There are, however, more fundamental causes of factionalism and partisanship in our politics, namely, *human nature, democracy*, and *Madison's Constitution*. Since the "latent causes of faction" and the "spirit of party" are natural to man, Madison sought to control the effects of factions, rather than remove their causes. Madison did not think it possible to take factionalism, partisanship or politics out of politics; therefore, he sought instead to multiply factions and control their effects by means of republican institutions governed by constitutional structure.

No two citizens ever share the same interests, passions, and opinions; preservation of those differences is critical to any successful liberal regime. Thus the solution may be not to remove or eliminate partisan polarization but to harness its effects in a productive way. Partisan polarization is inherent in the nature of both man and our political institutions. Removing partisan polarization carries the threat of compromising liberty and compromising party principles. The competition of parties gives greater weight to the diverse voices of a democratic people. In fact, democracy itself may be part of the problem. Robert Samuelson observes:

> People complain about government gridlock. But what often obstructs constructive change is public opinion. The stalemates on immigration and retirement spending are typical. We avoid messy problems; we embrace inconsistent and unrealistic ambitions. We want more health care and lower health costs; cheap energy and less dependence on foreign energy; more government spending and lower taxes. The more unattainable our goals, the more we blame "special interests," "lobbyists," and other easy scapegoats.[52]

Partisan gridlock, of course, is another one of those easy scapegoats. We may denounce partisan polarization, yet we *are* partisan polarization. Voters and members of Congress may complain about partisan polarization, yet they are unwilling to compromise their ideological positions and party loyalty. Like the cartoon character Pogo, perhaps we have met the enemy and it is us. Winston Churchill's famous observation that democracy is the worst form of government except for all the rest seems apt. What after all is the alternative? It is certainly not the elimination of democracy and liberty, nor the attendant factionalism and partisanship.

So is the problem today hyperpartisanship or hypersensitivity to partisanship? Both. Partisanship and polarization are greater today, but so, too, is the overreaction to partisanship.

PARTISANSHIP IS NECESSARY, NATURAL, AND GOOD

Alexis de Tocqueville understood that "[p]arties are an evil inherent in free governments," although Tocqueville saw them as a necessary evil.[53] He expressed the same ambivalence toward our other two key mediating institutions, the press and associations, the media and interest groups:

> I do not feel toward freedom of the press that complete and instantaneous love which one accords to things by their nature supremely good. I love it more from considering the evils it prevents than on account of the good it does.[54]

Likewise about the perilous expedient of interest-group pluralism he says:

> The omnipotence of the majority seems to me such a danger to the American republics that the dangerous expedient [unleashing factionalism] used to curb it is actually something good.[55]

The intemperance of parties, interest groups, and the press are necessary evils in a liberal regime, which may explain why we love to hate them. Tocqueville shares Madison's ambivalence about the "mischiefs of faction" and the "spirit of party." Freedom of the press, parties, and interest groups provide a cure for the defects of liberalism. The excesses of partisanship, pluralism, and press freedom are therefore a *necessary evil*, and in some sense *good* according to both Tocqueville and Madison.

Partisanship is as necessary, natural, and good as pluralist accommodation. Professor Larry Sabato likes to tell his students that "politics is a good thing." Precisely. Politics is partisan, pluralistic, and permanent; it is sometimes polarizing, sometimes accommodating; it includes confrontation and compromise. The two inevitably go hand in hand.

Politics is good—or at least better than the alternative since the alternative is certainly not a politics free from factionalism, partisanship, and confrontation. Late in life, Madison rebutted John C. Calhoun's "concurrent majority" argument for nullification by defending majority rule in a compound pluralist republic like the United States. Madison reasoned that the perfect may be the enemy of the good: "no government of human device and human administration can be perfect; that which is the least imperfect is therefore the best government."[56] He thought the Constitution's liberal-democratic republic balancing pluralist factions and majority sentiment was best, despite its limitations. The least imperfect form of government, even with its defects, is the best.

In the prelude to the 2004 election, political scientist Bill Schambra questioned whether partisan polarization was altogether new:

> Is incivility a new and growing threat to American politics? No. American politics has always been robust, edgy, overstated, and "simplistic." Today's much-bemoaned 30-second attack ads are surely no more irrational, emotionally provocative, or unfair than posters of elephants stomping on Communism and New Dealism, which are meant to be viewed as two peas in a pod, according to the poster maker.
>
> Only in the eyes of certain elites is our politics today more than ordinarily nasty. And the solutions to that nastiness just happen to augment the influence of those very elites. Though they argue for a transcendence of the Founders' low expectations for American politics, even they live down to them. In the closing days of this election season, American citizens should celebrate, enjoy, and throw themselves into the exasperating, wonderful spectacle of our presidential election.
>
> And when they hear complaints about our debased politics, they should reflect on this lament: "The age of statesmen is gone. . . . God save the Republic . . . from the buffoon and gawk . . . we have for President."
>
> That was the *New York World* in 1864, commenting on the renomination of Abraham Lincoln.[57]

What we do not like is what Martin Diamond called "the solid but low foundation" of American politics; the by-products of liberty, democracy, and republicanism make us squeamish—and always have at least since the Founding.[58]

Like Schambra, historian Michael Kazin concludes the "permanent campaign" is a national tradition: "the nearly permanent campaign has been a feature of American politics since before the Civil War, when mass parties first emerged to contend for the votes of a mass electorate"[59]

Peter Trubowitz and Nicole Mellow draw on their quantitative analysis of "a century of roll-call voting in Congress" to argue that "[p]artisanship is politics as usual in the United States"; they cite former House Democratic leader Dick Gephardt saying "bipartisanship is abnormal."[60] In "'Going Bipartisan': Politics by Other Means," they argue bipartisan does not mean "apolitical"; nor does it mean "virtuous, understanding and open-minded"; nor does it mean placing "principle over electoral self-interest."[61] In fact, they argue that "bipartisanship is every bit as political as partisanship," thus "bipartisanship is best understood as an electoral strategy."[62] "In our view, lawmakers always face a choice between cooperation and confrontation, that is, between being more bipartisan or partisan."[63] Generally, "politicians must balance the risk of political retribution by partisans against a second worry: alienating swing or centrist voters."[64] As argued above, our constitutional separation of powers foists this acute conundrum in its distinct form upon members of Congress.

Just as Nicholas Lemann asked recently, "Does the wrangling of interests corrupt—or constitute politics?"[65] so, too, might we usefully ask, Does the wrangling of parties corrupt or constitute politics? Or is this merely the rough-and-tumble of a democratic people governing itself? In the 1830s in *Democracy in America*, Tocqueville remarked, "[A]lmost all the Americans' domestic quarrels seem at the first glance either incomprehensible or puerile, and one does not know whether to pity a people that takes such wretched trifles seriously or to envy the luck enabling it to do so."[66] Just as the political-science literature does not support the conventional view of our politics as special-interest-dominated, might not the same be said about partisan excesses? As Paul Quirk recognizes, partisanship in Congress may merely represent "a different and not necessarily a worse mode of representative democracy."[67] Perhaps these are the good old days.

Partisan combat and factional contention are a constant in our politics. Sometimes it takes the form of Red versus Blue party government confrontation; at other times factional combat occurs *within* each party more than *between* the two parties. Either way, factional divisiveness occurs. Why is intraparty factionalism preferable to interparty factionalism? It is not clear whether the bitterness and bile of partisanship and factionalism is any greater or less when it occurs *within* one of our two great parties or *between* them.

For example, the 2008 presidential primary competition between Barack Obama and Hillary Clinton, complete with the politics of personal destruction, may have been more rancorous than the presidential competition between Democrat Obama and Republican John McCain later in the year. The Democratic nomination fight between Obama and Clinton included charges and countercharges about playing the race card, along with divisive debates over Bitter-gate, Reverend Wright, the Weather Underground, and dodging bullets in Bosnia. In fact, Obama leveled the ultimate Democratic insult at Clinton, accusing her of acting like a Republican and adopting Karl Rove's purported tactics: "Senator Clinton has internalized a lot of the strategies and the tactics that have made Washington such a miserable place, where all we do is bicker and all we do is fight."[68]

Similarly, sharp internal Republican factionalism has a long history: Eisenhower vs. Taft in the 1950s, Goldwater vs. Rockefeller in the 1960s, and Ford vs. Reagan in the 1970s.[69] In the late 1980s, congressional conservatives began to defect from George H. W. Bush, and Gingrich eventually adopted his win-the-House-by-losing-the-White-House strategy in 1992. The history is similarly long within the House Republican leadership: Halleck versus Martin in the 1950s, Ford versus Halleck in the 1960s, Gingrich versus Michel in the 1980s, followed by the conservative coup against Gingrich in the 1990s and his eventual decision to step down.

Will Rogers's famous aphorism "I am not a member of an organized party—I am a Democrat," applies to the Republicans as well. Both parties are internally divided, just as Madison intended. No majority faction can rule for long, or really at all. Factionalism and partisanship are endemic to our constitutional system; in fact, our separation of powers needs factionalism and partisanship to function effectively according to Madison.

Our complex separation-of-powers system may preclude strict party accountability, yet internal party factionalism and competition between parties can promote an alternative form of accountability. Similarly, factionalism and partisanship can contribute to gridlock, but they can also energize our politics and promote change. Finally, partisanship can also provide an antidote to special-interest-dominated politics by giving voice to broad-based and even majority sentiment.

Accountability

In 2006, minority congressional Democrats held Republicans accountable in the lead-up to the midterm election; likewise, majority congressional Democrats held President Bush and Republicans accountable by defining the terms of the 2008 election. During the 2008 August recess, however, minority House GOP efforts to "keep the lights on" on the House floor also kept the pressure on Speaker Pelosi's party over the need for domestic offshore and Arctic National Wildlife Refuge (ANWR) oil exploration given rising gas prices. Such congressional oversight by either the majority or minority party promotes a reasonable form of party responsibility. While neither party is strictly speaking simply the government or the opposition, clearly election results suggest that at times voters hold one party or the other accountable.

Similarly, partisan rancor during the Clinton and Bush White House years helped promote institutional accountability in struggles over executive and legislative prerogative. The complexity of our constitutional separation of powers may promote a plethora of accountability, rather than merely preclude accountability as critics often suggest. In this way, partisan conflict is constitutionally necessary and good; in fact, institutional combat, including partisan conflict, may be preferable to legal prosecution of purported official malfeasance. Impeachment is a form of political, not legal, accountability; it is a two-edged sword as Gingrich learned. Both the president and Congress can be held accountable during such exercises. This may be another lesson Nancy Pelosi learned from Newt Gingrich, as witness her reining in Judiciary chair John Conyer's appetite for impeaching George W. Bush.

Energy

National Journal's Insider's Poll in December 2007 asked Democratic and Republican insiders if they considered members of Congress of the opposite party "principled" or "too partisan." Democrats answered 70 percent "principled" and 87 percent "too partisan," just as Republicans answered 67 percent "principled" and 87 percent "too partisan." Both may be right—both parties and both answers. The principles of both parties promote partisanship, providing voters a choice and not an echo. Principled partisanship, including sharp partisanship, provides accountability and energy, potentially fueling innovation and creativity.[70] As noted earlier, even divided government coupled with partisan competition can prove productive; Charles O. Jones and David Mayhew both puncture the commonplace myth of gridlock. For example, the 1986 Tax Reform, 1996 Welfare Reform, and 1997 Budget Accord might not have happened without the partisan competition that preceded all three. Similarly, divided government in the 104th Congress was more productive than "united party government" during the 103rd Congress.

Special Interests versus Majority Sentiment

The virtues of partisanship can include heightened voter turnout and political participation as we saw in both 2004 and 2008. As Milkis argues, partisanship can rouse us from our slumber, overcoming the scourge of apathy and alienation.[71] Political parties are instrumental in inspiring debate; parties can force consideration of what James W. Ceaser calls "foundational" concepts.[72] Tocqueville contrasts "great" and "small" parties. Great parties are "more attached to principles" and "ideas," while small parties are coalitions of selfish interests: "[g]reat parties convulse society; small ones agitate it. The former rend and the latter corrupt it; the first may sometimes save it by overthrowing it, but the second always create unprofitable trouble."[73] Periods of partisan polarization in America may approximate Tocqueville's great parties. Newt Gingrich and Nancy Pelosi may each have overthrown an existing order, although clearly and safely within the confines of Madison's constitutional system. In both cases, their ideological polarization at least temporarily offered a more principled politics. The American constitutional system not only allows for party polarization but actively encourages it. Partisan polarization may provide the premise for what party scholars call party realignments.[74]

Samuel Huntington argues that the American political system invites competition: "Conflict is the child of consensus."[75] Periods of realignment or reform eventually give way to a new status quo; we oscillate between conflict and consensus, disharmony and relative political quiescence. Similarly, Alan Ehrenhalt in *The United States of Ambition* cites the natural rhythm between establishment and movement politics in America.[76] Elites may be threatened by mass politics, but this is the natural ebb and flow of political tides. Both Huntington and Ehrenhalt see periods of consensus and conflict, and establishment or movement politics, as having both virtues and defects. Consensus and compromise can squelch needed change and discourage bold leadership; consensus can be a cover for domination by an established status quo. Nostalgia for the partisan tranquility of the 1950s, for example, may overlook failures during that decade to address needed change in civil rights.

It is no accident that our most successful and celebrated statesmen—Jefferson, Lincoln, FDR—were the founders of new party systems. They were party statesmen. So, too, were such enlightened statesmen as Madison and Hamilton both when they worked together in the 1780s and when they worked at cross-purposes in the 1790s. Partisanship is good. Parties have served us well. Both of our two great parties today are partisan—and appropriately so. Loyal partisan opposition, including vociferous opposition, is intrinsic to our politics, even when we are inclined to question the motives and good faith of our partisan opponents.

Nor is it only great party statesmen, like Lincoln or Roosevelt, who make a difference. Politicians like Gingrich and Pelosi, and Hastert and Gephardt, matter too. Sometimes the ebb and flow between the politics of conflict and consensus can be measured in terms of decades; sometimes it oscillates in years, months, weeks, and days. The purportedly gridlocked partisan 110th Congress moved in a quick, bipartisan fashion early in 2008 on an economic stimulus package; later that year the same Congress moved the landmark $700 billion Troubled Asset Relief Program (TARP) financial-services-sector rescue legislation in about a week. Congress received little praise for its bipartisan accomplishments.

During the first year of the 110th Congress, the *Washington Post* sharply rebuked the new Democratic Congress: "Forget about November's bipartisan promises of civility and cooperation in Congress. . . . [I]t is hard to believe that relations could have deteriorated so far so fast."[77] The *Post* elaborated: "On the House side, a major disappointment was the failure of Democrats to live up to their pledge to treat the new Republican minority better than Democrats were treated when Republicans held power . . . they, too, often used the same hardball tactics to muscle through legislation that Republicans had employed."[78] At the opening of the 111th Congress, the House Democratic majority added insult to injury with the first-day rules package; naturally, Democrats blamed Republican irresponsibility for inspiring the rules crackdown, while Republicans accused Democrats of majority tyranny.

But given the limits of strict party accountability in our separation-of-powers system, can either party or any outside critic, including journalists or political scientists, simply blame one party or the other? Blaming either Democrats or Republicans for partisan polarization presents the classic chicken or egg riddle. As with squabbling siblings, the question "Who started it?" often has no answer. There is plenty of blame to go around. Again, both parties are partisan—true to their nature—just as they should be. Partisanship is the virtue and defect of both Democrats and Republicans. When our two parties truly fail us, history suggests a corrective: third-party movements. If our parties are too polarized, they may inadvertently provide an opening for a third-party movement; more likely, they will provide an opening one or the other can exploit; this may explain, in part, the 2008 election.

When did partisanship begin? It began in the beginning. Just ask James Madison. The politics of the 1790s proves the "permanent campaign" begins with the Constitution.

TAKE MADISON SERIOUSLY

To understand contemporary congressional politics we must begin by taking the Founders seriously, both Federalists and Anti-Federalists, along with Tocqueville's synthesis of the two. We must take Madison and Wilson seriously, including the debate between them.

Both perspectives, especially taken together, provide insight into contemporary politics. Madison and his critics are two parts of a whole; a potentially healthy, dynamic tension exists between the Constitution and its critics. Madison's critics, old and new, offer balance by correctly identifying the defects of our constitutional system.

At the same time, though the criticisms of Madison's foes contain a large element of truth, their proffered solutions or alternatives—their cure to the defects—are wanting. In taking the Founders seriously, along with the echoing debate today, we need to recognize the limits of the Anti-Federalist and Wilsonian perspectives. We cannot make the weaker argument the stronger. We cannot turn the critique into the solution.

And yet we try. Contemporary critiques of American politics owe more to the Anti-Federalists and Wilson than Madison. Wilson's eclipse of Madison in the twentieth century affects the understanding of contemporary politics among politicians, journalists, and political scientists. We have lost sight of the importance of constitutional and institutional structures. We no longer appreciate Madison's central insight: institutions affect behavior; institutions count. We little recognize that the dual nature of Congress—committee and party—is founded in our complex separation of powers. We do not always appreciate how the separation of powers defines the central dynamic of Congress—government or opposition, compromise or confrontation, bipartisan or partisan, pluralism or party government. We fail to appreciate how the separation of powers limits and empowers Congress and president, House and Senate, Democrats and Republicans.

Contemporary critics have a narrow conception of the separation of powers premised on Wilson rather than Madison. Like Wilson, they reduce the separation of powers to the checks and balances. Consequently, they unnecessarily bifurcate pluralism and party government, which are, in fact, two sides of the same coin. Both are legitimate parts of the same rich constitutional system. Congress may change its personality—or at least its personalities—from term to term, but it does not change its essential character or nature. Understanding Congress as a pendulum swing between pluralism and party government—as encompassing compromise and confrontation, bipartisanship and partisanship—is a good starting point, though our constitutional context is richer still. We need to return to Madison's superior synthesis to understand how the separation of powers is the *solution*, not the *problem* as Wilson and too many today assume.

Can we find practical lessons in Federalist No. 10 and No. 51 for congressional party leaders? Absolutely. First, from experience, party leaders already know that ours is a "government of parties." Our two parties are really six parties, as witness the existence of six party headquarters on Capitol Hill: DNC, RNC, DCCC, NRCC, DSCC, and NRSC—or really 106 parties if we include the state parties. Second, congressional party leaders recognize that they are beset by the "mischiefs of faction," hence the challenge they face is to manage factionalism or be managed by factionalism. Third, Madison compounds this challenge by confronting party leaders with the impossible-to-answer "government or opposition" strategic dilemma. No one governs, not the Congress, president, House, or Senate—and certainly not the parties whether in the majority or in the minority. Fourth, party leaders understand that politics is infused with the "spirit of party." Politics is partisan.

Just as Madison manages factionalism, so, too, must congressional party leaders manage factionalism, which is why sharpened partisanship may not be particularly perilous. Madison manages factionalism in the nation, for example, by governing or taming partisanship by means of the constitutional separation of powers, bicameralism, and federalism. The Constitution limits government, limits parties, and limits partisanship. Bicameralism, for example, means that the "legislative authority" rarely "predominates."[79] For example, House Democratic Budget chair Dave Obey complained that the public thinks "we have control of the Senate when we merely have custody."[80] Factional and partisan differences within and between the two parties generally are lesser in the Senate than in the House in part because the Senate is less parochial than the House.

Yet precisely this difference bedevils the four congressional parties. Former House GOP leadership staffer Sam Langholz echoed a common sentiment among House Republicans: "The Democrats are the opposition; the Senate is the enemy."[81] No doubt House Democrats today concur.

Madison further manages factionalism and befuddles congressional party leaders by thrusting upon them the "government or opposition" conundrum. As an independent and powerful part of the government, for example, Congress created the standing committee system to be able to compete with the executive and engage in oversight. Congressional reformers, starting in the 1940s, also created party policy committees to better manage internal party factionalism. Yet ironically, these party policy committees, specifically designed by reformers to promote party discipline may be less independent and effective, and less able to foment "party government" when they are advantaged with a president of their own party.[82] United party government, so-called, is a mixed blessing for the majority party. In this way, too, Madison manages factionalism. If a party in the House is in the minority, they rarely feel as if they are part of the government, no matter who is in the White House.

Like Madison, congressional party leaders must manage factionalism between and within their parties. First, they must accept factionalism and the "spirit of party." Second, they cannot "remove the causes" by eliminating liberty or giving everyone the same opinions as some are wont to do. Zealous ideological "wingnuts" of the left and right are sometimes intolerant of the principled differences between the parties. Such ideologues are often intolerant of differences within their own party; promoting ideological purity, homogeneity, and a stultifying conformism within their party may be a good way to become or remain a minority party. In Madison's extended republic, a majority party must be a big tent. On the other hand, moderate centrists sometimes act as if the principled differences between parties do not matter in their rush to embrace a can't-we-all-get-along civility. Like it or not, a party must stand for something if it wishes to appeal to its base. Principled ideologues and centrists need one another.

If party leaders want to advance their party's ambition and agenda, they must effectively address the "government or opposition" conundrum, while also recognizing that there is no simply right answer. It depends. It depends on the institutional circumstances at the time in the White House, Congress, House, Senate, and whether they are in the majority or minority; yet under none of the possible institutional circumstances is the answer ever clear-cut. It also depends on the issue and timing. Party leaders need to know when to hold them and know when to fold them. They need to know when to find common ground and when to stand their ground. Learning to govern entails learning to campaign, and vice versa. Party leaders must at all times appreciate the synergy of political "jazz," simultaneously balancing "establishmentarian" and "revolution-ary" factions within their own coalition.[83]

Above all, congressional party leaders must adroitly manage faction-alism within their own party—including factionalism premised on the "government or opposition" compromise or confrontation dilemma. For example, both Gingrich and Pelosi deserve credit for uniting their parties in opposition as the minority party in the lead-up to the 1994 and 2006 elections respectively. Their full-throated unity in opposition enabled them to ride the electoral wave, even if political and institutional circum-stances beyond their control (for example, a president of the other party in the White House) helped create the wave. Even minority parties in the House are not powerless; they can, for example, recognize when all-politics-is-local gives way to a national wave, as did both Gingrich and Pelosi. Managing factionalism by controlling the effects is the answer to the Constitution's strategic conundrum confronting both congressional parties.

To govern, a party must govern Congress; to govern Congress, a party must govern itself. Madison has made this a daunting task. The greatest obstacle to the majority party's success may be the majority party itself. Majority parties often defeat themselves, or at least provide openings for the minority party to exploit. The majority party must manage factional-ism by controlling the effects of faction within their own party. The major-ity party in the House can get complacent and fall into one of two traps: either the excess of pluralism or the excess of party government (or both!). They can become the party of special interests or they can embrace the go-it-alone majority tyranny of party government. Either way, they make themselves vulnerable to the minority party.

The minority party always has at the ready the "culture of corrup-tion" charge and the accusation of "gridlock" if the majority party fails to act. If the majority party succeeds in advancing its agenda, the minority party can seek to hold the majority accountable if the legislative agenda proves unpopular. Adding to the challenge, majority parties may be more susceptible to corruption scandals; since they have more power, interest-group lobbyists shower them with more attention. Political impotence protects the minority; they cannot abuse power they do not have. How-ever, the minority party, too, can fall prey to the excesses of pluralism and party government. They can become a "permanent minority" by settling for crumbs from the tables of the majority committee barons in an effort to perpetuate their own personal reelection. Or they can become an ideo-logically pure minority party. Or, finally, they can perpetuate their own "permanent minority" status by continual infighting between the prag-matic "committee guys" and the ideological "party activists," or between moderates and the party base.[84] Either way, both parties must constantly manage their own internal party factionalism by controlling the effects.

Learning to govern requires understanding Madison's legislative play-ing field. Learning to oppose can mean adopting the Anti-Federalist cri-tique of Madison's system. At all times, however, both parties are part of the government and part of the opposition; thus, both must govern and campaign at all times.

STABILITY AND ENERGY

Political scientists can contribute to politics by clarifying the critical role of the Constitution's institutional playing field in promoting what Madison called "stability and energy."[85] Our separation-of-powers system with its confusing "government or opposition" calculus promotes both friction and fission. Just as the pluralism and party government paradigms re-main viable in political science, so, too, do the perspectives of Federalist and Anti-Federalist, Madison and Wilson, remain valid among legislative strategists. Madison embraces compromise and confrontation. Stability and energy are the two halves of the separation of powers.

Nelson Polsby recognized the role of "innovation and stalemate" built into our constitutional routines: "it is possible to discern an alternating and somewhat overlapping pattern of activity and retrenchment, of focus and stalemate in congressional affairs."[86] He added:

Neither one mode nor the other is exclusively "natural" to Congress. . . . [B]oth roles are historically characteristic of Congress, and both fully express the powers of Congress as contemplated in the overall constitutional design.[87]

Congress evolves, though perhaps not in a merely linear fashion.

Madison manages factionalism by unleashing and taming, inviting and channeling factionalism, including the majority factionalism of party. Congressional party leaders and members are confronted with a con-stant series of impossible questions: Is politics local or national? Should we govern or campaign? Do parties in the House really want to win a majority in the Senate or win the White House? Do minority parties win elections or do majority parties lose? And, of course, government or op-position? Compromise or confrontation? Bipartisanship or partisanship?

We can be sanguine about our constitutional system with its built-in balancing and equilibrium. Most of the time, we need not expect party leaders or members to be enlightened statesmen above partisanship and parochialism. Both partisan confrontation and pluralist compromise are necessary, as are the waxing and waning between Congress and presi-dent, House and Senate, majority and minority parties. Part of the balance and equilibrium is a simultaneously powerful Congress and president, House and Senate, along with humbled and empowered majority and minority parties. Minority parties can make a difference. Just ask Newt and Nancy. Part of the equilibrium is the balance between committees and parties, between committee government and party government in a powerful and independent legislature. Parties and their leaders should accept the equal legitimacy of both branches, both chambers, both parties; like two halves of a whole, they need each other.

The pendulum swings exist in both our theory and practice of politics. Both perspectives and approaches are important: pluralism and party government, *plus*, as argued in chapters 6 and 8. We need Madison's Constitution, along with the potentially constructive balancing of his critics. We need the enduring debate between Federalist and Anti-Federalists, Madison and Wilson. Madison's Constitution still governs, thus his critics' criticisms still stand.

THE 2008 ELECTION: HERE WE GO AGAIN?

In a December 2007 *National Journal* Special Report titled "Partisan Impulses," reporters Brian Friel, Richard Cohen, and James Barnes drew on their Insiders Poll to capture and articulate the debate over partisanship between and within the Democratic and Republican parties. They asked, "Bipartisan compromise. Partisan principle. Which is the devil? Which is the angel?"[88] The answers they received included "The answer is somewhere in the center," and "It's how the system was designed to work." Other respondents, however, rejected mushy unprincipled centrism as "namby-pamby" and "wimpy." Trent Lott insisted, "To you, bipartisanship means we do what you want." A Democratic insider disagreed: "Voters want solutions and an end to the finger-pointing." Another respondent observed, "It's the other folks who are the more partisan (and I'm sure they feel the reverse)." Finally, two differing Republican insiders commented, "People are fed up with the red state/ blue state divide," and "The two parties have fundamental and deep differences on foreign and domestic policy. And that won't change after 2008." Since there is an element of truth to all opinion, where does this leave us? Divided and united between and within both parties. Is there any end in sight?

Just before the 2008 election, a *Washington Post* story about the "perils of one-party rule," quoted political scientist David Rohde as noting "the potential pitfall is you can overreach, alienate the opposition party and alienate independents—sowing the seeds of your own destruction."[89] But former House Democratic leadership aide Steve Elmendorf insisted Democrats had learned from their experience in 1993 and 1994. Representative Rahm Emanuel, who soon would become White House chief of staff, concluded, "We'll be successful as a party, if we're known as the party of reform. We will be unsuccessful if we do things the way they've always been done." Always, of course, is a long time.

On election day 2008, columnist Anne Applebaum cited as an election "myth" the idea that

> *The Democratic Party will become more thoughtful and responsible when in power.* History tells a different story here, too. After decades in opposition, the Republicans took control of the House in 1994, vowing to reform Congress. For a while, they tried. Then they gave up. If anything, the subsequent Republican Congress proved to be bigger spenders and more avid consumers of pork than their predecessors had been. More to the point: The current Democratic Congress is, so far, no better.[90]

Both Newt Gingrich and Nancy Pelosi adopted confrontational partisan tactics in winning their majorities. Both were accused of trying to destroy Congress in the process, though both saw themselves as trying to save Congress. Neither, of course, was truly capable of destroying Congress with their verbal vitriol and partisan tactics. More likely, Congress would change them more than they changed Congress. Before the 2008 election, in fact, some Republicans admitted that though they had come to Washington to change Washington, instead Washington had changed them. They lost their majority, just as Democrats lost theirs in 1994, defeated in part due to the charge of corruption. Sure enough, the dust had barely settled on the 2008 election, when critics were already citing chapter and verse on purported Democratic corruption (e.g., Charlie Rangel, Tim Mahoney, William Jefferson, Roland Burris, Tom Daschle, and John Conyers).[91] At the same time, other critics were ready to accuse Speaker Pelosi of majority tyranny with her 111th Congress opening-day rules package further curbing minority party rights.[92] Is this yet another majority party already falling prey to the always-available criticisms of corruption and majority tyranny?

And what about the Republicans? Following the 2008 election *CQ Weekly* asked, "Can they climb back?" in a story titled "The Big Tent Collapses."[93] GOP strategist Joe Gaylord acknowledged "appealing to a shrinking base may not be the best election strategy." House Republican Chris Shays (R-CT), who lost his reelection bid, observed, "We were the party of ideas, and then we became the party in power and the party that would do anything to stay in power." Looking at the new House GOP leadership line, *CQ Weekly*'s Alan Ota concludes Republicans are likely to opt for a strategy of confrontation. House Republican Conference chair Mike Pence hopes to put Democrats on the defensive by promoting new ideas: "you can't beat a program without a program." Up-and-coming "young turk" Paul Ryan (R-WI) argues that good policy is good politics; he suggests Republicans need to promote innovative ideas, while at the same time remaining open to diverse perspectives within their conference.

Finally, according to the *Washington Post*, perhaps the ultimate rising star in House GOP ranks is the "pathfinder," Whip Eric Cantor:

> [Cantor] talks about creating a new kind of Republican conservative, one less concerned with ideology and more focused on practical solutions, more tech-savvy and less reflexively combative with Democrats, intolerant of ethical lapses and tolerant of new ideas. And especially one who communicates better to the middle class.[94]

The House Republicans, it seems, are ready to pursue majority status by a mix of strategies including both confrontation and compromise with congressional Democrats and President Obama. Yet House Republicans may have been the least of Barack Obama's worries. Majority parties must first contend with their own internal party factionalism, a factionalism often inspired by Madison.

Even before his inauguration, Barack Obama, according to a *Politico* article titled "O-bummer," was already running into flak from Democrats. "Congressional Democrats are firing a surprising number of unexpectedly sharp brush back pitches at President-elect Obama," they noted, adding, the "honeymoon isn't over" yet, and "Obama will face constant pushback from Reid and Pelosi."[95] The *Washington Post* headlined with "Democratic Congress Shows Signs It Will Not Bow to Obama," suggesting congressional Democrats expect "deference, humility and flexibility" from the new administration.[96] House majority leader Steny Hoyer went so far as to echo Senate majority leader Harry Reid's pronouncement "I don't work for Obama."[97] And the *Wall Street Journal* raised the specter of Democratic factions on the Hill stalling President Obama's plans.[98]

Still, President Obama and Speaker Pelosi were at least singing from the same song sheet in one regard. Within days of one another during negotiations over the huge economic stimulus package each made clear to House Republicans where they stood: "Yes, we wrote the bill. Yes, we won the election," Pelosi intoned. Similarly, "I won," President Obama reportedly responded to a Republican leader during a White House meeting.[99] Partisanship or bipartisanship? Which is the right strategy?

President Obama seemed to enjoy a rather short honeymoon due to controversies over nominations and conflict over the economic stimulus package. In an analytic article titled "Echoes from the Campaign Trail: Obama Returns to Aggressive Approach as Nominations Fail, Stimulus Teeters," reporters Michael Shear and Anne Kornblut concluded that after less than three weeks it was back to the "permanent campaign" and politics as usual for the Obama administration.[100]

Here we go again?

111TH CONGRESS DEMOCRATS: LEARNING TO GOVERN?

Following the 2008 election, Nancy Pelosi and congressional Democrats found themselves in more favorable circumstances than those confronting Newt Gingrich and Republicans at the outset of the 104th Congress. A popular Democratic president in the White House together with supermajorities in the House and Senate presented Democrats in 2009 with a clear opportunity to "govern" rather than "campaign," pursue policy rather than play politics. Did "united Democratic government," mean Democrats could afford to be bipartisan rather than further partisan polarization? After all, candidate Obama ran on the promise to promote a post-partisan politics. Did Democrats deliver? In Richard Fenno's words, did they learn to govern?

In *Learning to Govern* Fenno criticizes Gingrich and his House Republican revolutionaries for over-interpreting the mandate from their sweeping 1994 election victory and for failing to learn that governing entails pluralistic coalition-building, accommodation, and incrementalism.[101] As a longtime "permanent minority," House Republicans in the 104th Congress lacked the experience, according to Fenno, to understand that governing requires trade-offs and compromise. By Fenno's standard, how did the more experienced Democrats do in 2009?

Congressional Democrats already had experience as the majority party in the 110th Congress. Nancy Pelosi served as Speaker for two years during which congressional Democrats arguably contributed to electing a Democratic president in part by sharpening partisan differences with President George W. Bush. The outcome of the 2008 election was a reaction to an unpopular war and an economic crisis, and a rejection of Bush after the two-term presidential cycle. Yet Democrats in the 111th Congress, according to some observers, over-interpreted the meaning of the 2008 election as a mandate to dramatically expand the role of government.[102] In the first year of the 111th Congress, Pelosi and House Democrats adopted a sharp partisan strategy with Republicans responding in kind. Like Newt Gingrich before her, Nancy Pelosi is a partisan warrior.

Did the fall 2008 economic and financial crisis, along with a historic election victory, provide Democrats with an opening or box them in? Democrats scored important legislative victories in the early months of the Obama presidency, including expanding the Children's Health Insurance Program, passing gender discrimination legislation, enacting a $787 billion economic stimulus package, voting on a $4 trillion budget blueprint, confirming Supreme Court justice Sonia Sotomayor, and sending House-passed energy cap-and-trade legislation to the Senate, although the latter revealed fissures within the Democratic Party. Meanwhile, Democrats saw an opportunity. President Obama attempted to launch a health-care revolution premised on this opening, with White House Chief of Staff Rahm Emanuel famously observing, "You never want a serious crisis to go to waste." Did Democrats over-interpret their mandate? Was comprehensive health-care reform—potentially affecting fully one-sixth of the economy—a bridge too far?

By the August recess an apparent stalemate set in over health-care reform even though draft legislation had already passed three House committees and one Senate committee. Henry Waxman's Energy and Commerce Committee struggled in July to unite disparate Democratic factions of Blue Dogs and Progressives, while the bipartisan Senate Finance Committee "Gang of Six" negotiations led by Chairman Max Baucus (D-MT) slowed to a crawl. Congress headed into the August recess, having failed to meet the Democrats' self-imposed deadline on health-care reform, only to encounter protests at congressional town-hall meetings across the country. A Pandora's box of partisan recriminations ensued. Angry protesters packed constituent meetings shouting down members of Congress.

Democrats accused Republicans of "orchestrating" these protests, an ironic charge coming from the party that had seemingly mastered grassroots activism during the 2008 campaign. Harry Reid labeled the protesters "evil-mongers," while Nancy Pelosi penned a *USA Today* op-ed denouncing the disruptive town-hall protests as "un-American." In a seemingly sophomoric mistake, the Obama White House invited supporters to report "fishy" e-mails, thereby playing into the opposition's hands by enabling Senator John Cornyn (R-TX) to raise the specter of enemies lists chilling democratic discourse. Republicans naturally did their best to feed the flames of health-care reform dissent. The partisan blame game was in full flower with both sides demonizing the opposition. Candidate Obama's post-partisan promise fizzled.[103]

Which party was promoting partisanship and playing politics with health-care reform? The almost certain answer to this chicken or egg question is "both." In fact, the partisan blame game itself is inherently political and not readily susceptible to objective splicing by politicians, journalists or political scientists. While both parties, both chambers, and both branches contributed to governing on health-care reform in July, both were just as clearly campaigning in August. Congressional leaders armed their members with the usual talking-point cards, while Internet and TV ad wars commenced, fomenting, once again, a "permanent campaign" to advance or retard health-care reform. The irony, of course, was that Democrats were at times campaigning against themselves, as witness the Obama campaign's Organizing for America efforts targeting moderate Blue Dog Democrats.

Like Newt Gingrich and his House Republican revolutionaries before them, Democrats were tempted by energetic comprehensive "party government" reform. The difference is that while Gingrich sought to implement his "devolution revolution" limiting the role of government, Democrats in 2009 were seeking to expand it. Newly elected President Obama initiated the crisis-driven, comprehensive health-care reform effort, but not before Speaker Pelosi set out her agenda preemptively the day after he was elected president. House Democrats seemed especially impatient, like House Republicans in 1994. Let us look in turn at the party factions in our "government of parties" on health-care reform.

The Democratic White House

At the outset of the 111th Congress, President Obama's "hope-tastic juggernaut" of presidentially driven crisis politics promoting emergency-driven central planning on several fronts, especially health-care reform, seemed almost inevitable at first.[104] To his credit, President Obama began by aiming for bipartisanship; though, he also seemed to over-learn one lesson from the failed 1990s Hillary Clinton–led health-care reform effort. In place of secret White House councils drafting reform, Obama deferred to Congress; indeed, some thought too much so. His hands-off approach at times looked excessively deferential to the "First Branch" and weak. As *Congressional Quarterly* noted, it is "hard to steer using [a] hands-off approach."[105]

President Obama certainly did not seem to be "taming the beast" while enabling congressional Democrats to pass a pork-laden economic stimulus package and nine thousand earmarks during his first months. Similarly, on health-care reform in late July the White House seemed to be floundering, vacillating news cycle to news cycle on the public option, thereby driving allies to distraction. It did not help when the president inserted himself during a press conference into a local Cambridge, Massachusetts, imbroglio between a policeman and a professor. With his poll numbers dropping in July and August, President Obama became a potential liability for his own health-care reform effort. In 2010 President Obama replaced his 2009 hands-off strategy with more active intervention in the legislative process, thereby contributing to Democrats' eventual health care reform legislative victory.

Instead of modestly seeking incremental reform, Democrats exploited the economic crisis—as Rahm Emanuel urged—to advance comprehensive health-care reform designed to increase the size and role of government. Arguably, the very effort was partisan in scope. Comprehensive reform may be by definition confrontational. Unleashing liberal Democrats' pent-up ambitions for a comprehensive overhaul of one-sixth of the economy resembled nothing so much as yet another party giving in to the Wilsonian "party government" temptation, like Newt Gingrich and his House GOP revolutionaries who sought similarly sweeping reforms to limit the scope of government.

In a Madisonian system that invites "energy and stability," it is not surprising that a party would dream big dreams of advancing its agenda and ambitions. Nor is it surprising that such an effort would elicit partisan opposition—and eventually a groundswell of public resistance. Partisan intensity naturally surrounds the role-of-government questions that have been perpetually arising since the early republic. The interests and ideas, special interests and principles, of both parties are at stake. It is altogether appropriate that both parties mount the partisan barricades to defend themselves. Partisanship can be good.

Sometimes, of course, partisanship results in gridlock, as occurred during the Clinton health-care reform effort. At such times, the "pluralist" side of Madison's "energy and stability" equation may take hold. Do we know enough to undertake wholesale reform given the complexity of the massive American health-care system—or is incrementalism best? Hillary Clinton in retrospect concluded that her critical mistake was "trying to do too much, too fast"—a lesson Democrats rejected in 2010.[106] From time to time the American political system does bring about substantial change, for example, during the presidencies of Woodrow Wilson, FDR, LBJ, and Ronald Reagan. For that matter the contestation and collaboration of Bill Clinton and Newt Gingrich brought about a balanced budget and welfare reform.

House Democrats

The question for Speaker Pelosi is whether her legislative strategy is advancing her party's agenda and ambitions. Being the "responsible" majority party is difficult; the key to governing Congress rather than being governed by Congress is, of course, managing factionalism—especially within one's own party. Just as James Madison expected, the fight within the Democratic Party is as important as the fight between Democrats and Republicans. The health-care reform debate is defined as much by divisions between the Democratic White House and Congress, the Democratic House and Senate, and Democrats within the House, as it is by tensions between the two parties. As Stuart Rothenberg summarized, "Capitol Hill Democrats have met their enemy and it is them."[107] Arguably, Pelosi is perpetually caught between a rock and a hard place.

As the majority party, of course, Democrats have been willing to push the envelope on rules and procedures to make life easier for themselves. A Brookings study of the 110th Congress concluded, "The number and percentage of restrictive rules used by Democratic leaders to control debate and amending activity on the House floor exceeded the degree of control and departure from regular order exercised by their Republican predecessors."[108] In the 111th Congress, *Congressional Quarterly* cited Democrats' "unprecedented restrictions" on rules for debate, in part following from the draconian rules-package Pelosi passed on day one.[109] Similarly, Harry

Reid and Senate Democrats in 2010 used budget reconciliation to severely limit GOP options on health-care reform.

Still, Democrats had their hands full with their own factions. During late July 2009 Energy and Commerce Committee deliberations over the public option, the *Washington Post* observed, "Liberal and Conservative Democrats Feud over Bill." Liberal chairman Henry Waxman accused moderate Blue Dogs of lying and, the ultimate treason, "empowering Republicans."[110] As House Democrats attempted to wait out the Senate's "Gang of Six" negotiations, the Democratic White House began to waver on the public option. Suddenly House Democratic Progressive Caucus members found themselves toying with becoming the "opposition" to Senate Democrats and President Obama if they ultimately settled for consensus reforms, jettisoning the public option.

Senate Democrats

The bicameral minuet between House and Senate Democrats played out first on cap-and-trade energy legislation, and later on health-care reform. House Blue Dog Democrats were uncomfortable taking votes without first knowing what Senate Democrats would ultimately do. The health-care reform action in the Senate focused more on the Baucus-led "Gang of Six" deliberations consisting of senators from sparsely populated moderate states than on Majority Leader Harry Reid. Baucus's bipartisan strategy contrasted with Pelosi's partisan strategy. Liberal Democratic senators such as Chris Dodd (D-CT) were critical of Baucus for his bipartisan strategy, just as conservative Republican senators such as Jim DeMint (R-SC) were critical of moderate "Gang of Six" Republicans for potentially providing Democrats with bipartisan cover. Meanwhile, Senate individualism enabled Senators Ron Wyden (D-OR) and Robert Bennett (R-UT) to float their own bipartisan alternative bill in case all else failed. Both chambers and both parties had members wondering, "With friends like these, who needs enemies?"[111]

Senate Republicans

As senators are wont to do, Senate Republicans generally portrayed themselves on health-care reform as part of the government, not part of the opposition. Senate GOP leader Mitch McConnell (R-KY) counseled, at least in public, against both the politics of personal destruction and obstructionism: "[I]t's not about the president, it's about the policy"; health-care "[r]eform is no longer just a good idea—it's absolutely necessary."[112] Senate GOP Policy Committee chair John Thune (R-SD) intoned, "We have to have alternatives. It's got to be positive."[113] Senate Republican moderates such as Olympia Snowe (R-ME) and Charles Grassley (R-IA), and even conservatives like Mike Enzi (R-WO), accepted the bipartisan olive branch initially extended by President Obama and joined Senator Baucus's negotiations in good faith. On the other hand, Jim DeMint (R-SC) said, "If we're able to stop Obama on this, it will be his Waterloo." But this observation seemed to play into Democrats' hands given how eagerly the White House and liberal bloggers highlighted DeMint's strategy. Most attention focused on the "Gang of Six" bipartisan negotiations.

House Republicans

House Republicans feared Senate Republican moderates would sell them out and provide Democrats with a fig leaf of bipartisanship. They worried Democrats would divide and conquer Republican factions by splitting the House and Senate GOP or, more likely, by peeling off a few moderate Senate Republicans. The minority party in the House faces the same question as the other "parties" in our "government of parties" system: government or opposition, compromise or confrontation, bipartisanship or partisanship? However, the minority party in the majoritarian House has less leverage; hence, it is less tempted to opt for "government" over "opposition." It is therefore not surprising that House Republicans in a polarized House under "united Democratic government" would embrace obstructionism. Indeed, being the "Party of No" may even make sense if it forces the majority party to ultimately work with your party in a bipartisan fashion. Sometimes a party has to campaign in order to govern. Given President Obama's early popularity, the House GOP naturally targeted Speaker Pelosi. Like Newt Gingrich before her, Pelosi proved easy to demonize; not least because Congress is our national lightning rod.

Health-Care Reform 2009

In August knowledgeable observers began outlining endgame scenarios for health-care reform.[114] *National Journal*'s Richard Cohen and Brian Friel offered four possibilities: (1) "by the book," through regular order; (2) "done with 51," a partisan strategy resorting to the draconian budget reconciliation process; (3) "health reform-lite," entailing bipartisan compromise; and (4) "failure."[115] Henry Waxman (D-CA) insisted, "Failure is not an option."[116] Moderate GOP senator Richard G. Lugar (R-IN) suggested that initiating health-care reform during troubled economic times was a "mistake" and he advised President Obama to "postpone the decision" until next year or later.[117] Cohen and Friel seemed to highlight the bipartisan health reform-lite option: "Democratic pursuit of a smaller health care bill could allow the minority party to have an imprint on a high-profile initiative and demonstrate bipartisanship."[118] In 2010, however, Democrats opted for a partisan strategy exploiting budget reconciliation.

Each party faced a dilemma. Must Democrats pass a bill? Must the GOP provide creative, Republican, alternative proposals, or is it enough for the minority to be the "Party of No"? Should each party play to its base or to the center? Under the prevailing political circumstances, including united Democratic government so-called, Democrats seemed to need a health-care reform bill more than Republicans. Their fate was on the line in 2010 and 2012. Former Democratic senator Bob Kerrey saw Democrats as in a "potentially lose-lose" situation, "damned if you do and damned if you don't."[119] Managing factionalism within the two parties was as challenging as the contest between the two parties. James Madison made certain the fight within the two parties would be as critical as that between them.

Again, Madison's separation-of-powers system invites "energy *and* stability." While revolutions are not possible, serious reform is possible. Just as an earlier president and Congress passed welfare reform and a balanced budget in 1996 and 1997, so, too, health-care reform passed in 2010. Partisan confrontation can be the necessary prelude and predicate to either bipartisan compromise or sustained partisan confrontation. Legislating in our constitutional system is a constant-feedback loop of competing party and factional ambitions and agendas. Politics is, after all, how we make policy. Democrats and Republicans alike will naturally pursue partisan and bipartisan legislative strategies as appropriate, though the majority party may also bear the majority of risk.

Election observer Charlie Cook opined in late summer 2009, "Democrats can now assume that the charmed life they enjoyed in 2006 and 2008 is over. The wind, waves, and tides, which were strong and at their backs in those elections will at best be still in 2010. The chances of those forces being in their faces this time are rising."[120] Using a similar metaphor, Alexis de Tocqueville once observed, "A lawgiver is like a man steering his route over the sea. He, too, can control the ship that bears him, but he cannot change its structure, create the winds, or prevent the ocean stirring beneath him."[121] Lawmakers like Newt Gingrich and Nancy Pelosi, along with their respective parties, find themselves buffeted by the winds and waves, by the competing interests and ideas in the political environment. Yet Madison built the ship. In this sense, James Madison still rules America.

CONCLUSION

Even if partisanship marks the 111th Congress, this is politics as usual and would not surprise James Madison. Madison saw political parties as instrumental in inspiring debate and promoting innovation. No two citizens or group of citizens ever share the same interests, passions, and opinions; preservation and even encouragement of that diversity is critical to our liberal-democratic republic. The solution is not to remove or eliminate factionalism, including partisan polarization, but rather to harness its effects in a productive way.

The Founders understood that politics, partisanship, and polarization can be good in part because our constitutional concrete can withstand a contentious, cantankerous, and confrontational politics. Our institutions survive even when the latest partisan barbarians beat down the gate. Majorities may fall, but Congress and the Constitution stand.

Sometimes the best way to advance your agenda is to play politics, thereby first advancing your electoral ambitions. With congressional parties, ambition and agenda, politics and principle, campaigning and governing go hand in hand. Sometimes confrontation is the predicate for compromise, and playing politics can advance policy. Politics and policymaking remain inextricably intertwined in the American political system. Hence, bipartisan compromise and partisan confrontation both are natural, legitimate, and desirable. Hence, too, both parties must be on a constant war footing. There is a reason the Democratic Congressional Campaign Committee and National Republican Congressional Committee are permanent organizations headquartered close to the Capitol complex. Politics is rarely far removed from policymaking, campaigning is inevitably part of governing.

Are Democrats and Republicans part of the government or part of the opposition? Are the majority and minority party part of the government or part of the opposition? They are both. Our separation of powers humbles and empowers both branches, both parties, and both the majority and minority at all times. A party can be master of its own fate only if it succeeds in managing internal party conflict. Before either party can hope to govern Congress or the country, they must first learn to govern themselves. For better or for worse, James Madison does not make that task easy.

Learning to govern entails learning to campaign. Campaigning and governing are inseparable in our constitutional order because neither party is ever simply the government or the opposition. Both parties at all times are both government and opposition; hence, both parties must at all times juggle the politics of governing and the politics of campaigning. Both parties must at times promote policy by playing politics, and at other times successfully play politics by promoting policy. Both parties must advance their party ambitions in order to advance their policy agenda and advance their policy agenda in order to advance their party ambitions. Sometimes parties must narrow the scope of conflict and sit down behind closed doors to negotiate with the other side. At other times, parties must broaden the scope of conflict in order to set the political agenda. Both strategies are necessary and connected.

Critics of partisan polarization today denounce politics, especially partisan politics, in the name of civility and comity, as if politics were bad. Yet politics is good. It is how we govern ourselves and how we make policy. As the old adage has it, "a man who says he is not interested in politics, is like a drowning man who says he is not interested in water"—and this is true whether one means the politics of interest-group pluralism or the politics of party competition. One cannot take the politics out of politics, though Wilsonian reformers and Progressives sometimes wish they could. Our Madisonian system is fueled by politics, including both the "mischiefs of faction" and the "spirit of party," the politics of interest-group factionalism and the politics of partisan strife, the politics of intense minorities and the politics of aspiring majorities.

Civility and comity are virtues, but so, too, are competition and confrontation, especially in Madison's political free market premised on the unleashing of ambition, self-interest, factionalism, and the "spirit of party." Today, a favorite partisan ploy is to denounce partisan politics—as if the other party is solely responsible for such politics. Both parties are inevitably partisan. And both parties have regular recourse to confrontational tactics. Just ask Newt and Nancy.

Both parties are partisan because both parties are partial—neither ever represents the whole. Neither party ever is simply the government or simply the opposition. No party simply governs; both at all times are always government *and* opposition, whether they are in the executive or legislative branch, House or Senate, majority or minority. Consequently, both parties at all times must constantly campaign and govern.

Ultimately, the "broken branch" is not broken. We are not on the verge of a second Civil War. Both parties are learning to govern in part by constantly campaigning. Since we never form a government, the "permanent campaign" is permanent. While the party wars may seem never ending, in fact, our politics is marked by intermittent compromise and confrontation. Just as the waxing and waning of legislative and executive power is a normal feature of Madison's constitutional system, so, too, is the ebb and flow of partisanship to be expected. The separation of powers is dynamic, not static. Confrontational partisanship is part and parcel of a democratic people governing themselves. While not always pretty, it is in its own way a wonder to behold.

In conclusion, the Constitution governs. Compromise and confrontation are both good and constitutionally permissible. Politicians and political analysts are constantly tempted by the twin temptations of "pluralism" and "party government" built into our constitutional institutions. The separation of powers limits and empowers both majority and minority parties; hence politics, partisanship, polarization, and the "permanent campaign" are a permanent, normal, natural, and necessary part of our politics.

Appendix:
Research Interviews

MEMBERS OF CONGRESS AND FORMER MEMBERS

Congressman Dick Armey (R-TX)
Congressman Eric Cantor (R-VA)
Congressman Dick Cheney (R-WY)
Congressman Barber Conable Jr. (R-NY)
Congressman Jim Davis (D-FL)
Congressman Tom Davis (R-VA)
Congresswoman Jo Ann Emerson (R-MO)
Congressman Vic Fazio (D-CA)
Congressman Harold Ford Jr. (D-TN)
Congressman Barney Frank (D-MA)
Congressman Bill Frenzel (R-MN)
Congresswoman Connie Morella (R-MD)
Congressman Bill Thomas (R-CA)
Congressman Vin Weber (R-MN)

CONGRESSIONAL STAFFERS AND FORMER STAFFERS

Cory Alexander
Neil Bradley
Joseph Crapa
George Crawford
Dan Diller

Tom Eisenhauer
Jeff Eller
Steve Elmendorf
Mary Sue Englund
Suzanne Farmer
David Gogol
Terry Holt
Kerry Knott
George Kundanis
Mark Lagon
Sam Langholz
John McManus
Bill Moore
Paul Morrell
Tom O'Donnell
Bob Okun
Matt Pinkus
Billy Pitts
Vince Randazzo
Chris Scheve
Danielle Simonetta
Richard Spence
Jeffrey Taylor
David Thomas
Ted Van der Meid
Pete Weissman
Paul Wilkinson
Andy Wright

Notes

INTRODUCTION

1. During his tenure as a member of Congress, Cheney developed a reputation as a pragmatic problem-solver. At times he did adopt confrontational tactics—yet when he did so, many assumed he was acting out of character. During a 1985 fight over the disputed McIntyre-McCloskey Indiana House election, the *Washington Post*'s Dan Balz concluded Cheney's tough approach was noteworthy since he was "normally the moderate's moderate among House Republicans." In a similar story a few years later, Richard Cohen of *National Journal* said that Cheney's occasional partisanship clashed with "a timeworn image as an accommodating centrist." During Cheney's time as vice president, this perception had changed completely. Had Cheney changed? Or was he rather operating from a different institutional position and under different circumstances? See also Stephen Hayes, *Cheney* (New York: HarperCollins, 2007), 155–60.

2. One might add, and why? Is it the job of the minority to become the majority for the sake of advancing their ambition *or* their agenda? Are they interested in playing politics or promoting policy? Do they seek power for its own sake or rather as a means not an end in itself? Power alone may be explanation enough for a Machiavelli or perhaps for today's legions of political consultants, Democratic and Republican. Like gravity drawing an apple to the earth, ambition theory may alone be an adequate explanation. Yet politicians, Democratic and Republican, insist they serve the larger purpose of promoting their principles. Similarly, commentators from the Founders to Alexis de Tocqueville to Woodrow Wilson see politicians as more than mere rational actors pursuing personal ambition.

3. See William F. Connelly, Jr., and John J. Pitney, Jr., *Congress' Permanent Minority? Republicans in the U.S. House* (Lanham, MD: Rowman and Littlefield, 1994), 75.

4. House Republican Whip Newt Gingrich, typically a confrontational leader, found himself working with President Clinton as part of the "government" in support of NAFTA: "This is a vote for history, larger than politics, larger than reelection, larger than personal ego." *Washington Post*, 18 November 1993, A1.

5. Michael D. Shear and Paul Kane, "Obama vs. Own Party on Troop Increase," *Washington Post*, 26 November 2009, A1.

6. Herbert Croly, *Progressive Democracy* (New York: Macmillan, 1915), 256.

7. Woodrow Wilson, *Constitutional Government* (New Brunswick, NJ: Transaction Publishers, 2002), 22.

8. Alexander Hamilton, James Madison, and John Jay, *The Federalist*, Federalist No. 37, ed. Robert Scigliano (New York: Modern Library, 2000), 224.

9. James Madison to Richard Henry Lee, 25 June 1824, in *Writings of James Madison*, ed. Gaillard Hunt, 9 vols. (New York: Putnam's, 1904), 9:190–91.

10. Marvin Meyers, *The Mind of the Founder: Sources of the Political Thought of James Madison* (Hanover, NH: University Press of New England, 1973), 188–90.

11. Hamilton, Madison, and Jay, *The Federalist*, Federalist No. 10, 56.

12. Dan Balz, "Energized Republican Governors Aim for Majority Status," *Washington Post*, 20 November 2009, A1.

13. Renee Montagne and Steve Inskeep, "GOP Strategist: Obama Honeymoon Is Over," *National Public Radio*, 5 November 2009.

14. Montagne and Inskeep, "GOP Strategist."

15. Rhodes Cook, "Past May Be Prologue for Races," *Politico*, 10 November 2008.

16. Ceci Connolly, "Obama Readies Reform Specifics," *Washington Post*, 7 September 2009, A1.

17. Michael Gerson, "Obama Cedes the Center," *Washington Post*, 6 November 2009, A20.

18. David Broder, "Mr. Policy Hits a Wall," *Real Clear Politics*, 24 September 2009, www.realclearpolitics.com/articles/2009/09/24/mr_policy_hits_a_wall .html.

19. Alec MacGillis, "Grandiose Rhetoric Pushes Details Aside," *Washington Post*, 8 November 2009, A9.

20. Carrie Budoff Brown and Patrick O'Connor, "How Health Care Reform Could Fall Apart," *Politico*, 22 November 2009. See also, MacGillis, "Grandiose Rhetoric Pushes Details Aside."

21. David Paul Kuhn, "Democrats Again Lost in Divisions," *Real Clear Politics*, 28 September 2009, www.realclearpolitics.com/articles/2009/09/28/democrats_ still_lost_divisions_98486.html.

22. Naftali Bendavid and Jonathan Weisman, "Democrats Show Strain of Heated Battle," *Wall Street Journal*, 1 August 2009, A4.

23. Paul Kane and Perry Bacon, Jr., "Compromise Won over Democratic Holdouts," *Washington Post*, 9 November 2009, A5; MacGillis, "Grandiose Rhetoric Pushes Details Aside."

24. During the previous Congress, Speaker Pelosi actively squelched partisan overreach in the efforts by Judiciary Committee chair John Conyers and others to promote impeachment of President Bush.

25. Richard E. Cohen, "Help Wanted," *National Journal*, 3 October 2009, 36.

26. Daniel Henninger, "From Bismarck to Obama," *Wall Street Journal Europe*, 24 September 2009, A14.

27. Michael Barone, "Democrat Sees 'Huge Unknowns' in Health Care Bill," *Washington Examiner*, 15 October 2009, www.washingtonexaminer.com/opinion/blogs/beltway-confidential/Democrat-sees-huge-unknowns-in-health-care-bill-64370552.html.

28. Naftali Bendavid, "GOP Calibrates Role as Opposition," *Wall Street Journal*, 21 January 2009, A2.

29. Bendavid, "GOP Calibrates Role as Opposition."

30. Bendavid, "GOP Calibrates Role as Opposition."

31. Dan Balz, "Republicans Seek a Path to Revival," *Washington Post*, 8 November 2009, A1.

32. Reid Wilson, "Cantor Council to Hold Second Event on Wednesday," *The Hill*, 18 July 2009, 8.

33. Of course, one House Republican, Joseph Cao (R-LA), voted in favor on final passage, while Senate Republicans produced not a single vote to bring health-care legislation to the floor for debate.

34. James W. Ceaser, Andrew E. Busch, and John J. Pitney, Jr., *Epic Journey: The 2008 Elections and American Politics* (Lanham, MD: Rowman and Littlefield, 2009), 44.

35. Jim VandeHei and Mike Allen, "The Great Myth: Bipartisanship," *Politico*, 14 September 2009, www.politico.com/news/stories/0909/27110.html.

36. Dan Balz and Jon Cohen, "Deep Divisions Linger on Health Care," *Washington Post*, 17 November 2009, A3.

37. Rhodes Cook, "The GOP: Poised for Another Quick Comeback?" *Sabato's Crystal Ball*, www.centerforpolitics.org/crystalball/articlephp?id=FRC2009070201.

38. Newt Gingrich, "A Growth Vision for Health Reform," *Wall Street Journal*, 21 September 2009, A17. See also, Jessica Brady, "GOP Seeks to Push Debate toward Incremental Reform," *Roll Call*, 20 September 2009, 1.

CHAPTER 1

1. John Harris, "Clinton and Gore Clashed over Blame for Election," *Washington Post*, 7 February 2001, 1.

2. Stephen Dinan, "Frost Calls Pelosi Too Liberal to Lead Democrats," *Washington Times*, 8 November 2002, 1.

3. Dinan, "Frost Calls Pelosi Too Liberal," 1.

4. David Baumann, "Representative Returns to New Role, Same Agenda" *National Journal*, http://nationaljournal.com/members/buzz/2003/capitol corridors/022003.htm (20 February 2003).

5. William F. Connelly, Jr., and John J. Pitney, Jr., "Family Feuds," chap. 2 in *Congress' Permanent Minority? Republicans in the U.S. House* (Lanham, MD: Rowman and Littlefield, 1994).

6. See Connelly and Pitney, *Congress' Permanent Minority?* 45.

7. Connelly and Pitney, *Congress' Permanent Minority?* 14–15.

8. See, for example, Martin Frost, "Newt Gingrich and Nancy Pelosi: Two Peas in a Pod?" *FoxNews.com*, www.foxnews.com/story/0,2933,266378,00.html (accessed 17 April 2007).

9. Carl Cannon and David Bauman, "Performance Pressure," *National Journal*, 9 November 2002, 3269.

10. See, for example, Richard E. Cohen, "What, Me Worry?" *National Journal*, 22 February 2003, 588.

11. See, for example, Frank H. Mackaman, *Understanding Congressional Leadership* (Washington, DC: CQ Press, 1981).

12. See, for example, Jim VandeHei, "Democrats on Hill Split on Agenda: Divisions Weaken Attack on Bush," *Washington Post*, 4 March 2003, 1, 6.

13. See, for example, "GOP Takes Most State-Legislative Seats—a 50-Year First," *Christian Science Monitor*, www.csmonitor.com/2002/1112/p02s02-uspo.html (accessed 12 November 2002). Democratic success in 2000 and Republican success in 2002 suggests voter-turnout efforts matter in close elections.

14. See Connelly and Pitney, *Congress' Permanent Minority?* chap. 5.

15. The existence of a viable third party in the British system complicates this calculus, as does the existence of multiparty parliamentary systems in other nations.

16. It is important to note, however, that not all political scientists accept the notion that institutional structure affects behavior. For one famous example, see Robert Dahl's *A Preface to Democratic Theory* (Chicago: University of Chicago Press, 1956).

17. See, for example, David Rapp, "From the Editor," in "Women in Power," *CQ Weekly*, 28 December 2002, 6. Rapp says the purpose of this special 108th Congress issue is "to describe those skills, styles, and leadership personalities that will help shape legislation, political strategy and, ultimately, the law of the land." *CQ* journalists, unlike some political scientists, think leaders' skills, styles, and personalities matter.

18. See Richard Fenno, *Learning to Govern* (Washington, DC: Brookings Institution Press, 1997).

19. William F. Connelly, Jr., and John J. Pitney, Jr., "Leadership Riff: Jazzy Vision, Steady Beat," *L.A. Times*, 11 November 1998, B7.

20. Paul Quirk, "The Legislative Branch: Assessing the Partisan Congress," in *A Republic Divided*, ed. Kathleen Hall Jamieson (Oxford: Oxford University Press, 2007), 125.

21. As a House GOP leader, Congressman Dick Cheney might provide an exception to this observation. Despite his Western conservative voting record, many perceived Cheney as a moderate given his manner. As a "House institutionalist," however, he stood somewhere between Michel and Gingrich in his approach to legislative strategy, willing at times to be confrontational. See Connelly and Pitney, *Congress' Permanent Minority?*

22. Barber B. Conable, Jr. (R-NY), June 10, 1984, "Washington Report" to constituents. Personal copy.

23. Joseph M. Bessette, *The Mild Voice of Reason* (Chicago: University of Chicago Press, 1994).

24. Connelly and Pitney, *Congress' Permanent Minority?*

25. Tim Conlon, Margaret Wrightson, and David Beam, *Taxing Choices* (Washington, DC: CQ Press, 1990), 240.

26. Robert H. Davidson and Walter J. Oleszek, *Congress and Its Members*, 9th ed. (Washington, DC: CQ Press, 2004).

27. Although at times Congress certainly seems to delegate its responsibility to the executive.

28. Connelly and Pitney, *Congress' Permanent Minority?* 20.

29. Richard F. Fenno, *Learning to Govern: An Institutional View of the 104th Congress* (Washington, DC: Brookings Institution Press, 1997), 3.

30. Fenno, *Learning to Govern*, 20.

31. In this description of our constitutional separation of powers, Fenno echoes Richard Neustadt's famous "separate institutions sharing power" formulation.

32. In effect, Fenno argues that leadership and leadership understanding of constitutional institutions matter, contrary to those Congress scholars who conclude leaders and constitutional institutions do not matter.

33. Benjamin Ginsberg and Martin Shefter, *Politics by Other Means*, 3rd ed. (New York: Norton, 2002), 36.

34. Ginsberg and Shefter, *Politics by Other Means*, 18.

35. Ginsberg and Shefter, *Politics by Other Means*, 14. The authors echo Lloyd Cutler in this observation.

36. Vin Weber, personal interview with the author, 1993.

37. See Ginsberg and Shefter, *Politics by Other Means*, for example, 25–36. See also Larry Sabato, *Feeding Frenzy* (New York: Free Press, 1991).

38. William Schambra, "Nasty Politics? Puhleez! Get a Historic Grip," *Christian Science Monitor*, 21 October 2004, 9.

39. Lloyd Cutler, "To Form a Government," *Foreign Affairs*, www.foreign affairs.org/19800901faessay8153/lloyd-n-culter/to-form-a-government.html (Fall 1980). Cutler is a Wilsonian.

40. The volume *Responsible Partisanship?* edited by John C. Green and Paul S. Herrnson, is another fine example of serious political science.

41. For example, Ron Brownstein's *The Second Civil War*, or *Off Center* by Jacob S. Hacker and Paul Pierson. See also the enlightening critique of *Off Center* by John J. Pitney Jr. in the Berkeley Electronic Press Forum, along with the ensuing exchange between Hacker and Pierson and Pitney.

42. Nicol Rae, "Be Careful What You Wish For: The Rise of Responsible Parties in American National Politics," *Annual Review of Political Science* 10 (June 2007): 169–91.

43. David Broder, *The Party's Over* (New York: Harper and Row, 1972).

44. Rae, "Be Careful What You Wish For," 4–5, 21. Rae cites further impediments to party government in the form of progressive reforms including civil service, secret-ballot elections, initiative, and referendum, along with the rise of Social Security, suburbs, higher education, and a burgeoning middle class. See Rae, "Be Careful What You Wish For," 7–9.

45. Rae, "Be Careful What You Wish For," 12–19. It may be worth noting the unintended consequence of some of these progressive reforms designed specifically to weaken the role of parties.

46. Barbara Sinclair, *Party Wars* (Norman, OK: University of Oklahoma Press, 2006), 22, 33.

47. Thomas Mann and Norman Ornstein, *The Broken Branch* (Oxford: Oxford University Press, 2006), xi, 12, 83.

48. Ronald Brownstein, *The Second Civil War* (New York: Penguin Press, 2007), 22, 373.

49. Quirk, "The Legislative Branch," 123, 148–49. See also Juliet Eilperin, *Fight Club Politics*; Halperin and Harris, *The Way to Win*; and Brownstein, *The Second Civil War*, passim. Some commentators acknowledge Democrats' complicity in polarizing our politics, yet it seems clear that these same commentators lay most blame on Republicans.

50. Mark Halperin and John F. Harris, *The Way to Win* (New York: Random House, 2006), 413.

51. Rae, "Be Careful What You Wish For," 15.

52. Rae, "Be Careful What You Wish For," 18.

53. Rae, "Be Careful What You Wish For," 17–18. See also Sinclair, *Party Wars*, 30–31.

54. Rae, "Be Careful What You Wish For," 21.

55. Hahrie Han and David W. Brady, "A Delayed Return to Historical Norms: Congressional Party Polarization after the Second World War," *British Journal of Political Science* 37, no. 3 (July 2007): 505.

56. Han and Brady, "A Delayed Return to Historical Norms," 506.

57. Brownstein, *The Second Civil War*, 13.

58. Brownstein, *The Second Civil War*, 144.

59. Brownstein, *The Second Civil War*, 145. Note that Brownstein's observations about Bolling and Wright raise doubts as to whether Republicans started the party wars.

60. To understand the importance of evolution rather than revolution, see Nelson Polsby, *How Congress Evolves: Social Bases of Institutional Change* (Oxford: Oxford University Press, 2004).

61. Brownstein, *The Second Civil War*, 118–19

62. Brownstein, *The Second Civil War*, 119.

63. See Alan Ehrenhalt, *United States of Ambition: Politicians, Power, and the Pursuit of Office* (New York: Random House, 1991), and Jonathan Rauch, "Demosclerosis," *National Journal*, 15 May 1992, www.jonathanrauch.com/jrauch_articles/demosclerosis_the_original_article/.

64. Brownstein, *The Second Civil War*, 79, 137.

65. Brownstein, *The Second Civil War*, 369.

66. Brownstein, *The Second Civil War*, 373.

67. Brownstein, *The Second Civil War*, 369, 372.

68. The phrase "new American political system" is borrowed from Anthony King's edited volume *The New American Political System* (Washington, DC: American Enterprise Institute Press, 1978).

69. Brownstein, *The Second Civil War*, 11.

70. Brownstein, *The Second Civil War*, 11.

71. Brownstein, *The Second Civil War*, 11. Brownstein also cites a number of bipartisan pieces of legislation during Bush's first term besides the No Child Left Behind Act: the Patriot Act, formation of the Department of Homeland Security, the Afghan war, and authorization to use force in Iraq, pp. 233, 237.

72. Brownstein, *The Second Civil War*, 12.

73. Brownstein, *The Second Civil War*, 367.

74. Brownstein, *The Second Civil War*, 367.

75. Brownstein, *The Second Civil War*, 367.

76. See Mark Brewer's book review at www.bepress.com/forum/vol6/iss2/art13/.

77. Alexis de Tocqueville, *Democracy in America* (New York: Harper and Row, 1969), 177.

78. Brownstein, *The Second Civil War*, 376–85.

79. Brownstein, *The Second Civil War*, 395.

80. Brownstein, *The Second Civil War*, 23, 400–417.

81. Brownstein, *The Second Civil War*, 414.

82. See Mark Brewer's book review at www.bepress.com/forum/vol6/iss2/art13/.

83. Mann and Ornstein, *The Broken Branch*, 12. It is worth noting that the charge that Congress is delegating too much to the executive branch is at least as old as the New Deal. In fact, this criticism echoes the Anti-Federalist complaint about the tendency of the new Constitution to elevate the executive above the legislature. Patrick Henry famously observed that the new Constitution "squints toward monarchy."

84. Mann and Ornstein, *The Broken Branch*, 169–71.

85. Mann and Ornstein, *The Broken Branch*, 146.

86. Mann and Ornstein, *The Broken Branch*, 86.

87. See, for example, the discussion of Charles O. Jones in chapter 8: gridlock can be governing.

88. Larry Sabato, *The Crystal* Ball, www.centerforpolitics.org/crystalball/.

89. Richard F. Fenno, Jr., "If as Ralph Nader Says, Congress Is 'The Broken Branch,' How Come We Love Our Congressmen So Much?" Originally written as his contribution to an editorial project titled "The Role of Congress: A Study of the Legislative Branch." Copyright 1972 by Time, Inc. and Richard F. Fenno, Jr. See Peter Woll, *American Government: Readings and Case Studies*, 17th ed. (New York: Pearson Longman, 2008), 358–65.

90. Fenno in Woll, *American Government*, 364.

91. Mann and Ornstein, *The Broken Branch*, 14.

92. Mann and Ornstein, *The Broken Branch*, 20, 37.

93. Mann and Ornstein, *The Broken Branch*, 37–46. See also David K. Nichols, *The Myth of the Modern Presidency* (University Park: Pennsylvania State University Press, 1994).

94. Mann and Ornstein, *The Broken Branch*, 229.

95. Mann and Ornstein, *The Broken Branch*, 97, 103.

96. See William F. Connelly, Jr., "Newt Gingrich—Professor and Politician: The Anti-Federalist Roots of Newt Gingrich's Thought," *Southeastern Political Review* 27, no. 1 (March 1999), and William F. Connelly, Jr., "Newt, the Anti-Federalist," *Weekly Standard* (2 December 1996), 18–19. Mann and Ornstein, *The Broken Branch*, 98.

97. See Federalist No. 70 and No. 78.

98. See the discussion in chapter 6 of Martin Diamond on the Founders' separation of powers.

99. Mann and Ornstein, *The Broken Branch*, 236, 192–210. In the example of the Office of Public Integrity, apparently for the authors, politics and partisan competition and open elections are not adequate for policing Congress. To maintain the

continuity of Congress in the event of a large-scale terrorist attack on Washington, they propose appointing new members as needed to maintain the quorum Congress needs to operate. Much to the consternation of Mann and Ornstein, House Republicans countered this proposal, insisting on adherence to the constitutional provision requiring election of all House members. Mann and Ornstein see the latter process as too slow, leaving the country subject to "martial law" during the time it takes to elect new members. Yet when Congress is in recess or adjourns, or in the period between congressional elections and the opening of a new Congress, America is not subject to martial law. Mann and Ornstein, *The Broken Branch*, 198–204.

100. Mann and Ornstein, *The Broken Branch*, 242.

101. A further irony, entrenched in our party system, of course, is the fact that both parties have their libertarian and statist wings. Democrats want to limit the growth of the national security state; Republicans want to limit the growth of the social welfare state.

102. Mann and Ornstein, *The Broken Branch*, 242. See also Nelson Polsby's "Comment" in *Red and Blue Nation*, vol. 2 (Washington, DC: Brookings Institution Press, 2008), 285–87.

103. Quirk, "The Legislative Branch," 150, 125.

104. Quirk, "The Legislative Branch," 125. See also Mann and Ornstein, *The Broken Branch*, 212.

105. Quirk, "The Legislative Branch," 141–42, 148.

106. Quirk, "The Legislative Branch," 137. Were political scientists as solicitous of minority party concerns in the 1980s when Republicans were a "permanent minority"?

107. Quirk, "The Legislative Branch," 123, 136.

108. Quirk, "The Legislative Branch," 134–36.

109. Quirk, "The Legislative Branch," 138.

110. Quirk, "The Legislative Branch," 147.

111. Quirk, "The Legislative Branch," 132. See also Brownstein's discussion of the "Age of Bargaining," chapter 3. In their regard for bipartisan standing committees, the authors disagree with Woodrow Wilson in *Congressional Government*.

112. As an APSA Congressional Fellow working for the House Republican Policy Committee in the 1980s, I witnessed House Republican closed-party deliberations that were as thoughtful—and at times as contentious!—as those in the bipartisan standing committees or on the floor.

113. Quirk, "The Legislative Branch," 149.

114. David Brooks, *PBS NewsHour*, 8 August 2008, transcript: www.pbs.org/newshour/bb/politics/july-dec08/sbads_08-08.html.

115. Quirk, "The Legislative Branch," 139.

116. Quirk, "The Legislative Branch," 131.

117. Quirk, "The Legislative Branch," 148.

118. See Connelly and Pitney, *Congress' Permanent Minority?* chap. 4, "The War on the Floor." See also John J. Pitney, Jr., "The Roots of Rancor," *National Journal Online*, http://article.nationalreview.com/?q=NTA5ZWU2NmIxYjMyODZiOGIxM2M wZTIxYTFkN2I0MTc (accessed 15 February 2008).

119. Quirk, "The Legislative Branch," 148–49. As for a Republican Congress "uncritically accepting a vague, unsubstantiated administration case for pre-

emptive war," congressional Democrats had access to the same National Intelligence Estimate (NIE) as the Republicans. But they too failed to read beyond the Cliff Notes version, and the war vote was bipartisan. See www.washington post.com/ac2/wp-dyn/A44837-2004Apr26. Plus, the Obama stimulus package at the opening of the 111th Congress continued, if not expanded, Congress' appetite for pork.

120. Again, see John J. Pitney, Jr.'s analysis of the Pierson and Hacker argument in *Off Center*.

121. Mann and Ornstein, *The Broken Branch*, xii.

122. Mann and Ornstein, *The Broken Branch*, 216. See also pp. 122–23, 124, 129.

123. See Connelly and Pitney, *Congress' Permanent Minority?* 81–83.

124. Polsby, *How Congress Evolves*, 107–9, 115–17, 124–25.

125. See Stanley Bach, *Managing Uncertainty* (Washington, DC: Brookings Institution Press, 1988), 82.

126. Yes and no according to Mann and Ornstein, "Is Congress Still the Broken Branch?" in *Congress Reconsidered*, ed. Lawrence Dodd and Bruce Oppenheimer, 9th ed. (Washington, DC: CQ Press, 2009), 53–69.

127. Martin Frost, "Newt Gingrich and Nancy Pelosi: Two Peas in a Pod?" *FoxNews.com*, www.foxnews.com/story/0,2933,266378,00.html (accessed 17 April 2007).

128. The differences between Democrats and Republicans still pale relative to the differences between parties in some parliamentary systems, and certainly differences between our two parties pale relative to differences between sentiment in the U.S. and other countries: "For all their recent acrimony, Democrats and Republicans have more in common with each other on foreign policy than they do even with their closest allies in Europe and Asia," according to Timothy Lynch and Robert Singh in *After Bush* (Cambridge: Cambridge University Press, 2008). Found in Gary Schmidt, "Indispensable Nation," *Weekly Standard*, 28 July 2008, 34.

129. See Sidney Milkis, "The Virtues of Partisan Rancor," *The Chronicle Review: The Chronicle of Higher Education*, 2 March 2007, B9. See also Sinclair, *Party Wars*, 326.

130. Quirk, "The Legislative Branch," 144.

131. Quirk, "The Legislative Branch," 144, 149.

132. Quirk, "The Legislative Branch," 133. Quirk cites Rohde, Cox, and McCubbin.

133. See Samuel Huntington, *American Politics: The Promise of Disharmony* (Cambridge, MA: Harvard University Press, 1981).

CHAPTER 2

1. Josh Tyrangiel, "Looking Ahead to 2004," *Time*, www.time.com/time/magazine/article/0,9171,1003693-1,00.html (accessed 18 November 2002).

2. John Harwood and Helene Cooper, "For Democrats, Hope Is Scant," *Wall Street Journal*, 7 November 2002, A4.

3. Susan Ferrechio, "House Democrats Begin Anew," *CQ Weekly*, 9 November 2002, 2932.

4. Susan Page, "Dems Adopt a More Confrontational Stance," *USA Today*, www.usatoday.com/news/politicselections/2002-11-06-dems-usat_x.htm (6 November 2002).

5. Michael Barone, "Party Like It's 1962," *Wall Street Journal*, 7 November 2002, A14.

6. Peggy Noonan, *Hotline*, 8 November 2002. Italics added.

7. PBS, *Online NewsHour*, www.pbs.org/newshour/bb/political_wrap/july-dec02/bo_11-08.html, 6. Oliphant then proceeded to debate the correct course of action for Democrats.

8. Carl Hulse, "Democrats Seek Leader to Recover From Losses," *New York Times*, 8 November 2002, A23.

9. Adam Nagourney, "Gephardt Urges Democrats to Offer Alternative to GOP," *New York Times*, 8 November 2002, A27.

10. Dan Balz, "Gephardt Defends Election Strategy," *Washington Post*, 8 November 2002, A9.

11. Balz, "Gephardt Defends Election Strategy."

12. Nagourney, "Gephardt Urges Democrats."

13. Personality, style, and strategic sense may be connected as evidenced by Newt Gingrich.

14. NPR, *Morning Edition*, 14 November 2002, online transcript. Italics added.

15. NPR, *Morning Edition*. See also Carl Hulse, "Pelosi Says She's Secured Votes to Be House Democratic Leader," *New York Times*, 9 November 2002. Italics added.

16. Jim VandeHei, "Democrats Fight for the Future," *Washington Post*, 8 November 2002, A1, A8. Italics added.

17. David Firestone, "Getting Closer to the Top, and Smiling All the Way: Nancy Pelosi," *New York Times*, 10 November 1992, www.nytimes.com/2002/11/10/politics/10PELO.html. Italics added.

18. Gebe Martinez, "Solidly Backed by Her Colleagues, Pelosi Faces GOP's Sharpened Barbs," *CQ Weekly*, 16 November 2002, 3111.

19. PBS, *NewsHour*, "Party Picks," 14 November 2002, www.pbs.org/newshour/bb/congress/july-dec02/pelosi_11-14.html, online transcript.

20. *Wall Street Journal*, editorial, 11 November 2002, A12.

21. David Rogers, "Duel for Gephardt's Post May Shake Up the Democratic Caucus," *Wall Street Journal*, 8 November 2002, A4. It is worth noting that in 2006 the DCCC's Rahm Emanuel, in part, adopted Frost's recommendation by recruiting Democratic candidates who could win in Republican districts.

22. *CQ Midday Update*, "Quote of the Day," 7 November 2002.

23. Hulse, "Pelosi Says She's Secured Votes," A1.

24. Hulse, "Democrats Seek Leader."

25. Stephen Dinan, "Frost Calls Pelosi Too liberal to Lead Democrats," *Washington Times*, 8 November 2002, www.washingtontimes.com/national/20021108-504525.htm.

26. Dinan, "Frost Calls Pelosi Too Liberal."

27. Harold Ford, Jr., *Imus in the Morning*, MSNBC in *Hotline*, 7 November, 2002.

28. "Perspectives," *Newsweek*, 18 November 2002, 27.

29. Ford, *Imus in the Morning*. Italics added.

30. Ford, *Imus in the Morning*. Italics added.

31. Ford, *Imus in the Morning*. Italics added. Note that managing diversity of internal party factionalism may be key to effectively addressing the strategic dilemma legislative parties face.

32. Harold Ford, Jr., "Why I Should Be Minority Leader," *Washington Post*, 13 November 2002, A27. All quotations in this paragraph are from Congressman Ford's op-ed. Italics added.

33. Democratic campaign consultant, not-for-attribution personal interview with the author, 12 January 2003.

34. It is worth noting that Daschle's more confrontational approach during the 108th Congress made him a more tempting target for Republicans, which may have contributed to his defeat in 2004.

35. See chapter 1 discussion of Ginsberg and Shefter's *Politics by Other Means*.

36. NPR interview, 14 November 2002, online transcript.

37. Anthony Corrado, "Running Backward: The Congressional Money Chase," in *The Permanent Campaign and Its Future*, ed. Norman J. Ornstein and Thomas E. Mann (Washington, DC: American Enterprise Institute and the Brookings Institution, 2000), 75–107, 221.

38. Modern reform politics owes much to Woodrow Wilson and his disdain for Madisonian pluralism.

39. Firestone, "Getting Closer to the Top."

40. Hulse, "Democrats Seek Leader."

41. Hulse, "Pelosi Says She's Secured Votes."

42. *Hotline*, 12 November 2002, 32.

43. Carl Hulse, "In a New G.O.P. Era, DeLay Drives Agenda for Congress," *New York Times*, 5 January 2003, A1.

44. Janet Hook, "Winning Republicans Refrain from Gloating," *Los Angeles Times*, 10 November 2002, 22.

45. Hook, "Winning Republicans Refrain."

46. Hook, "Winning Republicans Refrain."

47. Richard E. Cohen, "What, Me Worry?" *National Journal*, 2 February 2003, 588.

48. Derek Willis, "Nurturing the GOP Agenda," *CQ Weekly*, 9 November 2002, 2930.

49. Hulse, "In a New G.O.P. Era."

50. Susan Benkelman, "Minority Rules," *CQ Weekly*, 23 November 2002, 3056. Also, PBS *NewsHour*, 23 January 2002, www.pbs.org/newshour/bb/congress/jan-june03/daschle_1-23.html.

51. PBS *NewsHour*, 23 January 2002.

52. PBS *NewsHour*, 23 January 2002. Of course, one has to wonder how "liberated" Daschle felt following the 2004 election, and whether he still thought obstructionism was the right strategy.

53. George Will, "The GOP's Sunny Senate Prospects," *Washington Post*, 24 November 2002, B7.

54. Hoy, *Newsday*, 10 November 2002, A07.

55. David Nather, "Still-Thin Edge Leaves GOP with a Cautious Mandate, *CQ Weekly*, 9 November 2002, 2888.

56. Mary Dalrymple and Emily Pierce, "The Chamber of Tactics," *CQ Weekly*, 9 November 2002, 2904.

57. *Fox News Sunday*, "FNC," 10 November 2002, in *Hotline*, 12 November 2002, 18.

58. David Rapp, "Editor's Notebook," *CQ Weekly*, 9 November 2002, 2880.

59. Juan Andrade, "1 Dem Leader Down, 1 to Go," *Chicago Sun Times*, 8 November 2002, 49.

60. Charlie Cook, "Balance Will Become Democrats' New Mantra," *National Journal*, 4 January 2003, 56.

61. R. W. Apple, "Listless on Election Day," *New York Times*, 6 November 2002, A1, early edition.

62. Connelly and Pitney, *Congress' Permanent Minority?* 15.

63. Chuck Todd, "On the Trail," *NationalJournal.com*, 6 November 2002, www .nationaljournal.com/members/buzz/trail.htm.

64. David Brooks, PBS *NewsHour*, 7 November 2002, online transcript.

65. David Brooks, PBS *NewsHour*, 10 December 2002, online transcript.

66. Albert R. Hunt, "Memo to Nancy Pelosi," *Wall Street Journal*, 14 November 2002, A15. All other quotations in this paragraph are from the same article.

67. E. J. Dionne, "With No Battle Plan," *Washington Post*, 12 November 2002, A25.

68. Morton Kondracke, "Special Report," *Fox News Channel*, 11 November 2002.

69. James Carville, "Quotables," *National Journal*, 9 November 2002, 3349.

70. *Washington Post*, "What Now for Democrats," editorial, 9 November 2002, A25.

71. Adam Nagourney, "A Change That Pleases Both Parties," *New York Times*, 9 November 2002, A16.

72. Tom Freedman and Bill Knapp, "How Republicans Usurped the Center," *New York Times*, 8 November 2002, A31. The following quotations from Freedman and Knapp are from the same source.

73. Nagourney, "A Change That Pleases Both Parties."

74. Charlie Cook, "A Landslide? That Talk Is Mostly Just Hot Air," *National Journal*, 9 November 2002, 3347.

75. Cook, "A Landslide?" 3358.

76. Cook, "Balance Will Become Democrats' New Mantra," 55.

77. Cook, "Balance Will Become Democrats' New Mantra."

78. Robin Toner, "In the House at Least, Moderation Is No Virtue," *New York Times*, "Week in Review," 17 November 2002, 3.

79. James A. Barnes, "Stumbling toward 2004," *National Journal*, 9 November 2002, 3342.

80. PBS *NewsHour*, "Democratic Fallout," 7 November 2002, online transcript.

81. Barnes, "Stumbling toward 2004."

82. Elaine C. Kamarck, "Democrats Lost the Power of Ideas," *Newsday*, 8 November 2002, A41.

83. PBS *NewsHour*, 7 November 2002, online transcript.

84. Gingrich favored an open politics of ideas, principles, and "grand partisanship" and was sharply critical of the bargaining, lobbying, and logrolling of

interest-group pluralism. Newt Gingrich, "Gingrich Address: New House Speaker Envisions Cooperation, Cuts, Hardwork," *CQ Weekly*, 12 November 1994, 3296.

85. Dana Milbank and Mike Allen, "White House Claims Election Is Broad Mandate," *Washington Post*, 7 November 2002, A27, A33.

86. Jim VandeHei, "Race Is On for Gephardt Post," *Washington Post*, 8 November 2002, A1, A8.

87. See the chapter 1 discussion of Ginsberg and Shefter on "revelation, investigation and prosecution" tactics.

88. Connelly and Pitney, *Congress' Permanent Minority?* 27.

89. *Washington Post*, "A Republican Revolution? Not Likely," 5 January 2003, A4.

90. PBS *NewsHour*, 6 November 2002, online transcript. Italics added.

91. David Broder, "Time Was GOP's Ally on the Vote," 23 November 2003, A01.

92. See Connelly and Pitney, *Congress' Permanent Minority?* 82–83.

93. David Rapp, "The Indiana Parable," *CQ Weekly*, 19 July 2003, 1798.

94. Erin P. Billings, "Pelosi Calls Caucus on 9/11," *Roll Call*, 28 July 2004, online.

95. Helen Dewar, "Tight Race in S.D. Constrains Daschle," *Washington Post*, 26 September 2004, A5.

96. Charles Babington, "Reid Tapped to Lead Senate Democrats," *Washington Post*, 16 November 2004, A3.

97. Babington, "Reid Tapped."

98. Babington, "Reid Tapped."

99. James Kuhnhenn, "Partisanship Stalls Important Work in the House," *Miami Herald*, 25 July 2003, online.

100. Charles Babington, "Pelosi Seeks House Minority 'Bill of Rights,'" *Washington Post*, 24 June 2004, A5.

101. Emily Pierce, "Democrats Set to Assail Do-Nothing GOP Congress," *Roll Call*, 20 July 2004, online.

102. Charles Babington and Brian Faler, "Hard-Line Policy to Secure House Majority," *Washington Post*, 29 July 2004, A26.

103. Erin Billings, "Pelosi Sets Long-Awaited Message Rollout," *Roll Call*, 13 September 2004, online.

104. ABC, *The Note*, http://abcnews.go.com/Politics/TheNote/story?id=226188 (1 February 2010).

105. Dana Milbank, "Halliburton, the Second-Term Curse?" *Washington Post*, 9 November 2004, A25.

106. Milbank, "Halliburton, the Second-Term Curse?"

107. Congressman Bill Thomas, personal interview with the author, 14 July 2004.

108. David Brooks, "Strength in Disunity," *New York Times*, 23 November 2004, online.

109. President Clinton, in effect, suffered his six-year election four years early in 1994 thanks to a shaky start.

110. For a contrary view of the six-year-itch phenomenon, see Stuart Rothenberg, "Midterms Spell Trouble, but 'Itch' Theory Is a Real Head Scratcher," *Roll Call*, 15 September 2005. What Rothenberg calls "inevitable souring," however, does seem to

occur, though perhaps in all midterms, not just six-year-itch elections as he notes. Bill Clinton's losses in 1994 minimized his party's potential losses in 1998.

111. C-SPAN, "AARP Panel on 2006 Midterm Election," 8 November 2006.

112. Bob Benenson, "Blue State Special," *CQ Weekly*, 14 August 2006, 2227.

113. Gregory L. Giroux, "Democrats Take House on Strength of Bush's Unpopularity and GOP Scandals," *CQ Weekly*, 9 November 2006, 20.

114. For example, a "local" event, Hurricane Katrina, clearly gained national political significance.

115. Ornstein and Mann, *The Permanent Campaign*. See especially chapter 1 by Hugh Heclo.

116. Lexington, "The Return of the Newt," *Economist*, 22 January 2005, 34.

117. Congressman Bill Thomas, personal interview.

118. Mark Shields, PBS *NewsHour*, 8 November 2006.

119. C-SPAN, "AARP Panel."

120. Zachary A. Godfarb, "Election Battles Are Over; Let the Infighting Begin," *Washington Post*, 19 November 2006, A5.

121. C-SPAN, "AARP Panel."

122. Stephen Skowronek, *The Politics Presidents Make* (Cambridge, MA: Belknap Press, 1993).

123. James W. Ceaser, "In Defense of Separation of Powers," in *Separation of Powers: Does It Still Work?* ed. Robert A. Goldwin and Art Kaufman (Washington, DC: American Enterprise Institute, 1986), 171. See also David K. Nichols, *The Myth of the Modern Presidency* (University Park: Pennsylvania State University Press, 1994).

CHAPTER 3

1. Connie Bruck, "The Politics of Perception," *New Yorker*, 9 October 1995, 73.

2. Michael Barone and Grant Ujifusa, *The Almanac of American Politics* (Washington, DC: National Journal, 1996), 372.

3. Barone and Ujifusa, *The Almanac of American Politics*.

4. John J. Pitney, Jr., "Understanding Newt Gingrich" (paper presented at the annual meeting of the American Political Science Association, San Francisco, CA, 1996).

5. James W. Ceaser and Andrew E. Busch, *Upside Down, Inside Out* (Lanham, MD: Rowman and Littlefield, 1993), 2.

6. Mark P. Petracca, "Rotation in Office: The History of an Idea," in *Limiting Legislative Terms*, ed. Gerald Benjamin and Michael Malbin (Washington, DC: CQ Press, 1992), 34.

7. In an adroit bit of political legerdemain, the original proponents of the Constitution managed to co-opt the term *Federalist* for themselves even though they favored a stronger, more centralized national government. In the late eighteenth century, *federal* meant what we today might call *confederal*, that is, a system more closely resembling the Articles of Confederation. See Joseph Ellis, *American Creation* (New York: Knopf, 2007), 114–15.

8. Newt Gingrich in an address to the Southern Republican Leadership Conference, Raleigh, NC, 30 March 1990.

9. Herbert J. Storing, *What the Anti-Federalists Were For* (Chicago: University of Chicago Press, 1981).

10. Storing, *What the Anti-Federalists Were For*, 5.

11. Storing, *What the Anti-Federalists Were For*.

12. Storing, *What the Anti-Federalists Were For*, 55.

13. Storing, *What the Anti-Federalists Were For*, 56.

14. Alexander Hamilton, James Madison, and John Jay, *The Federalist*, Federalist No. 10, ed. Robert Scigliano (New York: Modern Library, 2000), 56.

15. Hamilton, Madison, and Jay, *The Federalist*, Federalist No. 70, 451.

16. Adam Wolfson, "Cautious Federalism," *Crisis* (July/August 1995): 44.

17. Storing, *What the Anti-Federalists Were For*, see 7–14.

18. Robert Goldwin, *From Parchment to Power* (Washington, DC: AEI Press, 1997), 113.

19. Centinel, "The Small Republic Argument," in *Readings in American Government*, ed. Mary Nichols (Dubuque, IA: Kendall Hunt, 1983), 24.

20. Storing, *What the Anti-Federalists Were For*, see 48–52.

21. Brutus, "No. XI," in *American Constitutional Law*, ed. Alpheus T. Mason and D. Grier Stephenson (Englewood Cliffs, NJ: Prentice-Hall, 1987), 45.

22. Brutus, "No. XI."

23. Patrick Henry, "Speech against Ratification," in *The Power of the Presidency*, ed. Robert Hirschfield, 2nd ed. (Chicago: Aldine, 1973), 22.

24. Old Whig, in *The Power of the Presidency*, ed. Robert Hirschfield, 2nd ed. (Chicago: Aldine, 1973), 24.

25. Hamilton, Madison, and Jay, *The Federalist*, Federalist No. 70, 447.

26. Storing, *What the Anti-Federalists Were For*, 16.

27. Storing, *What the Anti-Federalists Were For*, 47.

28. Storing, *What the Anti-Federalists Were For*, 22–23.

29. Storing, *What the Anti-Federalists Were For*, 71.

30. Storing, *What the Anti-Federalists Were For*, 6.

31. Storing, *What the Anti-Federalists Were For*, 72.

32. Storing, *What the Anti-Federalists Were For*.

33. William Kristol, "The Politics of Liberty, the Sociology of Virtue," in *The Essential Neo-Conservative Reader*, ed. Mark Gerson (Reading, MA: Addison-Wesley, 1996), 438.

34. Newt Gingrich, *To Renew America* (New York: HarperCollins, 1995), 228.

35. Gingrich, *To Renew America*.

36. Hamilton, Madison, and Jay, *The Federalist*, Federalist No. 17, 102.

37. Harvey C. Mansfield, Jr., "Newt Take Note: Populism Poses Its Own Dangers," *Wall Street Journal*, 1 November 1994, A16.

38. Wolfson, "Cautious Federalism," 44–45.

39. Wolfson, "Cautious Federalism," 45.

40. Daniel Stid, "A Wilsonian Perspective on the Newtonian Revolution" (paper presented at the annual meeting of the American Political Science Association, Chicago, IL, September 1995).

41. Adam Clymer, "House Party: With Discipline, It Works Like Parliament," *New York Times*, 6 August 1995, E6.

42. See James W. Ceaser, *Presidential Selection* (Princeton, NJ: Princeton University Press, 1978), chap. 1, 4.

43. Newt Gingrich, "Gingrich Address: New House Speaker Envisions Cooperation, Cuts, Hardwork," *CQ Weekly*, 12 November 1994, 3296–97.

44. Newt Gingrich, "The Leader as Learner—and Legislator," *Futurist*, July 1995, 10.

45. Newt Gingrich, "The Leader as Learner."

46. Dan Balz and Ronald Brownstein, *Storming the Gates: Protest Politics and the Republican Revival* (Boston: Little, Brown, 1996).

47. Balz and Brownstein, *Storming the Gates*. Italics added.

48. CNN News, 20 February 1995, transcript no. 7, p. 7.

49. James Q. Wilson, "The Politics of Regulation," in *The Politics of Regulation*, ed. James Q. Wilson (New York: Basic Books, 1980), 363.

50. Herbert Croly, *The Promise of American Life* (New York: Capricorn Books, 1964), 213–14.

51. Balz and Brownstein, *Storming the Gates*, 125.

52. Balz and Brownstein, *Storming the Gates*, 158.

53. Balz and Brownstein, *Storming the Gates*, 371.

54. Newt Gingrich, "The Leader as Learner," 10. Italics added.

55. Katherine Seeyle, "Why Gingrich Trots for Presidency: It's Publicity," *New York Times*, 26 July 1995, A12.

56. Ronald G. Shaiko, "Lobby Reform: Curing the Mischiefs of Factions?" in *Remakng Congress*, ed. James Thurber and Roger Davidson (Washington, DC: CQ Press, 1995), 168.

57. Shaiko, "Lobby Reform."

58. Gingrich, "Gingrich Address," 3296.

59. Gingrich, *To Renew America*, 237.

60. Conceivably an even greater practical proof of the limits of Gingrich's experiment in congressional government might be the failure of the House Republican effort to impeach and remove Bill Clinton from the presidency. Did Gingrich in his heart of hearts think of impeachment as the parliamentary equivalent of a vote of no confidence?

61. Federalist No. 51, 331.

62. Elizabeth Drew, *Showdown* (New York: Simon and Schuster, 1996), 275.

63. Drew, *Showdown*, 277.

64. Newt Gingrich, *Lessons Learned the Hard Way* (New York: HarperCollins, 1998), 10.

65. Gingrich, *Lessons Learned the Hard Way*, 10.

66. See www.pbs.org/wgbh/pages/frontline/shows/clinton/chapters/4.html.

67. Gingrich, *To Renew America*, 57.

68. Gingrich, *To Renew America*, 104–5.

69. Bruck, "The Politics of Perception," 75.

70. Gingrich, *To Renew America*, 248.

71. Gingrich, "Gingrich Address," 3297.

72. Gingrich, *To Renew America*, 71, 77.

73. Gingrich, *To Renew America*, 77.

74. Newt Gingrich, "Renewing American Civilization: Toward an Opportunity Society," *Futurist*, July 1995, 10.

75. Ronald Reagan, "Reagan Tells Audience, Country: We Need George Bush," *CQ Weekly*, 22 August 1992, 2546.

76. Alexis de Tocqueville, *Democracy in America*, ed. J. P. Mayer (Garden City, NY: Doubleday/Anchor Books, 1969), 515.

77. Tocqueville, *Democracy in America*, 515.

78. Tocqueville, *Democracy in America*.

79. See, for example, William Schambra, "By the People: The Old Values of the New Citizenship," *Policy Review*, no. 69 (Summer 1994) 32–38.

80. Richard Fenno, *Learning to Govern* (Washington, DC: Brookings Institution Press, 1997).

CHAPTER 4

1. CNN News, 20 February 1995, transcript no. 7, p. 7. Woodrow Wilson called himself a "literary politician." See Sidney A. Pearson, Jr., "Reinterpreting the Constitution for a New Era: Woodrow Wilson and the Liberal-Progressive Science of Politics," introduction to *Constitutional Government in the United States*, by Woodrow Wilson (New Brunswick, NJ: Transaction Press, 2002), 2.

2. See, for example, Woodrow Wilson, *Congressional Government: A Study in American Politics* (New Brunswick, NJ: Transaction Press, 2002), 98–99, 117.

3. Wilson, *Congressional Government*, 268–70.

4. Wilson, *Congressional Government*, 254, 257, 266, 312, 318–19, 330.

5. See Wilson, *Congressional Government*, 85; and Newt Gingrich, "Gingrich Address: New House Speaker Envisions Cooperation, Cuts, Hardwork," *CQ Weekly*, 12 November 1994, 3296.

6. See Daniel D. Stid, "A Wilsonian Perspective on the Newtonian Revolution" (unpublished manuscript), 6. Also, Wilson, *Congressional Government*, 98.

7. Wilson shares with reformers such as John McCain and Ross Perot a fundamental dissatisfaction with the excesses of pluralism. Nevertheless, Wilson was not a simple-minded good-government reformer inclined to cast aspersions on the integrity of most politicians. See Wilson, *Constitutional Government*, 105. See also James W. Ceaser, *Presidential Selection* (Princeton, NJ: Princeton University Press, 1979), 38; and James W. Ceaser and Andrew Busch, "The Strange Career of Ross Perot," in *Upside Down and Inside Out: The 1992 Elections and American Politics* (Lanham, MD: Rowman and Littlefield, 1993). See also Michael Barone, "McCain vs. Madison," *National Review*, 20 March 2000, 19–20.

8. Wilson, *Congressional Government*, 41. See also Wilson, *Constitutional Government*, 165: "Every government is a government of men, not laws."

9. Wilson, *Congressional Government*, 207.

10. Wilson, *Congressional Government*, 208, 302–4.

11. Wilson, *Congressional Government*, 294–95, 297–99.

12. See William F. Connelly, Jr., "Newt Who?" *Extensions*, Fall 2000, 20–24.

13. American Political Science Association Committee on Political Parties, "Toward a More Responsible Two-Party System," *American Political Science Review*, 44 (September 1950), suppl.

14. For more extended discussions of Wilson's influence on twentieth-century political science, see, for example, Ceaser, *Presidential Selection*; James W. Ceaser, *Reconstructing America: The Symbol of America in Modern Thought* (New

Haven, CT: Yale University Press, 1997); David K. Nichols, *The Myth of the Modern Presidency* (University Park: Pennsylvania State University Press, 1994); Daniel D. Stid, *The President as Statesman* (Lawrence: University Press of Kansas, 1998); and Pearson, "Reinterpreting the Constitution," 28.

15. Wilson, *Congressional Government*, 1. See also pp. 1–5.

16. Wilson, *Congressional Government*, 332.

17. Wilson, *Congressional Government*, 5. It is perhaps odd that Wilson seems somewhat unfamiliar with Tocqueville's *Democracy in America*, which like *Congressional Government* both engages in comparative analysis and also examines the original Federalist/Anti-Federalist debate. See also Harvey C. Mansfield, "Separation of Powers in the American Constitution," in *Separation of Powers and Good Government*, ed. Bradford Wilson and Peter Schramm (Lanham, MD: Rowman and Littlefield, 1994), 15.

18. See Herbert J. Storing, *What the Anti-Federalists Were For* (Chicago: University of Chicago Press, 1981), 72 and passim, for a discussion of the echoes of Anti-Federalist thought throughout our history.

19. See Storing, *What the Anti-Federalists Were For*, 55.

20. See Storing, *What the Anti-Federalists Were For*, 56.

21. Wilson, *Congressional Government*, 210.

22. Wilson, *Congressional Government*, 58, 93, 97–99, 185–86, 281–82.

23. Samual Bryan, "Centinel I," in *The Complete Anti-Federalist*, ed. Herbert J. Storing (Chicago: University of Chicago Press, 1981), 2:139.

24. Wilson, *Congressional Government*, 282.

25. For an insightful discussion of Progressive Era echoes of the Federalists and Anti-Federalists, see William A. Schambra, "The Decline of National Community, and the Renaissance of the Small Republic," *Public Interest*, no. 79 (Spring 1985).

26. See Wilson, *Congressional Government*, 10.

27. Wilson, *Congressional Government*, preface and 100. See also Storing, *What the Anti-Federalists Were For*.

28. See Wilson to Ellen Axson, in *Woodrow Wilson: Life and Letters*, Ray Stanard Baker, 1:213. See also Stid, *The President as Statesman*, 3.

29. Wilson, *Congressional Government*, 333.

30. For an excellent discussion of the essential continuity between *Congressional Government* and *Constitutional Government* see Pearson, "Reinterpreting the Constitution," 26. Central to Wilson's critique of the separation of powers is his search for an organic, living (or Darwinian) premise to replace the Founders' purported Newtonian checks and balances. See *Constitutional Government*, 54–55.

31. Wilson, *Congressional Government*, xv–xvi.

32. Such reforms include having the president draw his cabinet secretaries from the ranks of Congress, allowing the executive to dissolve the legislature, extending House terms to six or eight years, and even subordinating the Senate to the House of Representatives. See Stid, *The President as Statesman*, 15, 20–21.

33. Woodrow Wilson, "Cabinet Government in the United States," August 1879, 1:498–99, and "Committee or Cabinet Government?" 1 January 1884, 2:627–31, in *The Papers of Woodrow Wilson*, ed. Arthur Link et al. (Princeton, NJ: Princeton University Press, 1966–1993).

34. Wilson, *Congressional Government*, 315.

35. Stid, *The President as Statesman*, 11.

36. Wilson to R. Bridges, 19 November 1884, in Link et al., *The Papers of Woodrow Wilson*, 3:465.

37. See Stid's excellent exploration of Wilson's need to balance "the statesmanship of thought" and "the statesmanship of action" in Stid, *The President as Statesman*, 2–5, 21–26, 48.

38. Stid, *The President as Statesman*, 26.

39. Ceaser, *Presidential Selection*, 174. In *Liberal Democracy and Political Science* (Baltimore: Johns Hopkins University Press, 1990), Ceaser notes that the modern critique of the separation of powers originates with Wilson. Progressive proponents of this critique, he argues, "often mistakenly equate governing with policymaking," 177, 195. Did Wilson's desire for reform and policy innovation blind him to the virtues of the separation of powers? Ceaser concludes that Progressive reformers' desire for change blinds them to the true nature of the separation of powers.

40. Wilson, *Congressional Government*, 311, 10. Pearson argues one defect of *Congressional Government* is Wilson's failure to define *constitution*. See Pearson, "Reinterpreting the Constitution," 5. Nichols argues in *The Myth of the Modern Presidency* that a written constitution is key to solving the central problem of liberal government, namely, how to limit the abuse of power by the executive ("how to kill the king"), while also providing for effective power. Nichols concludes that the solution requires empowering the president with independent constitutional authority, 165–67.

41. For example, Wilson, *Congressional Government*, 128–29, 267. In the context of British circumstances and culture, Wilson certainly seems correct on this point; however, it is worth contemplating the effect of parliamentary government in other national contexts, for example, Italy.

42. Wilson, *Congressional Government*, 117. Generally, Wilson follows Bagehot's lead in criticizing Congress. An important exception, however, is Wilson's approval of the bicameral nature of Congress. On balance, Wilson approves of having a second chamber structured like the Senate even though it essentially shares the same nature as the House. Wilson sees the Senate as a useful, albeit modest and temporary, check on democratic sentiment. "The Senate commonly feels with the House, but it does not, so to say, feel so fast," *Congressional Government*, 228.

43. Wilson, *Congressional Government*, 284. Italics in the original.

44. Wilson, *Congressional Government*, 283–84. Italics in the original.

45. Wilson, *Congressional Government*, 282.

46. See, for example, Lloyd Cutler, "To Form a Government," *Foreign Affairs* 59 (Fall 1980); or Committee on the Constitutional System, "A Bicentennial Analysis of the American Political Structure" (Washington, DC: Committee on the Constitutional System, 1987). But see also David Mayhew's discussion in *Divided We Govern: Party Control, Lawmaking, and Investigation, 1946–1990* (New Haven, CT: Yale University Press, 1991) of whether "divided government" has resulted in paralysis.

47. Wilson, *Congressional Government*, 85.

48. Wilson, *Congressional Government*, xvi.

49. Wilson, *Congressional Government*, 79.

50. Wilson, *Congressional Government*, 187. See Harry Clor, "Woodrow Wilson," in *American Political Thought: The Philosophic Dimension of American Statesmanship*, ed. Morton J. Frisch and Richard G. Stevens (New York: Charles Scribner's Sons, 1971), 191–218, and Peter Schultz, "Congress and the Separation of Powers Today: Practice in Search of a Theory," in *Separation of Powers and Good Government*, ed. Bradford Wilson and Peter Schramm (Lanham, MD: Rowman and Littlefield, 1994), 185–200.

51. Wilson, *Congressional Government*, 281, 330–31.

52. *The Papers of Woodrow Wilson*, 7:210–11, 370–71. See Stid, *The President as Statesman*, 36.

53. This contrasts, of course, with Madison's grounding of the legislative process in the local, parochial interests of members of Congress. See, for example, Federalist No. 56.

54. Wilson, *Congressional Government*, 315.

55. Wilson, *Congressional Government*, 231, 270. See Stid, *The President as Statesman*, 12–14.

56. Wilson, *Congressional Government*, 232, 277.

57. Wilson, *Congressional Government*, 45.

58. Wilson, *Congressional Government*, 189.

59. Wilson, *Congressional Government*, 92.

60. Wilson, *Congressional Government*, 61.

61. Wilson, *Congressional Government*, 204. Wilson reversed himself on this point in *Constitutional Government*.

62. Wilson, *Congressional Government*, 204–5.

63. Wilson, *Congressional Government*, 194, 206.

64. Clor, "Woodrow Wilson," 191–99.

65. Wilson, *Congressional Government*, 85.

66. Wilson, *Congressional Government*, 298–99.

67. Wilson, *Congressional Government*, 299.

68. Wilson, *Congressional Government*, 302–3, 318, 323–24.

69. Wilson, *Congressional Government*, 101.

70. Wilson, *Congressional Government*, 186–87.

71. Storing, *What the Anti-Federalists Were For*, 73.

72. Wilson, *Congressional Government*, 294, 299.

73. Wilson, *Congressional Government*, 303, 297, 299.

74. Wilson, *Congressional Government*, 304.

75. Wilson, *Congressional Government*, 298.

76. Wilson, *Congressional Government*, 209.

77. Wilson, *Congressional Government*.

78. For a criticism of Wilson on this point, see James W. Ceaser et al., "The Rise of the Rhetorical Presidency," in *Rethinking the Presidency*, ed. Thomas E. Cronin (Boston: Little, Brown, 1982), 233–51.

79. Thomas E. Mann and Norman J. Ornstein, *Renewing Congress*, first and second report (Washington, DC: AEI Press and Brookings Institution Press, 1992 and 1993). See also Wilson, *Congressional Government*, 300.

80. Mann and Ornstein, *Renewing Congress*, second report, 57. Italics added. The first report, 48–52, also echoes Wilson's language.

81. Federalist No. 10.

82. Federalist No. 55. See Joseph M. Bessette, *The Mild Voice of Reason* (Chicago: University of Chicago Press, 1994), 6–39.

83. Does the character of deliberation change depending on the intended audience? Deliberation addressed to fellow members of Congress may differ fundamentally from deliberation directed toward the public. Does Wilson risk diluting, or even corrupting, republican deliberation by making the public the primary audience? In today's context and parlance, will members be tempted to play to the C-SPAN cameras?

84. See Federalist No. 56 and Bessette, *The Mild Voice of Reason*, on the mix of "politics" (bargaining) and deliberation, 151–52 and passim. See also Ceaser, *Liberal Democracy and Political Science*, 201, 157–58.

85. In defense of the Federalist constitutional system against the charge that it takes for granted the need for republican virtue in a democratic republic, one can usefully note Tocqueville's praise for democracy in America. Tocqueville argues that the education of citizens to something other than mere self-interest occurs, in part, through participation in the pluralism of voluntary associations. Mediating institutions teach citizens an approximation of republican virtue he calls "self-interest rightly understood." Of course, this enlightened self-interest may not be as elevated and noble as Woodrow Wilson wished. A second defense of the Federalists can be found in Storing's *What the Anti-Federalists Were For*. Though the Anti-Federalists correctly argue that the Constitution tends to take republican virtue for granted, "veneration" for the Constitution may usefully uplift an otherwise individualistic people. The irony, of course, is that Wilson sets out to undermine this "veneration."

86. Wilson, *Congressional Government*, 284. See also Ronald J. Pestritto, *Woodrow Wilson and the Roots of Modern Liberalism* (Lanham, MD: Rowman and Littlefield, 2005), 226. Pestritto's book is an insightful and comprehensive examination of Wilson's thought, including on the separation of powers.

87. William F. Connelly, Jr., and John J. Pitney, Jr., *Congress' Permanent Minority? Republicans in the U.S. House* (Lanham, MD: Rowman and Littlefield, 1994), 8–9.

88. Wilson, *Congressional Government*, 285.

89. Wilson, *Constitutional Government*, 54–55.

90. Wilson, *Constitutional Government*, 56.

91. Jessica Korn, *The Power of Separation: American Constitutionalism and the Myth of the Legislative Veto* (Princeton, NJ: Princeton University Press, 1996), 12.

92. Martin Diamond, "The Separation of Powers and the Mixed Regime," in *As Far as Republican Principles Will Admit*, ed. William A. Schambra (Washington, DC: AEI Press, 1992), 61, 67.

93. William F. Connelly, Jr., and John J. Pitney, Jr., "The House Republicans: Lessons for Political Science," in *New Majority of Old Minority?* ed. Nicol C. Rae and Colton C. Campbell (Lanham, MD: Rowman and Littlefield, 1999), 181–87.

94. Nelson W. Polsby, *Political Innovation in America: The Politics of Policy Initiation* (New Haven, CT: Yale University Press, 1984), 165.

95. Daniel J. Palazzolo, *Done Deal? The Politics of the 1997 Budget Agreement* (New York: Chatham House, 1999), 115. See also pp. 1–9, 189–206.

96. Timothy J. Conlon, Margaret T. Wrightson, and David R. Beam, *Taxing Choices: The Politics of Tax Reform* (Washington, DC: CQ Press, 1990), see especially chap. 9.

97. For a classic example of a reductionist understanding of Madison, see Robert A. Dahl, *A Preface to Democratic Theory* (Chicago: University of Chicago Press, 1956).

98. Martha Derthick and Paul J. Quirk, *The Politics of Deregulation* (Washington, DC: Brookings Institution Press, 1985). See especially the chapter titled "The Politics of Ideas."

99. James Q. Wilson, "American Politics: Then and Now," *Commentary* 67 (February 1979): 39–46. See also James Q. Wilson, "Interests and Deliberation in the American Republic, or, Why James Madison Would Never Have Received the James Madison Award," *PS: Political Science and Politics* 23, no. 4 (December 1980): 558–62.

100. James W. Ceaser, "In Defense of the Separation of Powers," in *Separation of Powers—Does It Still Work?* ed. Robert A. Goldwin and Art Kaufman (Washington, DC: AEI Press, 1986), 178. See also Ceaser, *Liberal Democracy and Political Science*, chap. 8, "The Constitution and Its Critics."

101. Roger H. Davidson and Walter J. Oleszek, *Congress and Its Members*, 6th ed. (Washington, DC: CQ Press, 1998), 186.

102. Leonard Freedman, *Politics and Policy in Britain* (White Plains, NY: Longman USA, 1996), 45–48.

103. Nicol C. Rae, *Conservative Reformers: The Republican Freshman and the Lessons of the 104th Congress* (Armonk, NY: M. E. Sharpe, 1998), 25.

104. Nichols, *The Myth of the Modern Presidency*, 165.

105. Stid, "A Wilsonian Perspective on the Newtonian Revolution," 11. President Kennedy echoed Wilson's "third" thoughts by observing that the presidency looked a lot more powerful from the other end of Pennsylvania Avenue.

106. See, for example, Stephen Skowronek, *The Politics Presidents Make: Leadership from John Adams to George Bush* (Cambridge, MA: Harvard University Press, 1993).

107. Stid, *The President as Statesman*, 2.

108. Stid, *The President as Statesman*.

109. Stid, *The President as Statesman*, 170.

CHAPTER 5

1. Marc Plattner and Larry Diamond, "Introduction," *Journal of Democracy* 11, no. 1 (2000): 5–10; John J. Pitney, Jr., "Alexis de America," *Christian Science Monitor*, www.csmonitor.com/1997/0522/052297.opin.opin.1.html.

2. Donald J. Maletz, "The Union as Idea: Tocqueville on the American Constitution," *History of Political Thought* 19, no. 4 (1998): 599.

3. Maletz, "The Union as Idea."

4. Alexis de Tocqueville, *Democracy in America* (New York: Harper and Row, 1969), 305.

5. Tocqueville, *Democracy in America*, 173–95, 503–28.

6. Tocqueville, *Democracy in America*, 287.

7. Tocqueville, *Democracy in America*, 12.

8. Alexander Hamilton, James Madison, and John Jay, *The Federalist*, Federalist No. 47, ed. Robert Scigliano (New York: Modern Library, 2000), 308.

9. Harvey C. Mansfield and Delba Winthrop, "Editors' Introduction," in *Democracy in America* (Chicago: University of Chicago Press, 2000), xliii.

10. Tocqueville, *Democracy in America*, 86.

11. Tocqueville, *Democracy in America*, 184.

12. Tocqueville, *Democracy in America*, 156.

13. Hamilton, Madison, and Jay, *The Federalist*, Federalist No. 47, 225–26, 308.

14. Wilson Carey McWilliams, "Democracy and the Citizen," in *How Democratic Is the Constitution?* ed. Robert Goldwin and William Schambra (Washington, DC: AEI Press, 1980), 96.

15. Woodrow Wilson, *Constitutional Government* (New Brunswick, NJ: Transaction Press, 2002), 56.

16. Wilson, *Constitutional Government*, 57.

17. Herbert F. Weisberg, Eric Heberlig, and Lisa Campoli, "The Study of Congress: Methodologies and the Pursuit of Theory," in *Classics in Congressional Politics* (New York: Longman, 1999), 4.

18. Weisberg, Heberlig, and Campoli, "The Study of Congress," 4–5.

19. Tocqueville, *Democracy in America*, 204.

20. Tocqueville, *Democracy in America*, 305.

21. Tocqueville, *Democracy in America*, 163.

22. William F. Connelly, Jr., and John J. Pitney, Jr., *Congress' Permanent Minority?* (Lanham, MD: Rowman and Littlefield, 1994), chap. 5.

23. James W. Ceaser, *Reconstructing America: The Symbol of America in Modern Thought* (New Haven, CT: Yale University Press, 1997), 230.

24. Tocqueville, *Democracy in America*, 541.

25. Tocqueville, *Democracy in America*, 308.

26. Herbert J. Storing, *What the Anti-Federalists Were For* (Chicago: University of Chicago Press, 1981), 71–76.

27. Tocqueville, *Democracy in America*, 19.

28. Alexis de Tocqueville, *Recollections*, ed. J. P. Mayer (New York: Columbia, 1949), 63–64.

29. Marvin Zetterbaum, *Tocqueville and the Problem of Democracy* (Stanford, CA: Stanford University Press, 1967), 86–87.

30. David Mayhew, *America's Congress: Actions in the Public Sphere, James Madison through Newt Gingrich* (New Haven, CT: Yale University Press, 2000), 21–22.

31. Mayhew, *America's Congress*, 9, 17–21.

32. Mayhew, *America's Congress*, x.

33. Mayhew, *America's Congress*, xi.

34. Mayhew, *America's Congress*, 6.

35. Mayhew, *America's Congress*, 7.

36. Tocqueville, *Democracy in America*, 494.

37. Tocqueville, *Democracy in America*, 496.

38. Tocqueville, *Democracy in America*, 526.

39. Weisberg, Heberlig, and Campoli, "The Study of Congress," 9.

40. Weisberg, Heberlig, and Campoli, "The Study of Congress," 11.

41. Tocqueville, *Democracy in America*, 301.

42. Tocqueville, *Democracy in America*, 304.

43. Tocqueville, *Democracy in America*, 18, 20, 418.

44. Tocqueville, *Democracy in America*, 12.

45. Tocqueville, *Democracy in America*, 203.

46. Tocqueville, *Democracy in America*, 469.

47. Tocqueville, *Democracy in America*, 263, 269.

48. Tocqueville, *Democracy in America*, 264, 265.

49. Woodrow Wilson, *Congressional Government* (New Brunswick, NJ: Transaction Press, 2002), 228.

50. Tocqueville, *Democracy in America*, 153.

51. Tocqueville, *Democracy in America*, 20.

52. Walter J. Oleszek, *Congressional Procedure and the Policy Process*, 3rd ed. (Washington, DC: CQ Press, 1989), 23–28; Ross K. Baker, *House and Senate* (New York: W. W. Norton, 1995).

53. Tocqueville, *Democracy in America*, 200–201.

54. Tocqueville, *Democracy in America*.

55. Tocqueville, *Democracy in America*, 120.

56. Tocqueville, *Democracy in America*.

57. Tocqueville, *Democracy in America*, 118.

58. Tocqueville, *Democracy in America*.

59. Tocqueville, *Democracy in America*.

60. Tocqueville, *Democracy in America*, 156–57.

61. Tocqueville, *Democracy in America*, 159.

62. Tocqueville, *Democracy in America*, 159–60

63. Tocqueville, *Democracy in America*, 161.

64. Tocqueville, *Democracy in America*, 163.

65. Tocqueville, *Democracy in America*, 162. See William A. Schambra, "From Self-Interest to Social Obligation: Local Communities vs. the National Community," in *Meeting Human Needs*, ed. Jack Meyer (Washington, DC: AEI Press, 1982), 90.

66. Storing, *What the Anti-Federalists Were For*, 73.

67. For an insightful discussion of Progressive-Era echoes of the Federalist/Anti-Federalist debate, see William A. Schambra, "The Decline of National Community, and the Renaissance of the Small Republic," *Public Interest*, no. 79 (spring 1985).

68. Tocqueville, *Democracy in America*, 117, 120.

69. Martin Diamond, "The Separation of Powers and the Mixed Regime," in *As far as Republican Principles Will Admit* (Washington, DC: AEI Press, 1992), 61, 65.

70. Robert Dahl, *A Preface to Democratic Theory* (Chicago: University of Chicago Press, 1956), provides an example of such a reduction of Madison's argument.

71. David Mayhew, *Divided We Govern: Party Control, Lawmaking and Investigating, 1986–1990* (New Haven, CT: Yale University Press, 1991), 198.

72. Tocqueville, *Democracy in America*, 154.

73. Tocqueville, *Democracy in America*. In discussing the executive, Tocqueville notes that the president's "weakness, not his strength . . . allows him to carry on in opposition to the legislative power" (127). Congress has most of the lawmaking power; the president can remain in power in part because he is not responsible for passing laws.

74. Tocqueville, *Democracy in America*, 154.

75. Hamilton, Madison, and Jay, *The Federalist*, Federalist No. 47, 332.

76. Tocqueville, *Democracy in America*, 155.

77. Tocqueville, *Democracy in America*, 601.

78. Tocqueville, *Democracy in America*, 72.

79. Andrew E. Busch, *Horses in Midstream: U.S. Midterm Elections and Their Consequences, 1984–1998* (Pittsburgh, PA: University of Pittsburgh Press, 1999), 9.

80. Tocqueville, *Democracy in America*, 173.

81. Tocqueville, *Democracy in America*.

82. Tocqueville, *Democracy in America*, 398.

83. Tocqueville, *Democracy in America*, 241, 243–44.

84. Tocqueville, *Democracy in America*, 202. Tocqueville cites (202–3) the authority of Hamilton, Madison, and Jefferson on the dangers of legislative mutability, yet he seems sanguine about such legislative instability.

85. Tocqueville, *Democracy in America*, 244.

86. Norman Ornstein and Thomas Mann, *The Permanent Campaign and Its Future* (Washington, DC: AEI Press and Brookings Institution Press, 2000), xii. "Permanent campaign" can refer to seemingly ceaseless campaigning by politicians, the negative quality of such campaigning, or the trumping of politics over policy, campaigning over governing.

87. Tocqueville, *Democracy in America*, 398.

88. Tocqueville, *Democracy in America*, 638.

89. Tocqueville, *Democracy in America*, 262–76.

90. Tocqueville, *Democracy in America*, 275.

91. Wilson, *Congressional Government*, 101, 186–87, 297, 303.

92. Hamilton, Madison, and Jay, *The Federalist*, Federalist No. 10, 58–59.

93. The exception to this may, of course, be Tocqueville's praise of Senate oratory cited earlier.

94. Tocqueville, *Democracy in America*, 177.

95. Tocqueville, *Democracy in America*.

96. Tocqueville, *Democracy in America*, 498. Italics added. Tocqueville follows Federalist No. 51 in thinking the nation's size and diversity make it difficult to create and sustain "great parties." Tocqueville does not seem to think Wilsonian "party government" is likely in the American constitutional context.

97. One is reminded of Tocqueville's summary of the differences between democracy and aristocracy, *Democracy in America*, 245.

98. Joseph M. Bessette, *The Mild Voice of Reason* (Chicago: University of Chicago Press, 1994), 26.

99. Roger Davidson and Walter Oleszek, *Congress and Its Members* (Washington, DC: CQ Press, 1998), 4.

100. See Richard F. Fenno, Jr., *Learning to Govern* (Washington, DC: Brookings Institution Press), 1997, where he seems to reduce governing to compromise, perhaps slighting the importance of confrontation to policy innovation.

101. Tocqueville, *Democracy in America*, 499.

102. Tocqueville, *Democracy in America*.

103. Tocqueville, *Democracy in America*, 499–500. Italics added.

104. Tocqueville, *Democracy in America*, 395.

105. Tocqueville, *Democracy in America*.

106. Tocqueville, *Democracy in America*, 398.

107. Tocqueville, *Democracy in America*, 304.

108. Tocqueville, *Democracy in America*, 517, 525.

109. Tocqueville, *Democracy in America*, 522.

110. Everett Carl Ladd, *The Ladd Report* (New York: Free Press, 1999), 18–20; Peter Berger and Richard John Neuhaus, *To Empower People* (Washington, DC: AEI Press, 1996), 162–63.

111. Schambra, "From Self-Interest to Social Obligation," 89.

112. Tocqueville, *Democracy in America*, 510.

113. Tocqueville, *Democracy in America*.

114. Tocqueville, *Democracy in America*, 632.

115. Tocqueville, *Democracy in America*, 511.

116. Tocqueville, *Democracy in America*.

117. Tocqueville, *Democracy in America*.

118. Tocqueville, *Democracy in America*, 512–13.

119. Tocqueville, *Democracy in America*, 515.

120. Tocqueville, *Democracy in America*, 522. In a personal interview, then-congressman Dick Cheney once insisted one cannot understand House Republicans (in the 1980s) without understanding two member social groups: the SOS and the Chowder and Marching societies.

121. Paul Quirk, "Deregulation and the Politics of Ideas in Congress," in *Beyond Self-Interest*, ed. Jane Mansbridge (Chicago: University of Chicago Press, 1990), 197–99.

122. Donald Matthews, "The Folkways of the Senate," in Weisberg, Heberlig, and Campoli, *Classics in Congressional Politics*, 212.

123. Baker, *House and Senate*, 83–84.

124. One thinks of the influence of former senator Sam Nunn on defense issues, or Senator Richard Lugar on foreign-relations matters; careful attention to legislative work often empowers "work horses" over "show horses." Even today, the notion that knowledge is power applies to the legislative process. See, for example, "Lugar's Second Act," *National Journal*, 7 December 2002, 3592–94; or "Lugar's Passionate Plan for a Regained Chair," *Congressional Quarterly* 60:47, 3160–64. See also observations about Congressman Jim McCrery, Congressman Mac Thornberry, and Senator John Sununu, in Richard Cohen et al., "Republicans to Watch," *National Journal*, 18 January 2003, 158–72.

125. Tocqueville, *Democracy in America*, 442.

126. Tocqueville, *Democracy in America*, 541.

127. Bernard Asbell, *The Senate Nobody Knows* (Baltimore: Johns Hopkins University Press, 1978), 262.

128. Davidson and Oleszek, *Congress and Its Members*, 186.

CHAPTER 6

1. Harry M. Clor, "Judicial Statesmanship and Constitutional Interpretation," *South Texas Law Journal* 26, no. 3 (Fall 1985): 397–433.

2. Marvin Meyers, *The Mind of the Founder: Sources of the Political Thought of James Madison* (Hanover, NH: University Press of New England, 1973), 349. In 1825 Madison wrote, "The 'Federalist' may fairly enough be regarded as the most

authentic exposition of the text of the federal Constitution, as understood by the Body which prepared & the Authority which accepted it."

3. Herbert Storing, *What the Anti-Federalists Were For* (Chicago: University of Chicago Press, 1981), 72.

4. In his book *America's Congress* (New Haven, CT: Yale University Press, 2000), in which he reconsiders the "electoral connection," David Mayhew provides support for the idea that the Constitution matters. He suggests that it is a mistake for contemporary political science to treat constitutions as exogenous: "In the United States, it is impossible to comprehend the role of House and Senate members without seeing them as, at least sometimes, performers at a constitutional level" (27).

5. Note the "two Congresses" theme of the leading textbook on Congress, Roger H. Davidson and Walter J. Oleszek's *Congress and Its Members* (Washington, DC: CQ Press, 1998).

6. David K. Nichols, *The Myth of the Modern Presidency* (University Park: Pennsylvania State University Press, 1994), 15, 168–70.

7. See Nicol Rae, "Be Careful What You Wish For: The Rise of Responsible Parties in American National Politics," *Annual Review of Political Science* 10 (June 2007): 169–91.

8. Charles O. Jones, *Presidency in a Separated System*, 2nd ed. (Washington, DC: Brookings Institution Press, 2005), 8, xv.

9. Davidson and Oleszek, *Congress and Its Members*, 9.

10. See Rae, "Be Careful What You Wish For," 169–91.

11. Nichols argues effectively that Wilson's Progressive reduction of the separation of powers is rooted in Whig ideas. See Nichols, *The Myth of the Modern Presidency*, 15, 168–70.

12. Jones, *Presidency in a Separated System*, 343. "Seemingly infinite" may not mean utterly openended and flexible.

13. James W. Ceaser, "In Defense of Separation of Powers," in *Separation of Powers—Does It Still Work?* ed. Robert A. Goldwin and Art Kaufman (Washington, DC: AEI Press, 1986), 178.

14. Congressman Bill Thomas, personal interview with the author.

15. Congressman Vin Weber, personal interview with the author.

16. Andrew E. Busch, *Horses in Midstream: U.S. Midterm Elections and Their Consequences, 1894–1998* (Pittsburgh, PA: University of Pittsburgh Press, 1999), 8–9.

17. Alexis de Tocqueville, *Democracy in America* (New York: Harper and Row, 1969), 177.

18. Robert A. Dahl and Charles E. Lindblom, *Politics, Economics, and Welfare* (Edison, NJ: Transaction Press, 1991), 336.

19. Jones, *Presidency in a Separated System*, 74.

20. Jones, *Presidency in a Separated System*, 349, 241.

21. 1 Tucker 248, N.Y. Surr. 18. This quotation is often attributed to Mark Twain. See www.kudzuworld.com/Quotes/index.en.aspx.

22. Jones, *Presidency in a Separated System*, 240.

23. Storing, *What the Anti-Federalists Were For*, 56.

24. Jones, *Presidency in a Separated System*, 241–42.

25. Jones, *Presidency in a Separated System*, 317.

26. Jones, *Presidency in a Separated System*, 203.

27. Jones, *Presidency in a Separated System*, 223.

28. Alexander Hamilton, James Madison, and John Jay, *The Federalist*, Federalist No. 10, ed. Robert Scigliano (New York: Modern Library, 2000), 56.

29. Jones, *Presidency in a Separated System*, 223, endnote 5.

30. Jones, *Presidency in a Separated System*, 223.

31. James Q. Wilson, "Interests and Deliberation in the American Republic, or, Why James Madison Would Never Have Received the James Madison Award," *PS: Political Science and Politics* 23, no. 4 (December 1990): 558–60.

32. Wilson, "Interests and Deliberation," 561. Italics added.

33. Wilson, "Interests and Deliberation," 560.

34. Wilson, "Interests and Deliberation," 562.

35. Wilson, "Interests and Deliberation."

36. Arthur Bentley, *The Process of Government* (Chicago: University of Chicago Press, 1908), 208–9.

37. Hamilton, Madison, and Jay, *The Federalist*, Federalist No. 61. Italics added.

38. Thomas Mann and Norman Ornstein, *The Broken Branch* (Oxford: Oxford University Press, 2006), 14, 46.

39. Thomas Cronin and Michael Genovese, *The Paradoxes of the American Presidency* (Oxford: Oxford University Press, 1998), chap. 6, also 350–56.

40. Roger Davidson "Presidential Relations with Congress," in *Understanding the Presidency*, ed. James Pfiffner and Roger Davidson, 3rd. ed. (New York: Longman, 2003), 284.

41. Davidson, "Presidential Relations with Congress."

42. Hamilton, Madison, and Jay, *The Federalist*, Federalist No. 51, 332.

43. Hamilton, Madison, and Jay, *The Federalist*, Federalist No. 51.

44. Hamilton, Madison, and Jay, *The Federalist*, Federalist No. 53, 343. If the Federalists were solely interested in shackling power, they could have kept the Articles of Confederation. Note the reference to the Constitution being "paramount."

45. Hamilton, Madison, and Jay, *The Federalist*, Federalist No. 48, 316–17.

46. Hamilton, Madison, and Jay, *The Federalist*, Federalist No. 51, 332.

47. Ceaser, "In Defense of Separation of Powers," 178.

48. Martin Diamond, "The Separation of Powers and the Mixed Regime," in *As Far as Republican Principles Will Admit*, ed. William Schambra (Washington, DC: AEI Press, 1992), 58; and Nichols, *The Myth of the Modern Presidency*, 166–67.

49. Diamond, "The Separation of Powers," 58. The Federalists were also innovative in advancing the constitutional principles of bicameralism and federalism. One cannot understand the constitutional separation of powers, federalism, and bicameralism apart from one another.

50. See Harvey Mansfield, *Taming the Prince* (New York: Free Press, 1989): "An invitation to struggle is an incitement to excel" (278). See also Nelson Polsby, *The Evolving Congress* (Oxford: Oxford University Press, 2004), 145.

51. Polsby, *The Evolving Congress*, 145–46.

52. See, for example, Nicol Rae, *Conservative Reformers* (Armonk, NY: M. E. Sharpe, 1998), 25–26. See also Jones, *Presidency in a Separated System*, 235. Jones argues that the president is less important and Congress is more important than is commonly understood. He further notes that Congress continues to be significant and powerful in the policy process. Why has Congress, alone among Western liberal-democratic legislatures, remained especially powerful? It is because the constitutional separation of powers makes Congress *independent* and powerful within

its own sphere. On the other hand, while Congress remains powerful, it is not all powerful nor is it the government pure and simple. Did the House GOP's effort to impeach President Clinton follow naturally from Gingrich's overweening view of Congress' role in the separation of powers? Did he see it as the parliamentary equivalent of a vote of no confidence designed to bring the government down?

53. Davidson and Oleszek, *Congress and Its Members*, 131.

54. Michael Malbin, "Framing a Congress to Channel Ambition," *This Constitution* 5 (Winter 1984): 12.

55. Robert Spitzer, "Is the Separation of Powers Obsolete?" in Pfiffner and Davidson, *Understanding the Presidency*, 310.

56. Davidson, "Presidential Relations with Congress," 283–84. Davidson cites two studies making the point that Congress innovates.

57. Rae, *Conservative Reformers*, 25–26.

58. Malbin, "Framing a Congress to Channel Ambition."

59. See William F. Connelly, Jr., and John J. Pitney, Jr., *Congress' Permanent Minority? Republicans in the U.S. House* (Lanham, MD: Rowman and Littlefield, 1994), chap. 7.

60. See Connelly and Pitney, *Congress' Permanent Minority?* 20.

61. See Connelly and Pitney, *Congress' Permanent Minority?* chap. 2.

62. Jessica Korn, *The Power of Separation: American Constitutionalism and the Myth of the Legislative Veto* (Princeton, NJ: Princeton University Press, 1996), 14.

63. Korn, *The Power of Separation*, 12. Also Diamond, "The Separation of Powers," 61.

64. Diamond, "The Separation of Powers." As Michael Malbin notes, "[C]reating power and checking it had to go hand in hand"; see Michael J. Malbin, "Congress during the Convention and Ratification," in *The Framing and Ratification of the Constitution*, ed. Leonard W. Levy and Dennis J. Mahoney (Birmingham, AL: Palladium Press, 2003), 196.

65. Hamilton, Madison, and Jay, *The Federalist*, Federalist No. 22, 134–45.

66. Hamilton, Madison, and Jay, *The Federalist*, Federalist No. 22, 135.

67. Marvin Meyers, *The Mind of the Founder: Sources of the Political Thought of James Madison* (Hanover, NH: University Press of New England, 1973), xxx. See also Hamilton, Madison, and Jay, *The Federalist*, Federalist No. 26, 157; No. 37, 221; and No. 63, 407.

68. Hamilton, Madison, and Jay, *The Federalist*, Federalist No. 37, 224.

69. Hamilton, Madison, and Jay, *The Federalist*, Federalist No. 51, 330.

70. Hamilton, Madison, and Jay, *The Federalist*, Federalist No. 9, 48.

71. Hamilton, Madison, and Jay, *The Federalist*, Federalist No. 48, 315.

72. Hamilton, Madison, and Jay, *The Federalist*, Federalist No. 48, 316. In Federalist No. 66 Hamilton elaborates on the separation of powers "maxim," explaining how and why the checks and balances help preserve the principled separation of powers: "The true meaning of this maxim has been discussed and ascertained in another place, and has been shown to be entirely compatible with a partial intermixture of those departments for special purposes, preserving them, in the main, distinct and unconnected. This partial intermixture is even, in some cases, not only proper but necessary to the mutual defense of the several members of the government against each other" (423).

73. Congress is replete with deliberation, perhaps especially in committee and bicameral conferences, contrary to those who judge Congress wanting on this

front by applying the Wilsonian standard of British parliamentary deliberation. Congress is not Parliament, nor did the Founders intend it to be.

74. Hamilton, Madison, and Jay, *The Federalist*, Federalist No. 70, 449.

75. Hamilton, Madison, and Jay, *The Federalist*, Federalist No. 78, 496.

76. Hamilton, Madison, and Jay, *The Federalist*, Federalist No. 70, 451.

77. Hamilton, Madison, and Jay, *The Federalist*, Federalist No. 39, 246.

78. See Alexis de Tocqueville, *Democracy in America*, ed. J. P. Mayer (Garden City, NY: Doubleday/Anchor Books, 1969), 155–63.

79. Alexis de Tocqueville, *Democracy in America*, ed. J. P. Mayer, 156.

80. Walter Oleszek, "Legislative Procedures and Congressional Policymaking: A Bicameral Perspective," in Christopher J. Deering, *Congressional Politics* (Chicago: The Dorsey Press, 1989), 194. Italics added. Walter J. Oleszek, *Congressional Procedures and the Policy Process*, 3rd ed. (Washington, DC: CQ Press, 1989), 24, 189.

81. Ross Baker, *House and Senate* (New York: Norton, 1989), 213.

82. An obvious caveat is that the legislative process has become more party-leadership-driven in recent years.

83. See Barbara Sinclair, *The Transformation of the U.S. Senate* (Baltimore: Johns Hopkins University Press, 1989).

84. Woodrow Wilson, *Congressional Government* (New Brunswick, NJ: Transaction Press, 2002), 210.

85. Baker, *House and Senate*.

86. Timothy J. Conlon, Margaret T. Wrightson, and David R. Beam, *Taxing Choices: The Politics of Tax Reform* (Washington, DC: CQ Press, 1990), 239–55.

87. Hamilton, Madison, and Jay, *The Federalist*, Federalist No. 10, 57–59.

88. Hamilton, Madison, and Jay, *The Federalist*, Federalist No. 10, 56.

89. Hamilton, Madison, and Jay, *The Federalist*, Federalist No. 51, 335.

90. Hamilton, Madison, and Jay, *The Federalist*, Federalist No. 10, 61.

91. See Samuel Kernell, "Introduction: James Madison and Political Science," in *James Madison: The Theory and Practice of Republican Government*, ed. Samuel Kernell (Stanford, CA: Stanford University Press, 2003), 6, 10.

92. Malbin, "Framing a Congress to Channel Ambition," 6.

93. Arthur Maass, *Congress and the Common Good* (New York: Basic Books, 1983).

94. Hamilton, Madison, and Jay, *The Federalist*, Federalist No. 63, 403.

95. Hamilton, Madison, and Jay, *The Federalist*, Federalist No. 71, 458.

96. Hamilton, Madison, and Jay, *The Federalist*, Federalist No. 42, 270; No. 1, 3.

97. Hamilton, Madison, and Jay, *The Federalist*, Federalist No. 48, 325.

98. James Q. Wilson, "The Politics of Regulation," in *The Politics of Regulation*, ed. James Q. Wilson (New York: Basic Books, 1980), 363.

99. Randall Strahan, "Personal Motives, Constitutional Forms, and the Public Good: Madison on Leadership," in *James Madison: Theory and Practice of Republican Government*, ed. Samuel Kernell (Stanford, CA: Stanford University Press, 2003), 71. Strahan notes that Madison differs from Hume in one important particular: reason, for Madison, can govern the passions even if it is fallible.

100. Hamilton, Madison, and Jay, *The Federalist*, Federalist No. 55, 359.

101. Hamilton, Madison, and Jay, *The Federalist*, Federalist No. 76, 487–88.

102. Wilson, "Interests and Deliberation," 562.

103. Malbin, "Framing a Congress to Channel Ambition," 7.

104. Herbert F. Weisberg, Eric S. Heberlig, and Lisa M. Campoli, *Classics in Congressional Politics* (New York: Longman, 1999), 2–18. See also Mayhew, *America's Congress*, x.

105. Wilson, "Interests and Deliberation," 558, 561.

106. Wilson, "Interests and Deliberation," 558.

107. Tocqueville, *Democracy in America*, 526. See chap. 3.

108. Wilson, "Interests and Deliberation," 561.

109. Mayhew, *America's Congress*, x, 17.

110. Mayhew, *America's Congress*, 20.

111. Mayhew, *America's Congress*, 18, 20–21.

112. Martin Diamond, "The Dependence of Fact upon Value," in *As Far as Republican Principles Will Admit*, ed. William Schambra (Washington, DC: AEI Press, 1992), 311.

113. Hamilton, Madison, and Jay, *The Federalist*, Federalist No. 10, 58–59.

114. Hamilton, Madison, and Jay, *The Federalist*, Federalist No. 57.

115. Strahan, "Personal Motives, Constitutional Forms," 73–75.

116. In Morris Fiorina, *Congress: Keystone of the Washington Establishment*, 2nd ed. (New Haven, CT: Yale University Press, 1989), rational-choice theorist Fiorina notes, "On occasion a member will even take an electoral gamble because some other goal is sufficiently valued" (103).

117. Joseph Bessette, *The Mild Voice of Reason* (Chicago: University of Chicago Press, 1994), xii.

118. Bessette, *The Mild Voice of Reason*, see table 3, p. 152.

119. Martha Derthick and Paul J. Quirk, *The Politics of Deregulation* (Washington, DC: Brookings Institution Press, 1985).

120. Strahan, "Personal Motives, Constitutional Forms." Morris Fiorina says, "The term *self-interest* as used in rational choice analyses has . . . limited connotations. It simply means that individuals pursue their own goals, whether base or admirable, rather than the goals of others. It is true that on a scale ranging from base to laudable, rational choice goal assumptions tend to lie closer to the former than to the latter, but that simply reflects the subsidiary assumption that individuals have goals appropriate to the institutional positions around which their careers are centered" (Fiorina, *Congress: Keystone*, 102).

121. Bessette, *The Mild Voice of Reason*, 46.

122. Bessette, *The Mild Voice of Reason*, 26.

123. Hamilton, Madison, and Jay, *The Federalist*, Federalist No. 55, 356.

124. Maass, *Congress and the Common Good*.

125. Michael Mezey notes (Michael L. Mezey, "Legislatures: Individual Purpose and Institutional Performance," in *Political Science the State of the Discipline II*, ed. Ada W. Finifter [Washington, D.C.: American Political Science Association, 1993], 355–56) that comparative legislative scholars, unlike Congress scholars, tend to emphasize institutional factors more than individual incentives. Members of Parliament behave differently than members of Congress. For that matter, senators behave differently than House members. Evidence for this proposition can be found in the mutual distrust between the House and Senate.

126. Derthick and Quirk, *The Politics of Deregulation*. See also Conlon, Wrightson, and Beam, *Taxing Choices*.

127. Paul Quirk, "Deregulation and the Politics of Ideas in Congress," in *Beyond Self-Interest*, ed. Jane J. Mansbridge (Chicago: University of Chicago Press, 1990), 197.

128. See Quirk, "Deregulation"; also, Bessette, *The Mild Voice of Reason*, 140.

129. Stephen Kelman, "Congress and Public Spirit: A Commentary," in Mansbridge, *Beyond Self-Interest*, 200–201.

130. See chapter 5 on Tocqueville, especially the final section on "self-interest properly understood."

131. Strahan, "Personal Motives, Constitutional Forms," 84.

132. Robert Dahl, "James Madison: Republican or Democrat?" *Perspectives on Political Science* 3, no. 3 (September 2005): 442.

133. Strahan, "Personal Motives, Constitutional Forms," 65.

134. Strahan, "Personal Motives, Constitutional Forms," 77.

135. Strahan, "Personal Motives, Constitutional Forms," 87–88.

136. Strahan, "Personal Motives, Constitutional Forms," 77.

137. Strahan, "Personal Motives, Constitutional Forms," 79.

138. My experience working in the Connecticut General Assembly and Congress supports this observation. Members of Congress are on balance more talented than the average state legislator in Connecticut.

139. Strahan, "Personal Motives, Constitutional Forms," 73.

140. See James Madison, "Memorial and Remonstrance," in Meyers, *The Mind of the Founder*, 5–13.

141. Strahan, "Personal Motives, Constitutional Forms," 87.

142. Strahan, "Personal Motives, Constitutional Forms," 81.

143. Hamilton in Federalist No. 72, 464, calls love of fame the ruling passion of the noblest minds. A later statesman, Abraham Lincoln, lends credence to this observation in his famous Lyceum Address: "Many great and good men sufficiently qualified for any task they should undertake, may ever be found, whose ambition would inspire to nothing beyond a seat in Congress, a gubernatorial or a presidential chair; *but such belong not to the family of the lion, or the tribe of the eagle.* What! think you these places would satisfy an Alexander, a Caesar, or a Napoleon?—Never! Towering genius distains a beaten path. It seeks regions hitherto unexplored.—It sees *no distinction* in adding story to story, upon the monuments of fame, erected to the memory of others. It *denies* that it is glory enough to serve under any chief. It *scorns* to tread in the footsteps of *any* predecessor, however illustrious. It thirsts and burns for distinction; and, if possible, it will have it, whether at the expense of emancipating slaves, or enslaving freemen." If Lincoln is right, ambition defined as a desire for reelection to Congress does not encompass what motivates politicians.

144. Strahan, "Personal Motives, Constitutional Forms," 84.

145. Strahan, "Personal Motives, Constitutional Forms," 87.

146. Hamilton, Madison, and Jay, *The Federalist*, Federalist No. 70, 451.

147. Fiorina, *Congress: Keystone*, 127, 68.

148. Fiorina, *Congress: Keystone*, 127, 103.

149. Fiorina, *Congress: Keystone*, 104.

150. Fiorina, *Congress: Keystone*, 110.

151. Fiorina, *Congress: Keystone*, 56n30.

152. Fiorina, *Congress: Keystone*, 129.

153. Fiorina, *Congress: Keystone*.

154. Fiorina, *Congress: Keystone*, 89, 91.

155. Conable and Barber, "Washington Report," 10 June 1984.

156. Connelly and Pitney, *Congress' Permanent Minority?* 163.

157. Conlon, Wrightson, and Beam, *Taxing Choices*, 239–55.

158. Lloyd Cutler, "To Form a Government," *Foreign Affairs* 59 (1978): 79.

CHAPTER 7

1. In Sidney Milkis and Michael Nelson, *The American Presidency* (Washington, DC: CQ Press, 2009), 86, the authors note that Madison was a partisan in-fighter in the early Congress.

2. Joseph Ellis, *Founding Brothers: The Revolutionary Generation* (New York: Alfred A. Knopf, 2000), 16.

3. Gordon Wood, *Revolutionary Characters: What Made the Founders Different* (New York: Penguin Press, 2006), 56.

4. Wood, *Revolutionary Characters*, 63.

5. Marvin Meyers, *The Mind of the Founder* (Hanover, NH: University Press of New England, 1973), xlii, xlv; Garry Wills, *James Madison* (New York: Times Books, 2002), 161. See also Gary Rosen, *American Compact: James Madison and the Problem of Founding* (Lawrence: University Press of Kansas, 1999), 126, 128; and William Safire, *Scandalmonger* (New York: Harcourt, 2000), 277–78. Also, Ellis, *Founding Brothers*, 56.

6. Ellis, *Founding Brothers*, 16.

7. Alexander Hamilton, James Madison, and John Jay, *The Federalist*, Federalist No. 10, ed. Robert Scigliano (New York: Modern Library, 2000), 56. "Madison was suspicious of political parties" is Ronald M. Peters's observation in *The American Speakership*, 2nd ed. (Baltimore: Johns Hopkins University Press, 1997), 22. Harvey Mansfield notes that Madison in Federalist No. 10 equates factions and parties. See Harvey C. Mansfield, Jr., *Statesmanship and Party Government* (Chicago: Chicago University Press, 1965), 15.

8. Robert Goldwin, *From Parchment to Power* (Washington, DC: AEI Press, 1997), 9, 95.

9. Wills, *James Madison*, 36–37, 76, 163.

10. Rosen, *American Compact*, 126–28, 178.

11. Clinton Rossiter, *1787 The Grand Convention* (New York: Macmillan, 1966), 313.

12. Rossiter, *1787 The Grand Convention*, 312.

13. Rossiter, *1787 The Grand Convention*.

14. Meyers, *The Mind of the Founder*, 181.

15. Meyers, *The Mind of the Founder*, 189.

16. *The Federalist* was similarly both partisan advocacy and serious political science.

17. Meyers, *The Mind of the Founder*, 189.

18. Meyers, *The Mind of the Founder*.

19. Meyers, *The Mind of the Founder*. See Rosen, *American Compact*, 152.

20. Meyers, *The Mind of the Founder*.

21. Meyers, *The Mind of the Founder*, 190.

22. Meyers, *The Mind of the Founder*.
23. Meyers, *The Mind of the Founder*.
24. Meyers, *The Mind of the Founder*.
25. Ronald M. Peters, *The American Speakership*, 28. See also Safire, *Scandalmonger*, 253–61, 388–97, 415–30.
26. Peters, *The American Speakership*.
27. Peters, *The American Speakership*, 30.
28. Ellis, *Founding Brothers*, 199.
29. Ellis, *Founding Brothers*, 198.
30. Bradley A. Smith, "Time to Go Negative," *Wall Street Journal*, 8 October 1996, A16.
31. Ellis, *Founding Brothers*, 210.
32. Ellis, *Founding Brothers*, 190.
33. The phrase "politics by other means" comes from the Ginsberg and Shefter book by that title.
34. Safire, *Scandalmonger*, 93. See also 193, 215.
35. Safire, *Scandalmonger*, 352.
36. Safire, *Scandalmonger*, 395.
37. Safire, *Scandalmonger*, 422, 427.
38. See Suzanne Garment, *Scandal* (New York: Random House, 1991).
39. Hamilton, Madison, and Jay, *The Federalist*, Federalist No. 10, 55.
40. Michael Kazin, "Permanent Campaign? It's a National Tradition," *Washington Post*, 13 February 2007, A21.
41. Wills, *James Madison*, 39.
42. Goldwin, *From Parchment to Power*, 93.
43. Goldwin, *From Parchment to Power*, 100.
44. Goldwin, *From Parchment to Power*.
45. Hamilton, Madison, and Jay, *The Federalist*, Federalist No. 84. See also Goldwin, *From Parchment to Power*, 101, 125.
46. Herbert J. Storing, "The Constitution and the Bill of Rights," in *Toward a More Perfect Union*, ed. Joseph M. Bessette (Washington, DC: AEI Press, 1995), 128. See also Goldwin, *From Parchment to Power*, 93–95, 101.
47. Meyers, *The Mind of the Founder*, 164.
48. Storing, "The Constitution," 114.
49. Storing, "The Constitution," 115. See also Meyers, *The Mind of the Founder*, 162–64, 172.
50. Ellis, *Founding Brothers*, 113–14.
51. Ellis, *Founding Brothers*, 117.
52. Ellis, *Founding Brothers*, 113–19.
53. Ellis, *Founding Brothers*, 114.
54. Ellis, *Founding Brothers*, 119. In many ways, the founding generation adopted the same prudential posture on slavery that Lincoln did as president. What they could do, they did. What they could not accomplish, they did not. Like Lincoln, they in effect favored saving the Union over abolition of slavery. Arguably, had they tried to abolish slavery in the early republic, they would only have succeeded in abolishing the union of states. By firmly and securely establishing the republic, they may have accomplished all that was possible toward eventually eliminating slavery. Such an understanding of the political reality, of course, is little consolation to the genera-

tions of slaves following the Founding. On Lincoln, see Lucas Morel, "Forced into Gory Lincoln Revisionism," *Claremont Review of Books* 1, no. 1(Fall 2000): S12.

55. Jean Fritz, *The Great Little Madison* (New York: G. P. Putnam's Sons, 1989), 65.

56. Rosen, *American Compact*, 144–45.

57. Jack Rakove, *James Madison and the Creation of the American Republic* (Glenville, IL: Scott Foresman/Little Brown Higher Education, 1990), 91. See Rosen, *American Compact*, 145.

58. Rosen, *American Compact*, 151.

59. Rosen, *American Compact*, 152.

60. Rosen, *American Compact*, 156, 167.

61. Rossiter, *1787 The Grand Convention*, 310.

62. Rossiter, *1787 The Grand Convention*.

63. Rossiter, *1787 The Grand Convention*, 311.

64. *McCullough v. Maryland*, S. Ct. of U.S., 1819 17 U.S. (4 Wheat) 316, 4 L Ed. 579.

65. Cynthia Crossen, "After U.S. Revolution, Country Was Split over France's War," *Wall Street Journal*, 31 July 2006, B1.

66. Lloyd S. Kramer, "The French Revolution and the Creation of American Political Culture," in *The Global Ramifications of the French Revolution*, ed. Joseph Klaits and Michael H. Haltzel (Cambridge: Cambridge University Press, 1994), 27.

67. Crossen, "After U.S. Revolution."

68. Conor Cruise O'Brien, *The Long Affair* (Chicago: University of Chicago Press, 1996), 81.

69. Ellis, *Founding Brothers*, 138.

70. Ellis, *Founding Brothers*. On Madison's partisanship, see 183.

71. Meyers, *The Mind of the Founder*, 229. Italics added.

72. Ellis, *Founding Brothers*, 199–200.

73. Meyers, *The Mind of the Founder*, 229.

74. Meyers, *The Mind of the Founder*.

75. James Morton Smith, "Virginia and Kentucky Resolutions," in *James Madison and the American Nation: 1751–1836, An Encyclopedia*, ed. Robert A. Rutland (New York: Simon and Schuster, 1994), 421–23.

76. Wills, *James Madison*, 69–70.

77. Peters, *The American Speakership*, 33.

78. Ellis, *Founding Brothers*, 204–5.

79. Peters, *The American Speakership*, 26–30.

80. Wills, *James Madison*, 96.

81. Wills, *James Madison*, 150, 153.

82. Ellis, *Founding Brothers*, 67.

83. The phrase "matchless political savvy" is borrowed from Ellis, *Founding Brothers*, 74.

84. Meyers, *The Mind of the Founder*, 327. Phillip Kurland and Ralph Lerner, *The Founders' Constitution*, CD-ROM edition, chap. 15, document 50.

85. Alexis de Tocqueville, *Democracy in America*, ed. J. P. Mayer (New York: Harper and Row, 1969), 102.

86. Rosen, *American Compact*, 8.

87. Rosen, *American Compact*, 178–84.

88. Herbert J. Storing, *What the Anti-Federalists Were For* (Chicago: University of Chicago Press, 1981), 5.

89. Rossiter, *1787 The Grand Convention*, 311.

90. Storing, *What the Anti-Federalists Were For*, 72.

91. Peters, *The American Speakership*, 27.

92. Peters, *The American Speakership*, 28.

93. Peters, *The American Speakership*, 29.

94. Michael Malbin, "Framing a Congress to Channel Ambition," *This Constitution* 5 (Winter 1984): 12.

95. Roger H. Davidson and Walter J. Oleszek, *Congress and Its Members* (Washington, DC: CQ Press, 1998), 186.

96. Ellis, *Founding Brothers*, 15.

97. Ellis, *Founding Brothers*, 78.

98. Ellis, *Founding Brothers*, 15.

99. Ellis, *Founding Brothers*, 16. See also Samuel Huntington, *American Politics: The Promise of Disharmony* (Cambridge, MA: Harvard University Press, 1981).

100. Mansfield, *Statesmanship and Party Government*, 1.

101. Mac Farrand, ed., *The Records of the Federalist Convention of 1787* (New Haven, CT: Yale University Press, 1966), 3:452, appendix A.

102. Mansfield, *Statesmanship and Party Government*, 2.

103. The phrase "politics is a good thing" has been made famous today by University of Virginia politics professor Larry Sabato.

104. See John J. Pitney, Jr., *The Art of Political Warfare* (Norman: University of Oklahoma Press, 2000).

105. Thomas Mann and Norman Ornstein, *The Broken Branch* (Oxford: Oxford University Press, 2006).

106. Alexis de Tocqueville, *Democracy in America*, ed. J. P. Mayer (New York: Harper and Row, 1969).

107. Or so we are told; however, prime minister question period seems smitten with partisanship and even the "permanent campaign."

CHAPTER 8

1. Norman Ornstein, *Roll Call*, 2 August 1993.

2. Paul Johnson, *A History of the American People* (New York: HarperCollins, 1997), 326.

3. Johnson, *A History of the American People*, 332.

4. Johnson, *A History of the American People*, 332–33. See also James W. Ceaser, *Presidential Selection* (Princeton, NJ: Princeton University Press, 1978), chap. 3.

5. Johnson, *A History of the American People*, 333.

6. Alexis de Tocqueville, *Democracy in America*, ed. J. P. Mayer (New York: HarperCollins, 1969), 182.

7. Johnson, *A History of the American People*, 334–35.

8. Bill Frenzel, personal interview with the author.

9. Timothy J. Conlon, Margaret T. Wrightson, and David R. Beam, *Taxing Choices: The Politics of Tax Reform* (Washington, DC: CQ Press, 1990), 257.

10. See William F. Connelly, Jr., and John J. Pitney, Jr., *Congress' Permanent Minority? Republicans in the U.S. House* (Lanham, MD: Rowman and Littlefield, 1994), ch. 5.

11. Conlon, Wrightson, and Beam, *Taxing Choices*, 239–55.

12. Conlon, Wrightson, and Beam, *Taxing Choices*, 240.

13. James Q. Wilson, ed., *The Politics of Regulation* (New York: Basic Books, 1980), 370–72. See Conlon, Wrightson, and Beam, *Taxing Choices*, 240. See also, Martha Derthick and Paul Quirk, eds. *The Politics of Deregulation* (Washington, DC: Brookings Institution Press, 1985), 192–93, 197.

14. Conlon, Wrightson, and Beam, *Taxing Choices*, 240.

15. Conlon, Wrightson, and Beam, *Taxing Choices*, 240–41; Deborah A. Stone, *Policy Paradox and Political Reason* (Glenview, IL: Scotts Foresman, 1988), 25. John W. Kingdon, *Agendas, Alternatives, and Public Policies* (Boston: Little, Brown, 1984), 131–32. See also, Martin Diamond, "Facts and Values," in *As Far as Republican Principles Will Admit*, ed. William Schambra (Washington, DC: AEI Press, 1992).

16. Gary R. Orren, "Beyond Self-Interest," in *The Power of Public Ideas*, ed. Robert B. Reich (Cambridge, MA: Ballinger, 1988), 13. See Conlon, Wrightson, and Beam, *Taxing Choices*, 241.

17. Conlon, Wrightson, and Beam, *Taxing Choices*, 239.

18. Conlon, Wrightson, and Beam, *Taxing Choices*, 111.

19. Conlon, Wrightson, and Beam, *Taxing Choices*, 257, 247. See also, 188–89.

20. Nelson Polsby, *Political Innovation* (New Haven, CT: Yale University Press, 1984).

21. See James W. Ceaser, "In Defense of Separation of Powers," in *Separation of Powers—Does It Still Work?* ed. Robert A. Goldwin and Art Kaufman (Washington, DC: AEI Press, 1986).

22. Conlon, Wrightson, and Beam, *Taxing Choices*, 84.

23. See Steven Kelman, "Congress and Public Spirit: A Commentary," in *Beyond Self-Interest*, ed. Jane Mansbridge (Chicago: University of Chicago Press, 1990). See also, Arthur Maass, *Congress and the Common Good* (New York: Basic Books, 1983).

24. Conlon, Wrightson, and Beam, *Taxing Choices*, 104.

25. Ceaser, "In Defense of Separation of Powers," 178.

26. See Stephen Skowronek, *The Politics Presidents Make* (Cambridge, MA: Harvard University Press, 1993).

27. See V. Lance Tarrance, Walter De Vries, and Donna L. Mosher, *Checked and Balanced: How Ticket Splitters Are Shaping the New Balance of Power in American Politics* (Grand Rapids, MI: Eerdmans, 1998).

28. Ron Haskins, *Work over Welfare: The Inside Story of the 1996 Welfare Reform Law* (Washington, DC: Brookings Institution Press, 2006).

29. See, for example, Thomas E. Mann and Norman J. Ornstein, *The Broken Branch* (Oxford: Oxford University Press, 2006); Jacob S. Hacker and Paul Pierson, *Off Center* (New Haven, CT: Yale University Press, 2005).

30. Dan Balz and Ron Brownstein, *Storming the Gates: Protest Politics and the Republican Revival* (Boston: Little, Brown, 1996), 158.

31. Elizabeth Drew, *Showdown* (New York: Simon and Schuster, 1996), 275.

32. Drew, *Showdown*, 276.

33. Drew, *Showdown*, 277.

34. See Ronald M. Peters, Jr., "Institutional Context and Leadership Style: The Case of Newt Gingrich," in *New Majority or Old Minority?* (Lanham, MD: Rowman and Littlefield, 1999), 43–65. See also Eric M. Uslaner, *The Decline of Comity in Congress* (Ann Arbor: University of Michigan Press, 1993).

35. Drew, *Showdown*, 11.

36. In Gingrich's allusion to differing worldviews, or *weltanschauung*, as well as in Gingrich's observation above ("We don't resemble any previous system. There are no comparisons that make sense because you've never had an information-age, grassroots-focused, change-oriented structure"), one hears echoes of his fascination with Thomas Kuhn's paradigms and an undercurrent of historicism. Along with Heraclitus, Gingrich seems to think one cannot step into the same river twice, in which case, perhaps Gingrich is right to pay little heed to Madison's antiquated thought. And yet Madison's constitutional structure came back to haunt and halt Gingrich's revolution.

37. See Samuel Huntington, *American Politics: The Promise of Disharmony* (Cambridge, MA: Harvard University Press, 1981). See also Tocqueville's famous observation that in American politics our differences are often mere differences of "hue."

38. Newt Gingrich, *Lessons Learned the Hard Way* (New York: HarperCollins, 1998), 10.

39. Gingrich, *Lessons Learned the Hard Way*.

40. Drew, *Showdown*, 194.

41. See James L. Sundquist, *Dynamics of the Party System* (Washington, DC: The Brookings Institution, 1973), and Everett Carll Ladd, Jr., *American Political Parties* (New York: W. W. Norton, 1970).

42. Richard F. Fenno, Jr., *Learning to Govern* (Washington, DC: Brookings Institution Press 1997), 3.

43. Fenno, *Learning to Govern*, 13.

44. Richard Fenno is the dean of Congress scholars and probably the key founder of the APSA Congressional Fellowship Program. Fenno has taught generations of Congress scholars the importance of participant observation and interview-based research, in the process revolutionizing the study of Congress, most importantly by grounding legislative studies in a concrete, practical understanding of our national legislature. Fenno has written a number of the classic works on Congress. When Richard Fenno makes an argument about Congress, it is by definition worth taking seriously. In *Learning to Govern* Fenno cites the book I coauthored with John J. Pitney, Jr., *Congress' Permanent Minority? Republicans in the U.S. House*. In many ways, I am indebted to Richard Fenno, but in this instance I must beg to differ.

45. Fenno, *Learning to Govern*, 45, 49.

46. Fenno, *Learning to Govern*, 48.

47. Fenno, *Learning to Govern*, 39.

48. Fenno, *Learning to Govern*, 20.

49. Fenno, *Learning to Govern*. Italics added. If imitation is the sincerest form of flattery, then it is worth noting that Nancy Pelosi mimicked the Contract with her own Six for '06. Pelosi, unlike Fenno, thought the Contract served a useful purpose, including as a governing document.

50. Fenno, *Learning to Govern*, 21. Italics added.

51. Fenno, *Learning to Govern*, 22. One might usefully ask if the House ever governs?

52. See Charles O. Jones, *The Presidency in a Separated System*, 2nd ed. (Washington, DC: Brookings Institution Press, 2005), 349, 241, where Jones concludes, "[T]he prevention of legislation may also represent effective governance."

53. Alexander Hamilton, James Madison, and John Jay, *The Federalist*, Federalist No. 48, ed. Robert Scigliano (New York: Modern Library, 2000), 315–16.

54. Nicol C. Rae, *Conservative Reformers: The Republican Freshmen and the Lessons of the 104th Congress* (Armonk, NY: M. E. Sharpe, 1998), 25–26.

55. Fenno, *Learning to Govern*, 7. Italics in the original.

56. Hamilton, Madison, and Jay, *The Federalist*, Federalist No. 51, 331.

57. See Connelly and Pitney, *Congress' Permanent Minority?* 106. See also, William F. Connelly, Jr., and John J. Pitney Jr., "The House Republicans: Lessons for Political Science," in *New Majority or Old Minority?* ed. Nicol C. Rae and Colton C. Campbell (Lanham, MD: Rowman and Littlefield, 1999), 183.

58. Arguably, by sharpening differences with George W. Bush, congressional Democrats contributed to his low poll numbers, thereby paving the way for a Democrat to win the White House in 2008. Sometimes the bully pulpit of the presidency is no match for a cacophony of clamoring criticism coming from an opposition Congress. However, larger circumstances—an unpopular war, the economy, the constitutional cycle—explain more about the 2008 election than Hill partisanship.

59. Connelly and Pitney, *Congress' Permanent Minority?* 32–34.

60. Fenno, *Learning to Govern*, 46.

61. James W. Ceaser and Andrew E. Busch, *Losing to Win* (Lanham, MD: Rowman and Littlefield, 1997).

62. Fenno, *Learning to Govern*, 51.

63. Fenno, *Learning to Govern*.

64. Fenno, *Learning to Govern*.

65. Fenno, *Learning to Govern*.

66. James Barnes and Richard E. Cohen, "Divided Democrats," *National Journal*, 15 November 1997, 2304.

67. See Dan Palazzolo, *Done Deal?* (New York: Chatham House, 1999), 83.

68. See John Aldrich and David Rohde on House Democrats' abuse of rules in the 110th Congress in *Congress Reconsidered*, ed. Lawrence C. Dodd and Bruce I. Oppenheimer, 9th ed. (Washington, DC: CQ Press, 2009), 236.

69. Fenno, *Learning to Govern*, 3. One lesson Pelosi seems to have learned from Gingrich's experience is to avoid impeachment, as witnesses her struggle in the 110th Congress to fend off efforts by Congressmen Conyers and Kucinich to try to impeach George W. Bush.

70. See Hacker and Pierson, *Off Center*, and Ronald Brownstein, *The Second Civil War* (New York: Penguin Press, 2007).

71. Fenno, *Learning to Govern*, 16.

72. Fenno, *Learning to Govern*, 51.

73. An important difference between Gingrich in 1996 and Pelosi in 2008 is that Bill Clinton had only served one term by 1996, while George W. Bush was finishing his second term in 2008. At times, constitutional cycle may matter more than legislative strategy.

74. Fenno, *Learning to Govern*, 30.

75. Drew, *Showdown*, 184.

76. Donald Lambro, "Kerry Has Advice for Democrats," *Washington Times*, 25 June 1995, A1.

77. Fenno, *Learning to Govern*, 50.

78. See Palazzolo, *Done Deal?* 83–84.

79. Fenno, *Learning to Govern*, 40.

80. Rae, *Conservative Reformers*, 209.

81. Rae, *Conservative Reformers*, 93.
82. Rae, *Conservative Reformers*, 167.
83. Rae, *Conservative Reformers*, 161.
84. Rae, *Conservative Reformers*, 208.
85. Rae, *Conservative Reformers*.
86. Rae, *Conservative Reformers*, 214.
87. Rae, *Conservative Reformers*, 216.
88. Ornstein, *Roll Call*.
89. Woodrow Wilson, *Congressional Government* (New Brunswick, NJ: Transaction Publishers, 2002), 210.
90. Palazzolo, *Done Deal?* 9.
91. Palazzolo, *Done Deal?* 40, 47.
92. Palazzolo, *Done Deal?* 97.
93. Palazzolo, *Done Deal?* 102.
94. Palazzolo, *Done Deal?* 97.
95. Palazzolo, *Done Deal?* 93, 115.
96. Palazzolo, *Done Deal?* 115, 117, 133, 166, 195.
97. Drew, *Showdown*, 276.
98. Peters, "Institutional Context and Leadership Style," 43–65.
99. Mark Halperin and John F. Harris, *The Way to Win* (New York: Random House, 2006). Of course, it is at a minimum ironic that Halperin and Harris (and many critics of the Republican Party today) look back to the 1990s as a golden age of accommodation.

CHAPTER 9

1. James Q. Wilson, "Interests and Deliberation in the American Republic," *PS: Political Science and Politics* 23, no. 4 (December 1990): 558–61.
2. Alexis de Tocqueville, *Democracy in America*, ed. J. P. Mayer (New York: Harper and Row, 1969), 102.
3. Alexander Hamilton, James Madison, and John Jay, *The Federalist*, Federalist No. 78, ed. Robert Scigliano (New York: Modern Library, 2000), 499.
4. Hamilton, Madison, and Jay, *The Federalist*, Federalist No. 51, 331.
5. Daniel D. Stid, *The President as Statesman: Woodrow Wilson and the Constitution* (Lawrence: University Press of Kansas, 1998), 175.
6. See Harvey Mansfield, "The Law and the President," *Weekly Standard*, 16 January 2006.
7. See Randall Strahan, *Leading Representatives: The Agency of Leaders in the U.S. House* (Baltimore: Johns Hopkins University Press, 2007).
8. See Nicholas Lemann, "Conflict of Interests," *New Yorker*, 11 August 2008, 86–92.
9. *Weekly Standard*, "In Praise of Bipartisanship," in *Scrapbook*, 28 June 1999, 2.
10. Charles O. Jones, *The Presidency in a Separated System*, 2nd ed. (Washington, DC: Brookings Institution Press, 2005), 349, 241.
11. Hamilton, Madison, and Jay, *The Federalist*, Federalist No. 51, 335.

12. Herbert J. Storing, *What the Anti-Federalists Were For* (Chicago: University of Chicago Press, 1981), 3.

13. Robert Goldwin, *From Parchment to Power* (Washington, DC: AEI Press, 1997).

14. Woodrow Wilson, *Constitutional Government* (New Brunswick, NJ: Transaction Publishers, 2002), 22.

15. Wilson, *Constitutional Government*. See Donald Wolfensberger, "How and Why Does Congress Change? An Introductory Essay" (paper presented at the Congress Project Roundtable, Woodrow Wilson Center, Washington, DC, 13 November 2006). See also, Stid, *The President as Statesman*, 179–80.

16. Herbert J. Storing, "American Statesmanship: Old and New," in *Toward a More Perfect Union*, ed. Joseph M. Bessette (Washington, DC: AEI Press, 1995), 403–28.

17. Wilson, *Constitutional Government*, 83.

18. Wilson, *Constitutional Government*, 106.

19. Wolfensberger, "How and Why Does Congress Change?" 3.

20. Opposition politicians naturally resort to the perspective of the critic, and Wilson provides a clear articulation of that perspective. As for journalists and political scientists, perhaps Joseph Schumpeter's famous observation about intellectuals naturally embracing an adversarial posture helps explain criticism of the existing constitutional order.

21. Storing, *What the Anti-Federalists Were For*, 6, 71–72.

22. James W. Ceaser et al., "The Rise of the Rhetorical Presidency," in *Rethinking the Presidency*, ed. Thomas Cronin (Boston: Little, Brown, 1982), 249.

23. David S. Broder, "Stench of Partisanship," *Washington Post*, 29 January 2006, B7.

24. See Brian Friel, "Bipolarization," *National Journal*, 1 December 2007, 20.

25. Jonathan Rauch, "Post-Partisanship," *Atlantic Monthly*, July/August 2008, www.theatlantic.com/200807/partisanship-rauch (accessed 22 January 2009).

26. Donald Wolfensberger, "Woodrow Wilson on Presidents, Campaigns, Congress, and Governing" (introductory essay given at the "Seminar on Presidential Campaigns and Congressional Agendas: Linkage or Disconnect?" The Congress Project, Woodrow Wilson Center, Washington, DC, 15 September 2000), www.wilsoncenter.org/events/docs/prescampintro.pdf (accessed 11 August 2008).

27. Thomas Patterson, *Out of Order* (New York: Vintage, 1994), 18–19, 25–26, 246. Political scientists Thomas Cronin and Michael Genovese explicitly ground their own thoughtful analysis of politics in the Progressive perspective, including that of Wilson. See Thomas Cronin and Michael Genovese, *The Paradoxes of the Modern Presidency*, 2nd ed. (Oxford: Oxford University Press, 2004), 327–28.

28. See James W. Ceaser and Andrew E. Busch, *Upside Down and Inside Out* (Lanham, MD: Rowman and Littlefield, 1993).

29. Sidney Milkis, "The Virtues of Partisan Rancor," *Chronicle Review: The Chronicle of Higher Education*, 2 March 2007, B9. See also, Storing, "American Statesmanship," 91–102.

30. Storing, "American Statesmanship," 410.

31. David Brooks, *Bobos in Paradise* (New York: Simon and Schuster, 2000), 249–56, 271.

32. Tocqueville, *Democracy in America*, 242–49, 254–55.

33. Hamilton, Madison, and Jay, *The Federalist*, Federalist No. 10, 56.

34. See Michael Malbin, "Rethinking the Campaign Finance Agenda," *Berkeley Online Forum* 6, no. 1 (2008), art. 3, www.cfinst.org/books_reports/Participation/Malbin_Rethinking.pdf.

35. Hamilton, Madison, and Jay, *The Federalist*, Federalist No. 10.

36. Harvey C. Mansfield, *A Student's Guide to Political Philosophy* (Wilmington, DE: ISI Books, 2001), 2.

37. Mansfield, *A Student's Guide*, 8–9.

38. See Terry Sullivan, ed., *Nerve Center: Lessons in Governing from the White House Chiefs of Staff* (College Station, TX: Texas A&M University Press, 2004), xvi.

39. Sullivan, *Nerve Center*, 62.

40. Sullivan, *Nerve Center*, 79–80, 86.

41. Marc Hetherington, "Resolved, the President Is a More Authentic Representative of the American People Than Is Congress: Pro," in *Debating the Presidency*, ed. Richard Ellis and Michael Nelson (Washington, DC: CQ Press, 2006), 78.

42. Frances E. Lee, "Agreeing to Disagree: Agenda Content and Senate Partisanship, 1981–2004," *Legislative Studies Quarterly* 33, no. 2 (May 2008): 199–222.

43. An example of the Progressive presumption is the "public interest group" pretense. According to Madison in Federalist No. 10, all factions are, by definition, partial and adverse to the public interest; there are no public interest groups.

44. Tim Groeling and Samuel Kernell, "Congress, the President, and Party Competition via Network News," in *Polarized Politics*, ed. Jon R. Bond and Richard Fleisher (Washington, DC: CQ Press, 2000), 79.

45. Sidney Blumenthal, *The Permanent Campaign* (Boston: Beacon Press, 1980), 9.

46. Barbara Sinclair, "Hostile Partners," in Bond and Fleisher, *Polarized Politics*, 144.

47. Jason Mycoff and Joseph Pika, *Confrontation and Compromise* (Lanham, MD: Rowman and Littlefield, 2008), 249. The more fragmented and competitive "new media" also contributes to audience "cocooning," further polarizing political discourse.

48. Barbara Sinclair, *Party Wars* (Norman: University of Oklahoma Press, 2006), 368.

49. Roger H. Davidson and Walter J. Oleszek, *Congress and Its Members*, 6th ed. (Washington, DC: CQ Press, 1998), 9.

50. Michael J. Robinson coined the term "journalistic Naderism." See Karen Johnson-Cartee, *News Narrative and News Framing* (Lanham, MD: Rowman and Littlefield, 2005), 298.

51. Constance Morella, personal interview with the author, 25 September 2008.

52. Robert Samuelson, "The Candor Gap," *Washington Post*, 9 July 2008, A15.

53. Tocqueville, *Democracy in America*, 174.

54. Tocqueville, *Democracy in America*, 180.

55. Tocqueville, *Democracy in America*, 192.

56. James Madison, "Defense of Majority Rule: The Least Imperfect Government," in *The Mind of the Founder: Sources of the Political Thought of James Madison*, ed. Marvin Meyers (Hanover, NH: University Press of New England, 1981), 416.

57. William Schambra, "Nasty Politics? Puhleez! . . . Get a Historic Grip," *Christian Science Monitor*, 21 October 2004, www.csmonitor.com/2004/1021/p09s01 -coop.html.

58. Martin Diamond, "Ethics and Politics: The American Way," in *As Far as Republican Principles Will Admit*, ed. William Schambra (Washington, DC: AEI Press, 1992), 355.

59. Michael Kazin, "The Permanent Campaign? It's a National Tradition," *Washington Post*, 13 February 2007, A21.

60. Peter Trubowitz and Nicole Mellow, "'Going Bipartisan': Politics by Other Means," *Political Science Quarterly* 120, no. 3 (Fall 2005): 434.

61. Trubowitz and Mellow, "'Going Bipartisan,'" 433–53.

62. Trubowitz and Mellow, "'Going Bipartisan,'" 433.

63. Trubowitz and Mellow, "'Going Bipartisan,'" 435.

64. Trubowitz and Mellow, "'Going Bipartisan.'"

65. Lemann, "Conflict of Interests," 86–92.

66. Tocqueville, *Democracy in America*, 177.

67. Paul Quirk, "The Legislative Branch: Assessing the Partisan Congress," in *A Republic Divided*, ed. Kathleen Hall Jamieson (Oxford: Oxford University Press, 2007), 133.

68. Jonathan Weisman, "Obama's Gloves Are Off," *Washington Post*, 23 April 2008, A1.

69. John J. Pitney, Jr., "Republicans: Divided as Usual," *Roll Call*, 27 June 2006.

70. See Nelson Polsby, *Political Innovation in America* (New Haven, CT: Yale University Press, 1984), 165.

71. Milkis, "The Virtues of Partisan Rancor," B8.

72. James W. Ceaser, "True Blue vs. Deep Red: The Ideas That Move American Politics" (paper presented at the 2006 Bradley Symposium, Hudson Institute, Washington, DC), http://pcr.hudson.org/files/publications/Ceaser2006Bradley Symposium.doc, p. 24.

73. Tocqueville, *Democracy in America*, 175.

74. Everett Carll Ladd, *American Political Parties* (New York: Norton, 1970); and James Sundquist, *Dynamics of the Party System* (Washington, DC: Brookings Institution Press, 1973).

75. Samuel Huntington, *American Politics: The Promise of Disharmony* (Cambridge, MA: Harvard University Press, 1981), 33.

76. Alan Ehrenhalt, *The United States of Ambition: Politicians, Power, and the Pursuit of Office* (New York: Random House, 1991), chap. 4.

77. *Washington Post*, "The Congress So Far," editorial, 5 August 2007, B6.

78. *Washington Post*, "The Congress So Far."

79. Hamilton, Madison, and Jay, *The Federalist*, Federalist No. 51, 332.

80. David Herszenhorn, "How the Filibuster Became the Rule," *New York Times*, 2 December 2007, 45.

81. Sam Langholz, personal interview with the author, Lexington, Virginia, 22 February 2005.

82. William F. Connelly, Jr., "Party Policy Committees in Congress" (paper presented at the annual meeting of the Western Political Science Association, Seattle, Washington, 21–23 March 1991).

83. See Bill Gavin's observation highlighted in chapter 6.

84. William F. Connelly, Jr., and John J. Pitney, Jr., *Congress' Permanent Minority? Republicans in the U.S. House* (Lanham, MD: Rowman and Littlefield, 1994), 20.

85. Hamilton, Madison, and Jay, *The Federalist*, Federalist No. 37, 223–24. See also, 225–27 on how the separation of powers and federalism promote both stability and energy.

86. Nelson Polsby, *How Congress Evolves: Social Bases of Institutional Change* (Oxford: Oxford University Press, 2004), 145.

87. Polsby, *How Congress Evolves*, 145–46.

88. Brian Friel, Richard Cohen, and James Barnes, "Partisan Impulses," *National Journal*, Special Report, 1 December 2007, 18. The quoted observations in this paragraph are taken from pages 20, 21, 22, 27, 28, and 37 respectively.

89. Shailagh Murray, "GOP Candidates Warn about the Perils of One-Party Rule," *Washington Post*, 26 October 2008, A1. Quotations in this paragraph are from the same story.

90. Anne Applebaum, "Five Election Myths," *Washington Post*, 4 November 2008, A17.

91. Peter Wehner, "Democrats and the Culture of Corruption," *Commentary*, www.commentarymagazine.com/blogs/index.php/wehner/47191 (accessed 6 February 2009).

92. John Fund, "Pelosi Turns Back the Clock on House Reform: Moderate Democrats Will Be Frozen Out," *Wall Street Journal Online Journal*, www.online.wsj.com/article/SB123146274483166511.html (accessed 9 February 2009).

93. David Nather, "The Big Tent Collapses," *CQ Weekly*, 17 November 2008, 3082. *CQ* citations in this paragraph are all from this article, pages 3084, 3085, 3086, 3089, and 3090 respectively.

94. Manuel Roig-Franzia, "The Pathfinder," *Washington Post*, 11 December 2008, A1.

95. Jim VandeHei and Mike Allen, "O-bummer," *Politico*, January 9, 2009.

96. Shailagh Murray and Paul Kane, "Democratic Congress Shows Signs It Will Not Bow to Obama," *Washington Post*, 11 January 2009, A5.

97. Murray and Kane, "Democratic Congress Shows Signs."

98. Naftali Bendavid and Greg Hitt, "Democrats' Factions Could Stall Grand Plans," *Wall Street Journal Online Journal*, 6 January 2009, http://online.wsj.com/article/SB123120199307655729.html (accessed 11 February 2009).

99. Paul Kane, "Stimulus Plan Meets More GOP Resistance," *Washington Post*, 30 January 2009, A1; and Michael Fletcher, "Obama Using His Personal Appeal to Put Change into Motion," *Washington Post*, 26 January 2009, A9.

100. Michael Shear and Anne Kornblut, "Echoes from the Campaign Trail," *Washington Post*, 8 February 2009, A2.

101. See chapter 1 discussion of Fenno.

102. Peggy Noonan, "You Are Terrifying Us," *Wall Street Journal*, 8 August 2009, A13.

103. Jonathan Weisman, "Post-Partisan Promise Fizzles," *Wall Street Journal*, 18 August 2009, A4.

104. Matt Welch and Nick Gillespie, "What Next Mr. President—Cardigans?" *Washington Post*, 19 July 2009, B1.

105. Adriel Bettelheim, "Overhaul Hard to Steer Using Hands-Off Approach," *CQ Weekly*, 10 August 2009, 1894. See also, Charlie Cook, "Feeling Cautious," *National Journal*, 8 August 2009, 64.

106. James A. Barnes and Marilyn Werber Serafini, "Taking Instruction from Failure," *National Journal*, 1 August 2009, 27.

107. Stuart Rothenberg, "Capitol Hill Democrats Have Met Their Enemy and It Is Them," *Roll Call*, 27 July 2009, 13.

108. Sarah A. Binder, Thomas E. Mann, Norman J. Ornstein, and Molly Reynolds, *Assessing the 110th Congress, Anticipating the 111th* (Washington, DC: Brookings Institution Press, 2009), 3: 8.

109. Paul Krawzak, "Rules Let Democrats Move Faster, Avoid Tough Votes," *CQ Online News*, 27 July 2009.

110. Perry Bacon, Jr., Paul Kane, and Ben Pershing, "Liberal and Conservative Democrats Feud," *Washington Post*, 25 July 2009, A1.

111. Rothenberg, "Capitol Hill Democrats."

112. Alexis Simendinger, "The Echo Chamber," *National Journal*, 1 August 2009, 20–21.

113. Simendinger, "The Echo Chamber," 20.

114. Jonathan Weisman and Naftali Bendavid, "New Rx for Health Plan: Split Bill," *Wall Street Journal*, 20 August 2009, A1; Gerald F. Seib, "Scaled-Down Health Bill Is Democrats' Less Risky Path," *Wall Street Journal*, 21 August 2009, A2; Brian Friel and Richard E. Cohen, "Health Care Endgames," *National Journal*, 8 August 2009, 30–35.

115. Friel and Cohen, "Health Care Endgames."

116. Friel and Cohen, "Health Care Endgames," 35.

117. Gary Fields, "Health-Bill's Pace Prompts Calls for Delay," *Wall Street Journal*, 24 August 2009, A4.

118. Friel and Cohen, "Health Care Endgames," 34.

119. Kirk Victor, "A Lose-Lose Situation?" *National Journal*, 1 August 2009, 28.

120. Charlie Cook, "The Edge Shrinks," *National Journal*, 1 August 2009, 64.

121. Tocqueville, *Democracy in America*, 163.

Selected Bibliography

American Political Science Association Committee on Political Parties. "Toward a More Responsible Two-Party System." *American Political Science Review* 44, suppl. (September 1950).

Asbell, Bernard. *The Senate Nobody Knows*. Baltimore: Johns Hopkins University Press, 1978.

Bach, Stanley. *Managing Uncertainty*. Washington, DC: Brookings Institution Press, 1988.

Baker, Ray Stannard. *Woodrow Wilson: Life and Letters*. New York: Greenwood Press, 1968.

Baker, Ross K. *House and Senate*. New York: W. W. Norton, 1995.

Balz, Dan, and Ron Brownstein. *Storming the Gates: Protest Politics and the Republican Revival*. Boston: Little, Brown, 1996.

Barone, Michael, and Grant Ujifusa. *The Almanac of American Politics*. Washington, DC: National Journal, 1996–2009.

Benjamin, Gerald, and Michael Malbin, eds. *Limiting Legislative Terms*. Washington, DC: CQ Press, 1992.

Bentley, Arthur. *The Process of Government*. Chicago: University of Chicago Press, 1908.

Berger, Peter, and Richard John Neuhaus. *To Empower People*. Washington, DC: AEI Press, 1996.

Bessette, Joseph M. *The Mild Voice of Reason*. Chicago: University of Chicago Press, 1994.

Blumenthal, Sidney. *The Permanent Campaign*. Boston: Beacon Press, 1980.

Bond, Jon R., and Richard Fleisher, eds. *Polarized Politics*. Washington, DC: CQ Press, 2000.

Broder, David S. *The Party's Over*. New York: Harper and Row, 1972.

Brooks, David. *Bobos in Paradise*. New York: Simon and Schuster, 2000.

Brownstein, Ronald. *The Second Civil War*. New York: Penguin Press, 2007.

Brutus. "No. XI." In *American Constitutional Law*, edited by Alpheus T. Mason and D. Grier Stephenson. Englewood Cliffs, NJ: Prentice-Hall, 1987.

Bryan, Samual. "Centinel I." In *The Complete Anti-Federalist*, edited by Herbert J. Storing. Vol. 2. Chicago: University of Chicago Press, 1981.

Busch, Andrew E. *Horses in Midstream: U.S. Midterm Elections and Their Consequences, 1894–1998*. Pittsburgh, PA: University of Pittsburgh Press, 1999.

Ceaser, James W. "In Defense of the Separation of Powers." In *Separation of Powers—Does It Still Work?* edited by Robert A. Goldwin and Art Kaufman. Washington, DC: AEI Press, 1986.

———. *Liberal Democracy and Political Science*. Baltimore: Johns Hopkins University Press, 1990.

———. *Presidential Selection*. Princeton, NJ: Princeton University Press, 1978.

———. *Reconstructing America: The Symbol of America in Modern Thought*. New Haven, CT: Yale University Press, 1997.

———. "True Blue vs. Deep Red: The Ideas That Move American Politics." Paper presented at the 2006 Bradley Symposium, Hudson Institute, Washington, DC.

Ceaser, James W., and Andrew E. Busch. *Losing to Win*. Lanham, MD: Rowman and Littlefield, 1997.

———. *Upside Down, Inside Out: The 1992 Elections and American Politics*. Lanham, MD: Rowman and Littlefield, 1993.

Ceaser, James W., Glen Thurow, Jeffrey Tulis, and Joseph M. Bessette. "The Rise of the Rhetorical Presidency." In *Rethinking the Presidency*, edited by Thomas E. Cronin. Boston: Little, Brown, 1982.

Clor, Harry M. "Judicial Statesmanship and Constitutional Interpretation." *South Texas Law Journal* 26, no. 3 (Fall 1985).

———. "Woodrow Wilson." In *American Political Thought: The Philosophic Dimension of American Statesmanship*, edited by Morton J. Frisch and Richard G. Stevens. New York: Charles Scribner's Sons, 1971.

Conable, Barber. "Washington Report," 10 June 1984.

Conlon, Timothy J., Margaret T. Wrightson, and David R. Beam. *Taxing Choices: The Politics of Tax Reform*. Washington, DC: CQ Press, 1990.

Connelly, William F., Jr. "Newt, the Anti-Federalist." *Weekly Standard*, 2 December 1996, 18–19.

———. "Newt Who?" *Extensions*, Fall 2000, 20–24.

Connelly, William F., Jr., and John J. Pitney, Jr. *Congress' Permanent Minority? Republicans in the U.S. House*. Lanham, MD: Rowman and Littlefield, 1994.

———. "The House Republicans: Lessons for Political Science." In *New Majority or Old Minority?* edited by Nicol C. Rae and Colton C. Campbell. Lanham, MD: Rowman and Littlefield, 1999.

———. "Leadership Riff: Jazzy Vision, Steady Beat." *L.A. Times*, 11 November 1998.

Croly, Herbert. *The Promise of American Life*. New York: Capricorn Books, 1964.

Cronin, Thomas, and Michael Genovese. *The Paradoxes of the American Presidency*. Oxford: Oxford University Press, 1998.

Cutler, Lloyd. "To Form a Government." *Foreign Affairs* 59 (fall 1980).

Dahl, Robert A. "James Madison: Republican or Democrat?" *Perspectives on Political Science* 3, no. 3 (September 2005).

———. *A Preface to Democratic Theory.* Chicago: University of Chicago Press, 1956.

Dahl, Robert A., and Charles E. Lindblom. *Politics, Economics, and Welfare.* Edison, NJ: Transaction Press, 1991.

Davidson, Roger H., and Walter J. Oleszek. *Congress and Its Members.* 6th–9th ed. Washington, DC: CQ Press, 1998.

Derthick, Martha, and Paul J. Quirk. *The Politics of Deregulation.* Washington, DC: Brookings Institution Press, 1985.

Drew, Elizabeth. *Showdown.* New York: Simon and Schuster, 1996.

Ehrenhalt, Alan. *The United States of Ambition: Politicians, Power, and the Pursuit of Office.* New York: Random House, 1991.

Eilperin, Juliet. *Fight Club Politics.* Lanham, MD: Rowman and Littlefield, 2006.

Ellis, Joseph. *Founding Brothers: The Revolutionary Generation.* New York: Alfred A. Knopf, 2000.

Ellis, Richard, and Michael Nelson, eds. *Debating the Presidency.* Washington, DC: CQ Press, 2006.

Fenno, Richard F., Jr. *Learning to Govern.* Washington, DC: Brookings Institution Press, 1997.

Fiorina, Morris. *Congress: Keystone of the Washington Establishment.* 2nd ed. New Haven, CT: Yale University Press, 1989.

Freedman, Leonard. *Politics and Policy in Britain.* New York: Longman USA, 1996.

Fritz, Jean. *The Great Little Madison.* New York: G. P. Putnam's Sons, 1989.

Garment, Suzanne. *Scandal.* New York: Random House, 1991.

Gerson, Mark, ed. *The Essential Neo-Conservative Reader.* Reading, MA: Addison Wesley, 1996.

Gingrich, Newt. "The Leader as Learner—and Legislator." *Futurist*, July 1995, 10.

———. *Lessons Learned the Hard Way.* New York: HarperCollins, 1998.

———. *To Renew America.* New York: HarperCollins, 1995.

Ginsberg, Benjamin, and Martin Shefter. *Politics by Other Means.* 3rd ed. New York: Norton, 2002.

Goldwin, Robert A. *From Parchment to Power.* Washington, DC: AEI Press, 1997.

Goldwin, Robert A., and Art Kaufman, eds. *Separation of Powers—Does It Still Work?* Washington, DC: AEI Press, 1986.

Goldwin, Robert A., and William Schambra, eds. *How Democratic Is the Constitution?* Washington, DC: AEI Press, 1980.

Green, John C., and Paul S. Herrnson, eds. *Responsible Partisanship? The Evolution of American Political Parties since 1950.* Lawrence: University Press of Kansas, 2003.

Hacker, Jacob S., and Paul Pierson. *Off Center.* New Haven, CT: Yale University Press, 2005.

Halperin, Mark, and John F. Harris. *The Way to Win.* New York: Random House, 2006.

Hamilton, Alexander, James Madison, and John Jay. *The Federalist*, edited by Robert Scigliano. New York: Modern Library, 2000.

Han, Hahrie, and David W. Brady. "A Delayed Return to Historical Norms: Congressional Party Polarization after the Second World War." *British Journal of Political Science* 37, no. 3 (July 2007).

Haskins, Ron. *Work Over Welfare: The Inside Story of the 1996 Welfare Reform Law.* Washington, DC: Brookings Institution Press, 2006.

Huntington, Samuel. *American Politics: The Promise of Disharmony*. Cambridge, MA: Harvard University Press, 1981.

Johnson-Cartee, Karen. *News Narrative and News Framing*. Lanham, MD: Rowman and Littlefield, 2005.

Jones, Charles O. *The Presidency in a Separated System*. 2nd ed. Washington, DC: Brookings Institution Press, 2005.

Kernell, Samuel, ed. *James Madison: The Theory and Practice of Republican Government*. Stanford, CA: Stanford University Press, 2003.

King, Anthony, ed. *The New American Political System*. Washington, DC: AEI Press, 1978.

Kingdon, John W. *Agendas, Alternatives, and Public Policies*. Boston: Little, Brown, 1984.

Klaits, Joseph, and Michael H. Haltzel, ed. *The Global Ramifications of the French Revolution*. Cambridge: Cambridge University Press, 1994.

Korn, Jessica. *The Power of Separation: American Constitutionalism and the Myth of the Legislative Veto*. Princeton, NJ: Princeton University Press, 1996.

Kurland, Philip, and Ralph Lerner. *The Founders' Constitution*. CD-ROM ed. Chicago: University of Chicago Press, 1987.

Ladd, Everett Carl. *American Political Parties*. New York: Norton, 1970.

———. *The Ladd Report*. New York: Free Press, 1999.

Lemann, Nicholas. "Conflict of Interests." *New Yorker*, 11 August 2008, 86–92.

Link, Arthur, ed. *The Papers of Woodrow Wilson*. Princeton, NJ: Princeton University Press, 1966–1993.

Maass, Arthur. *Congress and the Common Good*. New York: Basic Books, 1983.

Mackaman, Frank H. *Understanding Congressional Leadership*. Washington, DC: CQ Press, 1981.

Malbin, Michael. "Framing a Congress to Channel Ambition." *This Constitution* 5 (Winter 1984): 12.

Mann, Thomas E., and Norman J. Ornstein. *The Broken Branch*. Oxford: Oxford University Press, 2006.

———. "Is Congress Still the Broken Branch?" In *Congress Reconsidered*, edited by Lawrence C. Dodd and Bruce I. Oppenheimer. 9th ed. Washington, DC: CQ Press, 2009.

———. *Renewing Congress*. First and Second Report. Washington, DC: AEI Press and Brookings Institution Press, 1992 and 1993.

Mansbridge, Jane J. *Beyond Self-Interest*. Chicago: University of Chicago Press, 1990.

Mansfield, Harvey C. *A Student's Guide to Political Philosophy*. Wilmington, DE: ISI Books, 2001.

Matthews, Donald. "The Folkways of the Senate." In *Classics in Congressional Politics*, edited by Herbert F. Weisberg, Eric S. Heberlig, and Lisa M. Campoli. New York: Longman, 1999.

Mayhew, David. *America's Congress: Actions in the Public Sphere, James Madison through Newt Gingrich*. New Haven, CT: Yale University Press, 2000.

———. *Congress: The Electoral Connection*. 2nd ed. New Haven, CT: Yale University Press, 2004.

———. *Divided We Govern: Party Control, Lawmaking and Investigating, 1986–1990*. New Haven, CT: Yale University Press, 1991.

Meyers, Marvin. *The Mind of the Founder: Sources of the Political Thought of James Madison.* Hanover, NH: University Press of New England, 1973.

Milkis, Sidney. "The Virtues of Partisan Rancor." *Chronicle Review: The Chronicle of Higher Education*, 2 March 2007, B9.

Mycoff, Jason, and Joseph Pika. *Confrontation and Compromise.* Lanham, MD: Rowman and Littlefield, 2008.

Nichols, David K. *The Myth of the Modern Presidency.* University Park: Pennsylvania State University Press, 1994.

O'Brien, Conor Cruise. *The Long Affair.* Chicago: University of Chicago Press, 1996.

Oleszek, Walter J. *Congressional Procedure and the Policy Process.* 3rd ed. Washington, DC: CQ Press, 1989.

Ornstein, Norman J., and Thomas E. Mann. *The Permanent Campaign and Its Future.* Washington, DC: AEI Press and Brookings Institution Press, 2000.

Palazzolo, Daniel J. *Done Deal? The Politics of the 1997 Budget Agreement.* New York: Chatham House, 1999.

Patterson, Thomas. *Out of Order.* New York: Vintage, 1994.

Pearson, Sidney A., Jr. "Reinterpreting the Constitution for a New Era: Woodrow Wilson and the Liberal-Progressive Science of Politics." In Woodrow Wilson, *Constitutional Government in the United States.* New Brunswick, NJ: Transaction Press, 2002.

Pestritto, Ronald J. *Woodrow Wilson and the Roots of Modern Liberalism.* Lanham, MD: Rowman and Littlefield, 2005.

Peters, Ronald M. *The American Speakership.* 2nd ed. Baltimore: Johns Hopkins University Press, 1997.

Pfiffner, James, and Roger Davidson. *Understanding the Presidency.* 3rd ed. New York: Longman, 2003.

Pitney, John J., Jr. *The Art of Political Warfare.* Norman: University of Oklahoma Press, 2000.

Plattner, Marc, and Larry Diamond. "Introduction." *Journal of Democracy* 11, no. 1 (2000): 5–10.

Polsby, Nelson W. *How Congress Evolves: Social Bases of Institutional Change.* Oxford: Oxford University Press, 2004.

———. *Political Innovation in America: The Politics of Policy Initiation.* New Haven, CT: Yale University Press, 1984.

Quirk, Paul. "The Legislative Branch: Assessing the Partisan Congress." In *A Republic Divided*, edited by Kathleen Hall Jamieson. Oxford: Oxford University Press, 2007.

Rae, Nicol C. "Be Careful What You Wish For: The Rise of Responsible Parties in American National Politics." *Annual Review of Political Science* 10 (June 2007): 169–91.

———. *Conservative Reformers: The Republican Freshman and the Lessons of the 104th Congress.* Armonk, NY: M. E. Sharpe, 1998.

Rakove, Jack. *James Madison and the Creation of the American Republic.* Glenville, IL: Scott Foresman/Little Brown Higher Education, 1990.

Rauch, Jonathan. "Demosclerosis." *National Journal*, 15 May 1992.

Rosen, Gary. *American Compact: James Madison and the Problem of Founding.* Lawrence: University Press of Kansas, 1999.

Rossiter, Clinton. *1787 The Grand Convention*. New York: Macmillan, 1966.

Rutland, Robert A., ed. *James Madison and the American Nation, 1751–1836: An Encyclopedia*. New York: Simon and Schuster, 1994.

Sabato, Larry. *Feeding Frenzy*. New York: Free Press, 1991.

Safire, William. *Scandalmonger*. New York: Harcourt, 2000.

Schambra, William, ed. *As Far as Republican Principles Will Admit*. Washington, DC: AEI Press, 1992.

———. "By the People: The Old Values of the New Citizenship." *Policy Review*, no. 69 (Summer 1994): 32–38.

Shaiko, Ronald G. "Lobby Reform: Curing the Mischiefs of Factions?" In *Remaking Congress*, edited by James Thurber and Roger Davidson. Washington, DC: CQ Press, 1995.

Sinclair, Barbara. *Party Wars*. Norman: University of Oklahoma Press, 2006.

———. *The Transformation of the U.S. Senate*. Baltimore: Johns Hopkins University Press, 1989.

Skowronek, Stephen. *The Politics Presidents Make: Leadership from John Adams to George Bush*. Cambridge, MA: Harvard University Press, 1993.

Stid, Daniel D. *The President as Statesman: Woodrow Wilson and the Constitution*. Lawrence: University Press of Kansas, 1998.

Stone, Deborah A. *Policy Paradox and Political Reason*. Glenview, IL: Scotts Foresman, 1988.

Storing, Herbert J. *Toward a More Perfect Union*. Edited by Joseph M. Bessette. Washington, DC: AEI Press, 1995.

———. *What the Anti-Federalists Were For*. Chicago: University of Chicago Press, 1981.

Strahan, Randall. *Leading Representatives: The Agency of Leaders in the U.S. House*. Baltimore: Johns Hopkins University Press, 2007.

Sullivan, Terry, ed. *Nerve Center: Lessons in Governing from the White House Chiefs of Staff*. College Station: Texas A&M University Press, 2004.

Sundquist, James. *Dynamics of the Party System*. Washington, DC: Brookings Institution Press, 1973.

Tarrance, V. Lance, Walter De Vries, and Donna L. Mosher. *Checked and Balanced: How Ticket Splitters Are Shaping the New Balance of Power in American Politics*. Grand Rapids, MI: Eerdmans, 1998.

Tocqueville, Alexis de. *Democracy in America*. Edited by Harvey C. Mansfield and Delba Winthrop. Chicago: University of Chicago Press, 2000.

———. *Democracy in America*. Edited by J. P. Mayer. Garden City, NY: Doubleday/Anchor Books, 1969.

———. *Recollections*. Edited by J. P. Mayer. New York: Columbia, 1949.

Weisberg, Herbert F., Eric S. Heberlig, and Lisa M. Campoli, eds. *Classics in Congressional Politics*. New York: Longman, 1999.

Wills, Garry. *James Madison*. New York: Times Books, 2002.

Wilson, Bradford, and Peter Schramm, eds. *Separation of Powers and Good Government*. Lanham, MD: Rowman and Littlefield, 1994.

Wilson, James Q. "American Politics: Then and Now." *Commentary* 67 (February 1979): 39–46.

———. "Interests and Deliberation in the American Republic, or Why James Madison Would Never Have Received the James Madison Award." *PS: Political Science and Politics* 23, no. 4 (December 1990): 558–62.
———. ed. *The Politics of Regulation*. New York: Basic Books, 1980.
Wilson, Woodrow. *Congressional Government*. New Brunswick, NJ: Transaction Publishers, 2002.
———. *Constitutional Government in the United States*. New Brunswick, NJ: Transaction Publishers, 2002.
Wolfensberger, Donald. "How and Why Does Congress Change? An Introductory Essay." Paper presented at the Congress Project Roundtable, Woodrow Wilson Center for Scholars, Washington, 13 November 2006.
———. "Woodrow Wilson on Presidents, Campaigns, Congress, and Governing." Wilson Center, Congress Project, 15 September 2000.
Wolfson, Adam. "Cautious Federalism." *Crisis*, July/August 1995, 44.
Zetterbaum, Marvin. *Tocqueville and the Problem of Democracy*. Stanford, CA: Stanford University Press, 1967.

Index

About the Author

William F. Connelly, Jr., is John K. Boardman Politics Professor at Washington and Lee University. He has a master's in political philosophy from Boston College and a Ph.D. in American government from the University of Virginia. He was an American Political Science Association Congressional Fellow and a guest scholar at the Brookings Institution. In 2007, Professor Connelly received the Virginia Council of Higher Education Outstanding Faculty Award.